DARWIN'S BARDS

To Jo,
Amy and Hannah

DARWIN'S BARDS
British and American Poetry in the Age of Evolution

JOHN HOLMES

Edinburgh University Press

Edinburgh University Press Ltd
22 George Square, Edinburgh

www.euppublishing.com

Typeset in 11/13 pt Goudy Old Style
by Servis Filmsetting Ltd, Stockport, Cheshire, and
printed and bound in Great Britain by
CPI Antony Rowe Ltd, Chippenham and Eastbourne

A CIP record for this book is available from the British Library

ISBN 978 0 7486 3940 3 (hardback)

Contents

Acknowledgements

Institutionally, my first thanks must be to the Leverhulme Trust, who awarded me a two-year Research Fellowship from 2006–8 to work on Darwinism, poetry and poetics. Without the Trust's generous support, this book could not have been written in such good time. I owe a great debt too to my employers and colleagues at the University of Reading, whose generosity during my leave of absence was also fundamental. Thirdly, I am very grateful indeed to the British Society for Literature and Science for giving me the opportunity to meet so many like-minded scholars. Their enthusiasm for this project has been a great encouragement to me throughout. I have presented work towards this book at conferences of the British Society for Literature and Science, the British Association for Victorian Studies, the British Society for the History of Science, the North American Victorian Studies Association and the International Cultural History Association; at conferences at the universities of Keele, Ghent and Durham; and at research seminars at the universities of Oxford, Sheffield, Warwick and Keele. I am grateful to all these societies and universities for the opportunity to try out my ideas, to the colleagues who invited me or accepted my papers, and to the audiences, whose feedback has been invaluable. I would particularly like to thank the staff and students of Randolph College (then Randolph-Macon Women's College) in Lynchburg, Virginia, for the opportunity to explore my ideas in classes on Victorian history, American literature, environmental studies, evolution and animal behaviour, as well as in a public lecture, during a week as a visiting professor in 2007. I would like too to thank the staff of the Bodleian Library, the British Library and the library of the Royal Society.

Individually, I am most indebted to David Amigoni, Doug Shedd and Rebecca Stott, whose advice, encouragement, friendship and practical support have been indispensable. I am particularly grateful too to Geoff Harvey, Simon Eliot, Ronan McDonald and Dinah Birch, who were all instrumental in getting this work off the ground, and to my commissioning editor Máiréad McElligott and her colleagues at Edinburgh University

Press for accepting the book for publication and seeing it through into print. Other friends and colleagues who have helped and encouraged me along the way, and without whom this book would not be what it is, include Marie Banfield, Ian Bell, Giles Bergel, Kirstie Blair, Barrie Bullen, Alice Jenkins, Mike Londry, Peter Middleton, Keith Moore, Kirsten Shepherd-Barr, Helen Small, Kelley Swain, Andrew van der Vlies, Marianne van Remoortel and Michael Whitworth, and my copy editor Felicity Marsh. As always, my mother, Margaret Holmes, has been a great help, reading plans and proposals with a frankness born of unbreakable affection on both sides, while the keen interest that both my parents have taken in my work has been an encouragement throughout. I would also like to take this opportunity to thank Isobel Armstrong and Angela Leighton, whose masterly readings of sonnets by Dante Gabriel and Christina Rossetti at the conference in Ghent inspired me to try my hand at more formalist readings of poems myself. (Needless to say, any mistaken scientific claims, stylistic faults and other errors remain strictly my own.) Finally, I want to thank Jo, Amy and (latterly) Hannah, for making the last few years while I have been writing this book the happiest of my life so far.

Grateful acknowledgement is made to the following sources for permission to reproduce material in this book previously published elsewhere. Every effort has been made to trace copyright holders, but if any have been inadvertently overlooked the publisher will be pleased to make the necessary arrangement at the first opportunity.

Holt and Company, copyright © 1936, 1940, 1942, 1944 by Robert Frost, copyright © 1964, 1970 by Lesley Frost Ballantine. Reprinted by permission of Henry Holt and Company, LLC, and The Random House Group Ltd.

'Adultery' and 'The Garden of the Gods', from *Collected Poems* by Thom Gunn. Copyright © 1994 by Thom Gunn. Reprinted by permission of Faber and Faber Ltd and Farrar, Straus and Giroux, LLC.

'Rock and Hawk', copyright 1934 and renewed 1962 by Donnan Jeffers and Garth Jeffers, 'Vulture', copyright © 1963 by Garth Jeffers and Donnan Jeffers, from *Selected Poetry of Robinson Jeffers* by Robinson Jeffers. Used by permission of Random House, Inc.

'The Fawn' and 'I shall forget you presently, my dear', by Edna St Vincent Millay. Copyright © 1922, 1934, 1950, 1962 by Edna St Vincent Millay and Norma Millay Ellis. Reprinted by permission of Elizabeth Barnett, Literary Executor, The Millay Society.

'Eohippus', 'The Archaeopteryx's Song' and 'Trilobites' by Edwin Morgan, from *Collected Poems*. Copyright © 1990 by Edwin Morgan. Reprinted by permission of Carcanet Press Ltd.

Pattiann Rogers, 'The Possible Suffering of a God During Creation,' 'Geocentric,' and 'Against the Ethereal,' in *Song of the World Becoming: New and Collected Poems 1981-2001* (Minneapolis: Milkweed Editions, 2001). Copyright © 2001 by Pattiann Rogers. Reprinted with permission from Milkweed Editions.

'My Father Shaving Charles Darwin', from *A Spillage of Mercury* by Neil Rollinson. Copyright © 1996 by Neil Rollinson. Reprinted with permission from the author.

Preface

Since the first publication of *On the Origin of Species* 150 years ago, Charles Darwin's ideas and the discipline of biology founded upon them have changed our understanding of the natural world and our place within it radically and definitively. As a discourse, Darwinism has transformed Western culture. More fundamentally, it has transformed nature as we apprehend it. The sciences of palaeontology, ecology, ethology, evolutionary biology and genetics through which we understand the natural world are all Darwinian sciences. The processes of Darwinism – genetic mutation and recombination, natural and sexual selection – are the processes of biological creation by which, in the last words of Darwin's book, 'endless forms most beautiful and most wonderful have been, and are being, evolved' ([1859] 2003: 398). We ourselves are one of these forms, one twig on the tree of life, to use Darwin's own image.

Darwin himself has been dead for well over a century, yet his thinking has never been more vital nor more contentious than it is today. Now more than ever, with fundamentalism on the rise and ecosystems changing and collapsing around us on a global scale, we need to understand where Darwin's discoveries leave us, to feel for ourselves what it means to live in, to be born of, a Darwinian world. In this book I will be arguing that poetry has a unique and important role to play in helping us to reach that accommodation with Darwinism. More than any other art, poetry is equipped to knit together our immediate experience and our understanding, to make us feel for ourselves the impact of the ideas that it sets out before us. At the same time, poetry need not speak with a single voice. Many of the most gifted poets of the last 150 years, in Britain and the United States, have wrestled with Darwinism, from Alfred Tennyson, Thomas Hardy and Robert Frost to Ted Hughes, A. R. Ammons and Amy Clampitt. Each has confronted the implications of Darwin's ideas, yet for each those implications and their responses to them are different. By reading their poetry, we can gain for ourselves a more comprehensive sense of the human condition after Darwin and of the distinct ways of living within it.

Since the 1980s, the library of books on Darwin and Darwinism has mushroomed. A small but distinguished group of these have been literary critical studies. A very few (John Barnie's *No Hiding Place*, a collection of essays on post-war poetry and science writing, Robert Faggen's *Robert Frost and the Challenge of Darwinism*) have been on poetry. The last comprehensive account of the subject, Georg Roppen's *Evolution and Poetic Belief*, was written in the middle of the last century, while the standard authority, Lionel Stevenson's *Darwin Among the Poets*, is older still. When Stevenson's book was first published in 1932 the Modern Synthesis of Darwinism and Mendelism was not yet complete, while many of the most incisive poets who have tackled Darwinism were barely able to read, let alone write.

This book aims to plug this gap in our understanding, both of poetry and of the Darwinian condition itself. My hope is that it will have as much to say to scientists, environmentalists, philosophers and theologians – indeed, to anyone who finds themselves on the frontline of the struggle to comprehend Darwin's legacy – as it does to scholars, students and readers of poetry *per se*. To make the book as useful a tool in this struggle as possible, I have reprinted many of the poems I discuss in detail in full, so that readers may experience them for themselves.

In Chapter 1 I lay the foundations for my discussion of poetry and Darwinism, setting out my overall argument and its place within contemporary debates on the relationship between literature and science. I argue that both the so-called eclipse of Darwinism around the turn of the last century and disputes between current evolutionists have been overplayed. Instead, I make the case that there has been a broad theoretical consensus among specifically Darwinian evolutionists from Darwin himself onwards, regardless of the differences in the details of their theories. While this Darwinian understanding of evolution has been challenged, it has at no point been supplanted within the biological sciences, and has always been available to the laity, poets included. I then provide an overview of the history of Darwinian poetry in England and the United States, outlining a tradition that stretches from the 1860s to today and sketching out the distinct idea of modern poetry that it embodies. Finally, I address the practical question of how exactly poetry can affect how we see and respond to a scientific theory such as Darwinism by looking closely at three poems by the leading Scottish poet Edwin Morgan that do just that.

In Chapter 2 I provide a brief survey of non-Darwinian and pseudo-Darwinian evolutionary poetry in the late Victorian period, including poems which articulate Social Darwinist visions grounded in different political ideologies. I then look in more detail at specific poems and collections by A. C. Swinburne, Mathilde Blind, George Meredith and Tennyson. A clear understanding of the distinctions between different evolutionary theories both enables us to interpret these poems more precisely and exposes the fallacies, limits and contradictions of non-Darwinian evolutionism, many of which remain current as misinterpretations or misrepresentations of Darwinism today.

The remaining six chapters are organised not chronologically but thematically. In Chapter 3 I address what for many is the most fundamental challenge Darwinism poses to their thinking and their way of life – the implications of evolution and natural selection for belief in God. I argue that Darwinism poses two particular problems for theology. Firstly, the theory of natural selection appears to render a divine creator superfluous to the history of life on Earth. Secondly, it suggests that, if there is a creator, he has so little concern for suffering as to choose a creative process that is dependent on aggressive competition, premature death and the failure to breed. I explore how Hardy, Frost and Robert Browning interrogate the idea of a Darwinian natural theology in three poems, each concluding that it leads either to a bad God or to no God at all. Taking a lead from recent essays by the contemporary American poet Robert Pack, I go on to examine how two of his contemporaries, Philip Appleman and Pattiann Rogers – one an atheist, the other a Christian – reconcile a Darwinian God to the biblical God as represented in the Book of Job.

In Chapter 4 I examine how poets have responded to the related question of immortality. Darwinism poses a problem for belief in immortality because it is unclear how a process that works through gradual change can give rise to a being with an immortal soul, when the distinction between mortality and immortality is an absolute one. On the other hand, if we attribute immortality to a direct gift from God, we are faced with the question of why God would bestow immortality on a chosen organism having denied it to its parents. Meredith and Robinson Jeffers both accept that, after Darwin, death is final, yet they seek through their poetry to make that finality less distressing. Hardy too accepts the finality of death, but in his famous elegies for his wife Emma he does not reconcile himself to it. Instead, he uses poetry to create a space within which he can knowingly suspend disbelief and imagine for a time that death is not the end after all.

In Chapter 5 I look at how Darwinism alters our perception of our place in the universe. This chapter forms a bridge between the previous two, which are concerned with religious questions, and the next, which has an emphasis on ecology. Both these concerns come up here. I begin with Hughes's 'Wodwo', which draws attention to humanity's solipsistic preoccupation with its own significance through the figure of a proto-human aquatic ape. Darwinism compounds the impression astronomy gives us of our own littleness and marginality in relation to the universe as a whole. After a brief glance at how disturbed many Victorians were by this realisation, I look at Jeffers's homage to the universe's transcendence of merely human concerns in 'Night' and other poems. I then go on to look at how three contemporary American poets (Ammons, Pack and Appleman) pull the focus back in their poetry from the astronomical scale of Jeffers's poem to the planetary and human scales. On the planetary scale, they see the current ecological crisis as bearing witness to humanity's power of destruction. On the human scale, they emphasise the vital importance of our relationships with one another as the only guarantee of meaning we have in an otherwise inscrutable universe.

In Chapter 6 I look at how poets have responded to Darwinism in poems about animals. The realisation that we are animals ourselves, not merely taxonomically but by nature, is another of the blows that Darwinism has struck at humanity's self-image. But it also changes fundamentally how we think about other animals, as we recognise that they are our kin and that they too are conscious creatures who, in Hardy's word, know 'Earth-secrets' to which we are oblivious ('An August Midnight', l. 12). In this chapter, I concentrate on three types of animal that have played particular symbolic roles in poetry since Darwin. In birds of prey, Jeffers, Hughes, Richard Eberhart and others have discerned a symbol of the deliberate violence of nature after Darwin. Through songbirds, Meredith, Hardy, Frost and Clampitt have articulated post-Romantic Darwinian visions of nature to set against Shelley's 'To a Skylark' and Keats's 'Ode to a Nightingale'. Through encounters with deer, Hardy, Frost and others have explored the divide between humans and wild animals and the yearning to cross it.

In Chapter 7 I explore the implications of the fact that we are animals for how we think about love and sexual desire. In the 1880s, Constance Naden used comic poetry to good and funny effect to critique Darwinian hypotheses about the evolutionary psychology of love. More radically, other poets have taken our animal nature itself as a starting point for explorations of sexual psychology and morality. Both Meredith in *Modern Love* and Edna St Vincent Millay in her sonnets extrapolate from a Darwinian understanding of desire as natural to a feminism which insists on an equal status for female and male desire. In his poetry, including his response to the impact of AIDS on the gay community in *The Man with Night Sweats*, Thom Gunn extends this realisation to insist on the naturalness of homosexual as well as heterosexual desire.

In Chapter 8 I look back over the previous five chapters to ask whether, on balance, poets have found hope or despair in the Darwinian worldview, and where their leads might take us. There are two approaches to answering this question. The first is to look at poems in which the poets themselves weigh up the Darwinian condition as a whole and pass judgement upon it. I discuss a selection of these poems by Hardy, Frost, Clampitt, Ammons, Gunn and Rogers. The second approach is to weigh up different poets' views and their impact upon us for ourselves. In the last section of this chapter, I contrast two of the earliest and most comprehensive masterpieces of Darwinian poetry: Meredith's 'Ode to the Spirit of Earth in Autumn', with its optimistic, exuberant, pagan view of nature, and Tennyson's 'Lucretius', which finds nothing but madness and despair in a materialist worldview.

I close with one final reading, of 'Kew Gardens' by the contemporary Scottish poet D. M. Black, a poem which captures both the need for a source of meaning that transcends scientific materialism and the potential for poetry to provide that meaning, without withholding assent from science itself.

Poetry in the Age of Darwin

SCIENCE, POETRY AND LITERARY CRITICISM

At the end of the last century, the American naturalist Edward O. Wilson called for the arts and sciences to unite in a new harmony of knowledge. With characteristic panache, the founder of 'sociobiology' and prophet of 'Biophilia' called his new project 'Consilience' (1999). A term from the philosophy of science, 'consilience' refers to the 'jumping together' of distinct facts within the same explanation. Wilson was not alone in looking to bring the arts and the sciences together. As Wilson called for literary criticism to become more scientific, Richard Dawkins was calling on 'real poets and true scholars of literature' to join him in the inspirational world view of science (1999: 24). In reply, Mary Midgley (2001) called on Dawkins to accept that poets and critics had a responsibility to scrutinise science as well as to celebrate it, while the late Stephen Jay Gould (2004) called Wilson to account, insisting that the questions asked by the humanities could not be answered by scientific methods alone, but agreeing that scientists and scholars could learn from one another nonetheless.

In spite of their influence as public intellectuals, this debate between these leading Darwinians has received very little attention from the humanities. Not that literary critics have ignored science. Indeed, literary critics had been thinking about science in general and Darwinism in particular for some years before the scientists repaid the compliment. But in approaching science they have mostly preferred to use the tools of their own discipline, as Midgley and Gould suggest, rather than to imitate the practice or pay homage to the truths of science, as Wilson and Dawkins would prefer. The pattern for this literary critical approach to science was set in the 1980s with pioneering books by Gillian Beer ([1983] 2009), George Levine (1988) and others. For such critics science was very much part of culture, and culture was best understood in its historical context. On this model, literary criticism has more in common with the history of science than with science itself. The critic may well appreciate the force of

Darwin's arguments, for example, but he or she is concerned primarily with the language in which he formulates them and with their impact on his contemporaries (or vice versa). The aim is to write the novelists and poets back into the history of science, and the scientists and their science back into literary and cultural history. Within this project what Darwin himself wrote, or what other people wrote about him in his own time, is more significant than Darwinian biology today.

This historicist approach is typical of most literary criticism that takes an interest in science. It has greatly enriched our understanding of both literature and the history of science. But there are also critics who see Darwinism itself as the key to reading literary texts. Led by Joseph Carroll they have sought to turn Wilson's model of consilience into a critical methodology. As earlier generations of critics appealed to Freudian psychoanalysis or Marxist social theory, these self-styled literary Darwinists or biopoetic critics cite evolutionary psychology as the key to understanding human nature and therefore literature. Literary Darwinism has generated a number of more or less plausible models of how literature works but rather fewer productive critical methods. The most suggestive criticism to have arisen from this school so far – Peter Graham's work on Jane Austen, for example, or Marcus Nordlund's work on Shakespeare – takes Darwinian theory as a starting point rather than a predetermined conclusion. As Nordlund himself remarks,

> it is a mistake to suppose that any theory of human nature can ever be more than a reference point in the study of literary texts. To apply evolutionary principles directly to literary texts will often prove either uninteresting or reductive, and usually both. (2007: 72)

Under the banner of consilience, Wilson proclaims an alliance of the arts and the sciences on equal terms. In practice, his project subordinates the critical (if not the creative) arts to the sciences, specifically biology. Wilson wants 'scholars in the humanities' to embrace 'the knowledge of science' and 'lift the anathema placed on reductionism' (1999: 234). But as Gould points out, while the first half of this demand is sensible, the second is methodologically nonsensical (2004: 234–9). Literary interpretations and aesthetic judgements cannot be reduced to empirical facts. We may find new documents which give us a better idea of exactly what Shakespeare wrote, but that knowledge can never resolve once and for all what *Hamlet* means, nor whether it is a better play than *Macbeth*.

For literary criticism, Gould's more balanced model of consilience is ultimately more promising than Wilson's. Instead of an ambitious plan to unify the sciences and the arts, Gould suggests a more modest but less Quixotic approach to bringing them together. He proposes a 'consilience of equal regard' which 'respects the inherent differences' between the sciences and the humanities (2004: 259). 'Leading scholars in the humanities', he suggests, should 'seek out, and struggle to understand' 'factual information in scientific form', on the grounds that such information 'will be extremely helpful and relevant to the discussion of almost any important question in nonscientific subjects of the humanities, ethics, and religion' (ibid.: 235).

Gould could be charged (not for the first time) with overstating his case here. Whether or not a question is important is a matter of judgement, not fact, so to imply that only (or even 'almost' only) those questions on which science has a bearing can be important runs counter to his own argument. All the same, 'factual information in scientific form' surely is relevant to many important questions in the humanities. At the very least, as Jonathan Gottschall has remarked, many questions asked by literary scholars are 'contingent on specific fact claims about empirical reality' (2008: 58). (Gottschall too says 'most', but again this is questionable.) Scholars asking such questions will benefit from a knowledge of science and even have a responsibility to seek it out and 'struggle to understand' it, if only, as Gottschall insists, to ensure that their truth-claims do 'not conflict with well-established knowledge' in the physical and biological sciences (ibid.: 37).

Although his intellectual allegiances lie with Wilson, Gottschall's ideal of consilience as 'a catholic philosophy' which includes 'weak and strong forms' (ibid.: 37–8) seems closer to Gould. His weak form of consilience amounts to little more than the avoidance of error. What, then, might a more productive form of consilience look like on Gould's model? Are there other, more positive, ways for us, in Midgley's words, to 'sit down together and exchange our visions' (2001: 57), aside from the less doctrinaire developments of Wilson's work in evolutionary psychology?

One way in which literature – and literary criticism – can enhance our understanding of science is in helping us to grasp more fully its implications for ourselves. Over the last four centuries, science has transformed our understanding of the universe we inhabit and of our own place within it. In other words, it has changed fundamentally our perspective on the human condition. No other scientific development has had so profound a bearing on our perception of ourselves and our world as Darwin's discovery of evolution by natural selection. The philosopher John Dupré is right on both accounts when he remarks that, even as 'it is easy to overstate' how far Darwin's theory can generate 'detailed insight into our nature', it is 'hard to overstate' its importance 'to our general view of our place in the order of things' (2001: 19). A supposedly Darwinian idea of human nature does not look set to advance literary criticism very far, for all that Graham's and Nordlund's work, and indeed Gottschall's statistical analyses of folktales, suggest that it has its place within a Gouldian consilience. But an awareness of the human condition within a Darwinian universe is crucial if we are to understand what it is that literature offers us.

For all their differences, the historicist critics and the literary Darwinists have one thing in common. Both cross the line between disciplines by claiming the territory of another discipline for their own. The historicist critics claim books written by scientists about science for literary studies and cultural history. The literary Darwinists claim novels, plays and epic poems for the science of evolutionary psychology. What I am aiming for in this book is a more equal meeting of the disciplines – literary criticism and evolutionary biology – on their own terms. Through close and informed critical reading, we can draw out the significance of texts which explore the world view put forward by science today. Darwinism has been lucky in numbering some of the most lucid and engaging prose writers of the last 150 years among its leading exponents, from Darwin himself to Gould and Dawkins. Literary critics have at last begun treating such scientists as authors in their own right. Both Beer ([1983] 2009) and Levine (2006) have drawn out the importance of Darwin himself as a writer for our times as well as his own.

But it is not only the scientists themselves who concern us. To anyone with an interest in Darwinism – and we all have an interest in the world view of science, whether or not we think we are interested by it – the thoughts and feelings of poets and novelists who share that interest are equally and profoundly significant. Broadly speaking, poets and novelists stand in the same relation to science as the rest of the laity. They receive their understanding of science largely at second hand, and they respond to it in the light of their wider experience and ideas. In this regard, the poet or novelist is an everyman, as far as his or her perspective on Darwinism is concerned. Yet, at the same time, we value artists of all kinds for the imaginative richness of their art and for the depth of the feelings and ideas which they explore within it. By reading poems and novels which respond to Darwinism we can reach a fuller and more complex sense of our own Darwinian condition as we ourselves experience it.

Among the different literary genres which have engaged with Darwinism poetry addresses most directly the question of what it is to be a human being in a Darwinian universe. Novels assume an objective or ironic distance between the reader, the author and the third-person narrator (if there is one) on one side and the characters themselves on the other. Poetry, in particular lyric poetry, invites us to take on and experience for ourselves the emotions and perspectives of another human being as we read. Both transport us, but where novels transport us into a fictional world poems transport us to another state of mind, one in which we seek to grasp for ourselves the moods and ideas that led the poet to create the poem in the first place. Poetry has this effect in part because it makes use of the visceral power of language. Like a piece of music, a poem – especially when read aloud – is a felt experience, not just an object of study.

The poets I discuss in this book share a fundamental commitment to what the contemporary American poet Robert Pack calls 'the willingness to pay the price of consciousness'. As Pack writes, 'thought and feeling are not separable' (Hall and Pack 1962: 181). The confrontation with the reality of Darwinism is not merely an abstract intellectual or philosophical exercise. It is a profoundly moral, some would say spiritual, matter. Like poetry itself, deep engagement with moral or spiritual questions is a powerfully visceral experience. It requires both honesty and courage to undertake it. As we read the poetry of Darwinism we retrace the paths the poets themselves took as they explored our shared Darwinian condition. Some of these paths open onto more attractive vistas than others. Some may never open out at all. Some are too alarming or inhospitable for many readers to venture far along. Others may be false trails. Some run alongside one another, others across one another, others in different directions altogether. The more of them we explore, with the poets themselves as our guides, the fuller our mental map of the Darwinian condition, and the better we can grasp what it means for different people – ourselves included – to live in a Darwinian world.

In this book, I hope to show that poems written in response to Darwin's thinking from the early 1860s onwards are still profoundly relevant to how we think about Darwinism today. My argument implies that two claims routinely dismissed by cultural historians and historians of science are in fact at least partly correct. The first is that there was a 'Darwinian revolution', an epiphany in the history of ideas, marking a single radical break with the intellectual traditions of the past. The second is that Darwinism has remained largely consistent ever since Darwin first published *On the Origin of Species* in 1859. In the next section of this chapter, I make the case for why these claims, if not absolutely true, are at least sufficiently true to warrant reading Victorian or early twentieth-century poems as still pertinent to our understanding of the Darwinian condition. I will then set out briefly the tradition of Darwinian poetry that runs from Darwin's own day to the present. Finally, I will use three poems by the contemporary

Scottish poet Edwin Morgan to set out a number of ways in which a poet can approach Darwinism and shed light upon it.

Whose 'Darwinism'?

In an essay on 'The Nature of the Darwinian Revolution', Ernst Mayr, an openly partisan Darwinian, admitted that Darwin's ideas needed to be seen as contributing to a long process of change, which set in in the eighteenth century and would not be completed until over fifty years after his death (1976: 277–94). More recently, Philip Kitcher has itemised the impact of Darwinism, separating it into three separate ideas: an ancient Earth, a single tree of life and natural selection. As Kitcher sees it, each of these ideas took hold within science at a different stage, with only the middle one of the three being accepted as an immediate consequence of Darwin's own work (2007: 14–22). One of the leading historians of evolution, Peter Bowler, has even argued that the triumph of evolutionism over creationism in the nineteenth century is best seen not as a Darwinian revolution at all, but as a 'non-Darwinian revolution'. While Darwin played a major role in converting the scientific community and the public at large to evolution, Bowler argues, very few people accepted his argument that natural selection was the primary mechanism for evolutionary change. As a result, the evolution that people believed in after Darwin looked more like the evolution proposed by evolutionists earlier in the century (and largely rejected at the time) than it did Darwin's own model (Bowler 1983; 1992; 2003: 224–73). As Mark Ridley puts it in one of the standard textbooks on evolutionary biology, 'While evolution – of a sort – was being accepted, natural selection was just as surely being rejected' (2004: 10).

As these evolutionists and historians argue, many central elements of Darwin's world view were in place or at least under discussion before Darwin published his theory, including old-earth geology and the idea of evolution itself. Evolution had been a theme within English poetry too for at least seventy years. At the end of the eighteenth century, Darwin's own grandfather, Erasmus Darwin, proposed a teleological theory of evolution in his rococo verse treatises *The Botanic Garden* and *The Temple of Nature*, while in the mid-nineteenth century both Alfred Tennyson and Robert Browning explored evolutionary ideas in their poetry.

Evolutionism has indeed changed significantly since Darwin's day too. Most famously, Darwin himself knew nothing of genetics. It was not until 1900 that biologists began to take notice of the experiments conducted by the Bohemian monk Gregor Mendel in the 1860s showing that inheritance worked by recombining not blending genetic particles. As the early geneticists were largely hostile to Darwinian evolution, the so-called Modern Synthesis of Darwinism and Mendelism was a slow process. Initiated around the end of the first of the world wars, in the early papers of R. A. Fisher, it was not definitively completed until Julian Huxley declared victory for the new Darwinism in the book that gave the synthesis its name, *Evolution: The Modern Synthesis*, in the middle of the second. Prior to the Modern Synthesis, Darwinism itself had to struggle to survive alongside other competing theories of evolution and inheritance. These included Lamarckism (evolution through the inheritance of characteristics acquired through use and disuse and, in stronger forms of the theory, through willpower), orthogenesis (evolution along naturally – or divinely – pre-determined channels) and saltationism (evolution proceeding by random but drastic mutation, the theory preferred by most early Mendelians).

If the early history of Darwinism seems inauspicious for my claim that Victorian or early twentieth-century poetry which engages with Darwinism can be relevant on the same terms today, the second half of the story, from the Modern Synthesis onwards, appears to be little more promising. Even today Darwinists cannot agree among themselves what exactly 'Darwinism' means. The disputes between Wilson, Dawkins and Daniel Dennett on one side and Gould, Midgley and Steven Rose on the other are too technical to go into in detail here, but they are well known and have been rehearsed many times. Like any living science, post-war Darwinism has been far from monolithic, and it is far from certain which of the key players will be judged in the longer run to have been most consistently right.

How, then, can a poem by Alfred Tennyson or Thomas Hardy or even Robert Frost speak to Darwinism as we understand it now, when even the leading authorities do not agree on what 'Darwinism' means, beyond agreeing that, whatever it means today, it certainly does not mean what it meant when Tennyson, Hardy and Frost were alive? And why should we draw a line at 1859 when looking at poetry that grapples with the Darwinian world view when poets were already responding to some of the key elements of that world view before Darwin?

Before I can answer these questions, I have to concede that not every poem written in response to evolutionary thinking in the last century and a half remains current in the way that I want to suggest many do. Much, even most, of the poetry inspired by evolution in the last thirty years of the nineteenth century, for example, is indeed 'non-Darwinian' in Bowler's sense of the word, in that it engages with or reproduces models of evolution that are teleological in ways that Darwinian natural selection is not. This includes poems by Tennyson, Swinburne and Wilde, as well as a catalogue of poets now known only to specialists in Victorian poetry. To do justice to the history of poetry's responses to evolution since Darwin, and to shed light on how even such non-Darwinian poetry can illuminate reactions to Darwinism, I will discuss this poetry in the next chapter.

Here I want to make the case that even if many of the poems that responded to evolutionary theory before the triumph of the Modern Synthesis are only indirectly relevant to how we understand ourselves and our place in the modern Darwinian age there remain some, indeed many, that have a direct bearing on that understanding. There are four main reasons why this is true, in spite of the received history of Darwinism. Firstly, both Huxley and Bowler describe Darwinism as in eclipse around the turn of the last century. But for Darwinism to be eclipsed it must first have been shining. Huxley dated the reaction against Darwinism to the 1890s (1942: 22–8). Bowler has shown that it set in as early as the 1870s. But that still leaves a good decade when poets who were responding afresh to evolutionary thinking were responding predominantly to Darwin himself, and to a lesser extent to his close allies such as Alfred Russel Wallace and T. H. Huxley. Setting aside for a moment the distance between Darwin's Darwinism and our own we can at least agree that poets who grappled with evolution in the 1860s had in mind a set of ideas that were Darwinian by Darwin's own standards, whether they accepted them or rejected them.

Secondly, Darwinian evolution may have been under pressure from rival theories around the turn of the century, but it was by no means in abeyance. The eclipse of Darwinism was a partial not a total eclipse. My point is not to dispute that Darwinian evolution – evolution by means of natural selection – was a hotly contested subject in the late nineteenth and early twentieth centuries, nor that other non-Darwinian versions of evolution had a comparable currency within the wider culture of the time. But I do want to redress the balance somewhat by acknowledging that many of those who contributed to or followed these debates remained convinced throughout that Darwin's was the correct account of evolution. Bowler himself admits that the picture he paints in his influential study *The Non-Darwinian Revolution* may be somewhat exaggerated, remarking in his preface, 'If I have deliberately overstated my case in some respects, it should be remembered that my chief intention is to stimulate debate' (1992: x). Bowler's own work and the debate he has stimulated have deepened our understanding of the history of evolutionary theory immensely. But in spite of his disclaimer, his overstated case has become a misleading orthodoxy, as Ridley's textbook shows.

Bowler's thesis that the transition from creationism to evolutionism was a non-Darwinian revolution is based on a set of fine discriminations which leave Darwin standing almost entirely on his own. For example, Bowler identifies the German evolutionist Ernst Haeckel as a pseudo-Darwinian, rather than a Darwinian, partly (though not wholly) on account of his famous adage that ontogeny (individual growth) recapitulates phylogeny (evolutionary history). As Bowler remarks, 'Although Haeckel claimed that growth merely followed the path established by evolution, his use of the analogy with growth seemed to carry the implication that evolution, too, was a purposeful process' (1992: 13). As we shall see in the next chapter, this was indeed the case. Haeckel's argument did *seem* to imply that evolution was directed and developmental. But Bowler becomes carried away by these erroneous implications himself, affirming by the end of his book that Haeckel's recapitulationism is 'perhaps the most blatant late-nineteenth-century expression of the analogy between growth and evolution' (ibid.: 192), in spite of Haeckel's own insistence that 'ontogeny recapitulates phylogeny' is an analogy that holds good in one direction only.

Bowler even identifies T. H. Huxley, Darwin's famous bulldog, as a pseudo-Darwinian because of his affinities with the pre-Darwinian morphological tradition grounded in philosophical idealism; because he openly expressed doubts about natural selection; and because he tended within his own work towards linear and progressive rather than branching and directionless models of evolution, and then only from the late 1860s onwards (ibid.: 76–82). Yet, although Huxley consistently conceded that Darwin's theory of natural selection was unproven, in a review published within weeks of the *Origin* itself, he nonetheless declared it to be the only plausible explanation for evolution yet proposed. He reiterated this point in 1863 in two substantial lecture series, *Man's Place in Nature* and his lectures to working men, *On Our Knowledge of the Causes of the Phenomena of Organic Nature*. It is clear from these works and from his other early responses to Darwin that Huxley accepted evolution and understood it in Darwinian terms of common descent, as a branching and not necessarily progressive process, from the early 1860s onwards.

There were certainly differences between how Darwin, Haeckel and Huxley understood and represented evolution. Historians of science are rightly concerned to establish these differences. But looking not for the fine distinctions so much as the broad tendencies, it is clear that the broadly Darwinian contingent within late Victorian biology was powerful and vocal. After Darwin's death in 1882, prominent biologists including Wallace, Joseph Hooker, Francis Galton, Karl Pearson, Edwin Ray Lankester, August Weismann and Edward B. Poulton continued to make the case that natural selection was indeed the main motive force behind evolution in nature. As Bowler acknowledges (1992: 167), Huxley too presupposed that nature operated according to these same brutal principles in his masterful attack on Social Darwinism and eugenics, *Evolution and Ethics*. So did the political philosopher and professor of sociology L. T. Hobhouse, in his compendious *Morals in Evolution: A Study in Comparative Ethics*. Hence their insistence that we cannot take nature as an ethical or political model. Even Herbert Spencer, routinely set up as the philosophical spokesman for a deluded Victorian Lamarckism, retained a key role – if, as Bowler rightly points out, a secondary one (ibid.: 158, 165) – for natural selection. None of these men were mavericks, while most were professional scientists with strong institutional backing and substantial public reputations.

At the celebrations in honour of Darwin's centenary and the fiftieth anniversary of the *Origin* held at Cambridge University in July, 1909, Lankester was invited to speak as the representative of British biology, alongside other representative biologists from Germany, Russia and the United States. In what the journal *Nature* described as 'an eloquent appreciation of Darwin's work and an unequivocal vindication' of natural selection (Anon. 1909: 9–10), Lankester declared it to be the judgement of 'the large majority of British naturalists' that Darwin's 'theory of the origin of species by means of natural selection or the preservation of favoured races in the struggle for life' remained 'whole and sound and convincing, in spite of every attempt to upset it' ([1910] 1932: 34). The previous issue of *Nature*, which went to press the same day as Lankester's speech, carried as its lead article a review of a collection of essays entitled *Darwin and Modern Science*. Although this collection was published in Darwin's honour, and although its contributors included Hooker, Weismann and Poulton, the reviewer nevertheless detected an anti-selectionist bias in the absence of Wallace, Galton, Pearson and others. Even so, the 'educated layman' would still be able to conclude from the conflicting views set out in the collection 'that for the great majority of living biologists natural selection is still a working power in organic evolution' (Meldola 1909: 482–3).

Lankester's remarks and the stance taken by *Nature* run counter to Bowler's view that by the first decade of the twentieth century 'the majority of biologists had turned their backs on Darwinism' (1992: 169). They form a valuable counterpoint too to Stephen Jay Gould's account of the state of the debate on natural selection fifty years after the *Origin*. Gould had his own particular axe to grind, as he was keen to present what he saw as the rigid adaptationism of the Modern Synthesis and its heirs (the so-called ultra-Darwinians, led by Wilson and Dawkins) as an aberration in a more pluralist history of broadly Darwinian thought. Even the evidence Gould cites, however, does not justify his hyperbolic remark 'I can imagine no contrast more stark, no reversal so complete, as the comparison of these doubts in 1909 with the confidence and near unanimity expressed fifty years later at the *Origin*'s centennial in 1959' (2002: 569–70). The contrast would have been far more stark if natural selection had been thoroughly repudiated. As it is, even the leading Mendelian William Bateson, characterised by Gould as 'the least Darwinian' of the contributors to *Darwin and Modern Science*, is quoted as admitting that 'for some the perception of the principle of Natural Selection stands out as [Darwin's] most wonderful achievement' (ibid.: 569).

As Lankester and *Nature* saw it, that 'some' concealed a solid majority in favour. Lankester was of course a partisan in this debate, so his remarks need to be handled with care. Clearly he felt that Darwinism was under attack, or he would not have felt the need to defend it. But equally clearly he was not a lone voice nor an insignificant one. Lankester was feted by his peers, who awarded him the Darwin-Wallace Medal of the Linnaean Society in 1908 and the prestigious Copley Medal of the Royal Society in 1913. The invitation to speak at the centenary celebrations as the representative British biologist was an accolade in itself.

Lankester was also an influential educator, as a professor at University College London, Oxford and the Royal Institution and, publicly, as the Director of the British Museum's Natural History collection until 1907. Perhaps most significantly, from 1908 he was the author of a column on 'Science from an Easy Chair' in *The Daily Telegraph*. This column – which included a reprint of his Cambridge address in an article entitled 'Darwin's Theory Unshaken' – reached up to half a million readers each week. These 'Easy Chair' essays were periodically collected into volumes, which Lankester's biographer Joseph Lester estimates sold nearly 140,000 copies in total. According to Lester, 'no other science writer of the time enjoyed the same level of success' (1995: 155, 159). Whether or not we take Lankester's remarks in Cambridge at face value, it would have been far from clear to the generations of biologists taught by him or to the wider public who read him or visited his museum that Darwinism was in eclipse, whatever the 'calumny' (as he put it) spread by those who wanted 'to alarm the public mind with the preposterous statement that [Darwin's] celebrated and universally accepted theory . . . is undermined and discredited' ([1910] 1932: 27).

The prevailing history of science notwithstanding, since 1859 there have always been eminent and influential biologists for whom natural selection was the best available hypothesis. Even after the First World War, when Bernard Shaw remarked that 'every puny whipster may say what he likes about Darwin' ([1921] 1939: xxxiv) and W. R. Inge proclaimed that 'the legacy of Darwin is now in a state of chaos' (1925: 369), Lankester's books continued to sell in new editions, while R. A. Fisher, J. B. S. Haldane, Julian Huxley and others began publishing the papers and essays which would form the basis of the Modern Synthesis. At the same time, there was never a solid consensus among anti-Darwinian biologists as to which was the correct non-Darwinian theory of evolution. It is therefore reasonable to expect that some poets at least would have responded to what we still recognise as Darwinian ideas, even at the darkest moments of the eclipse of Darwinism. As it is, Lankester's claims, *Nature*'s and, indeed, Bateson's suggest that that eclipse was not in fact as dark as many historians of science believe.

The third reason why Darwinian poetry from before the mid-twentieth century is still pertinent today is that the differences between Darwin's Darwinism and the versions of Darwinism current now are not as dramatic as they seem. The reconciliation of Darwinism and genetics in the Modern Synthesis is something of a red herring. As Bowler observes, 'the selection theory was conceptually sound even on the basis of blending heredity' (1992: 91). Nor were the Darwinian and Mendelian parties as starkly divided as they are typically presented as being. Anticipating the Modern Synthesis by a decade or two in his Cambridge address, Lankester remarked that he was sure that Darwin 'would have been deeply interested in the numerical and statistical results associated with the name of Mendel'. In Lankester's eyes, these results illuminated 'the mechanisms concerned in hereditary transmission' but were not 'opposed in any way to the truth of Darwin's great theoretical structure – his doctrine of the origin of species' ([1910] 1932: 35). As Lankester predicted, Mendelian genetics corroborated Darwin's theory. To put it another way, genetics transformed our understanding of how precisely natural selection works without transforming the theory of natural selection itself.

An arguably more significant difference between Darwin's Darwinism and our own is the trust Darwin himself placed in the Lamarckian mechanism of the inheritance of characteristics acquired through use and disuse. This weak form of Lamarckism played an increasingly important part in Darwin's thinking, in part because it seemed a plausible means of speeding up the process of evolution, in response to erroneous calculations by the famous physicist William Thomson, later Lord Kelvin, which appeared to show that the Earth was not old enough for natural selection alone to explain the diversity of life. *The Descent of Man* and later editions of *The Origin of Species* can seem disappointingly Lamarckian today. But while the inheritance of acquired characteristics always had a place in Darwin's theory, from the first edition of the *Origin* onwards, Darwin consistently maintained that natural selection was the primary means by which evolution occurred. Lamarckism was only ever supplementary for Darwin, while for many of his closest allies, including Wallace and Huxley, it was superfluous.

On the other side, even today Darwinism retains elements which look not unlike the supplementary Lamarckism espoused by Darwin. The most well known of these is the Baldwin effect, named after the American evolutionist James Mark Baldwin, who was among a number of Darwinian biologists who identified it in the 1890s. Dawkins sums up the Baldwin effect in three sentences: 'Learning doesn't imprint itself into the genes. Instead, natural selection favours genetic propensities to learn certain things. After generations of such selection, evolved descendants learn so fast that the behaviour has become "instinctive"' (2005: 401n.). In contrast with Darwin's own Lamarckian account of the inheritance of acquired characteristics, the Baldwin effect allows evolution to give the impression that it is getting ahead of natural selection without violating what we now think of as orthodox Darwinian principles.

In their recent book *Evolution in Four Dimensions*, Eva Jablonka and Marion Lamb demonstrate that learning itself can be an agent of evolutionary change as behaviours develop which can isolate populations from one another, leading at least theoretically to speciation. As Jablonka and Lamb point out, the evidence is mounting too that characteristics acquired as a result of developmental and environmental conditions can be inherited, either as they activate inherited potentials within the genes themselves (as in chromosomal marking) or directly through the structural templating of proteins (as in prion diseases such as Creutzfeldt-Jakob disease and 'mad cow' disease). Jablonka and Lamb argue that such so-called epigenetic inheritance may even have played a crucial part in determining the path of evolution in the very early stages of the evolution of multicellular life.

Jablonka and Lamb like to call themselves Lamarckians, but their self-proclaimed Lamarckism is a long way from Darwin's, let alone Lamarck's. It has no role for use and disuse, and certainly no place for teleology or the will. Nonetheless, their work and the research they draw on suggest that the divide between Darwinian natural selection and the Lamarckian inheritance of acquired characteristics which became established soon after Darwin's death may be breaking down. Both in this and in the debate which Lamarckism still generates, Darwinism today looks more Victorian, and indeed more Darwinian, than it has for a long time.

Bowler (1992: 201–2) makes a similar point with reference not to Lamarckism but to the emergence of a more pluralist model of evolution which challenges some of the more rigid assumptions of the Modern Synthesis. Gould's work has been central in introducing into modern

Darwinism concepts which look superficially like the other non-Darwinian evolutionary theories of the late nineteenth and early twentieth centuries. Gould and Niles Eldredge's famous thesis that evolution occurs not steadily but at moments of punctuated equilibrium seems almost saltationist when set against the gradualism of Darwin himself. When the clock is slowed down to match the geological time periods that they have in mind, however, it is clear that they are still talking of evolution occurring over many generations, not in a single bound. Similarly, Gould's promotion of the new field of evolutionary developmental biology, or 'evo-devo', looks at first glance like a revival of orthogenesis or directed evolution. On closer inspection, however, evolution in Gould's work is not impelled in given directions, merely channelled. Insofar as this resembles older versions of evolutionary theory it is more akin to those of Bowler's pseudo-Darwinians such as Huxley and Haeckel, whose work was accepted by Darwin himself as complementing his own.

Neither the absence of genetics nor the presence of weak Lamarckism and developmental analogies make Darwin's Darwinism inaccessibly remote from our own. Nor, for all the heated debate between them, are Dawkins and Gould or any of the other architects of today's Darwinism remote from one another. This is the fourth reason why it makes sense to speak about poetry, whether Victorian or modern, as engaging with Darwinism. Aside from evolutionary psychology, where many of the disagreements between its practitioners and their critics are substantive, the most well-known spats among current Darwinians come down more to differences in emphasis or interpretation than to disagreements over fundamental principles. A palaeontologist like Gould has a different perspective on what is important within evolution from a population geneticist like Dawkins or a field naturalist like Wilson. Dawkins happily accepts many of Gould's arguments, just not the claim that they represent a fundamental departure from orthodox Darwinism. As for criticisms of Dawkins's own work, even the famous arguments over the 'selfish gene' result partly from a selective reading of Dawkins's occasionally overblown rhetoric, partly from a presumption that his thesis has political implications, which he himself frankly disavows, and partly from a reluctance on the part of molecular geneticists to recognise that population geneticists mean something else by the word 'gene' from what they mean themselves.

Once these disciplinary differences and political disagreements – real or imagined – are set aside, contemporary Darwinism looks less like a battlefield and much more like a consensus within which, as in any living science, there are healthy disagreements over how data should be interpreted and which might be the most productive models for further enquiry. It is the broad consensus rather than the finer details which makes up the basic description of the Darwinian condition. This consensus has remained remarkably consistent within Darwinian (as opposed to non-Darwinian) evolutionary theory ever since the first publication of *The Origin of Species* 150 years ago. Hence Gould's assessment that the *Origin* 'exceeds all other scientific "classics" of past centuries in immediate and continued relevance to the basic theoretical formulations and debates of current practitioners' (2002: 58). Hence, too, my argument that poetry engaging with Darwinism from Darwin's own time onwards remains relevant today.

What is this consensus, the core of Darwinism, which has remained constant across the last 150 years? Here is a short list of the key tenets of Darwinism:

1. Biology, including human biology, is a strictly secular science. The entire history of life on Earth since its origin can be explained without recourse to teleology or supernatural causes through the known mechanisms of evolution. The origin of life itself remains unknown.

   The only leading Darwinian who would not have accepted this point is Wallace, whose conversion to Spiritualism in the mid-1860s led him to isolate humanity from his strictly Darwinian understanding of evolution in the natural world. All Darwinians accept that the origin of life itself is currently unknown, for all that there are a number of hypotheses as to how Darwinian selective processes may have transformed self-replicating inorganic matter into living forms.

2. The history of life on Earth is one of branching evolution or descent with modification. All living organisms on Earth are thus related to one another to a greater or lesser degree.

   The only illustration included in the original edition of *The Origin of Species* illustrates this principle of common descent. Since the discovery of DNA in 1953, it has been clear that the shared chemistry of all life on Earth bears witness to this common ancestry.

3. The enormous diversity of species which have existed during the history of life has arisen over the course of immense stretches of time.

   Precise estimates as to the age of the Earth and of life on Earth have changed considerably since the nineteenth century. But the principle that it is geological reaches of time which have allowed natural selection to bring the observable diversity of life into being has remained constant. Current estimates place the age of the Earth at 4.6 billion years. There is good evidence that life had arisen by 3.8 billion years ago and multicellular life forms by more than a billion years ago. The earliest fossils of multicellular animals themselves are around 600 million years old.

4. The primary motor for evolutionary change is the natural selection of heritable variations.

This is the central thesis of *The Origin of Species*, and the core of Darwinism. Given variation, inheritance and competition, natural selection follows not merely in fact but as a logical necessity. Competition between different organisms to survive and reproduce leads inevitably to the spread of those inheritable traits or combinations of traits which tend towards relative competitive success. The motors for evolutionary change are thus premature death and the failure to reproduce.

5. Evolution can result from competition for mates as well as competition to survive. Traits which evolve as a result of sexual selection need not have any direct survival value or advantage.

Sexual selection has come relatively in and out of favour with Darwinian biologists. Darwin himself introduced the idea in the first edition of the *Origin*. He went on to devote the better part (in both senses) of *The Descent of Man and Selection in Relation to Sex* to it. Wallace refused to accept the argument that sexual selection could have much impact in the ruthlessly competitive world of natural selection, although he accepted that sexual selection could be a surrogate for natural selection, arguing that traits with beneficial survival value might also be more attractive to potential mates. As a rule, among more recent Darwinians, sexual selection has been given more weight by field naturalists, population geneticists and sociobiologists than by molecular geneticists and palaeontologists.

6. Some variations may be neither advantageous nor disadvantageous. While this tends to maintain broadly static populations, it can result in population drift and speciation when populations of the same species become isolated from one another.

Population drift is a relatively recent concept within Darwinian biology, although it follows from Darwin's own work on island populations. Gould is the leading champion of population drift as a major factor in evolution among recent Darwinians. Population drift inevitably remains a relatively weak evolutionary force in that it can be trumped by either natural or sexual selection.

7. The physiological variations on which these three motors for evolution (natural selection, sexual selection and population drift) operate arise largely as a result of random mutation and sexual reproduction. Patterns of behaviour, whether wholly innate or partly learnt, may also be selected.

Within any population of organisms, there will be a wide range of genetic variation which will be subject to natural selection as environmental pressures change. The mutations and recombinations of genes which give rise to these variations are random, in that the process of mutation is blind to whether or not a variation will be beneficial to the organism itself. They are not mathematically random, in that certain mutations will be more likely than others. As Jablonka and Lamb argue, natural selection can in theory choose between learnt behaviours as well as genetic variations, while the Baldwin effect explains how the propensity to learn behaviours can also be selected. It looks increasingly as though environmental factors may lead to heritable variations too, particularly in cases of stress (Kaati et al. 2007).

8. Natural selection adapts species to their ecosystems and environments, but only within parameters close to the current form of the given species and to the degree required for that species to survive alongside the other species which make up its ecosystem. To understand fully the biology of any species it is therefore necessary to understand both its history and its ecology.

The ecological implications of Darwin's theory are vividly illustrated in his famous image of life as an 'entangled bank' in the closing paragraph of *The Origin of Species* ([1859] 2003: 397).

9. The precise history of evolution is contingent upon climatic, geological and astronomical events.

Although Darwin acknowledged that environmental conditions form a key factor in natural selection, the gradualism of his own account of evolution, derived from Charles Lyell's uniformitarian (as opposed to catastrophist) geology, did not allow for drastic changes to environmental conditions on the scale of the meteor strikes and super volcanoes that have since been identified as major causes of mass extinctions. In the extreme conditions that follow from such extreme events the criteria for fitness and survival are liable to sudden and radical change. The traits that have enabled a given species to survive thus far may no longer serve, while the extinction of individual species or lineages in these circumstances may be more largely a matter of chance. This does not imply that natural selection is in abeyance, however, merely that the nature which is selecting has itself been radically changed. The motor of evolution remains differential survival; that is, death and the failure to reproduce.

10. Insofar as evolution is progressive this is to be understood in local and relative, not universal nor absolute, terms. There is no evidence that evolution progresses towards a single, predetermined goal.

In *The Descent of Man*, Darwin insisted that 'we must remember that progress is no invariable rule' ([1871] 2004: 166). In Hobhouse's words, 'progress is not something that goes on of itself by an automatic law or an inherent tendency of things' (1906: II, 280). As Lankester argued in his short book *Degeneration: A Chapter in Darwinism*, natural selection is perfectly capable of favouring traits that seem to us intellectually, morally or aesthetically degenerate – a point vividly illustrated by H. G. Wells in the 1890s in his essay 'Zoological Regression' and his novels *The Time Machine* and *The War of the Worlds*. Even Julian Huxley, the twentieth-century Darwinian most committed to the idea of progress, accepted that, while evolutionary progress (defined as an organism's 'increased control over and independence of the environment' (1942: 564–5)) remained for him an objective fact this was nonetheless progress 'of a particular and limited nature' (ibid.: 569), which is entirely explicable according to the mechanism of natural selection. More recently, Gould argued that even the 'vaunted trend to increasing complexity in the history of life' is an artefact of history, recording 'little more than the constraint of life's origin right next to the lower bound of preservable complexity in the fossil record'. In Gould's eyes, 'only one direction – towards greater complexity – remained open to "invasion," and a small number of species dribble in that direction through time' (2002: 730). Like his close colleague John Maynard Smith (Smith and Szathmáry 1997), Dawkins sees the same trend less as a dribble than as a series of breakthroughs, each of which has dramatically increased the scope for further evolution and has been in that sense progressive. Dawkins argues too that the 'arms races' between species, where the individuals of each species are in direct competition with one another and with those of the other species, for example as predator and prey, lead to progress in local cases and relative terms along individual trajectories (2005: 611–28). Simon Conway Morris (2003) also disagrees with Gould. In his view – largely shared by Dawkins (1991: 77–109; 2005: 609–11) – the prevalence of convergent evolution in nature indicates that there are relatively few evolutionary solutions to a given problem. These solutions are therefore, in effect, the goals towards which evolution progresses, not through orthogenesis, but because it cannot efficiently go anywhere else.

Wallace's rejection of the first clause aside, all the leading Darwinian biologists of the last 150 years would have been able to subscribe to this list, although any individual scientist would of course identify some points as more significant than others and might quibble as to the detail of the wording of certain clauses.

Returning to the question of whether Darwin's theory marked a new departure in the history of ideas, or merely an extension of earlier developments such as uniformitarian geology and Lamarckian evolutionism, it is clear from this summary that Darwin initiated some truly radical shifts in our understanding. Pre-Darwinian evolutionism was an essentially providential, teleological thesis. There was no clear secular explanation for the design of life, no fully secular biology, before Darwin. There was no branching tree of life either, as even those who accepted evolution understood it to move in effectively parallel lines towards the same basic goals. And there was no natural, nor sexual, selection. While some pre-Darwinian poems – Erasmus Darwin's evolutionary reveries or Tennyson's *In Memoriam* – anticipate aspects of the Darwinian world view, even raising some of the questions Darwin would raise himself, they cannot by definition be meditations on that world view itself, and it would clearly be a mistake to read them as if they were.

The broad Darwinian consensus I have outlined has formed an influential strand in scientific thinking since 1859 and has been accepted as correct across the scientific community since the 1940s. It has been supported by findings not only in comparative anatomy, palaeontology, microbiology, epidemiology, ethology and ecology, but also in geology, climatology, organic and inorganic chemistry and nuclear physics. Gould praised *The Origin of Species* as the perfect example of 'the power and efficacy of consilience as a method of proof in natural history' (2004: 211). The subsequent development of biology has progressed along the same Darwinian lines, bringing ever more findings to bear from different disciplines and producing one of the fullest and most coherent theories in modern science.

There are many competing accounts of Darwinism, but they all fall within the broad Darwinian consensus. There are no scientifically credible alternatives to Darwinism. If we want to avoid confronting the implications of Darwinism we have only three options, none of them satisfactory. We can deny Darwinism outright, as religious fundamentalists do. This is the boldest and frankest move, but it requires such prodigious ignorance or bloody-mindedness that no one blessed with both curiosity and intellectual honesty can sustain it.

Secondly, we can take refuge in an extreme form of cultural relativism. This has an air of philosophical sophistication. It draws on the tendency in the history of science for one paradigm to give way to another, apparently proving that no scientific theory can claim to be 'true' in an absolute or eternal sense. This argument effaces the differences between the processes and contexts of scientific research at present and in the past. Counting the hours of research undertaken and the quantity of data amassed,

Darwinism has long outlasted all earlier biological paradigms put together. Furthermore, short of a debilitating and unwarranted position of absolute scepticism, or the equally untenable position that redundant science is as correct as current science, it is hard to see where extreme relativism leads. The argument that beliefs other than those of science have an equal claim to be true is only consistent if all beliefs are deemed to be equally and utterly unwarranted. As soon as we accept any grounds for reasonable belief at all, we have little choice but to accept that the established facts of science, including Darwinian biology, lay the best claim to that belief, the errors and paradigm shifts of the past notwithstanding.

The third option is to embrace the thesis of Intelligent Design or ID. ID has been well publicised and has a certain amount of currency at large. But it not only lacks the support of mainstream science, it has virtually no support at all among practising biologists. In his recent book, *The Edge of Evolution*, the ID theorist Michael J. Behe declares, 'Like it or not, the more science has discovered about the universe, the more deeply fine-tuning is seen to extend – well beyond laws, past details, and into the very fabric of life, perhaps beyond the level of the vertebrate classes' (2007: 230). Behe's claim to speak for 'science' is mere posturing. In the words of the American National Academy of Sciences – which could reasonably be said to speak for science – 'The scientific consensus around evolution is overwhelming' (cited Appleman 2001: 619). As with the question of climate change, the 'debate' is largely an artefact of media representation and of individuals' unwillingness to accept science. At best, it is a marginal issue within the philosophy and sociology of science. It is not a reflection of the state of science itself.

The proponents of ID see themselves as posing a strong scientific challenge to the ossified orthodoxy of Darwinism. As a molecular geneticist, Behe is arguably the ID theorist best-qualified to do so. And yet, taking *The Edge of Evolution* as representative of the science of ID as it stands, it is riddled with holes. Behe's major claim in this book is that the limited evolution of malaria and of resistance to it to date proves that Darwinism is hamstrung. He accepts that life on Earth has evolved from common ancestors over billions of years. He accepts too that random mutations and natural selection can explain the spread of drug-resistance among malaria parasites and of sickle-cell anaemia among humans, which provides a high-level of resistance to malaria for people with one copy of the relevant gene but is fatal to those with two. What he insists, however, is that if that is all natural selection can do, then it is not up to much.

Behe's arguments are based on a number of misconceptions. He repeatedly represents evolution as a process of getting from A to B, something he suggests that the drunken stagger of random variation and natural selection could never achieve. But evolution is not the process of getting from A to B, but the process of getting from A to anywhere a bit better than A in the circumstances. It is only in retrospect, once evolution has taken place, that B can be identified, and even then it would be a mistake to presuppose that there were not a number of alternative possibilities. Behe attempts to prove mathematically that the rate of evolutionary change by natural selection is far too slow to account for the complexity of life on Earth. But his assumption that we can generalise from the rate of evolution among malaria and HIV over the last fifty years to the rate of evolution of other organisms in other conditions is clearly unwarranted. As for the evolution of different lineages of multicellular life, he makes no mention whatever of the part played by sexual reproduction in generating new variations within species which are then open to natural selection.

Behe's book is subtitled *The Search for the Limits of Darwinism*. It fails in this aim. After Behe, the limits of Darwinism are where they have been for the last 150 years: at the origin of life itself. But even if Behe's critique of Darwinism was fatal, it would not substantiate ID. Evidence of weakness in one scientific theory is not of itself evidence of strength in another. As Philip Kitcher remarks in his excellent study of Creationism and ID, *Living with Darwin*, 'Neither in Behe's writings, nor in those of any other intelligent design-er, is there the slightest indication of how Intelligence performs the magic that poor, limited, natural selection cannot' (2007: 104).

Whatever the limitations of Behe's book, his professed aim remains legitimate. Science is there to be scrutinised, probed, interrogated. It depends upon such interrogation for its validity, indeed for its own methodology. Subjected to the same interrogation, ID is exposed as a will-o'-the-wisp. But even if it were not – even if ID proves able to mount a more robust scientific challenge to Darwinism than it has so far – it would be irresponsible and dishonest for anyone with a genuine commitment to the truth to ignore the vast weight of scientific opinion against it.

Creationism, relativism and Intelligent Design notwithstanding, Darwinian evolutionary theory remains the core of modern biology. As such, it has more profound implications for ourselves as living beings than any other science. We are the product of Darwinian processes and the inhabitants of a Darwinian world. These are facts, as robustly supported as any other facts we know. Indeed, the most fundamental argument of all, that evolution occurs through natural selection, is more secure still, as it is a logical corollary of three conditions (variation, inheritance and competition) which are self-evident.

Given these facts, we need to grapple with them if we are to understand ourselves and our place in the universe. But if we are to grapple with Darwinism where should we turn for guidance? Who, in short, should we read? One answer is the scientists themselves. Darwin himself is a rich, wise and humane writer, and *The Origin of Species* in its first edition remains the most persuasive case ever made for the thesis that the diversity of life is the product of evolution by means of natural selection. Darwin and later scientists capture the fascination of natural history in their prose too. Then there are philosophers and theologians, who lead us through the implications of Darwinism to their own conclusions. Their asides aside, however, few of these writers can help us to realise for ourselves what it is to be a Darwinian being in a Darwinian world. Their prose, even at its most humane or passionate, is too much bent on persuading us of their case. This is not a fault. It is simply the nature of prose argument. But that is why we need the poets as well.

THE DARWINIAN TRADITION IN MODERN POETRY

The oldest poets to respond to Darwin's ideas were of an age with Darwin himself. Darwin was fifty when he published the *Origin* in 1859. The predominant English poets of the time were Tennyson, the Poet Laureate, born like Darwin in 1809, and Elizabeth Barrett and Robert Browning, born in 1806 and 1812 respectively. Barrett Browning died in 1861, leaving no poetry responding to Darwin. For their part, Tennyson and Browning were already evolutionists when they read Darwin, and his world picture did not have a marked effect on their own. But while they may not have been influenced much by Darwin in their beliefs they nonetheless explored the theological implications and the psychological impact of his naturalistic world view in their poetry, particularly in the 1860s. Neither Tennyson nor Browning accepted Darwinism, yet their responses to it, particularly in 'Lucretius' and 'Caliban upon Setebos' respectively, remain incisive and indicative of how unsettling Darwinism can be if given serious thought.

It was the next generation, born from the late 1820s to the 1840s, who felt the impact of Darwin's ideas most acutely. For them, Darwinism was, as John Addington Symonds put it, 'a theory which startled the world' ([1890] 1907: 71). They were neither so old as to be settled in their thinking nor so young as to have been born into an age in which evolution was already accepted as science. Of the poets of this generation, George Meredith and Thomas Hardy engaged most profoundly and persistently with Darwinism. Meredith is remembered as one of the most challenging Victorian novelists. He is also one of the most difficult Victorian poets. Like grappling with Darwinism itself, reading Meredith is an intellectually bracing experience.

Hardy, by contrast, is always lucid, whether in his novels or his poetry. With that lucidity comes a remarkable ability to touch and move his readers with an unanticipated idea or image. The poetry of both will be central throughout this book.

Other poets of the same generation also responded to Darwinism. In the next chapter I will discuss the pseudo-Darwinian evolutionary poetry of Algernon Swinburne, Mathilde Blind and others. The Scottish poet James Thomson found in Darwinism a confirmation of the atheism he was already imbibing from other sources. His allegorical nightmare *The City of Dreadful Night* will be a point of reference in a number of later chapters. On the opposite side, Christina Rossetti and Gerard Manley Hopkins saw Darwinism as a threat to be faced down through an affirmation of the incarnation of Christ and the truth of the revealed word. Their strategy was more one of denial than engagement, however, so their poetry will not play a major role in this book.

For the next generation of English poets, evolution was an accepted fact. They were cushioned from the blows that struck their parents on first reading Darwin, both by this general acceptance and by the availability of apparently scientifically credible non-Darwinian versions of the theory. The polite and often genuine entente between liberal theology and natural science tended to conceal any underlying conflicts between them. All told, the full intellectual and emotional challenge of Darwinism rarely presented itself. Surviving Victorians like Hardy aside, English poets largely ignored Darwinism after the turn of the century. It was their parents' and grandparents' controversy, not their own.

Darwinian poetry did not become extinct, however. The poetic engagement with Darwinism which began in Victorian England took hold in the United States between the wars. Since the 1920s, religious belief has been a more contentious issue there than in Britain, and Darwinism has consequently been more hotly debated and aggressively interrogated there. It is largely because the religious seriousness that characterised the Victorians still pertains in the United States that the American poetry of Darwinism has been so substantial and profound.

The leaders of the first generation of American poets to respond to Darwinism were Robert Frost, Robinson Jeffers and Edna St Vincent Millay. Stylistically and geographically, each of these poets was wholly independent of the others. Frost wrote measured blank-verse narratives and stanzaic lyrics set in the woods and farmsteads of New England. Many of his poems are dark, even Gothic, but his manner is muted and restrained, quietly unsettling rather than shocking. Jeffers wrote book-length narratives and frankly didactic lyrics in his own brand of long rhythmic lines, freighted with meaning and heightened in intensity. His setting is the harsh landscape of northern California and his plots are derived from Greek tragedy. Where Jeffers's poems expand seemingly without limits, Millay is at her best within the precise confines of the sonnet. She was one of the first women poets to write openly and powerfully about sexual desire in English since the heady days of the Restoration. While her mores are thoroughly modern, her verse feels at times almost Renaissance, and she uses the rhetoric and imagery of Petrarchism with more wit and assurance than any poet since Shakespeare.

For all these differences of style and subject matter, Frost, Jeffers and Millay shared with Hardy an idea of what it meant to be a modern poet distinct from that of the modernist poets and critics who tend to dominate histories of twentieth-century poetry. In *New Bearings in English Poetry*, F. R. Leavis insisted that a poem should 'exhibit modernity' not 'by mentioning modern things, the apparatus of modern civilization', nor 'by being about modern subjects or topics'. Instead, he suggested, 'All that we can fairly ask of the poet is that he shall show himself to have been fully alive in our time. The evidence will be in the very texture of his poetry' ([1932] 1963: 24). For Leavis, to be modern was to be modernist. Taking challenging, even perplexing, innovations in poetic form and language to be the only true indicators of a poet's modernity, he named Hopkins, T. S. Eliot and Ezra Pound as the three crucial modern poets.

Countering Leavis, the American poet and critic Yvor Winters argued that the view that 'the chaos of modern thought' meant it was no longer possible to write good poetry except in the modernist mode was a form of 'group hypochondria' ([1937] 1960: 101). Jeffers agreed. As he wrote in 1948 in his essay 'Poetry, Gongorism, and a Thousand Years', 'it is not necessary, because an epoch is confused, that its poet should share its confusions'. A great modern poet, Jeffers proposed, would indeed 'be seeking to express the spirit of his time', but would also 'have something new and important to say' and 'would wish to say it clearly' (2001: 724).

To speak clearly virtually presupposes an anti-modernist aesthetic. In a letter to Pound, Hardy remarked,

> As I am old-fashioned, and think lucidity a virtue in poetry, as in prose, I am at a disadvantage in criticizing recent poets who apparently aim at obscurity. I do not mean that *you* do, but I gather that at least you do not care whether the many understand you or not. (1978–88: VI, 77)

Hardy's edgy politeness reveals how out of sympathy he too was with the modernist project. His sardonic dismissal of his own view that poetry should be lucid as 'old-fashioned' neatly affirms the opposite: that lucidity is indeed a virtue in poetry regardless of fashion. As Hardy's own poetry demonstrates, this commitment to lucidity does not equate to simplicity of form or ideas, nor to a transparent relation between the speaking voice of a poem and its author. But it does require that the language of the poem itself is not too opaque, disjointed or allusive to be readily understood. Frost too shared this commitment to lucidity, if not transparency, in poetry, as did Millay.

Given their shared sense of the demands of modern poetry, it is less surprising than it might seem that Hardy, Frost, Jeffers and Millay were linked too by their admiration for one another. Frost called Hardy 'an excellent poet and the greatest living novelist' in England and 'one of the most earthly wise of our time' (Frost 1965: 104, 147). For all their differences, Frost and Jeffers came to see each other as rural and regional allies against the urban, cosmopolitan modernists led by Eliot and Pound (Norwood 1995). Hardy was Jeffers's favourite novelist (Jeffers 1968: 272–3), while Millay admired him enough to send him a complimentary copy of her play *The King's Henchman*. Hardy returned the compliment, praising her lyric poetry in letters to Amy Lowell and to Millay herself (Hardy 1978–88: VI, 186; VII, 64), and provocatively remarking that America's two great contributions to the culture of the 1920s were its architecture and Millay's poems (cited in Walker 1996: 173). Millay and Jeffers were friends who admired each other's poetry. Jeffers was particularly impressed by Millay's sonnet sequence *Fatal Interview*, which I discuss in Chapter 7 (Jeffers 1968: 170; Epstein 2001: 214, 225). For her part, Millay considered Jeffers to be the best poet writing in America in her day (Milford 2001: 330).

The Darwinian tradition in modern English and American poetry centres on the work of Meredith, Hardy, Frost, Jeffers and Millay. It is an important and powerful counterweight to modernism. The two traditions saw both modernity and poetry differently. For modernists such as Leavis the *Zeitgeist* manifested itself in a distinctive modern manner born of a metropolitan environment in which 'Urban conditions, a sophisticated civilization, rapid change, and the mingling of cultures have destroyed the old rhythms and habits, and nothing adequate has taken their place' ([1932] 1963: 50). For the anti-modernist poets, poetry does not need to reflect the alienated life of the modern city back upon itself in order to be distinctively modern. What is crucial is rather to grapple with the challenges of modern thought, to explore how they have changed, perhaps permanently, our perspective on what Jeffers called 'permanent things' (2001: 728).

For all five of these poets, the most fundamental of these challenges is posed by Darwinism. Darwinism is the foundation stone of Meredith's, Hardy's and

Jeffers's poetry. It underpins their work, and their poems frequently consider it directly. It underlies Millay's work too, albeit less obviously. Frost is more equivocal about Darwin's legacy and the validity of his ideas. Although he named Darwin as the greatest thinker of the previous 100 years, he retained a degree of scepticism towards his account of evolution, partly because he was deeply and rightly suspicious of the eugenics seemingly premised on Darwinism in the mid-twentieth century, and partly because he saw Darwin as substituting the fallacy of infinite growth for the bleaker reality of finite growth rounded off with inevitable extinction (see Frost 2006: 317–18, 383–4, 484, 486, 522–4). Darwinism is nonetheless one of Frost's central preoccupations, a problem he worries at repeatedly in his poetry. His partial scepticism towards it, like Tennyson's and Browning's in the 1860s, does not impair his ability to scrutinise its implications, particularly as his own pessimistic view of evolution shares many of those implications itself.

The Anglo-American tradition initiated by these late nineteenth- and early twentieth-century poets persists in a more diffuse form in contemporary poetry. The second generation of American poets to grapple extensively with Darwinism was born in the 1920s. In the preface to his collection *Darwin's Ark*, published in 1984, Philip Appleman writes:

> I was conceived in the same month that John Thomas Scopes was arrested and indicted by a grand jury for the crime of teaching evolution to the schoolchildren of Dayton, Tennessee, and . . . born in the same month that the legislature of the state of Mississippi duplicated the Tennessee anti-evolution law. My memory of those events is imperfect, but I conjure up the temper of the times from the historical fact that, in the year of my birth, the famous evangelist Aimee Semple McPherson, concocting an alibi for an extended rendezvous with her lover, claimed to have been kidnapped by gamblers, dope peddlers, and evolutionists; and from the establishment, a year after my birth, of the American Anti-Evolution Association, an organization open to all citizens *except* 'Negroes, Atheists, Infidels, Agnostics, Evolutionists, and habitual drunkards.' (1996: 123)

For Appleman, the upshot of this stigmatizing of evolution – which, incidentally, gives the lie to the casual assumption that Darwinism and racism go hand-in-hand – was that he and his generation were taught biology without reference to evolution. As he puts it, 'Across the nation, the invisible government of church fathers and school boards had in effect abolished a natural law from the schools' (ibid.: 124). It is because Appleman feels the shadow of those times falling over these that he feels the need to champion Darwin so robustly. The leading American poets of his generation to engage with Darwinism (Amy Clampitt, A. R. Ammons and Robert Pack, together with their younger contemporary Pattiann Rogers) have felt a similar need to stand up and be counted.

The pre-eminent English poets of the same generation (Philip Larkin, Ted Hughes and Thom Gunn) all respond to Darwinism in their poetry too. Unlike their American contemporaries, however, they rarely make a point of addressing Darwinism directly. Instead, it defines their world views from the outset. In Larkin's case, Darwinism is one factor contributing to his secular disillusionment and his fear of mortality, and its specific place in his poetry is hard to isolate. More positively, Darwinism lies at the heart of how Hughes and Gunn think and write about nature. For Hughes, it is central to his understanding of the natural world as intrinsically violent – a leitmotiv of his poetry, typified by 'Hawk Roosting', which I discuss in Chapter 6. For Gunn, it leads rather to an understanding of human nature as fundamentally and positively animal, as I show in Chapter 7.

As with the earlier generations of Darwinian poets, there is little to identify these poets stylistically. What unites them is rather their open and persistent engagement with the questions raised by Darwin and his successors. This engagement is often realised in intertextual dialogues that cross the different generations of Darwinian poets. As Pack, Rogers and Clampitt respond to Frost who himself reworks ideas from Hardy, while Millay rewrites Meredith's *Modern Love* from her own vantage point, Hughes makes Jeffers's core imagery his own, and all of these poets write back to Darwin himself, the Darwinian tradition emerges as a substantial and shaping presence within modern poetry.

POETRY AND DARWINISM IN PRACTICE: THREE POEMS BY EDWIN MORGAN

I have suggested that poetry can affect how we think and feel about Darwinism. But how can a poem alter our perspective on a scientific world view such as Darwinism? How can a poem's tone, for example, affect our responses not only to the poem itself but to the questions it addresses? Again, what kinds of poetry are most effective for exploring the Darwinian condition? Do all Darwinian poems do similar things, or can poetry approach Darwinism in different but equally productive ways? The Darwinian condition may be a serious business, but is Darwinian poetry itself necessarily serious? If not, what might be the effect of humour in a Darwinian poem?

To suggest some answers to these questions, I want to look at three poems by Edwin Morgan. Morgan belongs to a distinct Scottish tradition of Darwinian poetry, looking back less to Frost, Hardy or Jeffers than to the great twentieth-century Scots poet Hugh MacDiarmid, who himself looked back to John Davidson. I will be looking briefly at Davidson's Nietzschean Social Darwinism in the next chapter. MacDiarmid's own grapplings with Darwinism have dated less than Davidson's, but his decision to write poems such as 'Gairmscoile', 'Whuchulls' and A Drunk Man Looks at the Thistle in Scots inevitably puts them beyond the reach of most English and American readers, who cannot hope to realise for themselves the nuances of sound or meaning in his poetry as fully as a native Scot. For this reason, MacDiarmid will not feature as much in this book as he deserves to.

Aside from his place in this lineage, Morgan stands on the sidelines of the Anglo-American tradition of Darwinian poetry for another reason. Where Davidson and MacDiarmid both aspired to be major poets of what they saw as an expressly Darwinian age – an aspiration MacDiarmid achieved in his Scots poetry – Morgan apparently has no such ambition. He is undoubtedly a major modern poet – he was appointed Scotland's first Makar, or poet laureate, in 2004 – but Darwinism has not been a central concern of his career as a poet. Instead it is an occasional consideration. Paradoxically, the very sparseness of Morgan's Darwinian poetry helps guarantee its significance. He may have written only a handful of poems drawing on Darwinism, but precisely because it is not a preoccupation, Morgan thinks about Darwinism in a new way each time he returns to it in a new poem.

Morgan's poetry may have no overarching Darwinian vision, but it is an excellent starting point for exploring the different things a poet can do with Darwinism. His most well-known evolutionary poem is 'Eohippus', published in 1970 as one of a series of poems entitled The Horseman's Word. It looks like this:

```
e e t l
p u r i
k i t l
k a t l
h u f f
w i d l
t r i g
s n e p
k l o p
k l i f
p t o t
s e e p
s i p l
```

```
t r i p
t o i p
t o r p
h o r p
h o r s
```

This poem is a verbal, visual and aural representation of the evolution of the horse. *Eohippus*, the 'dawn horse' (also called *Hyracotherium*), lived around 50 million years ago. The palaeontologist Robert Savage describes it as 'lamb-sized' (Savage and Long 1986: 200), a felicitous analogy which provokes something of the same sentimental affection for this ancient animal as Morgan's Scots-babyish 'eetl'. As Gould pointed out, the evolution of the swift, tall, handsome, one-toed *Equus* from this diminutive, undistinguished, four-toed ancestor is one of the iconic myths of evolution. In *The Structure of Evolutionary Theory*, Gould reproduces two representative illustrations of this lineage, one from the 1920s, another from 1973, a few years after Morgan's poem was published. Both of them present it as a model of progressive evolution. Each illustration is made up of a series of images representing the heads or skulls, feet and teeth of different extinct species, all ascending as they increase in size towards the modern horse (Gould 2002: 581, 906; see also Bowler 2003: 195; Savage and Long 1986: 200–1). Gould's point is that the subtext of these images is given the lie by modern palaeontology, which has shown that different extinct species of horses belonged to different lineages, that some of the more successful species were dwarf forms and that horses are currently doing much less well than they did when they were smaller and had more toes, in terms both of the number of species currently alive and of their populations relative to those of other large herbivores.

Visually, Morgan's depiction of this evolutionary path through his patterns of letters is more neutral than Gould's illustrations. Time passes downwards, not up, and he makes no allowance for differences of size or value. *The Horseman's Word* is a series of ten so-called concrete poems, each of which uses the layout of the poem as much as the words themselves to achieve its impact. As each poem is visually different from the others, Morgan could easily have chosen to use typography to represent these progressive features had he wanted to, although it would be an over-interpretation to read the fact that he does not as any kind of definite comment akin to Gould's on the myth of progressive evolution.

Morgan gives us less detail too. We do not see the stages through which the evolving horse passes, for all that the steps from one word or line to the next mirror the fossil record, with its pattern of incremental change – one letter at a time – punctuated by gaps that leave the impression of dramatic evolutionary leaps. Instead, in these nonsense words we catch the sound of the primeval horses as they trot, trip, snort and piss. These movements are both the sounds of their daily lives and moments on their evolutionary journey. We can even hear something of their growth over time even if we cannot see it, as the incremental changes of the last five lines stretch out their sounds, first elongating the vowels, then substituting an 'h' for the more pronounced 't', and at last giving us the open 's' of 'hors(e)' in place of the closed 'p'. (The closed or stop consonants P, B, T, D, C/K and G are distinct moments in speech which cannot be prolonged either before or after the main consonantal sound, as other consonants can. For example, the resonant consonants L, M, N, R, W and Y can be sounded indefinitely before the main consonantal sound, while in the so-called fricative consonants, F and S, the consonantal sound itself can be prolonged indefinitely.)

'Eohippus' passes no comment on evolutionary theory or the Darwinian condition. Its achievement as a piece of Darwinian poetry is rather to transform evolution itself into a poem. On a first reading, it can seem little more than a delightful piece of light verse, dressed up as concrete poetry and abstract art. But it is also a window onto a world of deep time, a time when there was no language, only sound. This sounds dreadfully pompous as a reading of such a whimsical poem, but then it is only by indulging our imaginations whimsically ourselves that we can catch these sounds from the deep past. Morgan invites us to share with him a moment of transcendence, but only if we are willing to let ourselves be a little silly.

Even though, indeed because, it largely eschews recognisable vocabulary, grammar and syntax, 'Eohippus' is a surprisingly full template for the things that more complex poems can do with Darwinism. Morgan uses the evolution of the horse both to depict that evolution as a trajectory and to establish a bond between the 'eetl' horse in the Darwinian past and his readers in the Darwinian present. He responds both to the popular iconography of Darwinism and to the natural history that it reveals. And he gives us both a light poem which parodies that iconography and a lyric which can transport us into the world of that natural history.

These three pairings, united in 'Eohippus', map out the range of poetic responses to Darwinism. A poem can interpret Darwinism diachronically, emphasising change through time, or synchronically, emphasising the unchanging conditions of life in a Darwinian universe. In other words, it can identify Darwinism with evolution or with natural selection. It can scrutinise Darwinism as a discourse – a set of myths, assumptions and ideas alive within a culture – or it can accept Darwinism as scientific truth. And it can respond to Darwinism with satirical scepticism or with lyric sincerity. Some poems, like 'Eohippus', combine both parts of each pair. Others tend towards either the first alternative in each pair or the second. Still others inadvertently bring them into conflict, as Swinburne, Blind and Meredith do in the poems I discuss in the next chapter, where non-Darwinian models of evolution clash with a Darwinian understanding of natural selection.

The tendency of many poems towards one of these sets of alternatives or the other is nicely illustrated – along with other, more ubiquitous poetic techniques – by two more poems by Morgan, written a few years after 'Eohippus', each of them again inspired by an ancient, extinct animal. 'The Archaeopteryx's Song' exemplifies the first alternative in each of these three pairings:

I am only half out of this rock of scales.
What good is armour when you want to fly?
My tail is like a stony pedestal
and not a rudder. If I sit back on it
I sniff winds, clouds, rains, fogs where
I'd be, where I'd be flying, be flying high.
Dinosaurs are spicks and
all I see when I look back
is tardy turdy bonehead swamps
whose scruples are dumb tons.
Damnable plates and plaques
can't even keep out ticks.
They think when they make the ground thunder
as they lumber for a horn-lock or a rut
that someone is afraid, that everyone is afraid,
but no one is afraid. The lords of creation
are in my mate's next egg's next egg's next egg,
stegosaur. It's feathers I need, more feathers
for the life to come. And these iron teeth
I want away, and a smooth beak
to cut the air. And these claws
on my wings, what use are they
except to drag me down, do you imagine
I am ever going to crawl again?
When I first left that crag
and flapped low and heavy over the ravine
I saw past present and future
like a dying tyrannosaur

and skimmed it with a hiss.
I will teach my sons and daughters to live
on mist and fire and fly to the stars.

This poem responds to Darwinism in terms of evolution rather than natural selection. Outside our own ancestry, Archaeopteryx is the most famous 'missing link' in evolutionary history. One of the clear, testable predictions of Darwin's theory of the origin of species was that fossil animals would be found which would combine features from distinct but related living types. Such finds would strongly suggest that the apparently fixed taxonomical boundaries between these types were the result of evolutionary divergence, not separate acts of creation. A few of these intermediate types were known to be still living. Darwin himself drew attention to lungfishes, and to the egg-laying but lactating duck-billed platypus ([1859] 2003: 160). But none of these was as vivid a fulfilment of his prediction as Archaeopteryx. A dinosaur with wings and feathers, or a bird with teeth, hands and a tail-bone, it was first discovered in Bavaria in 1861, only two years after *The Origin of Species* was published.

For a moment in the first line of Morgan's poem it seems as if we are listening to one of these famous fossils itself, speaking as a fossil 'only half out of this rock'. By the end of the line, it is clear that it is one of the first birds themselves who is speaking, alive and in its own time. The 'rock' is the Archaeopteryx's own metaphor for the condition of being still half-reptile. Morgan is a master of poetic metre who uses it sparingly and deftly as it suits him. Here he registers the Archaeopteryx's transmutation into a bird in the texture of the verse itself. The first four lines are more or less regular iambic pentameter or blank verse. The tone of Morgan's poem is conversational, and there are enough irregularities to disguise the verse form. Nonetheless, the pace of the verse is slow and relatively formal. In the fifth line Morgan slows it down further by keeping a five-beat line but giving us only seven syllables. After that, the staged repetition in the sixth line leads up to a crescendo when the bird takes flight, not actually, but in its imagination. From then on, the poem rattles freely along in variants on the faster, more informal, four- and three-beat lines typical of popular rhymes and ballads.

The Archaeopteryx's vision of the next great evolutionary leap forwards is inspiring. But, as the last lines of Morgan's poem suggest, it is science-fiction, not science. By putting these thoughts into the head of a non-human missing link, Morgan holds up a mirror to our myths of our own evolution. When Morgan wrote this poem in the late 1970s the dubious presumption that the dinosaurs might have died out not because of a global catastrophe but because they were out-competed by little, warm-blooded, dinosaur-egg-eating mammals was still current. This particular myth helped foster our sense, like the Archaeopteryx's, of our own manifest destiny. Looking in Morgan's mirror, we see a distorted, strange, half-comic image of ourselves.

Evolutionary trajectories are not foreordained, and history has belied the Archaeopteryx's song as Morgan sings it. It is mammals, not birds, that show the most plausible signs, albeit extremely slight ones, of ever being able to 'fly to the stars'. Equally though, as the poem reminds us, it might have been birds after all. The poem invites us to consider a possible world in which that was going to happen. Through the Archaeopteryx's self-consciousness about his own evolution, the poem reminds us too that evolution is precisely not a self-conscious process, not even for humanity, science fiction and the bogus science of eugenics notwithstanding. But even without this particular kind of self-consciousness, other animals might well dispute our claim to be the 'lords of creation', just as the Archaeopteryx pours scorn on the dinosaurs. Are we the Archaeopteryx in this poem, then, as we might like to think, or are we rather just another 'dying tyrannosaur'?

It is not only the poem's scenario that invites us to question humanity's inflated sense of its own evolutionary destiny. It is its tone too. Characteristically, Morgan enjoys playing with sounds in this poem. The play on eggs and Stegosaurs is an obvious and funny example, especially when the poem is read aloud. But there are more complex patterns too which have a subtler impact. As at the end of 'Eohippus', Morgan plays on the contrast between open and closed consonants. Here the closed consonants are repeatedly associated with the reptilian dinosaurs and with the Archaeopteryx's own reptilian qualities, those 'Damnable plates and plaques'. By contrast, the open consonant 'f' voices his self-proclaimed destiny to become a bird, as the Archaeopteryx imagines 'fogs where / I'd be, where I'd be flying, be flying high', or insists 'It's feathers I need, more feathers / for the life to come'. This interplay of consonants appears to reinforce the Archaeopteryx's perspective, much as Morgan's use of metre does, by identifying the dinosaurs with more restricted, retarding sounds, and the birds with freer, easier, more open sounds.

But 'The Archaeopteryx's Song' is spoken (or more implausibly sung) by the Archaeopteryx himself. Technically, it is a dramatic monologue, a poem spoken in a more or less identifiable scenario (in this case, a Cretaceous landscape) by a character clearly distinct from the poet (the Archaeopteryx). Reading a dramatic monologue, we are invited to ask ourselves how we respond to this character, whether we admire him, for example, or trust him, whether his opinions, values and arguments stand up. In steering our responses to these questions, the poet reveals something of where he or she stands too.

Morgan's handling of his verse in 'The Archaeopteryx's Song' is a master class in how a poet may direct us without our realising it. As we read this poem aloud we impersonate the Archaeopteryx for ourselves, and the values we hear in the sounds of the verse are his, not Morgan's. These patterns of sound characterise the Archaeopteryx as not only aspiring but arrogant. The tone caught in those closed consonants in particular is one of contempt. It is hard to speak these sounds in these words without spitting them out. That contempt is betrayed too by the Archaeopteryx's vocabulary as he dismisses the dinosaurs as 'spicks' and half imagines scorning a dying tyrannosaur with a 'hiss'. By the end of the poem his aspirations and his arrogance have shown themselves to be interdependent, as 'fire and fly' echo 'dying tyrannosaur' and 'mist' echoes that 'hiss'. As the poem holds up a mirror to our own evolutionary self-image, we see that that self-image itself is born as much of arrogance as of aspiration.

'The Archaeopteryx's Song' is an excellent example of a poem which takes evolution as its theme, examining the myths people tell about it and satirising them for believing in them. Like 'Eohippus', it is far from earnest, but it has serious implications and is genuinely thought-provoking. Another of Morgan's poems, inspired by yet another of the iconic creatures of evolutionary natural history, is more openly serious. This is 'Trilobites':

> A grey-blue slab, fanned like a pigeon's wing,
> stands on my record cabinet
> between a lamp and a speaker.
> Trapped in a sea of solid stone
> the trilobites still almost swim;
> the darker grey of their backs,
> thumbnail-sized and thumbnail-shaped,
> gives out a dull shine as I switch on the lamp.
> I have eight of them; half are crushed, but
> two are almost perfect, lacking nothing but the antennas.
> My fingertip, coarse and loutish
> tracing the three delicate rows of furrowed plates,
> tries to read that paleozoic braille
> as vainly as the blast of Wagner at their ear
> searches for entrance five hundred million years
> and a world of air too late. But I would not trade
> my family torn by chance from time
> for Grecian urn or gold Byzantium.

There are a number of similarities between this poem and the last. Both are conversational free verse poems, yet both resonate at the outset with an echo of the iambic pentameter. In 'Trilobites' Morgan establishes this echo in the very first line, only to let it vanish straightaway in the second. This would barely be significant except that he returns to this same metre at the very end of the poem. Both poems also use the aural contrast of closed and open consonants to suggest the fixity of fossils on the one hand and the free movement of living animals on the other. Where birds fly trilobites swam, so here Morgan takes 's' not 'f' as his open consonant. Fittingly too, he takes 't' as his key closed consonant, accompanied by the rasping, retarding 'r'. So 'Trapped in a sea of solid stone / the trilobites still almost swim'. The illusion of movement created by these 's's is only an illusion, and the trilobites remain fixed, fossilised within the poem.

These similarities between 'The Archaeopteryx's Song' and 'Trilobites' put into relief the more striking differences between them. Where 'The Archaeopteryx's Song' is a dramatic monologue, 'Trilobites' appears to be in Morgan's own voice. Where 'The Archaeopteryx's Song' is a satirical version of a popular scientific myth, 'Trilobites' is a lyric meditation on an object in the light of certain scientific facts. And where 'The Archaeopteryx's Song' considers Darwinism diachronically, as the narrative of evolution, 'Trilobites' considers it synchronically, as the condition of the world in which extinction, borne out by fossilisation, occurs.

'Trilobites' is a meditation on the Darwinian condition. It consists of a series of observations framed in words that subtly suggest the underlying significance that these observations have for Morgan himself. The trilobites are not merely fossilised, they are 'trapped', as if they were still alive. They are 'delicate' and 'almost perfect', in contrast with his own 'coarse and loutish' finger. Even to touch them seems somehow disrespectful. We are a world away here from the image of ourselves as 'lords of creation' satirised in 'The Archaeopteryx's Song'. There is too, trapped within the trilobites, a meaning, a script like Braille, but a Braille to which we are, as it were, blind, just as our music would have no meaning to the trilobites themselves, even if they could have heard it at all in the 'world of air'.

These long-dead animals are for Morgan fellow individuals, unique in their own experience of the world – an experience as hopelessly beyond our reach as ours is beyond theirs. Morgan's egalitarian respect and even tenderness towards them earns our respect in turn, and with it a sympathetic ear for his declaration at the end of the poem. The last three lines are dense with meaning. Morgan ensures we listen to them and take them seriously by returning to a clear iambic measure, the metre that underpins the most famous poetry in English. He alludes directly to three such poems in his richly evocative closing line: Keats's 'Ode on a Grecian Urn' and Yeats's 'Sailing to Byzantium' and 'Byzantium'. Keats's poem in particular is a close parallel to Morgan's. In both, the speaker contemplates an object in which a moment in time is preserved seemingly forever. But Morgan does not ally himself with Keats or Yeats. Instead, he puts forward his haphazard collection of broken trilobites as of more value, at least to him, than Keats's urn or the artificial songbirds made by the goldsmiths of Yeats's Byzantium.

In 'Trilobites' palaeontology triumphs over poetry, Palaeozoic nature over classical art – somewhat paradoxically, as the victory is won through poetry itself, and a poetry which owes its power to the poetic tradition. The reason nature triumphs over art for Morgan is captured in that surprising, puzzling word 'family'. Morgan imagines his eight trilobites as a family, choosing to identify a bond of kinship between them. But the phrase 'my family' goes further, establishing that same bond between the poet himself and these ancient arthropods. In this penultimate line, the literal fact of this kinship, which follows from Darwin's theory of descent with modification, is bound together with the knowledge that we each live or lived because our ancestors were 'torn by chance from time', happening to survive, and that, in a very different sense, we will each be 'torn by chance from time' ourselves on the day when we happen to die. This knowledge of our shared heritage and fate brings with it an honest solidarity that is, Morgan implies, worth more than all the finest transcendental fictions of poetry and art.

As well as being enjoyable and stimulating in their own right 'Eohippus', 'The Archaeopteryx's Song' and 'Trilobites' give us a good sense of the range of techniques a poet might employ in responding to Darwinism. These include several different genres: the lyric, the dramatic monologue, satire, concrete poetry, even – at a stretch, reading 'Eohippus' for the evolutionary journey – narrative verse. They include, too, the manipulation of metre, phonemic patterning, the choice of vocabulary and intertextual references to other poems, all of which have a profound impact on the tone of a poem as well as its content. And while a poet may begin with specific examples from natural history – the fauna of the Ordovician seas, or the evolution of birds from dinosaurs or of *Equus* from *Eohippus* – the implications of a poem always reach beyond its starting point. As Morgan's poems show, poetry can even change how we think about Darwinism itself.

Poetry and the 'Non-Darwinian Revolution'

Non-Darwinian evolution in late Victorian poetry

Before I engage with Darwinian poetry in detail, I want to consider the responses of late Victorian poets to what Peter Bowler calls the 'non-Darwinian revolution' in evolutionary biology. In the last chapter I argued that Bowler's thesis that late Victorian evolutionism was overwhelmingly non-Darwinian was an overstatement. Nonetheless, much of the poetry, as well as the science, of the 1870s and 1880s tallies with Bowler's account. These poems have a place in this book not only because the poets considered themselves to be responding to Darwinism as they understood it, but also because their very errors and doubts still have a bearing on evolutionary theory as it is understood today.

Take 'Darwinism', by the English poet Agnes Mary Robinson, published in 1888:

When first the unflowering Fern-forest
   Shadowed the dim lagoons of old,
A vague unconscious long unrest
   Swayed the great fronds of green and gold.

Until the flexible stem grew rude,
   The fronds began to branch and bower,
And lo! upon the unblossoming wood
   There breaks a dawn of apple-flower.

Then on the fruitful Forest-boughs
   For ages long the unquiet ape
Swung happy in his airy house
   And plucked the apple and sucked the grape.

Until in him at length there stirred
   The old, unchanged, remote distress,

That pierced his world of wind and bird
  With some divine unhappiness.

Not Love, nor the wild fruits he sought,
  Nor the fierce battles of his clan
Could still the unborn and aching thought,
  Until the brute became the man.

Long since . . . And now the same unrest
  Goads to the same invisible goal,
Till some new gift, undreamed, unguessed,
  End the new travail of the soul.

Like many writers before and since, Robinson transforms the narrative of evolution into a myth. Her originality lies in fusing a typical myth of evolutionary progress with imagery of the Fall, crucially the apple. At each stage of evolution, Robinson suggests, there is a loss of innocence as well as an advance. Progress requires a cycle of dissatisfaction as a stimulus. This cyclical pattern is repeated in the poem itself, as the rhymes of the first stanza reappear in the last, with a slight evolutionary change from 'gold' to 'goal' and 'soul'. A similar evolutionary metamorphosis takes place in the middle of the poem, as the 'vague unconscious long unrest' (due to recur as 'the same unrest' in the last stanza) manifests itself as 'The old, unchanged, remote distress'. Here again there is an echo in the rhyme, as well as the repeated pattern of three adjectives. Robinson's use of the prefix 'un-' here and throughout builds up a sense of absence and yearning, again enacting the poem's main theme. The internal rhymes this creates, together with the overt, even intrusive alliteration, give 'Darwinism' an incantatory quality fitting in a poem that casts its eye over such distances of time in order to spy out the mythic patterns underlying evolutionary history.

'Darwinism' may not be a perfect poem. The alliteration is heavy-handed at times, some of the rhymes seem forced and there are too many portentous clichés. Yet it remains an appealing piece of evolutionary myth-making. It plays on both hope and nostalgia in fairly obvious but nonetheless pleasing ways. It has an easy psychological veracity too, for all that the promise of a final fulfilment for the 'travail of the soul' may sound more hollow and less frank to us than it did to Robinson herself. But however effective this poem may be in these terms one thing it certainly is not is an appropriate response to the Darwinian condition as we understand it today. 'Darwinism' no longer works as a poem about Darwinism, except historically, because Robinson's understanding of Darwinism is shaped by a number of ideas which formed part of the mélange of Victorian evolutionary thinking but which modern science has discarded.

Evolution in Robinson's poem is driven by a yearning for something to come into being, not by the haphazard and undirected processes of natural selection. This yearning implies too that the stages of evolution in a given lineage are in some sense predetermined. The ape was always reaching towards becoming a human rather than, say, a bat. The image of the tree as Robinson uses it reinforces this impression. For Darwin, the tree of life is an image of ever-branching evolution with each new branch setting off in its own direction. For Robinson, the power of the tree as a symbol depends partly on Genesis but also on a parallel between evolution and the growth of an individual organism. According to this analogy evolution is again a directed process. A baby will always grow into a human, a puppy into a dog, a foal into a horse, and so on. By analogy, a particular lineage will pass through various stages, perhaps a fish, a lizard, something shrew-like, a monkey, an ape, as it grows towards its fully mature state as a human being or, as Robinson imagines it here, a being beyond the human. The yearning towards this condition suggests that this apparently orthogenetic evolution may be brought about by a Lamarckian act of will, albeit largely unconsciously, while the distinct stages of evolution in Robinson's poem suggest saltationism.

Robinson's poem is an epitome of the non-Darwinian theories of evolution circulating during the so-called eclipse of Darwinism. That she chose to call it 'Darwinism' nonetheless is a sign both of the confusion between these different ideas among the Victorian lay public and of the extent to which Darwin's name had become identified with the accepted fact of evolution rather than the contested theory of natural selection. The same confusion and identification can be seen in a letter Robert Browning wrote in 1881 to the founder of the Browning Society; in it he seeks to explain the difference between his own view of evolution and Darwin's. Browning remarks that all Darwin had proven was 'the progressive development from senseless matter to organized until man's appearance', a view of life he had articulated himself in a number of poems from *Paracelsus*, published in 1835, onwards. Darwin's own argument, that 'changes in organization' are 'brought about by desire and will in the creature', Browning found unconvincing (1933: 199–200).

Like Robinson, Browning neatly fits Bowler's thesis. He mistakes Darwin's arguments for the strong version of Lamarckism recently advocated by Samuel Butler in *Life and Habit* and *Evolution, Old and New*. That Browning is able to make this mistake shows that he has not read either Darwin or Butler at all recently. Even at his most Lamarckian, Darwin never argues that evolution can be brought about by willpower, while Butler makes it abundantly clear that he is arguing against Darwin not for him. Instead, Browning's comments mark him out as a man who has kept at best a cursory eye on recent debates in evolutionary theory. Having read Darwin in the early 1860s he has already made up his mind that the case for evolution has been proven but that the mechanism behind it remains up for grabs. A generation or two older than Robinson, Browning does not merely settle for an account of evolution that resembles his own pre-Darwinian ideas, he simply reiterates those ideas themselves.

Robinson's response to evolutionism is in one sense more typical of her time than Browning's. Browning saw biological evolution as the physiological correlative of spiritual progress. He was not much interested in it in its own right, and he disliked the materialist tendency which emphasised physical evolution at the expense of the metaphysical soul. For these reasons (and because he had formulated his view of evolution so early himself) he was largely unimpressed by the ferment of evolutionary thinking in Victorian science and social theory that followed the publication of the *Origin*. On the few occasions when Browning engages with evolutionary theory in his poetry from the 1860s onwards he does so as a critic, not a convert. This is particularly so in 'Caliban upon Setebos' in 1864 (which I discuss in the next chapter) and in 'Parleying with Francis Furini' in 1887.

For her part, Robinson celebrates the 'invisible goal' promised by evolution, albeit with some trepidation. This view of evolution as a new revelation of the cosmic purpose – and a scientific one at that – is a leitmotiv of a great deal of late Victorian poetry. Much of it is pedestrian, like this earnestly plodding passage from Frederic Myers's 'The Passing of Youth':

> Each wish unfilled, impracticable plan,
> Goes to the forging of the force of Man;
> Thro' thy blind craving novel powers they gain,
> And the slow Race developes [sic] in its pain: –
> See their new joy begotten of thy woe,
> When what thy soul desired their soul shall know; –
> Thy heights unclimbed shall be their wonted way,
> Thy hope their memory, and thy dream their day.
>   (1882: 130–1)

On rare occasions, non-Darwinian evolutionary poetry rises to such heights of awfulness as to become almost a treat, as in this account of evolution from the immensely popular Welsh poet Lewis Morris's 'Ode of Creation', the opening section of his *The Ode of Life*, published in 1880:

Myriads on myriads of years! if Time there were yet,
When no soul was by to remember or to forget;
The fin growing stronger, and changing to wing or to claw,
Struggle on struggle, sentience, consciousness, ravin, and pain,
Monstrous and mailèd forms in the ooze, or hurtling thro' air,
Waging through aeons of time the ineffable struggles which gain
Order thro' waste and thro' wear.
Till the mastodon stalks forth in might with hoof and with jaw,
And the law of the Higher prevails, the Ultimate Law,
And the cooler earth teems with life, on land and in sea:
Life organic in beast, fish, or bird, in herb or in tree,
Life dominant, life exulting with quick-coming breath,
Life that fades down and sinks in the silence and slumber of Death.
But no soul to mark the struggle nor thought which might turn
To whence those weird fires burn.
Successions, progressions, a scheme of insensible life,
One Will alone directing the infinite strife,
One Force, one Eye, one Sole and Regarding Mind,
In a Universe deaf and blind!

And was it some Inner Law,
Some hidden potency of Force,
Or some creative breath Divine,
Which sped the creature on its upward course?
Until at last it woke and saw,
With visual forces fine,
The Godhead that was round it everywhere,
The spiritual essence fair,
Which doth innerve this outward show of things –
And filled the brute with high imaginings,
And winging it with new-found wings
Lifted its aspect to the infinite sky,
Where, in the Light of the Creative Eye
Its ancient slough away it cast,
And rose to Man at last!

(ll. 40–73)

Setting aside the portentousness, the gratuitous poeticisms ('mailèd', 'ooze'), the vacuous abstractions ('sentience, consciousness'), the tautologies ('Life organic', 'potency of Force', winging – or being winged? – with wings), the scientific posing ('visual forces'!), the ill-conceived imagery (a stalking mastodon?) and the over-enthusiastic use of capitals (giving a delightful if fleeting impression of God as a transcendental 'Sole' or flat-fish), setting all these aside, Morris's account of evolution is to say the least eclectic.

At the beginning of this passage, Morris tips his hat to Darwin's struggle for existence, although it is unclear whether he has in mind Darwin's version of this struggle, in which organisms compete to survive, or Herbert Spencer's, in which, as Bowler points out (1992: 38–9), the individual struggles to better itself and so better its chances. Myers is certainly thinking in these Lamarckian terms in his poem, whether his 'blind craving' expresses a weak Lamarckism in which the wishes, plans, hopes and dreams are spurs to actions which then effect evolutionary change, or a strong Lamarckism in which they are the motors of that change themselves. The 'infinite strife' of 'insensible life' in Morris's ode expresses the same nexus of Lamarckian ideas. Alongside Darwinism and Lamarckism Morris puts forward both the orthogenetic idea that organisms are compelled to evolve by something in their own nature and the argument (put by both Wallace and the Roman Catholic evolutionist St George Mivart in the early 1870s) that the creation of the human soul in particular required an additional 'creative breath Divine'. Rather than synthesising these distinct evolutionary hypotheses, Morris acknowledges them as alternatives, interpreting them both in theistic terms.

In 'Through the Ages', written in 1879, William Canton paints a gently comic picture of an elderly professor expounding evolution to a class of girls. Like Canton's professor, Morris, Myers and Robinson are all 'Murmuring wondrous cosmic secrets never quite distinctly told' (1927: 55). Their accounts of how exactly evolution works are imprecise, but it remains clear in all of them that it tends towards one particular object: 'Man'. For Morris, humanity appears to be the end point of the 'upward course' of evolution. For Myers, as for Robinson, the process is ongoing. Through cravings and travail, humanity is able to advance its own progress. Here Myers and Robinson gesture towards another of the doctrines of late Victorian evolutionism rejected by modern Darwinism: Social Darwinism.

Social Darwinism is the argument that our political ideals should imitate and so advance the evolutionary processes of nature. The ideological conclusions derived from this argument depend on the ideological assumptions brought to it in the first place. Social Darwinism is often used as a by-word for right-wing arguments that rapacious capitalism – or more drastically conquest, warfare and extermination – are the natural competitive practices of humanity. But Social Darwinist arguments, or social evolutionist as Bowler more comprehensively calls them, have been put by liberals too, including Darwin himself, as well as by anarchists such as Kropotkin, feminists such as Olive Schreiner and socialists such as Wallace and Ramsay MacDonald. The diversity of the competing theories and interpretations put forward within late Victorian evolutionism ensured that almost anybody could declare their political programme to be in keeping with nature and hence the right goal for mankind. Even a non-teleological understanding of nature such as Darwinism itself could be taken as a warrant for teleological politics if the end point was the better equipping of mankind for the struggle for existence.

The poetry of Social Darwinism begins with the cosmic evolutionism of the 1870s and 1880s. By the 1890s confidence that progress was the inevitable outcome of the cosmic process was waning. Instead, progress had to be taken in hand. Like Social Darwinism itself, the increasingly programmatic poetry of Social Darwinism covers the full political range. In *The March of Man*, Alfred Hayes put forward a Christian Socialist interpretation of Darwinism:

Fitness alone surviveth; ay! but who
Shall gauge the fitness, – God or Devil? – Fit
To tear at one another's throats? Or fit
To wisely rule this world of tooth and claw,
Which yet is man's high empire, wherein claws
Have sheaths, and teeth have lips to smile and kiss,
And help o'ermasters hate?

(1891: 81)

Hayes reinterprets Spencer's epitome of Darwinism as 'the survival of the fittest' in altruistic terms. He makes a nod too to Tennyson's famous account of 'Nature, red in tooth and claw' from *In Memoriam* (LVI, l. 15) – a phrase which has become almost as closely identified with the Darwinian vision as Spencer's, for all that Tennyson's poem predates *The Origin of Species* by almost a decade. For Hayes humanity's potential for co-operation and love has changed the rules of natural selection so that a society that smiles and kisses has a better chance of survival (and is thus fitter) than one that bites.

Where Hayes uses Social Darwinist arguments to advocate a socialist utopia Robert Bridges uses them to defend the status quo. Bridges's poetic epistle 'To a Socialist in London', published in the *Monthly Review* in 1903, is an exuberant if self-satisfied restatement of the argument that socialism runs counter to the natural human instincts for self-advancement, owning property and idealising young men who shoot tigers and fight wars. For

Bridges Darwinism's reminder that 'LIFE LIVETH ON LIFE' (l. 118) confirms what is already self-evident, as he reproaches his socialist addressee:

> What madness works to delude you,
> Being a man, that you see not mankind's predilection
> Is for Magnificence, Force, Freedom, Bounty; his inborn
> Love for Beauty, his aim to possess, his pride to devise it.
>
> (ll. 220–3)

The Scottish poet John Davidson took these same right-wing arguments to their logical conclusions. For Davidson natural selection was a brutish fact, and the only admirable course was to throw oneself wholeheartedly into the struggle for domination. At the end of *The Testament of an Empire-Builder*, published in 1902, Davidson creates a fantasy of Hell into which he casts a motley assortment of those he despises, beginning with the very people Hayes believes to be fittest:

> Materials of Hell? The altruists;
> Agnostics; dreamers; idiots, cripples, dwarfs;
> All kinds of cowards who eluded fact;
> Dwellers in legend, burrowers in myth;
> The merciful, the meek and mild, the poor
> In spirit; Christians who in very deed
> Were Christians; pessimistic celibates;
> The feeble minds; the souls called beautiful;
> The slaves, the labourers, the mendicants;
> Survivors of defeat; the little clans
> That posed and fussed, in ignominy left
> By apathetic powers; the greater part
> Of all the swarthy all the tawny tribes;
> Degenerates; the desultory folk
> In pleasure, art, vocation, commerce, craft;
> And all deniers of the will to live,
> And all who shunned the strife for wealth and power.
>
> (ll. 658–74)

With a flourish, Davidson tells us that heaven and hell are merely the world itself, and that 'Only a splendid Hell keeps Heaven fair' (l. 725) for the 'Beauty and power and splendour and delight / Of chosen ones, elect ere Time began' (ll. 688–9).

Davidson's empire-builder is a Nietzschean Superman, a frankly martial imperialist driven to conquest by a will for power. Adopting this persona, Davidson damns to hell those he sees as self-deceiving, like agnostics who will not admit that material science has revealed a godless universe. He damns, too, those who do not thrive by his ruthless ethic of 'the strife for wealth and power' (and implicitly sex), either because they do not accept it, like Christians, or because they cannot be bothered, like the 'desultory folk'. Finally, he damns many people routinely despised by right-wing Social Darwinists simply for being who they are, including cripples, blacks, Indians and the working classes. For Davidson, the non-white races are by nature inferior, while the working-classes acquiesce in their own slavery because they do not have the will to challenge it.

Aside from being appalling, Davidson's Social Darwinism is outdated as a scientific political theory; so too are Hayes's and Bridges's. Together their poems illustrate the danger of beguiling ourselves into believing that any one ideology can claim the supposed authority of 'Nature'. The very fact that the same logic can sustain such violently opposed positions indicates that the logic itself is flawed. Social Darwinism falls down not only by its more grotesque results but by the fact that any politics derived from nature is invariably selective, whether it sees itself as imitating the natural world at large or an idea of human nature in particular. As the grounds for selection are themselves already political, the logic of Social Darwinism is circular.

The model of programmatic Social Darwinist poetry typified by these poems flourished in the 1890s and the early 1900s. The logic of Social Darwinism continued to be used to justify and underpin right-wing ideologies in particular, but as the Victorian appetite for philosophising in verse faded this type of poem became obsolete, although Bridges himself revived it for one last hurrah in *The Testament of Beauty* in 1929. Social Darwinism itself persisted in poetry between the wars not in sustained treatises but in individual images. Examples from T. S. Eliot's poetry include the presentation of an epileptic woman, the working-class Irishman Sweeney and the Jew Bleistein as simian and subhuman, degenerate or only half evolved, in 'Sweeney Erect', 'Sweeney Among the Nightingales' and 'Burbank with a Baedeker: Bleistein with a Cigar' respectively. As in Davidson's *Testament*, it is the congenitally ill, the working-classes and the 'swarthy tribes' who are the failures of evolution.

Eliot aside, this account of non-Darwinian evolutionary poetry in the late nineteenth and early twentieth centuries looks so far like a catalogue of bit-part players. This is partly because minor poets are often more representative than major ones as they follow rather than setting or challenging the prevailing trends. By the same token, better poets may be more revealing in the use they make of the ideas around them, in how they interrogate them or in the images or symbols through which they embody them. Over the rest of this chapter, I will look at the poetry of some of the more impressive late Victorian poets who articulated non-Darwinian ideas of evolution. In the first of these case studies I will look at how their attempts to reconcile Darwinian and non-Darwinian ideas of evolution in their poetry led Algernon Charles Swinburne and Mathilde Blind to acts of bad faith. In the second, I will look at how the non-Darwinian elements in George Meredith's later poetry have tended to obscure the more exclusively Darwinian perspectives of his earlier poetry. Finally, I will look at the struggle between Tennyson's yearning to believe in evolutionary progress and his deep-seated doubts about it in the last years of his life.

Pseudo-Darwinism and bad faith:
A. C. Swinburne and Mathilde Blind

In February 1870 the *enfant terrible* of Victorian poetry, Algernon Charles Swinburne, wrote to his friend and mentor the Pre-Raphaelite poet and painter Dante Gabriel Rossetti to tell him that he was putting the finishing touches to a new book of poems aimed at 'the promulgation of the double doctrine, democratic and atheistic, equality of men and abolition of gods' (1959–62: II, 98). In 1866, Swinburne had shocked the Victorian establishment with the paganism and perverse sexuality of his *Poems and Ballads*. Now he was preparing a second blow. Inspired by Shelley, Walt Whitman and the Italian patriot and socialist Giuseppe Mazzini, Swinburne was about to throw himself – or at least his verse – into revolutionary politics.

Like many late Victorian would-be revolutionaries, Swinburne took inspiration from evolution. But the precise role played by evolution in his thinking and his poetry has been widely debated. Swinburne prided himself on his 'not . . . unscientific' 'habit of mind' (1959–62: II, 335). At the same time, he was adamant that he was no optimist (ibid.: II, 80). Many scholars have taken him at his word (McGann 1972: 38, 248–53; Murfin 1978: 48, 54; Riede 1978: 38, 72, 111–12, 213). For such critics, *Songs before Sunrise*, which came out in 1871, interprets history as purposeless change within a pattern that is cyclical not progressive. As in existentialism, any purpose or meaning must come from our own actions, not as a gift of nature. Other critics disagree, however. For them, Swinburne depicts, in George Ridemour's words, 'a natural order which, while ultimately not moral, moves (and can be helped to move) toward good for man' (1971: 130–1). This Swinburne is expressly an evolutionist, and his evolutionism leads to what Kerry McSweeney, contradicting Swinburne without compunction, calls 'a facile optimism' (1981: 134; see also Beach 1936: 455–69; Roppen 1956: 175–209; Stevenson 1932: 49–52; Tillyard 1948: 91, 96).

The disagreements between Swinburne's critics follow in part from the different emphases and implications of the different poems in his collection. In 'Genesis' Swinburne presents 'The immortal war of mortal things' (l. 25) as the state of existence, on-going and ever-generative, but neither directed nor progressive. In 'On the Downs', on the other hand, an apparently similar Darwinian emphasis on nature as existent rather than created, as morally neutral and always changing, gives way to teleology:

One forceful nature uncreate
That feeds itself with death and fate,
    Evil and good, and change and time,
That within all men lies at wait
    Till the hour shall bid them climb
        And live sublime.

(ll. 127–32)

Swinburne glosses this idea of a latent human nature waiting to come into being in the next stanza, remarking, 'For all things come by fate to flower / At their unconquerable hour' (ll. 133–4). Here, like Robinson, he interprets evolution as growth, with predetermined outcomes occurring at set stages.

Poets are not obliged to be self-consistent, and Swinburne never identifies *Songs before Sunrise* as putting forward a single coherent scientific world view. Both 'Genesis' and 'On the Downs' draw on contemporary evolutionary theory. As a non-scientist himself Swinburne is within his rights to explore the possible implications of different versions of evolutionary theory in his poems. Yet the contradictions in Swinburne's conception of evolution occur not only between poems but within them. In 'On the Downs' the orthogenetic progress of nature is driven by death and change, like natural selection. In 'Genesis' a bleak, Darwinian vision of creation is excused on the grounds that 'if death were not, then should growth not be' (l. 41).

This self-contradiction, between a Darwinian vision of life as direction-less struggle and a teleological idea of evolution as inevitable progress, is clearest in 'Hertha'. This is Swinburne's fullest exposition of his evolutionary world view. It is also the poem in which he identifies that world view most explicitly with his revolutionary politics. In making this Social Darwinist move, Swinburne exposes his inconsistencies most directly.

'Hertha' takes its name from its speaker, a variation of Nerthus, the personification of Mother Earth in an ancient German religion recorded by Tacitus in the *Germania* (Tacitus 1935: 317; 1938: 187–8). Hertha introduces herself as follows:

> I am that which began;
>> Out of me the years roll;
> Out of me God and man;
>> I am equal and whole;
> God changes, and man, and the form of them bodily; I am the soul.
>
> (ll. 1–5)

Persisting in the same gnomic vein, she explains (if that is the right word):

> Beside or above me
>> Nought is there to go;
> Love or unlove me,
>> Unknow me or know,
> I am that which unloves me and loves; I am stricken, and I am the blow.
>
> (ll. 16–20)

Like Ralph Waldo Emerson's Brahma (to whom she bears a more than passing resemblance), Hertha appears to be in all places and all deeds at once. Indeed, she is all places and all deeds. She is the undifferentiated whole of which all persons and things are merely fleeting parts. She is 'the life-tree' of which we are the 'buds' (ll. 99–100) – an image drawn from Teutonic mythology, like Hertha herself, but at the same time recalling the branching tree of life sketched out in *The Origin of Species*.

The oracular riddling of 'Hertha' may be irritating but the philosophical position Swinburne sets out, albeit obliquely, seems so far to be self-consistent. The problem comes when he tries to identify his political goal of freedom as Hertha's own commitment to 'The free life of thy living' (l. 83). As Swinburne himself remarked in a letter to William Michael Rossetti, 'it was not at first evident *why* the principle of growth, whence and by which all evil not less than all good proceeds and acts, should *prefer* liberty to bondage, Mazzini to Buonaparte [. . .] Christ to de Sade'. In his letter, Swinburne quoted this stanza from his work-in-progress, declaring 'This much I think may be reasonably supposed and said':

> I bid you but be;
>> I have need not of prayer;

I have need of you free
　　As your mouths of mine air;
That my heart may grow greater within me, beholding the fruits of me fair.
　　　　　　　　(1959–62: ii, 79–80; ll. 156–60 var.)

In spite of Swinburne's protestations to Rossetti, it is not clear why Hertha should 'need' humanity to be free. Why should our liberation from religious delusion or political tyranny mean anything to her? Why should the 'principle of growth' have a political preference one way or the other?

The connotations of Swinburne's image of the life-tree in 'Hertha' shift from the Darwinian notion of the ever-branching bush into a more teleological idea of growth, with mankind as 'One topmost blossom / That scales the sky' (ll. 198–9). These lines themselves hint at Swinburne's ambivalence towards the idea of evolution as progress. We are a 'topmost blossom' and reaching ever further up. Yet we are still only 'One' such blossom, not the sole pinnacle of evolution, as Lewis Morris, for example, would have it. If Swinburne were more wholehearted in his commitment to the teleology he expresses in 'On the Downs' then he could argue that it is simply our natural destiny to be free. But he does not merely want to prophesy freedom: he wants to inspire us to claim it for ourselves. By placing this exhortation in the mouth of Mother Nature herself, however, he undermines it. If it is the natural order that we be free, how can we not be? And if it is not, in what sense, again, can Nature be said to care?

Swinburne's letter to William Michael Rossetti shows that he was aware of the contradictions within his view of evolution. In attempting to square a properly Darwinian understanding of evolution as direction-less with a desire to 'ma[k]e the All-Mother a good republican' Swinburne falls back on a pseudo-Darwinian view of evolution as the 'principle of growth'(1959–62: ii, 80). But this is not enough either, as he understands Darwinism too well to be able to put his faith in progressive evolution alone. So he invokes Social Darwinist arguments he knows to be unten-able within his own morally neutral vision of nature. This act of bad faith is written into the structure of 'Hertha' itself, with its self-contradictory imagery and arguments.

A similar act of bad faith occurs in another of the major poems of the late Victorian evolutionary vision. This is Mathilde Blind's evolutionary epic *The Ascent of Man*, first published in 1889 and reissued in 1899, after her death, with an admittedly somewhat apologetic preface by no less an evolutionist than Alfred Russel Wallace himself. Born in Mannheim in Germany in 1841, Blind moved to England in 1848 after her stepfather was exiled for his part in the year of revolutions. True to her origins, she became a vocal and active socialist, internationalist, free-thinker and feminist. As well as poetry, she wrote a novel, biographies, literary criticism and translations.

The Ascent of Man is Blind's most ambitious poem. It is made up of three main parts preceded by a prelude. Each part consists of one long narrative section, with the first two each rounded off by two or three sonnets. The first narrative, 'Chaunts of Life', tells the story of evolution from the creation of the universe to the battle of Waterloo before reflecting on the story so far and prophesying what might come next. The second and third narratives stage allegorical tours. In 'The Pilgrim Soul' – written in *terza rima* to recall Dante's *Divine Comedy* and Shelley's 'The Triumph of Life' – the narrator wanders through a modern city which is a vision of social injustice and depravity. On the edge of the city she encounters a small lost boy, personifying outcast Love. Through her impulse to cherish him he is transformed into a godlike redemptive power. In 'The Leading of Sorrow', the narrator has been deserted by Love, although it is not clear whether we should read this as a sequel to her encounter with him in 'The Pilgrim Soul' or as an alternative, parallel allegory. A shadowy phantom appears and takes her on a journey to show her the whole world. They visit the sea, woods, deserts and savannahs, then a market town set amid fields, then a modern city. At each stage, the immediate impression of beauty and order masks vicious conflict. The narrator is on the brink of an existential collapse, when 'a Voice' from 'the peaks of time' (III, l. 398) urges her not to despair and to become instead the means by which nature can be redeemed from violence. The poem closes with her shadowy guide transformed again into 'Love re-arisen / With the Eternal shining through his eyes' (III, ll. 455–6).

The three parts of Blind's poem might be expected to form a narrative or argumentative sequence. In fact each repeats the same moves. In all three Blind begins with the Darwinian realisation that life in the natural world is struggle. She then sees the same conflict taking place within human society. Humanity, she implies, has made no moral advance on nature whatsoever. In 'The Leading of Sorrow', the first stage of the narrator's tour, around the natural world, ends with this plea:

> What of antelopes crunched by the leopard?
>   What if hounds run down the timid hare?
> What though sheep, strayed from the faithful shepherd,
>   Perish helpless in the lion's lair?
> The all-seeing sun shines on unheeding,
>   In the night shines the unruffled moon,

Though on earth brute myriads, preying, bleeding,
   Put creation harshly out of tune.

Cried I, turning to the shrouded figure –
   'Oh, in mercy veil this cruel strife!
Sanguinary orgies which disfigure
   The green ways of labyrinthine life.
From the needs and greeds of primal passion,
   From the serpent's track and lion's den,
To the world our human hands did fashion,
   Lead me to the kindly haunts of men.'

(III, ll. 97–112)

These lines spell out a disjunction between what the narrator would like to believe about life and what she has to believe when she sees it. Blind had made the same point a few years earlier in a lecture on *Shelley's View of Nature Contrasted with Darwin's*. Citing Shelley's early poem *Queen Mab*, where he declares that in nature 'all things speak / Peace, harmony, and love', Blind replies that

> if we open our Darwin, the very opposite fact meets us at every turn . . .
> For gnawing at the root of life itself seems this power of evil from which
> the poet's sensitive soul shrank with such horror – lust, hunger, rapine,
> cruelty. (1886: 14)

Like Shelley, Blind's naïve narrator is appalled by this truth, in part because it is genuinely appalling to witness but also because it is utterly discordant with her prior view of life as an ordered, moral and harmonious creation. Cosmic physics may remain perfectly in tune but biology is jarring and painful.

Blind's narrator comes close to admitting that she would prefer ignorance to this Darwinian knowledge. Unable to regain that ignorance regarding nature at large she puts her trust in human kindness. The pastoral and Christian idyll to which she is transported is menaced after only three more stanzas and collapses into war in the fourth. The town burns as 'With her children's blood the green earth's turning' (III, l. 155), recalling the orgies of blood which disfigure green nature fifty lines before. Humanity at large having failed her, the narrator urges her guide to 'Seek the pale of some imperial city / Where the law rules starlike o'er man's life' (III, ll. 179–80). But here too the vision of astronomical order is dispelled by the biological imperatives of hunger and lust which Blind discerns in the economic relations and moral degradation of capitalism and prostitution.

As the expectation of a moral order rises with the ascent from nature to humanity to civilisation, so the narrator's disgust at not finding it grows too. Now it is 'the human myriads, preying, bleeding,' who 'Put creation harshly out of tune' (III, ll. 335–6). This realisation brings down the fury of the narrator and Blind upon the self-satisfaction of the Victorian elite. It is a corollary of the narrator's naïvety that her disillusionment is so intense. But with that naïvety goes a moral authority that the hypocrites around her lack. Her rage is righteous, even if her misanthropy is excessive, and her declaration that 'Life is but a momentary blunder / In the cycle of the Universe' (III, ll. 359–60) amounts to a defeatist retreat to the harmony of physics cleansed of biology.

In her allegories, Blind makes plain her socialist–feminist critique of capitalism and of those forms of Social Darwinism which claim that because competition is natural it is good regardless of its effects. She gives the lie too to her own title. The thrust of her indictment of society is that man has not ascended at all, at least not morally. He – particularly *he* – remains as much within the brutal economy of 'lust, hunger, rapine, cruelty' as the rest of nature. If he believes otherwise, he is deluding himself.

Yet at the end of each section of her poem Blind holds out the hope of an ascent after all, through Love, especially the love between mothers and children, and also through the mirror that literature and art hold up to life to influence its future development. She makes the same case in her lecture on Shelley and Darwin, where she argues that 'the true conflict consists in man's struggle with the irresponsible forces of Nature, and the victory in his conquest over them', both within himself and in the world around him (1886: 19). Here Blind recalls *In Memoriam* and anticipates Huxley's famous repudiation of Social Darwinism in *Evolution and Ethics*. Darwinian nature is not a guide to morality or politics. Instead morality and politics are a check upon Darwinian nature.

In her essay, Blind makes it clear that the struggle to rein in nature is continuous and progressive. In her poem she focuses rather on the imagined final conquest, prefigured in revelatory encounters with allegorical beings. This is legitimate poetic licence, and an apt counter-balance to her narrator's vision of unmitigated evil. But Blind is not willing to settle for culture standing alone against nature. She wants our victory over nature to be assured, to be our destiny. As an atheist, she cannot turn to revelation to guarantee this. So instead she turns back to nature itself.

Blind understands Darwinism better and faces it more honestly than most late Victorian poets. Yet at the end of her poem she pulls a teleological rabbit out of her Darwinian hat. The narrator hears a Voice which turns out, like Hertha, to be a personification of life itself:

'Long I waited – ages rolled o'er ages –
    As I crystallized in granite rocks,
Struggling dumb through immemorial stages,
    Glacial aeons, fiery earthquake shocks.
In fierce throbs of flame or slow upheaval,
    Speck by tiny speck, I topped the seas,
Leaped from earth's dark womb, and in primeval
    Forests shot up shafts of mammoth trees.

'Through a myriad forms I yearned and panted,
    Putting forth quick shoots in endless swarms –
Giant-hoofed, sharp-tusked, or finned or planted
    Writhing on the reef with pinioned arms.
I have climbed from reek of sanguine revels
    In Cimmerian wood and thorny wild,
Slowly upwards to the dawnlit levels
    Where I bore thee, oh my youngest Child!

'Oh, my heir and hope of my to-morrow,
    I – I draw thee on through fume and fret,
Croon to thee in pain and call through sorrow,
    Flowers and stars take for thy alphabet.
Through the eyes of animals appealing,
    Feel my fettered spirit yearn to thine,
Who, in storm of will and clash of feeling,
    Shape the life that shall be – the divine.'
                  (iii, ll. 401–24)

This whole passage is carried forward by movements upward. We are back with Lamarckian yearnings and a teleological drive towards an ideal humanity favoured by nature and equated with the divine. The project of taming nature has become nature's own, not merely circumstantially – we are all part of nature, after all – but purposively. Switching from natural selection as a process to evolution as a narrative Blind extrapolates from that narrative along morally progressive lines. Yet the bulk of her poem makes it clear that such an extrapolation is both theoretically and empirically unfounded. Strikingly, she makes exactly the same false move in her lecture, identifying Shelley himself as a prototype of the 'better, wiser, and more beautiful beings' who 'will inhabit this planet in ages to come, according to the laws of evolution' (1886: 20).

Late Victorian poets often took inspiration from non-Darwinian models of evolution, and they often argued for social evolutionism in verse. All the same, it is surprising that Blind should make these moves. She has no illusions about the harshness of the Darwinian state of nature, nor about the brutal and amoral economic realities of capitalism. Given this, for her to hold out the promise that, through us, nature will transcend both itself and our own brutality is an act of bad faith. Like Swinburne, Blind can only believe this by closing her eyes to what she already knows, and yet she does so because she cannot bear to believe what she knows to be true. As, in her poem, she lays out before us what she knows, we too can believe her promise only through forgetting that knowledge. Like the narrator of 'The Leading of Sorrow' we must take refuge in wilful ignorance. It is a sorry irony that a poem that exposes bad faith so boldly should be drawn back into a bad faith of its own.

In his biography of John Davidson, John Sloan writes that 'Although Davidson's ideas seem outdated in the twentieth century, a poet has to be judged not by the scientific accuracy of his world view, but by his effectiveness in transmuting this into poetry' (1995: 215). Sloan's judgement is fair, although any poet who invokes science to bear witness to his or her own transcendental vision inevitably leaves their poetry a hostage to fortune. Future changes in science may not affect how we judge the poem but they will surely affect how we read it, and how we respond to its claims to truth. In the cases of 'Hertha' and *The Ascent of Man*, however, scientific accuracy and the effectiveness of the poems themselves are interdependent. As verse, 'Hertha' is more accomplished than most late Victorian evolutionary poetry, while *The Ascent of Man* is more ambitious, although 'Hertha' remains pretentious and *The Ascent of Man* is often clumsy. Neither is an especially good poem, even on its own terms. But they are nonetheless worse as poems than they otherwise would be because their bad faith compromises their ability to transmute their world views into poetry.

At bottom, Swinburne and Blind know that the world views they want to set before us are grounded in lies. They know this because they really do understand Darwin's arguments. Robinson and Morris can salute progressive evolution honestly because they have not thought through the contradictions between the different scientific theories they allude to in their poems. Swinburne and Blind grasp these contradictions but cannot bring themselves to abandon the illusion. We may sympathise with their reluctance to face the full consequences of their knowledge but their poems remain, at the last reckoning, dishonest.

READING A *READING OF EARTH*: GEORGE MEREDITH'S LATER POETRY

Unlike those of Swinburne, Blind and the other non-Darwinian poets, many of George Meredith's poems remain current as Darwinian poetry today. To see this, however, we need to draw his earlier, Darwinian poetry out from under the shadow of his later, non- or only partly Darwinian philosophy. Ever since G. M. Trevelyan wrote *The Poetry and Philosophy of George Meredith*, in 1906, Meredith's critics have assumed that his philosophy of nature is broadly consistent from the early 1860s onwards, and that the main objective of his poetry is to teach that philosophy to its readers. As Lionel Stevenson puts it, although Meredith had given little thought to evolution before 1859, 'when he became acquainted with Darwinism, his philosophic system developed promptly and completely; so the stages of its growth cannot be chronicled' (1932: 183; see also Crum 1931: 207–27; Jones 1999: 124–38; Kelvin 1961: 114–64; Roppen 1956: 209–79; Strong 1921: 148–89. Beach 1936: 471 moves the origin of Meredith's evolutionary poetry back to the 1870s to justify his argument that Meredith was following the lead given by Swinburne in *Songs before Sunrise*, while Simpson 1970 pushes it back to around 1880, identifying Meredith's poetry before this date with an Arnoldian pessimistic humanism. Neither of these arguments is persuasive in itself, and both endorse the view that Meredith's nature poetry at least from the early 1880s onwards is all of a piece.)

The bulk of Meredith's nature poetry falls into two collections published five years apart: *Poems and Lyrics of the Joy of Earth*, published in 1883, and *A Reading of Earth*, published in 1888. On the grounds that 'Meredith's ideas . . . do not generally help to unify or integrate the individual poem, as a whole', Georg Roppen argues that the best approach to his poetry is to 'disregard the framework of the individual poem in order to trace more conveniently the larger unity of his vision and belief' (1956: 211). Roppen's assumption that poems can be broken down and reassembled in this way turns Stevenson's claim that Meredith's 'philosophic system' is self-consistent into a self-fulfilling prophecy, as superficially similar passages are read as confirming one another at the expense of the often more profound differences between them. Yet read independently of one another, these two collections reveal very different judgements on the significance of evolution, and implicitly on the role of poetry.

Poems and Lyrics of the Joy of Earth is a plural title for a diverse book. Meredith's first collection in over twenty years, it includes many poems that had been published before, some as early as the mid-1860s, one – a revised version of his once famous lyric 'Love in the Valley' – as far back as 1851. The poems are linked by the title as sharing the same optimistic outlook derived from the same ultimate source. But they are free to interpret 'the Joy of Earth' in different ways. Nor is this joy set up as all-encompassing. Four years later Meredith would publish another collection, *Ballads and Poems of Tragic Life*, again including a number of poems first published in the 1860s and 1870s. The implication of the two titles together is that the collections are complementary and that Meredith's poetry encompasses both 'the Joy of Earth' and a sense of 'Tragic Life', with a given poem treating one or other aspect of this dual vision.

The implications of A Reading of Earth as a title are very different. Where Poems and Lyrics are plural, A Reading of Earth is distinctly singular. Where they select one aspect of the Earth (its Joy) as their subject, it claims the Earth itself, as a whole. Where they are expressions of that Joy, it offers rather an interpretation, a 'reading', of the planet. It is not only the title that announces this book as an interpretation of the natural world. In poem after poem Meredith urges us to 'read' the meanings within nature, from the first poem, 'Seed-Time', where 'Earth discerns / Them that have served her in them that can read' (ll. 42–3), through 'Hard Weather' (ll. 60, 83), 'The Thrush in February' (l. 119), 'Outer and Inner' (l. 31), 'A Faith on Trial' (ll. 304, 501, 519), 'Hymn to Colour' (l. 74) and 'Meditation under Stars' (l. 68) right to the very last line of the last poem, 'The Year's Sheddings', 'Read that, who still to spell our earth remain' (l. 4).

A Reading of Earth is unrepentantly didactic. As we read, we are repeatedly being told, albeit cryptically, how 'to spell our earth'. Meredith's title implies that the 'readings' of nature put across in different poems – all bar two of which seem to have been written in the mid-to-late 1880s – constitute a single self-consistent 'Reading of Earth'. (The two earlier poems are 'Woodland Peace' and 'Dirge in Woods', both revised from sections of the composite poem 'In the Woods', which I discuss below in Chapter 4.) His title thus invites precisely the kind of reading Roppen undertakes, providing it is restricted to this collection alone.

What, then, is the 'Reading of Earth' that Meredith gives us in A Reading of Earth, and how far does it differ from any 'philosophy' implicit in his earlier collections? There are a number of revealing motifs that recur across different poems, alongside that of reading itself. One of these is the image of life as a battle. This idea, derived from the Darwinian notion of the struggle for life, leads Meredith to affirm a position that looks on the face of it like Social Darwinism. In 'Hard Weather', for example, he imagines Earth sharpening Life at a grindstone to 'String us for battle' (l. 63). In 'Nature and Life', he characterises a 'manful' confrontation with the challenges of life as a healthy exchange of gifts between humanity and a personified 'Battle' (ll. 17–20). In 'The Thrush in February', he tells us that the ancestral heroes 'scorned the ventral dream of peace, / Unknown in nature', that 'We breathe but to be sword or block', and that 'the sons of Strength' are Nature's 'cherished offspring'(ll. 101–2, 136, 145–6).

Meredith's imagery of battle is unfortunate as it gives the impression that his belief in natural selection and his admiration of strong leadership led him towards the same proto-fascist militarism that attracted Davidson. Writing at the beginning of the 1920s, when fascism was beginning its long march to political dominance in Europe, the critic Archibald Strong allowed himself a deliberate slip, remarking that 'Nature's chosen were, to Meredith, her strong men – I had almost said her supermen – disciplined by her ruthless schooling into iron self-reliance' (1921: 166). But although Meredith's rhetoric seems to anticipate Davidson's Nietzschean vision, his message is in fact very different.

Like Blind, Meredith calls not for the imitation of natural selection in ethics but rather for the frank recognition of it as the state of nature which needs to be transcended. This too takes strength, but not of the brutal self-serving kind characteristic of the competitive process itself. Instead, it takes what Meredith calls 'gentle heroic manhood' in his short epitaph on the Prussian king Frederick III, 'The Emperor Frederick of Our Time' (l. 3). Like the 'men who fare / Lock-mouthed' against the wind in 'Hard Weather' (ll. 47–8), the reformist and anti-militarist Frederick showed a determination born of natural selection but not in thrall to it.

There is a puzzle here, however, as Meredith also makes repeated calls for his readers not to repudiate Earth but to 'serve' her. In both 'Seed-Time' and 'Hard Weather', this ideal of service is tied to the act of interpretation. As Meredith writes of nature in 'Hard Weather', Earth's passion 'Devolves on them who read aright / Her meaning and devoutly serve' (ll. 101–2). This motif of service, here tied to native strength as well as insight, is repeated throughout the collection. The short lyric 'Woodland Peace', for example, first published as one section of 'In the Woods' in the *Fortnightly Review* in 1870, is expressly revised so that the lines 'Here all things say / "We know not," even as I' read 'Here all say, / We serve her, even as I' (ll. 7–8).

Serving nature in *A Reading of Earth* implies different things in different poems. In 'Woodman and Echo' and 'The Year's Sheddings', Meredith suggests that our greatest service lies in death, in making way for new wood. In 'Hard Weather' and 'The Thrush in February', on the other hand, to serve Earth is to lead others in their understanding and love of her. 'Woodland Peace' suggests that to serve nature is simply to be natural, like the animals in a wood, a point reinforced in 'The Thrush in February' too, as Meredith implies that we cannot in fact fail to serve her: 'This breath, her gift, has only choice / Of service, breathe we in or out' (ll. 131–2).

It is hard at first to see how these different ideals of service to nature can coexist in a single 'Reading of Earth'. They can, but only because Meredith's 'Reading' is informed by different competing theories of evolution at the same time. In his image of life as a battle, Meredith is thinking of evolution in terms of the on-going condition of life in a universe shaped by natural selection. In his various ideals of service he is thinking of it rather as a trajectory. All of these ideals are premised on furthering the future evolution of humanity, according to different methods prescribed by different evolutionary paradigms. In 'Woodman and Echo' and 'The Year's Sheddings' the process is Darwinian, as by allowing ourselves to be disposed of by natural selection we allow younger, more competitive stock to flourish. In 'Hard Weather', it is implicitly Lamarckian. In 'The Thrush in February', it is at once Darwinian, Lamarckian and orthogenetic.

In 'Hertha' and *The Ascent of Man*, the tension between Darwinian and non-Darwinian versions of evolution is an indicator of bad faith. Unlike Swinburne and Blind, Meredith is not guilty of bad faith in *A Reading of Earth*, for all that he understood Darwinism at least as well as they did. There are two reasons why not. The first is that, Meredith is fundamentally an optimist. Where Swinburne and Blind use Social Darwinist logic to articulate an optimism they do not believe in, Meredith genuinely believes it. The rationale behind Meredith's optimism is captured in another of the recurrent motifs of *A Reading of Earth*. For Meredith, the cosmic process is one of 'Beneficence'. As he writes at the end of 'The Question Wither':

We children of Beneficence
   Are in its being sharers;
And Whither vainer sounds than Whence,
   For word with such wayfarers.
(ll. 21–4)

Meredith's logic is impeccable. We cannot say with any assurance that Nature wills the good, that it is benevolent. But we can say that it makes for the good, that it is beneficent, and that we share in the goodness that is made. Whether or not we do say this is largely a matter of temperament. Meredith's disposition is towards optimism, so he is happy to take the good in life regardless of the bad, and to prize life for it.

For anyone who finds their own life to be on balance good the beneficence of nature is a fact. The promise that evolution will give rise to an ever-better humanity could never be certain, even according to Lamarckism or orthogenesis. For Meredith to affirm this belief in his poems is not an act of bad faith, however, because he frankly admits that it is an act of faith. He implies as much in 'The Question Whither' and makes it explicit in 'A Faith on Trial', one of Meredith's few overtly theistic poems, in which Earth herself whispers of an evolutionary destiny which will reveal the source of the Beneficence of nature as 'the Master I serve' (l. 627).

This poem is a restatement of his philosophy of nature in the light of his second wife Marie's death in 1885. Even Meredith's optimism was sorely tested by Marie's slow, painful dying of cancer (as it had been before by the collapse of his first marriage, which underlies the darkness of his most famous poem, *Modern Love*). As he meditates on her death, he realises that his willingness to put his trust in evolution is a matter of faith, not science. Many of the poets of the non-Darwinian revolution believed that science had vindicated their faith in progress and changed it into fact. Swinburne and Blind knew this was not the case but chose to write as if it were. For his part, Meredith was open about the fact that, whatever the science might suggest, the end was still unproven.

The contrast between Meredith's evolutionary philosophy in *A Reading of Earth* and his earlier outlook is clearest in one more motif recurrent within this collection. Like Tennyson calling on himself and his readers to 'Move upward, working out the beast, / And let the ape and tiger die' in *In Memoriam* (cxviii, ll. 27–8), Meredith repeatedly urges us to repudiate the animal within and strive towards a higher level of evolution. In 'Hard Weather', Earth's chosen 'see how spirit comes to light, / Through conquest of the inner beast' (ll. 79–80). In 'The Thrush in February' their role is 'to lead / The tidal multitude and blind / From bestial to the higher breed' (ll. 97–9). In 'A Faith on Trial' too, Meredith imagines us 'quivering upward' in evolution, as 'from flesh unto spirit man grows', leaving 'Our animal tangle' behind us (ll. 400, 485, 487).

These images (grounded like Tennyson's in non-Darwinian models of evolution) contrast markedly with Meredith's attitude to animal life and our own animal nature in a number of the *Poems and Lyrics of the Joy of Earth*. The opening section of 'The Woods of Westermain', the lines of which also open that volume as a whole, challenges us:

Enter these enchanted woods,
   You who dare.
Nothing harms beneath the leaves
More than waves a swimmer cleaves.
Toss your heart up with the lark,
Foot at peace with mouse and worm,
   Fair you fare.
Only at a dread of dark
Quaver, and they quit their form:
Thousand eyeballs under hoods
   Have you by the hair.

Enter these enchanted woods,
   You who dare.

With its direct address and the brilliantly bizarre image of hooded eyeballs gripping us by the hair – an inventive but utterly unimaginable fusion of the sense of being watched with the feeling that your hair is standing up on end – this opening is at once arresting and perplexing. It sets us an interpretative challenge even as it challenges us to enter the woods. Yet it is clear that the poem is urging us to live like animals, not to reject our animal nature. The fear of nature, Meredith implies, is born not of nature itself but of our suspicion towards it. Our own 'dread of dark' transforms nature into something menacing. If we take nature as it comes, we can learn to love, not hate, it.

Meredith endorses nature and animal life as models throughout *Poems and Lyrics of the Joy of Earth*. In 'Melampus', he stresses the fundamental sanity of the natural order as 'all sane / The woods revolve' and 'the rooted life / Restrains disorder' (ll. 28–31). This insistence on the fundamental sanity of nature recurs in the 'Pleasures that through blood run sane, / Quickening spirit from the brain' in 'The Woods of Westermain' (IV, ll. 167–8); in the sweet, 'sane' harmonies as Skiágeneia sings about nature in 'The Day of the Daughter of Hades' (VIII, ll. 44–5); and in the contrast between the raving of those who reject Earth and the calm of Earth herself in 'Earth and Man' (ll. 29–32). The clearest emblem of this is the skylark in 'The Lark Ascending', which I discuss in Chapter 6.

This contrasts starkly with Meredith's philosophy in *A Reading of Earth*, where sanity is identified not with wild nature but with the 'conquest of the inner beast, / Which Measure tames to movement sane, / In harmony with what is fair' ('Hard Weather', ll. 80–2). Here the idea of healthy restraint, identified in 'The Woods of Westermain' and 'Melampus' with the love of animals, is directed against the animal within. The Tennysonian repudiation of the inner beast that typifies *A Reading of Earth* runs wholly counter to the spirit of the *Poems and Lyrics of the Joy of Earth*, which aim to transform our preconceptions of ourselves and the natural world through cultivating a love of and respect for our fellow animals. Far from affirming the same 'philosophic system', these two collections are in this regard diametrically opposed because they are grounded in different readings of late Victorian evolutionary theory.

In 1862, Meredith attended the British Association for the Advancement of Science in Cambridge. There he witnessed T. H. Huxley's final, crushing demonstration that the anti-Darwinian palaeontologist Richard Owen's claim that the human brain was unique in including a hippocampus minor was false. Owen claimed that this organ was the site of human rationality. To prove him wrong, Huxley, newly elected to Owen's old job as the Hunterian Professor at the Royal College of Surgeons, had the Conservator of the College's museum publicly cut up an ape's brain to show that it too had a hippocampus. All thinking men, Meredith wrote to his friend William Hardman, sided with Huxley (1970: i, 165).

This remark identifies Meredith as a card-carrying Darwinian in the early 1860s. From then to the early 1880s his understanding of evolution remained essentially Darwinian. Taking Darwinism to be a description of the natural order, his earlier poems aim to teach the healthiest and best response to that order. From the mid-1880s onwards, however, Meredith begins to understand evolution in non-Darwinian as well as Darwinian terms. On one level, this is simply a matter of Meredith keeping pace with science itself, which now consisted of a lively debate between competing theories, rather than a single Darwinian orthodoxy. But the speed with which this transition occurs in Meredith's case points too to his need, as he watched his wife dying, to pin his hopes to something more concrete than his own optimism.

As Meredith moves from a Darwinian understanding of evolution to a more catholic evolutionism which incorporates other theories alongside Darwinism, he moves too from a synchronic reading emphasising natural processes happening at the same time to a diachronic reading emphasising change over time. As a result, he stops seeing humans and animals as fellow beasts. Instead, he sees humans as descendents of beasts who are putting their ancestors behind them. Still an optimist, but struggling with his grief, Meredith identifies this as nature's crucial positive process. In turn, this leads him to value humanity increasingly in opposition to animals, rather than alongside them, and to value evolution itself above the evolved world.

A Reading of Earth is not wholly remote from Darwinism. In some ways, it looks more outdated than it is, particularly in its apparent Social Darwinism. Meredith's espousal of teleological evolutionism is also less clearly non-Darwinian than that of most of his contemporaries because he openly admits that it depends as much on faith as on science. On the other hand, for all that Meredith's ethics are close to those Huxley would articulate in *Evolution and Ethics* a few years later they gesture too towards the eugenics that Huxley would expose as scientifically bogus and morally corrupting in the same lecture, while his repudiation of the beast within is premised on a concept of evolution which makes little sense in strictly Darwinian terms. In recognising these obsolete elements within Meredith's later poetry, we can understand the dynamics of that poetry more clearly, enabling us to read it both on its own terms and for those elements and ideas which remain relevant to our understanding of Darwinism today.

DOUBTING PROGRESS: SCIENCE AND EVOLUTION IN TENNYSON'S LAST POEMS

As Meredith was finding a new faith in evolution as progress, Tennyson was losing his. It was a commonplace among the Victorian intelligentsia that, of all their poets, Tennyson had the best grasp of science. Even the scientists themselves thought so. In 1865 they elected him a Fellow of the Royal Society, while after his death T. H. Huxley paid tribute to him as 'the first poet since Lucretius who has understood the drift of science' (cited Desmond 1998: 595). The physicist Sir Oliver Lodge wrote a laudatory essay on how Tennyson had managed to square faith and science (1911), while the astronomer Sir Norman Lockyer published an entire book of excerpts from Tennyson's poems which demonstrated his careful and correct understanding of the full range of natural sciences from astronomy to botany (Lockyer and Lockyer, 1910). Swinburne even joked that Tennyson's poems had been written by Darwin himself, by analogy with the famous Baconian heresy attributing the works of Shakespeare to Sir Francis Bacon ([1887] 1926).

Myers, a pioneering experimental psychologist and psychical researcher as well as a dull poet, went so far as to suggest that Tennyson had played a key role in science itself through his contribution to 'the intuition, discovery [and] promulgation of fundamental cosmic law' (1893: 93). To the three cosmic laws or principles already known through science (the uniformity of nature, the conservation of energy, and evolution) Myers claimed that Wordsworth and Tennyson between them had added a fourth: 'the interpenetration of the spiritual and the material worlds'. For Wordsworth, this was a matter of intuition alone. Tennyson, on the other hand, built on that intuition in the light of science. In Tennyson's poetry, 'the fourth law at once completes the third, and is confirmed by it. For with the affirmation of a spiritual universe he links a claim for moral evolution' (ibid.: 106).

For Huxley, Lodge and Lockyer, Tennyson was a poet who understood science and accepted it. For Myers, he was the crowning poet of the tele-ological evolutionism he himself believed in. And yet, in the poetry that he wrote after the publication of *The Origin of Species*, and especially in the last few years of his life, Tennyson himself was increasingly doubtful about the promises of science at large and of evolution in particular. As Sir Charles Tennyson noted, his grandfather's 'attitude to science was *defensive*' (cited Millhauser 1971: 32). Michael Tomko has observed that in *In Memoriam*

Tennyson erects 'an absolute and prophylactic barrier between the physical and spiritual world' to preserve a space for faith insulated from the shocks of science (2004: 113–14). As science became increasingly menacing after Darwin, so Tennyson policed this barrier ever more scrupulously in his later poetry.

A subtle and economical expression of Tennyson's position is this short lyric, published in 1869:

Flower in the crannied wall,
I pluck you out of the crannies,
I hold you here, root and all, in my hand,
Little flower – but *if* I could understand
What you are, root and all, and all in all,
I should know what God and man is.

For late Victorian and Edwardian scientists and scientifically-minded critics, this poem seemed to capture what Edward Dowden called the scientific idea of 'ensemble', that all causes and all phenomena are ultimately interconnected (1878: 100–2). As the entomologist and anthropologist Sir John Lubbock glossed it, with 'careful, patient, and reverent study' we can hope to solve 'some of the greatest mysteries of Nature' contained within 'all that the smallest flower could tell us' ([1892] 1900: 118). For Tennyson, science might even lead us to God, as the antiquarian J. W. Hayes (1909: 43) and the American evolutionary philosopher John Fiske (1900: 177–8) both remarked. These men of science and others read Tennyson's poem as expressing science's potential to bring us positive knowledge of the most profound kind (see also Huxley 1910: ix; Lodge 1910: 103–5; Pearson [1892] 1937: 114). What none of them notice is Tennyson's choice to italicise '*if*' in the fourth line of the poem. That stress on '*if*' as we read directs us to realise that Tennyson is not saying that we can understand God through science, but that we cannot. Such knowledge will never be within reach, as to know the flower 'all in all' would be to have knowledge only God can have. The poem is not an endorsement of the project of science as natural theology, but an insistence on the limits on that very project.

The doubts Tennyson encapsulates in 'Flower in the crannied wall' about science's ability to reach the truth or teach what really matters are repeated again and again in his later poetry. In 'The Ancient Sage', set 1,000 years before Christ and inspired in part by the *Tao Te Ching*, Tennyson's spokesman the sage insists to a wayward young protégé that 'Thou canst not prove the Nameless, O my son, / Nor canst thou prove the world thou movest in . . . For nothing worthy proving can be proven' (ll. 57–8, 66). In 'Akbar's

Dream', the last of Tennyson's long philosophical poems, written in the last year of his life, the enlightened Mogul emperor Akbar quotes with approval a hymn which declares 'All the tracks / Of science making toward Thy Perfectness / Are blinding desert sand' (ll. 27–9). In 'Vastness', one of Tennyson's most compelling late lyrics, the misery of the phenomenal world imagined in purely material terms is reinforced again and again until the final line:

> What the philosophies, all the sciences, poesy, varying voices of prayer?
> All that is noblest, all that is basest, all that is filthy with all that is fair?
>
> What is it all, if we all of us end but in being our own corpse-coffins at last,
> Swallowed in Vastness, lost in Silence, drowned in the deeps of a
>   meaningless Past?
>
> What but a murmur of gnats in the gloom, or a moment's anger of bees
>   in their hive? –
>   *   *   *   *
> Peace, let it be! for I loved him, and love him for ever: the dead are not
>   dead but alive.

> (ll. 31–6)

That row of asterisks is a vivid typographic symbol of Tomko's 'prophylactic barrier', walling off the cry of faith in immortality from the threat of a meaningless materialism.

In these poems from the 1880s and 1890s, Tennyson is careful to circumscribe the power of science to lay claim to the truth. On the other hand, he does continue to invoke the non-Darwinian science of teleological evolution as a source of hope within his poetry. In 'The Ancient Sage', the sage urges his disciple to 'curb the beast would cast thee in the mire, / And leave the hot swamp of voluptuousness' (ll. 276–7), repeating the evolutionary step onto firm ground through his own moral effort. In 'The Ring', Tennyson imagines that 'Æonian Evolution, swift or slow, / Through all the Spheres' is the destiny planned for mankind by 'the Will of One who knows and rules' (ll. 39–42). In 'De Profundis', he at last published in 1880 verses begun in 1852, greeting his infant son Hallam as the end-product of 'all this changing world of changeless law, / And every phase of ever-heightening life' (ll. 6–7) – bearing witness to the fact that Tennyson's view of evolution, like Browning's, was not significantly changed by Darwin.

Yet none of these poems affirm the promise of evolution as a fact with any conviction. The sage, as we have seen, is deeply sceptical about scientific proof. In 'De Profundis', subtitled 'The Two Greetings', the earlier, evolutionary greeting is superseded by an idealist message preoccupied not with the phenomenal world but with 'that true world within the world we see' (l. 30), and walled off from science by a structural divide equivalent to the row of asterisks in 'Vastness'. As for 'The Ring', it is a dramatic poem not written in Tennyson's own voice. More specifically, it is a ghost story. Tennyson allows one of his characters to articulate a version of the Spiritualist cosmology that was so attractive to Myers as a topical and atmospheric framing device for a story that depends upon the plausibility of haunting. He does not endorse that cosmology himself.

Tennyson's most well-known pronouncement on evolution after *In Memoriam* is from 'Locksley Hall Sixty Years After', published in 1886. This is not an endorsement of the theory either, but a sarcastic repudiation of it:

Is there evil but on earth? or pain in every peopled sphere?
Well be grateful for the sounding watchword 'Evolution' here.

Evolution ever climbing after some ideal good,
And Reversion ever dragging Evolution in the mud.

(ll. 197–200)

Increasingly sceptical that progressive politics can bring about material progress, Tennyson calls into question the idea that collective as opposed to individual moral progress is anything other than a myth. Tennyson counters his own view of evolution as an upward movement towards an ideal of humanity with Lankester's argument that natural selection can as readily lead to degeneration. In doing so, he recasts Lankester's arguments in pre-Darwinian terms, imagining humanity reverting to an earlier, less advanced type, rather than degenerating to new but by our own standards lower forms. His scathing rebuke to those who sound the 'watchword "Evolution"' is a vivid sign of how his own faith, even in non-Darwinian evolution, was slipping.

Tennyson's most concentrated engagements with evolution in his late poetry occur in three short lyrics. Published in 1889, 'By an Evolutionist' sets out in parallel the thoughts of a materialistic and a theistic evolutionist. It begins with a framing parable. The next two stanzas record the thoughts of an evolutionist, first in his youth and then in old age, to which Old Age itself replies. These stanzas are then paralleled by two more, spoken by a second evolutionist. Here is the poem as a whole:

The Lord let the house of a brute to the soul of a man,
  And the man said 'Am I your debtor?'
And the Lord – 'Not yet: but make it as clean as you can,
  And then I will let you a better.'

I

If my body come from brutes, my soul uncertain, or a fable,
  Why not bask amid the senses while the sun of morning shines,
I, the finer brute rejoicing in my hounds, and in my stable,
  Youth and Health, and birth and wealth, and choice of women and
    of wines?

What hast thou done for me, grim Old Age, save breaking my bones on
    the rack?
Would I had past in the morning that looks so bright from afar!

OLD AGE

Done for thee? starved the wild beast that was linkt with thee eighty
    years back.
  Less weight now for the ladder-of-heaven that hangs on a star.

II

If my body come from brutes, though somewhat finer than their own,
  I am heir, and this my kingdom. Shall the royal voice be mute?
No, but if the rebel subject seek to drag me from the throne,
  Hold the sceptre, Human Soul, and rule thy Province of the brute.

I have climbed to the snows of Age, and I gaze at a field in the Past,
  Where I sank with the body at times in the sloughs of a low desire,
But I hear no yelp of the beast, and the Man is quiet at last
  As he stands on the heights of his life with a glimpse of a height that
    is higher.

The materialist within this poem sees evolution as confirming his own identity as a 'finer brute'. 'Finer' to him means merely refined. He sees no purpose in life beyond self-indulgence. The theist, by contrast, understands evolution progressively and determines to 'rule the Province of the brute' within himself, fulfilling the moral purpose towards which evolution has

been working. Faced with the trial of old age, the materialist merely grum-
bles, while the theist 'stands on the heights of his life with a glimpse of a
height that is higher'. This closing line seems to spell out a prophetic view
of evolution, bridging the divide that Tennyson himself has constructed and
so rigorously policed between science and theology. A closer reading shows
that this higher height is not mankind's evolutionary destiny, however, but
the individual man's translation into a purely spiritual (and so no longer
animal) being through death. By the end of his life, the old evolutionist
has achieved a serene state of moral peace in which he is indeed no longer
troubled by bestial urges. He is now better placed to anticipate his future
ascent, as he leaves his sinking body behind him. Ironically, the materialist
has attained a not dissimilar condition through sheer dissipation.

Tennyson prefers his second evolutionist on moral grounds, although he
characteristically stacks the deck in implying that a materialist philosophy
inevitably leads to self-indulgence and moral bankruptcy. The second evolutionist's evolutionary ethic chimes with conventional Christian morality, as Tennyson believes it should. Even so, Tennyson still holds back from
affirming that it is evolution itself as a 'fundamental cosmic law' that has
led to his moral and spiritual betterment. Instead he leaves us with a riddle.
His poem is called 'By an Evolutionist', and yet at least two evolutionists
speak within the poem. Are they alternative portraits of the same imagi-
nary evolutionist, each transformed by his chosen version of the theory? Or
is Tennyson himself the evolutionist of the title, with the two evolutionists
inside the poem alternative projections of him?

The two evolutionists in Tennyson's poem seem diametrically opposed,
but what distinguishes them is less their science than their theology. Both
accept human evolution from animals, but one holds 'my soul uncertain, or
a fable' while the other elevates the 'Human Soul' into his moral ideal. The
opening parable endorses the latter view through its image of God leasing
'the house of a brute', the body, to 'the soul of a man'. But this is a divine
act, as it was for Wallace and Mivart, not the outcome of evolution itself.
Once again, Tennyson gives priority to theology over science as a source
of truth, while insisting that science on its own cannot bring us moral
enlightenment.

Tennyson's last two evolutionary poems were published in *The Death
of Œnone, Akbar's Dream, and Other Poems* in 1892, a fortnight after his
death. Even by the diminished standards of Tennyson's later poetry, this
last collection is a disappointment. These two lyrics and their place within
the collection as a whole remain revealing, however. After a touching
dedication to his wife, the book begins with narrative poems. Many of their
heroes (St Telemachus, Akbar, the widow who tends her dead husband's

ex-lover through childbirth in 'Charity', the Hawaiian queen Kapiolani who defies the superstitions of her priests) are figures of religious enlightenment who expose the moral failings of their age by rising above them. The two poems which follow 'Kapiolani' attempt to map a similar moral transcendence onto the evolutionary process itself. Here, however, Tennyson's belief in the potential for individuals to advance morally is compromised by his disgust at the brute nature of humanity at large.

This is most apparent in the first of these poems, 'The Dawn':

> Red of the Dawn!
> Screams of a babe in the red-hot palms of a Moloch of Tyre,
> > Man with his brotherless dinner on man in the tropical wood,
> Priests in the name of the Lord passing souls thro' fire to the fire,
> > Head-hunters and boats of Dahomey that float upon human blood!
>
> Red of the Dawn!
> Godless fury of peoples, and Christless frolic of kings,
> > And the bolt of war dashing down upon cities and blazing farms,
> > For Babylon was a child new-born, and Rome was a babe in arms,
> And London and Paris and all the rest are as yet but in leading-strings.
>
> Dawn not Day,
> > While scandal is mouthing a bloodless name at *her* cannibal feast,
> And rake-ruin'd bodies and souls go down in a common wreck,
> > And the press of a thousand cities is prized for it smells of the beast,
> Or easily violates virgin Truth for a coin or a cheque.
>
> Dawn not Day!
> Is it Shame, so few should have climb'd from the dens in the level below,
> > Men, with a heart and a soul, no slaves of a four-footed will?
> > But if twenty million of summers are stored in the sunlight still,
> We are far from the noon of man, there is time for the race to grow.
>
> Red of the Dawn!
> Is it turning a fainter red? so be it, but when shall we lay
> > The Ghost of the Brute that is walking and haunting us yet, and be free?
> > In a hundred, a thousand winters? Ah, what will *our* children be,
> The men of a hundred thousand, a million summers away?

In this poem, as in 'Vastness' and 'Locksley Hall Sixty Years After', Tennyson assumes the role of a modern Jeremiah, castigating his contemporaries for their failure to put their native immorality behind them. His uncompromising rhetoric is enhanced by his assertive metre. Aside from the first line of each verse, the lines in this poem have six stressed syllables, with a seventh thrown in on the italicised words in the third and fifth verses. Through its metre, Tennyson's poem detains us, forcing us to listen to his tirade as he jabs us insistently with his finger.

In 'The Dawn', Tennyson rehearses a number of the clichés of Victorian evolutionism. Human evolution is imagined as an ascent from savagery to civilisation. Recorded history, instead of being the near-negligible tail-end of an immensely long evolutionary process, is therefore taken as a record of human evolution itself. As in the models of evolution that Tennyson learnt from Lamarck in the 1830s (via Charles Lyell's refutation of him in the *Principles of Geology* (see Dean 1985: 12)) and from Robert Chambers's *Vestiges of the Natural History of Creation* in the 1840s, evolution proceeds progressively, with different groups travelling in parallel but at different speeds along the same broad path. Contemporary savages are thus identified with our own predecessors. Hence Tennyson's eclectic list of barbarities representing the bloody and fiery dawn of mankind in the first stanza. Biblical human sacrifice is set alongside timeless cannibalism, the *autos-da-fé* of the Spanish Inquisition and atrocities said to have been committed by Dahomey, an infamous African slave-making state recently at war with France.

In his second stanza, however, Tennyson begins to unpick the progressive assumptions underlying this view of human history. Like Joseph Conrad in *Heart of Darkness*, Tennyson collapses the distance between the past and the present, the savage and the civilised. As in Conrad's novel, savagery remains unredeemed. Yet modern Western man is shown to be little more than a savage himself. The centuries that have passed since the rise and fall of Babylon and Rome count for precious little, as even in London and Paris humanity remains in its infancy. The characteristic Victorian idea of the savage as a child to the European adult is cut down to size, as we too are mere moral infants. As the poem's epigraph, quoted from an Egyptian priest speaking to Solon, remarks, 'You are but children'.

Tennyson equates the modern crimes of slander, casual exploitation and corruption with those of the savages themselves. We may not eat people literally, but we feed scandal, personified here by Tennyson, on their reputations and so on their livelihoods and ultimately their lives. In the image of the violated virgin Truth, and in the vile smell of the beast that pervades the modern city, Tennyson also suggests the sexual corruption of civilisation. The Victorian moral outrage at the fate of girls forced into prostitution, their bodies and souls 'rake-ruined', is another component of

Tennyson's jeremiad. It is not only virgin Truth who is violated but virgins themselves, not by force, but 'for a coin or a cheque'.

The smell of the beast reinforces Tennyson's point that even civilised man is barely evolved. He picks up on this image twice more, in the striking image of a 'four-footed will', and in the 'Ghost of the Brute' who is 'haunting us yet'. Typically, Tennyson imagines evolution as mankind's gradual emergence from a bestial to a fully human state. In Darwinian evolutionary theory, it makes no sense to talk about evolution as complete or incomplete, as there is no goal to be reached, only a sequence of present moments within a perpetual transformation. As Huxley remarked in *Evolution and Ethics*, 'the theory of evolution encourages no millennial anticipations' (1893–4: IX, 95). Non-Darwinian models of evolution, on the other hand, allow for an imagined moment when the process will finally be completed. Unlike Huxley's, Tennyson's understanding of evolution is again largely untouched by Darwin.

And yet Tennyson's faith in this non-Darwinian process looks ever more attenuated. The culmination of human evolution is projected at 'a hundred, a thousand winters' then 'a hundred thousand, a million summers' away. The hoped-for 'noon of man' recedes, and promises to recede still further. Even the twenty million summers before the sun cools off allowed us by Victorian thermodynamics seem likely to be used up. Tennyson's appeal to a further twenty million years of evolution seems desperate, even if we take it to be sufficient. As Milton Millhauser observes, all he can offer is 'a thin gleam of millennially distant hope' which Tennyson himself 'would find insupportable without faith' (1971: 27). Were the science of evolution all we have to take hope in, Tennyson implies, then it would be a feeble hope indeed.

'The Dawn' begins with statements about the past and the present – bleak ones at that – and ends with questions. These questions crowd on top of one another, leaving the poem's uncertainties all too apparent. What will the descendents of human beings be, a million years on? H. G. Wells would ask the same question in *The Time Machine* three years after Tennyson. The beautiful and playful Eloi that his time traveller encounters in the year 802,701 seem at first to have lain the 'Ghost of the Brute' to rest, yet it haunts them still in the form of their own imbecility and their gruesome, predatory sister species, the Morlocks. Wells was a Darwinian. Tennyson was not, but he too had his doubts about where the process of evolution would take us.

'The Dawn' is not Tennyson's last poem on evolution. That is 'The Making of Man', which follows it in his last volume, although the order in which he wrote the two poems is unknown. This second poem is markedly more hopeful:

Where is one that, born of woman, altogether can escape
From the lower world within him, moods of tiger, or of ape?
　　Man as yet is being made, and ere the crowning Age of ages,
Shall not aeon after aeon pass and touch him into shape?

All about him shadow still, but, while the races flower and fade,
Prophet-eyes may catch a glory slowly gaining on the shade,
　　Till the peoples all are one, and all their voices blend in choric
Hallelujah to the Maker 'It is finished. Man is made.'

This short poem might have been written by the second of the two evolutionists in 'By an Evolutionist'. It is resolutely theistic. Evolution in
this poem is the process by which God touches His creation into shape,
with man as the culmination of that creation. Like Robinson and Myers,
Tennyson sees this as an ongoing process. Like Morris, however, he imagines it will reach an end. For Morris, this end has already come with the
creation of the human soul, and evolution is now complete. For Tennyson,
the same end is deferred to an indefinite point in the future, with evolution due to reach its climax in the Christian millennium, foreshadowed in
Christ's last words on the Cross, 'It is finished' (John 19: 30).

'The Making of Man' views evolution from the perspective not only
of the Maker but also of the made. Forty years on from *In Memoriam*
Tennyson is still thinking of evolution as the process of letting the ape and
tiger die. This tenacious image reveals again how little impact Darwin's
image of evolution as a branching tree of life made upon him. According
to Tennyson's pre-Darwinian models of evolution, all lineages of animals
follow parallel evolutionary tracks upwards towards increasingly human
forms and states. We are thus no more closely related to modern apes than
we are to modern tigers. Rather, we ourselves passed through both ape-like
and tiger-like stages in our own evolutionary past. Tennyson's tigers are
not purely metaphorical, then. They mark out an earlier stage of evolution
through which we too have passed on our ascent towards humanity. In *In
Memoriam*, this progressive vision of evolution plays a role (albeit a minor
one, as a handmaiden to faith) in redeeming Tennyson from his alternative
vision of 'Nature red in tooth and claw'. In 'The Making of Man', it lies at
the heart of the divine plan. Here, if anywhere, Tennyson shows himself to
be the prophet of cosmic evolution that Myers claimed he was (although
Myers himself does not mention this poem).

'The Making of Man' is a hymn in celebration of the Maker. One of
the most deliberate artists of all English poets, Tennyson chooses the
ancient Greek metre known as the paeon – virtually unknown in English

poetry – for his poem. This metre, characteristic of paeans, or hymns of thanksgiving to Apollo, comprises metrical units or feet with three short or in English poetry unstressed syllables for every long or stressed syllable. Each line of Tennyson's poem consists of an anapaest (two unstressed syllables followed by a stressed one) followed by three paeons. The effect is that the poem moves with remarkable rapidity, as only four syllables out of every fifteen emphasise themselves as we read.

This extraordinary momentum drives the poem on, like evolution itself as Tennyson understands it, towards its millennial conclusion. Yet even here Tennyson's progress towards this point is not all easy. Following on from the ending of 'The Dawn', the first stanza of 'The Making of Man' is made up of questions, suggesting in themselves Tennyson's doubt as to whether evolutionary progress is inevitable. Certainly, Tennyson implies, none of us have as yet 'let the ape and tiger die', at least not completely. Indeed, the subtle change in Tennyson's imagery implies that he no longer sees this as a matter of Lamarckian self-control, so much as an 'escape' less deliberate than desperate, with success determined less by our own efforts and more by the Maker's interventions.

Tennyson's rhymes too hold back his prophecy of our evolutionary destiny. The hope that we will be touched into 'shape' is haunted by the echo of our failure to 'escape' from our own 'ape'-like moods. Similarly, the prospect that one day 'Man' will be 'made' is seen only dimly through 'the shade', and, like the ephemeral 'races', the vision, true or not, will surely 'fade'. These rhymes, together with Tennyson's hesitant syntax – 'Shall not. . .?', 'may catch' – and the repetition in 'aeon after aeon' combine to give the impression that his millennial vision is far from sure, and far, far beyond our reach.

Tennyson's last evolutionary poems give little warrant to the self-satisfaction of the secular prophets of progress. Instead, the movement from one to the other affirms yet again his faith in revealed religion. The mainly trite lyrics that comprise the remainder of this last book – his last poems, together with some earlier fugitive pieces – chime with the uncomplicated morality of the earlier narrative poems as they repeatedly reaffirm this faith.

The last poems of all return to the real source of Tennyson's hope: not the evolution of life, but death. In 'Faith', Tennyson echoes both 'The Dawn' and 'The Making of Man', as if to make explicit his repudiation of both the threat of Darwinism and the consolation of progressive evolutionism:

Doubt no longer that the Highest is the wisest and the best,
Let not all that saddens Nature blight thy hope or break thy rest,

Quail not at the fiery mountain, at the shipwreck, or the rolling
Thunder, or the rending earthquake, or the famine, or the pest!

Neither mourn if human creeds be lower than the heart's desire!
Thro' the gates that bar the distance comes a gleam of what is higher.
  Wait till Death has flung them open, when the man will make the Maker
Dark no more with human hatreds in the glare of deathless fire!

Reprising the form of 'The Making of Man', Tennyson exhorts his readers
and himself to reject the doubt that can follow from a Darwinian recognition of the bloodiness of nature. His poem has its logic as well as its rhetoric.
If death is the promised revelation, the moment when the characteristic
Tennysonian 'gleam' becomes a full illumination, then there are no grounds
to fear volcanoes, earthquakes, disease and other causes of death. It is this
glimpse of heaven, for Tennyson, not the evolutionary destiny prophesied
in 'The Dawn' and 'The Making of Man', which truly reveals God the Maker
to us and saves us from the hatefulness of human beasthood. Tennyson's last
word on evolution is not, ultimately, about evolution at all.

Tennyson wanted to believe that evolution was a progressive force
destined to give rise to happier and better forms of humanity. But, like
Swinburne and Blind, he found it hard to believe, not, as they did, because
he understood evolution in Darwinian terms, but because he doubted the
evidence. Indeed, in one sense his position is almost exactly the reverse of
theirs. They persuaded themselves of progress even though they knew that
Darwinian evolution is undirected. He doubted progress even though the
non-Darwinian models of evolution he broadly accepted seemed intrinsically progressive. Like Meredith, Tennyson realised that the betterment
of humanity through evolution was a matter of faith, not fact. Unlike
Meredith, he did not have enough faith in science itself to put his trust
in evolution. His doubts remain salutary even today, as the idea of evolution as a movement upwards towards humanity is still current within the
popular imagination, even if not in science itself.

A decade before Tennyson wrote his last poems, Oscar Wilde wrote,

From lower cells of waking life we pass
  To full perfection; thus the world grows old:
We who are godlike now were once a mass
  Of quivering purple flecked with bars of gold,
Unsentient or of joy or misery,
And tossed in terrible tangles of some wild and wind-swept sea.

                                                    ('Panthea', ll. 103–8)

As Wilde sees it, evolutionary theory transforms the transcendental ideal of human perfection into a reality. We are perfect, near enough, judged against the basic and imperfect life-forms from which we have grown. And if we are not yet quite perfect, the process of evolution itself will surely perfect us. Wilde's verse is vapid, but even if the poetry were better, the ideas themselves are illusions. In their different ways Swinburne, Blind, Meredith and Tennyson all expose the hollowness at the heart of the Victorian enthusiasm for progressive evolution and of the non-Darwinian biology that sustained it.

3

God

DARWINISM, CHRISTIANITY AND THEOLOGY

If you know only one thing about Darwin, the chances are it concerns the fact that his theory has provoked intense religious debate. People who have only a vague idea of evolution and have never heard of natural selection know that. The most mythologised moments in the history of Darwinism – the triumph of T. H. Huxley over Bishop Wilberforce at Oxford, Darwin's own loss of faith and the false counter-myth of his deathbed conversion, the Scopes trial – all centre on this clash between science and religion. It has been loudly proclaimed by atheists and fundamentalists alike, and as assiduously denied by moderates on both sides of the fence and on it.

Amid this cacophony, it can be hard to look steadily at the question of how and how far Darwinism and religion really conflict. One problem is that the question itself will not hold still. It depends whose Darwinism and which religion you have in mind. Discussions of the conflict between science and religion generally restrict themselves to Christianity, and for now at least I shall do the same. As the dominant Western religion, the history of Christianity repeatedly intersects with that of Western science, and it remains the most popular and influential religion in the United States and Europe where these questions are most often debated. Furthermore, once we move beyond Christianity and its Mediterranean sister religions Judaism and Islam to consider Buddhism, for example, or Tao, or animism, none of which are straightforwardly theistic, it becomes increasingly hard to define what the term 'religion' means.

Even limiting ourselves to Christianity (with an eye on monotheism more widely), the view that Darwinism and faith are incompatible is at the very least ahistorical. Many leading Darwinian biologists have been devout Christians, including R. A. Fisher, Theodosius Dobzhansky, Simon Conway Morris and Kenneth Miller. For these scientists, faith and science are complementary, not irreconcilable. On the other hand, the argument that science and religion are not in conflict can be equally ahistorical. The historian J. H. Brooke makes this point in his important book *Science and Religion*. When modern liberal and ecumenical believers (or polite non-believers like Stephen Jay Gould) claim that Darwinism poses no problems for faith, they gloss over the often radical differences between 'Christianity *as it was*' and 'Christianity *as they now wish it to be*'. As Brooke notes, 'They may wish to say that their religion no longer needs a geocentric universe, a physical location for heaven and hell, a personal devil, or even divine intervention in the physical world', but this risks overlooking 'the importance of such beliefs for the Christian societies of the past', and indeed for many Christians today (1991: 44).

We have to grapple with this problem if we are to understand how other people think about science and religion. But we also have to face it honestly when thinking about science and religion ourselves. Brooke's point is that we can have no access to any 'correct and timeless view, against which historical controversies can be judged' (ibid.: 42). Whatever the ultimate truth of religion, each individual's perspective on it is a perspective from within history. This applies as much to us as to our discredited forebears and contemporaries. We (whoever 'we' are) have no monopoly of religious enlightenment nor of religious honesty. From the perspective of a Victorian Catholic or a Tennessee fundamentalist, it is the liberal Anglican or Episcopalian who is not facing the implications of Darwinism honestly. For an out-and-out atheist, it is just as much the agnostic.

Another difficulty in determining the implications of Darwinism for religion lies in isolating the problems posed by Darwinism itself from those which arise at least as much from other sources. Today the conflict between atheism and religion is often fought on the battlefield of Darwinian biology. But the Victorian crisis of faith was not precipitated by Darwin, nor was the general trend towards a more secular world view. Instead, Darwin's discoveries contributed to these shifts, in part by reinforcing positions already manned from within other disciplines. As a historical science, Darwinism compounded the evidence that geologists, historians and biblical critics had already gathered to demonstrate that the Bible could not be literally true – a position many sophisticated theologians had been arguing for since the days of St Augustine. Darwinism played its part too, alongside enlightenment philosophy, history, anthropology and psychology, in reducing religion to a cultural phenomenon that could be explained, even explained away, in essentially secular terms. Darwinism has been a significant plank in these arguments, but not an essential one.

In its own right, however, Darwinism has solved one key problem long-faced by non-believers: the problem of how life on Earth comes to be so fit for purpose if it was not deliberately designed. At the same time, it has exacerbated a key problem for Christians: the problem of how a good God could be responsible for so much suffering. In this chapter, I am going to explore how poets have responded to these two strictly theological challenges posed by Darwin's theory. Later chapters will examine other points of conflict between Darwinian and Christian world views, over personal immortality and the place of humanity in the universe. The questions I will be asking here are, what bearing might Darwinism have on whether or not we should believe in God? And if God does exist, what if anything does Darwinism suggest about Him?

Darwinism raises two critical problems for belief in the Christian God which will not simply go away. Both were realised and confronted by Darwin himself. The first problem is that Darwinian theory renders God largely or wholly superfluous as an explanation for why we are here. As Darwin put it in the autobiography he wrote for his children, 'The old argument of design in nature . . . fails, now that the law of natural selection has been discovered' (2002: 50). Insofar as natural selection and God's design fulfil the same explanatory function, then either one makes the other superfluous. As the evidence for natural selection mounts, so the space left for teleology shrinks. We are left with the choice of doing without it altogether, or identifying natural selection as God's chosen method. As Darwin points out, however, 'there seems to be no more design in the variability of organic beings and in the action of natural selection, than in the course which the wind blows' (ibid.). Natural selection explains the appearance of design in organisms, but it does not bear the hallmarks of design itself. A Christian may claim that, in determining the laws of nature, God determined all their consequences and so in effect designed them after all. He or she might take heart as well from the fact that Darwinism has yet to demonstrate how, or even that, living matter can arise from non-living components. But the more we know about the science of evolution, the more ineffable God's methods and purposes appear, and the less likely we are to deduce teleology from evolution unless we presuppose it in advance.

The theologian Alister McGrath declares that 'the alleged explanatory superfluity of God clearly has no bearing on the question of his existence' (2005: 60). But this is misleading. Insofar as God's existence is a question at all, it is a question of the plausibility of one answer relative to another. The old philosophical rule of thumb known as Ockham's Razor advises us that, when we are weighing up the merits of competing explanations, we should avoid multiplying causes unnecessarily. Before Darwin discovered natural selection, the argument that God designed living creatures was the most parsimonious explanation for their complexity and adaptation. With

natural selection, God becomes superfluous. The most parsimonious explanation is that he has played no part in evolution, as it could as readily have
followed the path it did without him. On the other side, as we will see, the
claim that natural selection is God's creative method raises problems of its
own without solving any that cannot be solved by other means. God may
be one explanation for the origin of life, for example, but there are plausible
materialist hypotheses as well.

Since Darwin, God has found himself on the wrong side of Ockham's
Razor. In her essay 'Darwinism in Morals', the Victorian commentator
Frances Power Cobbe sardonically remarked that 'it is a singular fact that
whenever we find out how anything is done, our first conclusion seems to
be that God did not do it' (1872: 1). Cobbe is right that the discovery of a
material process such as natural selection does not preclude the possibility
that it is God's way of bringing about his ends. But if God did do it, then we
can legitimately ask, what does this tell us about God? This is the second
problem that Darwinism poses for Christianity. McGrath claims that 'the
wonder of the creator can be known through the created order' (2005: 153).
But by the same logic, the barbarity of the creator can be known through
the horror that is the created order. Darwinism ratchets up the old problem
of suffering. How can a God who is at once omniscient, omnipotent and
benevolent permit – or cause – so much suffering?

There are four reasons why Darwinian biology makes this chronic
theological problem acute. Firstly, as a strictly secular science, Darwinism
emancipates natural history from natural theology, that is, the argument
that the design apparent in nature is evidence of a benevolent God.
Without a presumption in favour of deliberate design it is hard to deduce
benevolence from what we know about the natural world with any consist-
ency. To give one example, Darwin himself remarked in a letter to Asa
Gray, 'I cannot persuade myself that a beneficent and omnipotent God
would have designedly created the Ichneumonidae [a family of parasitic
wasps] with the express intention of their feeding within the living bodies
of Caterpillars' (cited 2003: 492). Yet, as he argues at the end of *The
Variation of Animals and Plants under Domestication* (his first substantial
sequel to *The Origin of Species*), if we give up the principle of benevolent
design in one case then we have no good grounds to hold to it in another
when we can explain both through the same material processes of undirected variation and natural selection (1868: ii, 431–2). We are back with
Ockham's Razor. Whatever benevolence we can find in nature falls victim
to the principle of parsimony.

The second reason why Darwinism makes the problem of suffering more
acute is that it blurs or even erases the line between humans and other

animals. I will return to this in more depth in Chapter 6. The relevant point here is that we are duty-bound to take the suffering of animals more seriously when we know that they share many of our emotions and much of our capacity for suffering than we are when we think of them as soulless automata. Darwin draws out the theological implications of this knowledge in his autobiography. Some theologians, he notes, have attempted to solve the problem of suffering by arguing that it helps to bring about mankind's moral improvement. 'But', Darwin points out, 'the number of men in the world is as nothing compared with that of all other sentient beings, and these often suffer greatly without any moral improvement.' 'What advantage can there be', he demands, 'in the sufferings of millions of the lower animals throughout almost endless time?' (2002: 52).

The third turn of the ratchet comes when we realise that natural selection is a process that operates by means of premature death and the failure to breed. It is, bluntly, murderous. If we argue that evolution is God's means of creation, then we have to answer the charge that he has chosen a bloody and brutal way of going about it. A year after Darwin published *The Descent of Man* the explorer and lay evolutionist Winwood Reade made this point in his universal history, *The Martyrdom of Man*. Reade argues that the proposition that God is both benevolent and omnipotent is self-contradictory. If he is omnipotent, then it follows that he has chosen 'cruelty' (in the form of natural selection) as his means of bringing about development through evolution. God 'therefore has a preference for cruelty or he would not choose it' (1872: 518). The argument that natural selection is God's creative mechanism for evolution begins as an attempt to rescue the divine designer. It ends as a gross stain on his character.

The final challenge Darwinism makes to Christian theology over the problem of suffering is not so much a further turn of the ratchet as an offer to release it. If we accept that life is not designed, that there is no overarching moral order or purpose, then the problem of suffering (in the theological sense) simply goes away. It is only the presumption that the world is morally ordered that leads us to be surprised and puzzled by suffering. Not that this makes any difference to our practical response. We can still lessen the suffering that follows from our own deeds, those of others and nature itself, as most secular moralists would urge us to do. But we need no longer be continually confronted by a radical disjunction between our world view and the world around us.

Whether or not the problems of superfluity and suffering are fatal to Christianity is hotly debated. But any Christian who acknowledges that Darwinism is correct science has to face them, and we all, believers and non-believers alike, need to think through for ourselves their implications for our own world views. In this chapter, I will explore how poets have imagined the nature of God in a Darwinian universe, from Robert Browning's 'Caliban upon Setebos', written in the very early 1860s in the immediate aftermath of *The Origin of Species*, to the essays and poems of the contemporary American poets Robert Pack, Philip Appleman and Pattiann Rogers. Before I do this, however, I want to look at two sonnets which focus our minds on the implications of the arguments for and against design in nature.

HAPPENSTANCE OR DESIGN? TWO SONNETS

In his autobiography, Thomas Hardy described himself as 'among the earliest acclaimers of *The Origin of Species*' (1962: 153). In 'Hap', written in 1866 but not published until 1898, Hardy gives us an epitome of the tragic vision his novels would make famous:

> If but some vengeful god would call to me
> From up the sky, and laugh: 'Thou suffering thing,
> Know that thy sorrow is my ecstasy,
> That thy love's loss is my hate's profiting!'
>
> Then would I bear it, clench myself, and die,
> Steeled by the sense of ire unmerited;
> Half-eased in that a Powerfuller than I
> Had willed and meted me the tears I shed.
>
> But not so. How arrives it joy lies slain,
> And why unblooms the best hope ever sown?
> – Cross Casualty obstructs the sun and rain,
> And dicing Time for gladness casts a moan. . . .
> These purblind Doomsters had as readily strown
> Blisses about my pilgrimage as pain.

The speaker of Hardy's poem does not claim that his suffering is unique, nor that such suffering is inevitable. Through him, however, Hardy insists that, where we do suffer, we cannot lay the blame at the feet of an unjust god. His most striking suggestion is that, if we could blame such a god, it would ease our pain. Developing a line of thought implicit in Matthew Arnold's *Empedocles on Etna* and Edward FitzGerald's *Rubáiyát of Omar Khayyám* – both pre-Darwinian poems of the Victorian religious crisis – Hardy argues that the haphazard miseries of a godless existence are harder to endure even than the arbitrary punishments of a malevolent god. This is both because we would be 'half-eased' if we could find someone to blame for our misery and because it is harder to cast ourselves in a heroic role if we are the victims of the arbitrary happenstance of events rather than some cosmic injustice.

Hardy's speaker imagines that, if he knew he suffered because of an unjust god, he would respond with defiance and stoic endurance. Faced with the realisation that there is no God at all, he falls back on cynicism, captured in his tone of voice. The harsh alliteration of 'Crass Casualty' and the spat-out plosives in the closing lines suggest the bitterness of his disillusionment. Yet this cynicism is itself a form of stoicism – a stoicism embodied in the very form that Hardy chooses for his poem. In place of an expansive Romantic ode or mid-Victorian elegy, he contains his complaint within the tight structures and fourteen lines of a Petrarchan sonnet. The self-discipline of his verse reflects the self-discipline of his persona. Hardy's speaker suffers, but he does not indulge his suffering.

The dignity of the sonnet form as Hardy handles it, with its measured division into two quatrains and a sestet, conveys a dignity on the speaker himself. The poem's diction too is strangely dignified. The closer Hardy's language comes to conventional poeticisms (the 'moan' of 'dicing Time', for example) the less it rings true. Instead, the poem's most powerful moments come when Hardy surprises us with the peculiarity of his idiom. The brutal reduction of God to merely 'a Powerfuller than I' is one example. So is that masterly 'unblooms', suggesting that a failure to come to fruition is a negative action rather than just a passive absence. Hardy's use of 'Casualty' as an abstract proper noun catches attention too, partly because of the snarling alliteration as it is dismissed as 'Crass', partly because it is unfamiliar and so unexpected. Hardy's creative confidence with language gives 'Hap' its distinctive authority. At the end of the sonnet he is left with no alternative but to struggle on with his godless pilgrimage in the full knowledge that his fate is arbitrary. It is this properly tragic attitude, rather than vainglorious defiance, that best fits the Darwinian condition as Hardy sees it.

Where Hardy's title 'Hap' (another example of his remote diction) implies from the outset that his sonnet will put misery down to happenstance, the title of Robert Frost's sonnet 'Design', drafted in 1912 and published after heavy revision in 1922, suggests a presumption of natural theology:

I found a dimpled spider, fat and white,
On a white heal-all, holding up a moth
Like a white piece of rigid satin cloth –

Assorted characters of death and blight
Mixed ready to begin the morning right,
Like the ingredients of a witches' broth –
A snow-drop spider, a flower like a froth,
And dead wings carried like a paper kite.

What had that flower to do with being white,
The wayside blue and innocent heal-all?
What brought the kindred spider to that height,
Then steered the white moth thither in the night?
What but design of darkness to appall? –
If design govern in a thing so small.

Where Hardy begins with human misery, Frost begins with natural history. The octet of 'Design' describes a natural scene; the sestet goes on to pose questions as to its purpose. Yet as soon as Frost begins to describe the scene in front of him, he starts directing our interpretation of it. To John Cunningham, the dimpled, fat, white spider seems at first 'most innocent' (2001: 271). But while each of these characteristics may imply innocence on their own, the combination of them suggests something much more sinister, like a bloated leech or vampire. Either way, Frost soon dispels any sense of innocence with a catalogue of sinister similes and rhymes that, as Cunningham notes, associate whiteness with 'blight' and later 'night'. As a result, even the more genuinely innocent similes which close the octet (the snow-drop, froth and paper kite) come to seem Gothic and grotesque.

These mounting similes are dark but also fanciful. Like Hardy, however, Frost uses the sonnet form to good effect. The Petrarchan sonnet typically includes a *volta* or 'turn' between the eighth and ninth lines. In 'Hap', this marks the point at which Hardy conclusively discards God as an explanation in favour of chance and time. In 'Design', the *volta* marks the shift from the description of the scene to the interrogation of it. But it also marks a change in tone as the Gothic chill turns from a frisson into real horror.

By asking about the purpose of this particular flower's particular colour – that recurrent white, rather than the usual blue – Frost suggests that this ghastly spectacle does in fact have a purpose. This impression is compounded by the implication that the spider's and the moth's movements have been directed to bring them to this point, and by the notion that in its whiteness the spider is somehow kin to the flower. These lines are horrifying partly because of the conclusion to which they lead: that all this whiteness is not innocence but a 'design of darkness' with no other purpose than to appal the human onlooker, who has presumably been 'brought' to this spot himself to witness it. But they are horrifying too because their logic is deranged. Frost does not ask whether these four organisms have been brought to the same spot, but what has brought them there. In his paranoid demand for meaning, Frost – who, it is increasingly apparent, is not Frost at all, but a dramatized mindset – attributes agency, and malevolent agency at that, to what is indeed an 'innocent' flower.

The argument from design, Frost implies, leads to, even is, a form of madness. It is not clear whether his poem's closing line exonerates this madness or persists in it. Does Frost really believe that natural theology might still be valid in larger matters, even if not in 'a thing so small'? The real menace of the scene he describes lies not in its littleness but in its ghastliness, which could surely recur on a larger scale. Indeed, the spectacle he shows us is typical of the horror of predation at large. Is he maintaining his dramatic voice instead then, implying that such an excuse is itself an insane evasion of the truth? Unlike the voice that Hardy creates in 'Hap', Frost's voice in 'Design' is hard to pin down – on a first reading it is not obviously dramatic at all – and the dash at the end of the penultimate line makes it even harder to tell whether he is remaining in character or ironically satirising his speaker by saying what he would have to say to excuse his God from the blame he appears to be laying at his feet.

Such equivocation is characteristic of Frost's poetry and of his response to Darwinism in particular. He is equivocal about his religious beliefs too. Unlike Hardy, whose unbelief, while not uncomplicated, is overt, Frost is persistently reluctant to declare a position. Like Swinburne's bad faith, Frost's ambivalences and ambiguities have led his critics to diametrically opposed accounts of his views on the relation between science and religion, with Albert Gelpi (1987: 12), Robert Faggen (1997) and Robert Pack (2004b) all seeing Frost's thinking as broadly aligned to Darwin's, even as Robert Haas argues that Darwin was 'for Frost the most threatening intellectual figure of the nineteenth century' (2002: 88).

Whatever the implications of 'Design' may be for Darwinism or Christianity *per se*, it is a powerful critique of natural theology. In 'Hap', Hardy suggests that even a belief in a vengeful god would be comforting, but that those who accept the Darwinian world view – 'We who believe the evidence', as he calls us in his later poem 'The Problem' (l. 2) – must do without even that consolation. In 'Design', Frost turns Hardy's logic on its head, implying that the belief in design yields up a universe which is not less but more terrifying. Neither poem has much to offer in the way of support, but Hardy at least reminds us that we are not alone. The speaker of 'Hap' may be too solipsistic to be wholly sympathetic, but his very existence raises the hope that, where he faces his trials alone, we may face ours together. In 'Hap', Hardy sets off on a poetic pilgrimage which leads him over forty years later to the conviction spelt out by the vanishing God at the end of 'A Plaint to Man', as he urges us to recognise

The fact of life with dependence placed
On the human heart's resource alone,
In brotherhood bonded close and graced

With loving-kindness fully blown,
And visioned help unsought, unknown.
(ll. 28–32)

Natural theology: Robert Browning's 'Caliban upon Setebos'

Both Hardy and Frost imply in their poems that, after Darwin, God is at best an absentee landlord, little better than no God at all. At worst, he has in Winwood Reade's words 'a preference for cruelty'. Hardy's contemporary James Thomson agreed, staging a debate between these two theologies in his macabre allegory *The City of Dreadful Night*. Thomson concluded that only atheism made sense:

The world rolls round for ever like a mill;
It grinds out death and life and good and ill;
It has no purpose, heart or mind or will.
(viii, ll. 36–8)

Where Thomson was a card-carrying atheist, Robert Browning was arguably the major Victorian poet most calmly confident in his Christianity. Yet he too saw the thrust of Darwinism as tending in this direction.

First published in 1864, Browning's dramatic monologue 'Caliban upon Setebos; or, Natural Theology in the Island' is one of the earliest responses to Darwin's theory by a major poet. The situation of the poem is this: Caliban, the sub-human native of Prospero's island from Shakespeare's *The Tempest*, is lounging in a muddy pool in front of his cave on a hot summer day. Taking advantage of Prospero's siesta to shirk, he ponders aloud to himself on the nature of God, called Setebos by his mother, the witch Sycorax. At the end of the poem, a storm gathers suddenly, or at least quickly enough for the preoccupied Caliban not to have noticed it. Afraid that the storm manifests the wrath of Setebos, he repents his presumptuous theologising, grovels and promises penance. Beyond Caliban beginning his pondering and abruptly winding it up because of a change in the weather, the poem has no narrative development or plot. Instead, it is an argument in a dramatic voice.

Caliban's God combines the qualities of the natural world as he observes it with extrapolations from his own character. The two tally remarkably well with one another. Two words recur throughout Caliban's explanations of Setebos's behaviour: 'spite' (ll. 56, 146, 202, 210) and 'sport' (ll. 61, 149, 177, 218). Both are apt to Caliban's own conduct, from which he draws the analogies which shape his theology. In the first of these analogies, Caliban ponders the relationship between a creator and his creations. He imagines how he himself might treat a creature that he had made if it were injured and appealed to him for help:

> if his leg snapped, brittle clay,
> And he lay stupid-like, – why, I should laugh;
> And if he, spying me, should fall to weep,
> Beseech me to be good, repair his wrong,
> Bid his poor leg smart less or grow again, –
> Well, as the chance were, this might take or else
> Not take my fancy: I might hear his cry,
> And give the mankin three sound legs for one,
> Or pluck the other off, leave him like an egg,
> And lessoned he was mine and merely clay.
> Were this no pleasure, lying in the thyme,
> Drinking the mash, with brain become alive,
> Making and marring clay at will? So He.
>
> (ll. 85–97)

Caliban casts God not only in his own image, but in the image of himself lolling drunk. The assonance and alliteration of the last three lines capture his playful but capricious self-indulgence. Caliban's whimsical cruelty is most tellingly suggested by his superficially kinder response to his creature's plea: not to restore its leg, but to give it 'three sound legs for one'. Extrapolating from himself, Caliban imagines a God who lacks any empathy for his creatures. He does not take pleasure in their pain directly, but because he does not empathise with that pain it does not inhibit him from toying with them and enjoying his power over them, the grotesque spectacle of their injuries, and the still more grotesque spectacles he can turn them into if he so chooses.

Caliban recognises his own lack of empathy in nature and so deduces it in God. For him, nature teaches us only that we are under God's power. Setebos is a drunken parody of the biblical image of God the Potter. In the

Book of Jeremiah, God instructs Jeremiah to go into a potter's house. There Jeremiah sees the potter accidentally spoil a pot as he makes it. The potter discards it and makes another. God tells Jeremiah, 'Behold, as the clay is in the potter's hand, so are ye in mine hand' (18:6). The crucial distinction between Caliban's God and the God of Jeremiah is that, where Jeremiah's God chooses to destroy that which happens to be marred, Setebos chooses to mar as well as to make.

As Caliban sees it, such misfits are not merely aberrant departures from a well-made order. Instead, God creates them for his own whimsical pleasure. But then they are of no great importance in themselves, because they are 'merely clay'. Caliban's theology has no place for a soul. Where his mother, Sycorax, believed 'that after death / He both plagued enemies and feasted friends' (ll. 251–2) – that is, she believed in Hell and Heaven, imagined in crudely material terms – Caliban merely "Believeth with the life, the pain shall stop' (l. 250).

In the second of his analogies between himself and Setebos, Caliban reflects on Setebos's morality:

'Thinketh, such shows nor right nor wrong in Him,
Nor kind, nor cruel: He is strong and Lord.
'Am strong myself compared to yonder crabs
That march now from the mountain to the sea,
'Let twenty pass, and stone the twenty-first,
Loving not, hating not, just choosing so.
'Say, the first straggler that boasts purple spots
Shall join the file, one pincer twisted off;
'Say, this bruised fellow shall receive a worm,
And two worms he whose nippers end in red;
As it likes me each time, I do; so He.
(ll. 98–108)

For Caliban, kindness and cruelty are categories of motivation, not of action. Setebos is not kind because his favour is not motivated by love, and he is not cruel because the suffering he inflicts is not motivated by hate. Caliban deduces Setebos's morality from this lack of motivation, suggesting that where kindness would be right and cruelty wrong, his arbitrary whims are neither. It does not occur to him that such arbitrary behaviour is itself immoral. Caliban's morality is of course awry. It does not follow that, because he (and by analogy Setebos) only destroys one in twenty-one crabs, 'He is good i' the main' (l. 109). Good cannot be determined statistically. A tyrant is not on balance a good man because he only kills one man for every twenty that he spares. Judged in these terms, God would be as immoral as any other arbitrary tyrant.

But this judgement follows from Caliban's anthropomorphism. If Setebos is simply a personification of the natural order, utterly remote from his creatures (as Caliban himself imagines him, when comparing himself with the crabs) then it may be meaningless to apply moral categories to him at all. And if his actions are thus truly beyond right and wrong, then the best assessment we can give is indeed statistical. Setebos may not be good morally, but the order attributed to him may be, on balance, more good than bad. Caliban smashing the crabs, plucking out their claws and feeding them titbits, on grounds that are at best whimsical, is a fitting symbol of natural selection, which as Darwin remarked blows like the wind. When you compare this with Tennyson's realisation in *In Memoriam* 'that of fifty seeds / She often brings but one to bear' (LV, ll. 11–12), Caliban's vision of nature looks positively benign. The odds are, after all, much better. Yet this is only true if we, like Caliban, exempt nature – and God – from the test of morality.

As Caliban seeks to explain Setebos's motivation, he moves from a vision of a God with a drunk's preference for cruelty to one in which he is purely arbitrary. Caliban's theology takes a further step in this direction as he imagines 'something quiet o'er His head, / Out of His reach' (ll. 132–3) that is responsible for creating this imperfect God. Being perfect, the Quiet 'feels nor joy nor grief, / Since both derive from weakness in some way' (ll. 133–4). The relationship between the Quiet and Setebos resembles that between God and Satan, except there is no sign that the Quiet is benevolent. Besides, Caliban does not attribute the creation of our world to it but to Setebos.

Nor can he see any evidence of a benevolent plan behind the suffering of nature:

His dam held that the Quiet made all things
Which Setebos vexed only: 'holds not so.
Who made them weak, meant weakness He might vex.
Had He meant other, while His hand was in,
Why not make horny eyes no thorn could prick,
Or plate my scalp with bone against the snow,
Or overscale my flesh 'neath joint and joint,
Like an orc's armour? Ay, – so spoil His sport!

(ll. 170–7)

Caliban rejects his mother's tradition which, like Christian mythology, attributes evil influence to a lesser being than the creator. Instead, misery is a deliberate object of the creative process. Caliban's logic is simple. Like Reade, he argues that if an effectively omnipotent God creates a world in which there is suffering, that suffering must have been created deliberately, as God could have chosen otherwise. Caliban can only conclude that he makes humans and animals weak and vulnerable because it makes it easier for him to toy with us, taking pleasure in our misfortunes and his power.

Taking a Darwinian view of nature, Caliban deduces from it a view of God as alternately beyond and so unconcerned with our moral categories, that is, amoral (the Quiet), or spiteful and callous, that is, immoral (Setebos), at least by our standards if not necessarily by Caliban's own. But what does Browning want us to make of this theology? On one side, he gives a Darwinian natural theology a surprisingly good shot. On the other, he puts this natural theology in Caliban's mouth.

Caliban is no fool. He does not follow his mother's traditional beliefs without question. Instead, as Michael Timko has remarked, he takes the rational and empirical project of natural theology as far as it can go and comes up with answers that are plausible on those terms (1965: 143). But while Caliban may not be a fool, he is a savage, with all the connotations that word had for a Victorian Englishman. Like the 'Head-hunters . . . of Dahomey' in Tennyson's 'The Dawn', he is an embodiment of mankind's evolutionary past and so a living symbol of evolution itself. Like them, he is brutal and morally repugnant, and while his thinking may be rational in parts, it is superstitious in others, as his crude and desperate bid for atonement at the end of poem makes vividly clear.

Neither is Caliban's voice what we would expect from a rational person. Browning's Caliban is a grotesque, a distorted exaggeration even of Shakespeare's tragicomic monster. Fittingly for a Shakespearean character, Caliban speaks in blank verse. But unlike Shakespeare's Caliban he speaks about himself in the third person, using archaic forms of verbs and omitting pronouns (their absence is marked with apostrophes). For all his rationality, then, Browning's Caliban is distanced from us by space, time and language. Indeed, his bizarre and idiosyncratic syntax suggests a mind that is alien in its very nature.

Through Caliban, Browning warns us that if we are to be Darwinians we must take the consequences, as – reversing Caliban's own analogies – the universe we live in will come to seem as brutal and alien as Caliban himself. At the same time, Caliban's moral backwardness is a stark warning against reversing his analogy in another sense and deriving our morality from the universe around us. Far from being the Social Darwinist path to progress, Browning insists, this would lead us back to the barbarism and brutality embodied in the as-yet-only-half-human Caliban.

Browning looks at Darwinism from a non-Darwinian vantage point. But his primary target, like Frost's, is not Darwinism itself, but natural theology. As Jeff Karr argues, Browning contrasts the world view of natural theologians such as William Paley with Darwin's 'in order to focus on the fundamentally flawed *process* of natural theology'. Browning's point, for Karr, 'is that the logical method of natural theology, applied to the Darwinian view of nature, alters revealed theology's conclusions concerning the nature of God' (1985: 38–9). In the last months of his life, Tennyson affirmed his faith that 'God *is* love, transcendent, all-pervading!' while admitting that 'We do not get *this* faith from Nature or the world. If we look at Nature alone, full of perfection and imperfection, she tells us that God is disease, murder and rapine' (cited Tennyson [1907–8] 1974: 4–5). Like Tennyson, Browning is not correcting a merely academic mistake in 'Caliban upon Setebos'. Instead he is pointing out the very real moral danger to which that mistake can lead as he traces a Darwinian natural theology to its logical conclusions: to a 'Being . . . wicked, foolish, and insane', as Thomson puts it in *The City of Dreadful Night* (VIII, ll. 33–4).

GOD AFTER DARWIN: THREE CONTEMPORARY AMERICAN POETS AND THE BOOK OF JOB

For all their differences over religious belief itself, Hardy, Frost, Thomson, Browning and Tennyson all agree that, since Darwin, natural theology leads us either to a bad God or to no God at all. All five reject the possibility of a bad God, leaving them again with two alternatives: to accept a godless universe, as Thomson and Hardy ruefully do, or to abandon natural theology as a method, as Frost, Browning and Tennyson all recommend. But even if we abandon natural theology and stop looking to nature for independent evidence of God, we still have to face the question of whether nature as we understand it through science is consistent with scripture. This is not the same question as whether Genesis read literally is consistent with science, to which the answer is a clear 'no'. Rather, it is a question of whether the relationship between God and his creation as represented in the Bible remains plausible in the light of Darwinism.

The clergyman, novelist and amateur naturalist Charles Kingsley had no doubt on this point. In his 1871 lecture 'The Natural Theology of the Future', he remarked of the Darwinian vision of nature, 'Whether or not it suits our conception of a God of love, it suits Scripture's conception of Him' (1880: 321). Ever the muscular Christian, Kingsley invites us to go back to the Bible and face up to the fact that the God revealed therein may not be the mild and benevolent being we might like him to be. In his autobiography, Darwin declared that 'it revolts our understanding to suppose that [God's] benevolence is not unbounded' (2002: 52). But perhaps such squeamishness is theologically misplaced. After all, who are we to judge God? In 1878, G. H. Lewes (George Eliot's common-law husband) argued in a persuasive essay 'On the Dread and Dislike of Science' that the true arbiter of morality should be our own moral sense. When moral propositions and statements about human nature are consistent with what we feel to be right, 'theology can give these no *extra* sanction'; when they are not, 'theology cannot make them acceptable' (1992: 324). Lewes's rationalist morality underlies Darwin's thinking but, as Kingsley points out, it is hardly scriptural.

In his essay 'The Long View: Darwin and the Book of Job', the contemporary American poet Robert Pack argues that Darwin's vision of the world is consistent with one book of the Bible in particular. In the Book of Job, God gives Satan permission to blight the life of Job, who to that point has been faultlessly upright and god-fearing, and happy and prosperous with it. Job's livestock is stolen, his servants and children slaughtered by bandits and he himself blighted with disease. While his wife urges him to curse God and die, his friends Eliphaz, Bildad and Zophar come to console him and mourn with him. Convinced that Job's suffering must be a just punishment for sin, they try to persuade him to confess. This the innocent Job adamantly refuses to do, reproaching God the while. The stalemate is broken when God himself appears in a whirlwind, berating Job for presuming that his suffering is of any significance, and his friends still more so for their mistaken understanding of natural morality. In the Book of Job, then, God expressly disavows any simplistic idea of suffering as divine punishment. Indeed, his words in this book are remote from anything we recognise as a moral code at all. Instead, as Pack remarks, 'Where Job has challenged God in the name of justice, God replies in the amoral terms of the joy of creation' (1991: 195).

Drawing on the Book of Job, Pack reconstructs an old theology for the new Darwinian condition. Darwinism does 'not negate the idea of God', he argues, 'but it does change the image of God from that of a compassionate intercessor to that of a profligate but potent creator' (ibid.: 182–3). According to Pack, 'there are two moralities in the Book of Job: God's morality of creation and humankind's morality of justice' (ibid.: 183). These two moralities are 'mutually exclusive' (ibid.: 184). As 'God's medium is power and creation' while 'man's medium is morality and social law', 'what is right for humans does not apply to God' (ibid.: 196). God is thus beyond our judgement, much as Browning's Caliban suggests. With this revival of an ancient theology we gain 'an enlarged sense' of (echoing

Darwin) the 'grandeur' in this view of life (ibid.: 199). The flip side of this is that, much as Hardy affirms in 'A Plaint to Man', 'this detachment carries with it a growing human need to express and offer sympathy precisely because such sympathy cannot be found in nature or in the God who created nature' (ibid.: 183).

Pack's conclusion that the God of Job fits a Darwinian universe is not unique. Indeed, it is a leitmotif of Darwinian poetry. Job is invoked explicitly by Frost in *A Masque of Reason* and by Jeffers in 'Birds and Fishes', as well as in responses to science by Christian poets as far apart as Christina Rossetti and R. S. Thomas in 'Later Life' and 'At It' respectively. In an interview, Hughes remarked that he drew on the depiction of the creator in Job for his personification of nature in 'Hawk Roosting' (Faas 1980: 199). Job also informs the presentation of God in Jeffers's 'Triad' and 'The Inhumanist'; in a number of Hardy's poems, including 'Doom and She', 'A Dream Question', 'New Year's Eve', 'God's Education' and 'A Philosophical Fantasy'; and in Pack's own poetry. Here I want to concentrate on three poems by two of Pack's contemporaries which recast this theology in their own opposing ways: 'Bildad' by Philip Appleman and 'Against the Ethereal' and 'The Possible Suffering of a God during Creation' by Pattiann Rogers.

Appleman is perhaps the most mercilessly anti-religious poet since Thomson. His targets include Christian Scientists ('Alive'), evangelical faith-healers ('The Faith-Healer Speaks'), biblical literalism ('Darwin's Ark', revised as 'Noah'), the Roman Catholic Church's stance on child abuse ('A Priest Forever') and modern Christians who disparage primitive religions as superstitious without admitting that their own faith is built on equally primitive superstitions of its own ('Credo'). Appleman's technique in these poems is not subtle, but then he is not aiming for subtlety. Having no truck whatever with those he is attacking, he makes his contempt felt. This approach is powerfully puritanical. Appleman's strength as a satirical poet lies in his unflinching moral gaze. His subjects, who often speak for themselves in dramatic monologues, give accounts of their moral and intellectual positions which become more desperate or grotesque as the poems unfold. Of course, they are his creations. No evangelical preacher or disgraced Catholic father would give the account of themselves that Appleman gives of them. But again, that is the point. Appleman does not want us to see these people as they see themselves, but for the monsters that in his eyes they really are.

In some ways 'Bildad' is of a piece with these other poems. Like 'Noah' and other poems from the same collection, sardonically entitled *Let There Be Light*, it takes a biblical narrative as its starting point. The speaker is Bildad himself, one of Job's three friends who demand he confess his sins.

The poem is spoken after God has appeared to Job and berated Bildad and the others for their false interpretation of divine morality. Bildad retells the story from his own perspective. Where many of Appleman's poems lampoon or deny the miraculous events in the Bible, Bildad's version of events is consistent with the Book of Job. It is rather his moral interpretation of them that differs.

As a result, the target of the poem shifts. At first Bildad himself is mocked. His conviction that Job must have sinned seems precisely the kind of dangerous, deluded self-righteousness that Appleman deplores. But our reaction to him is complicated by his reaction to God:

> But then God opened His mouth
> and in a whirlwind of rage
> blasted our beautiful logic.
> Out of a dust storm it came, that booming
> irrelevance: 'Where were you
> when I made the earth, the stars,
> the sea? Do you know the breadth of the world,
> the treasures of the snow?
> Out of whose womb comes the ice?
> Can you send down the lightning?' . . .
>
> Some scene, isn't it? There we are,
> making sense of things, putting Job in his place,
> proving the neat connection between
> crime and punishment – and just as our triumph
> burns in Job's bewildered eyes,
> God horns in with that scandalous
> non sequitur. 'No,' He says,
> 'You don't suffer because you sin.
> You suffer because I say so.'
>
> (ll. 88–97, 103–11)

God's first speech here is stitched together from different verses of Job, Chapter 38. Relative to Bildad's moral argument (his 'syllogism' that 'since God is just, / He cannot torment / an innocent man' (ll. 81–4)) it is indeed an 'irrelevance'. As Pack observes, God is not speaking in moral terms at all, and Bildad is frankly scandalised. His whole theology is grounded in that 'neat connection between / crime and punishment', and God has just given it the lie.

There is something hateful about Bildad's moral reasoning, or more precisely about the lengths to which he is prepared to go to prove it. He is an inquisitor, and his image of his triumph burning in Job's eyes, while strictly metaphorical, has connotations of torture. But his moral disgust at God is nonetheless compelling. On the one hand, he is galled at having been shown to be wrong. Through his pique, we are encouraged to laugh at his expense. But the words he puts into God's mouth are genuinely chilling, and the poem ends on an abrupt note of moral indignation which is not easy to dismiss:

> It's hard enough to bring up a family
> in these troubled times without admitting
> that almighty God has the morals
> of a Babylonian butcher.
>
> (ll. 135–8)

Appleman's poem is written in free verse, loosely knitted together with alliteration. In these closing lines – as in the last lines of the previous passage – Appleman uses this alliteration to hold our attention, binding these key passages into unified moments within the poem. The last lines in particular stay in the memory, partly because they close the poem, but more because of those scornful plosive 'b's and that evocative allusion to Babylon, and because here at last we find ourselves being directed to agree with Bildad. If you judge the God of Job by the standards of human morality, Appleman implies, He is indeed little better than an arbitrary despot.

'Bildad' is both a satire on the belief in a cosmic moral order and an indictment of any God who could preside over a cosmos that is not moral. Appleman is bullish in his attacks on Christianity, while by his own testimony Pack is a 'confirmed atheist' (1991: 49). For them both, the God of Job is the kind of God that might be believable within a Darwinian universe, rather than a God either of them actually believes in. He is God as a poetic symbol, not God as the theological truth.

For Pattiann Rogers, by contrast, he is God proper. Rogers's poetry is a valuable counterpoint to the poems I have discussed so far in this chapter, as she seeks, not merely hypothetically, to imagine a God who is true both to her religious impulses and to science. In 'Against the Ethereal', Rogers, like Appleman, takes her lead from Job:

> I'm certain these are the only angels
> there are: those with raised, sneering
> lips revealing razor-pure incisors that rip
> with a purpose, dominions in the moment

when they spread like flying squirrels,
sail like jaguarundi across the celestials
with sickle claws thrust forward.

This is the only rite of holiness
I know: fierce barb of bacteria, that hot,
hot coal, that smoldering challenge
glaring, for twelve millennia at least,
in all directions from its dark, subzero
cellar of frozen, glacial rock.

This is the noise of heavenly
hosts: trumpet-blaring chaparrals
and shinneries, cymbal-banging greasewood
and jojoba deserts, burble of hellbinders, slips
of heliotropes, tweakings of brush mice
and big-eared bats, wheezings of rusty wheels,
grasshopper sparrows, autumn leaves ticking
across gravel on their paper pricks.

I aspire devotedly and with all reverence
to the raspy links of lampreys, the tight
latchings of pawpaw apples and soursops,
the perfect piercings and fastenings
of sperms and ovipositors, clinging
grasps of titis and chacmas.

Aren't you peculiarly frightened, as I am,
by the vague, the lax, the gossamer
and faint, the insubstantial and all
submissive, bowing transparencies,
any wilfully pale worshipping?

This is the only stinging, magenta-cruel,
fire-green huffing, bellowing mayhemic
spirituality I will ever recognize:
the one shuddering with veined lightning,
chackling with seeded consolations, howling
with winter pities, posturing with speared
and fisted indignations, surly as rock, rude
as weeds, riotous as billbugs, tumultuous

as grapevine beetles, as large black, burying
beetles, bare, uncovered to every perception
of god, and never, never once forgiving
death.

Like 'Bildad', 'Against the Ethereal' is written in free verse bound together
with alliteration. But where Appleman uses alliteration to emphasise
certain moments in his poem, Rogers's entire poem is emphatic. Rogers
often couches her poems as suggestions or propositions, but here she asserts
boldly, even urgently, a perceived truth. This sense of urgency comes partly
from the alliteration itself, which keeps up the pace of the poem as we
read it. It comes too from the concentration of present participle verbs.
Everything in this poem is happening as she speaks. The animalistic angels'
lips are 'sneering', 'revealing' their predatory teeth; the challenge posed
by the bacteria is 'smouldering' and 'glaring' like a hot coal; the plants,
animals and objects in the third paragraph are 'blaring', 'banging', 'tweak-
ing', 'wheezing' and 'ticking'; and so on. There are no obvious pauses either,
as most lines run on into the next and each paragraph is a single sentence.
The only relief from this intensity comes in the fifth paragraph, an aside to
the reader in which both the participles and the alliteration briefly ease off.
Otherwise the pressure is sustained right up until the abrupt end on that
single word 'death'.

Like God in Job, Rogers dazzles us with the brilliance of life itself.
'Against the Ethereal' takes to an extreme a tendency within her poetry
for assembling haphazard lists of animals and plants, all busily living.
Characteristically, Rogers's menagerie includes some creatures that are
common worldwide (sparrows, lampreys and bacteria), others that are probably familiar to American readers (shinnery oaks, soursops and billbugs),
others that are native to America but nonetheless exotic (jaguarundi cats
and hellbender giant salamanders) and yet others that would be known to
most readers from zoos or documentaries if at all (titi monkeys and chacma
baboons). Rogers's delight in vocabulary seems to drive her imagination
as much as her love of natural history. This too contributes to the poem's
dazzling effect. Even those few readers who come close to Rogers's ency-
clopedic knowledge of plants and animals will not always recognise them
in this eclectic company, especially not when their names are oddly spelt,
like 'hellbinder', or abbreviated, like 'titis and chacmas', with nothing more
than the 'clinging / grasps' to suggest that these are kinds of monkey.

Rogers's vision of the natural world is dazzling, but it is not blinded.
Again, like God in Job, she is unashamed by the violence of nature, the
menace of predation and disease, and the noisy desperation of the struggle

to survive and reproduce. In nature, as she sees it, these are all bound indissolubly together. This is clearest in the fourth paragraph, where a single six-line sentence moves from the parasitic rasp of lampreys' jawless teeth first to the parallel 'latchings' of fruit, then to the cellular details of sexual reproduction and at last, in those 'clinging / grasps', to a hint of newborn primate life. This nexus of apparently conflicting tendencies within nature is epitomised even more economically in 'the perfect piercings and fastenings / of sperms and ovipositors'. Focussing on the sperm, these two lines are a vivid realisation of a microscopic view of the formation of a zygote as a sperm pierces an egg. But the 'piercing' ovipositors have a different set of associations. These lines are haunted by Darwin's appalling Ichneumonidae, as the ovipositor is the needle-like organ with which these parasitic wasps place their eggs within the bodies of growing caterpillars. Here reproduction and predation are intimately interlinked.

For Darwin, the Ichneumonidae were a bar to belief in God. In this poem Rogers takes them in her stride, suggesting that even they are 'perfect' in their way. She does this by identifying holiness with life itself. Her 'mayhemic / spirituality' is vibrantly celebratory but openly amoral. As Pack argues in his essay, morality is simply beside the point, in Job's spirituality as in Darwin's biology. But Rogers does not embrace this attitude with quite the conviction that she appears to. There are two moments in particular where this poem calls its own certainties into question. The first is that curious easing off in the fifth verse paragraph. What is puzzling about this paragraph is that it is not frightening. Rogers claims to be frightened, and yet her tone here is rather one of detached contempt or faint disgust than fear. Even so, it suggests that the speaker has a need to believe which is threatened by the 'insubstantial' and the 'pale', in short, by the 'Ethereal' of the poem's title. Her certainty comes to look more like desperation than conviction, as if she protests too much. The reason for this becomes clear in the poem's second, more abrupt change, not of tone so much as form, in the last line. Rogers's spirituality in 'Against the Ethereal' is a frantic affirmation of life in the face of death. Life itself is taken as the mark of God, and because life is morally neutral, so too is God.

The hints at desperation in 'Against the Ethereal' hint also at an equivocation over whether a Job-like spirituality is sufficient to sustain us in a Darwinian universe. Unlike Pack or Appleman, Rogers wants a spirituality that she can really feel and truly trust. In her reflexive essay *The Dream of the Marsh Wren* she characterises God as 'that essence, that benevolence, that presence so many human beings have sensed to be part of our experience' (1999: 92). Where 'Against the Ethereal' follows the tradition of Darwinian poetry in breaking the link between the essence or presence of

God and his benevolence, Rogers's earlier poem 'The Possible Suffering of a God during Creation' seeks to maintain that link within a Darwinian world view:

It might be continuous – the despair he experiences
Over the imperfection of the unfinished, the weaving
Body of the imprisoned moonfish, for instance,
Whose invisible arms in the mid-waters of the deep sea
Are not yet free, or the velvet-blue vervain
Whose grainy tongue will not move to speak, or the ear
Of the spitting spider still oblivious to sound.

It might be pervasive – the anguish he feels
Over the falling away of everything that the duration
Of the creation must, of necessity, demand, maybe feeling
The break of each and every russet-headed grass
Collapsing under winter ice or feeling the split
Of each dried and brittle yellow wing of the sycamore
As it falls from the branch. Maybe he winces
At each particle-by-particle disintegration of the limestone
Ledge into the crevasse and the resulting compulsion
Of the crevasse to rise grain by grain, obliterating itself.

And maybe he suffers from the suffering
Inherent to the transitory, feeling grief himself
For the grief of shattered beaches, disembodied bones
And claws, twisted squid, piles of ripped and tangled,
Uprooted turtles and rock crabs and Jonah crabs,
Sand bugs, seaweed and kelp.

How can he stand to comprehend the hard, pitiful
Unrelenting cycles of coitus, ovipositors, sperm and zygotes,
The repeated unions and dissolutions over and over,
The constant tenacious burying and covering and hiding
And nesting, the furious nurturing of eggs, the bright
Breaking-forth and the inevitable cold blowing-away?

Think of the million million dried stems of decaying
Dragonflies, the thousand thousand leathery cavities
Of old toads, the mounds of cows' teeth, the tufts
Of torn fur, the contorted eyes, the broken feet, the rank

Bloated odors, the fecund brown-haired mildews
That are the residue of his process. How can he tolerate knowing
There is nothing else here on earth as bright and salty
As blood spilled in the open?

Maybe he wakes periodically at night,
Wiping away the tears he doesn't know
He has cried in his sleep, not having had time yet to tell
Himself precisely how it is he must mourn, not having had time yet
To elicit from his creation its invention
Of his own solace.

Published a decade apart, the two poems are so close, not only thematically but structurally and in their imagery and vocabulary, that it is tempting to read them as companion pieces. Each consists of six verse paragraphs. In each, the first three paragraphs and the last repeat a single motif in two different phrases, 'It might be' and 'maybe' in the earlier poem, contrasting with 'I'm certain' and 'This is' in the later one. In each poem the fourth and fifth paragraphs depart from this model, with the fifth addressed directly to the reader. Both poems share too the same habit of listing, the same detailed interest in natural history and the same unromanticised vision of nature. As for specifics, the sand bugs in the earlier poem reappear as billbugs, the crushing 'winter ice' as bacteria-infested 'frozen, glacial rock'. The sperm and ovipositors are there in the fourth paragraph of each poem too, embedded in both in a cycle of images uniting pain and death with reproduction and rebirth.

The tone of the two poems is radically different, however. Where 'Against the Ethereal' is urgent and definite, 'The Possible Suffering of a God during Creation' is measured and provisional. The earlier poem is also the more unflinching. Rogers's acceptance of predation and disease in 'Against the Ethereal' does not sit easily with her abhorrence of death. In 'The Possible Suffering of a God during Creation', she recognises that death and suffering are inevitable consequences of the nature of time. In the first chapter I drew a distinction between poems which face Darwinism as an unchanging condition and those which look at it as a process. Like Edwin Morgan, Pattiann Rogers explores the implications of Darwinism viewed in these two distinct ways in different poems. In 'Against the Ethereal', she confronts the arbitrariness, waste and violence of natural selection. She faces these in 'The Possible Suffering of a God during Creation' too, but here she does so in the light of evolution over time as well.

Revealingly, Rogers's title for her collected poems is *Song of the World*

Becoming. In 'The Possible Suffering of a God during Creation' evolution is the process by which God brings creation into being. Each organism is not only itself; it is a stage in the coming-into-being of the organisms which come after it. The moonfish, for example, is a latent humanoid, as yet unrealised. If even a perfect creation is to come into being over time by means of evolution, then it must inevitably begin with imperfection and proceed through change – that is, through death and the 'Unrelenting cycles' of reproduction. Where other Darwinian poets interpret this suffering within nature as meaning that, if there is a God, he does not care that his creatures suffer, Rogers posits that he cares greatly and suffers in their suffering.

Rogers's own love of nature is so comprehensive that she imagines the whole of organic and inorganic nature to be worthy of God's compassion, even a slowly vanishing crevasse or some ripped and tangled kelp. Her poetic technique fits her subject especially well here. The authority with which she writes about nature readily gives the impression of omniscience and omnipresence. Hers is already a God's eye view. She sees everything, in specific detail. She names it too, implying a scientific or perhaps arcane knowledge beyond the name itself. Her verse compounds this impression, as the long free-verse lines and polysyllabic, Latinate words combine to give 'The Possible Suffering of a God during Creation' its stately pace and gravity.

The compassion Rogers's God feels for his creation distinguishes him from the Gods of other Darwinian poets. It is a fundamentally Christian response to nature as Darwin describes it. As Christ takes mankind's suffering upon himself on the cross, so Rogers's God takes on the suffering of all things through all time. Yet her theology is far from orthodox. Rogers repays God's compassion for nature with her own compassion for God. The image of a weeping God is oddly vulnerable, all the more so as Rogers holds out the prospect that something may come of evolution that can give him 'solace'.

In both *The Dream of the Marsh Wren* and her more recent essay 'Twentieth-Century Cosmology and the Soul's Habitation', Rogers imagines a reciprocal process of creation, in which God himself is completed or fulfilled only through the fulfilment of his creation (1999: 91–2; 2001b: 13). This poem gestures towards a similar process. Its culmination is a teleology that even God cannot wholly grasp because the 'solace' it will give him is yet to come. Both his omnipotence and his omniscience appear to be constrained by time.

Insofar as evolution has a goal in 'The Possible Suffering of a God during Creation', it exists only in the mind of God, and even he cannot know exactly what it is. Orthodox Darwinians may nevertheless see this as one goal too many. If natural selection blows like the wind, then evolution is not predetermined, and if evolution is not predetermined then it makes no sense to say that a specific future creature is latent within a current one – a man within a fish, for example – for all that some fish can in retrospect be seen to have had the potential to become people, alongside frogs, turtles, birds and countless possibilities as yet unrealised.

But Rogers is not so easily caught out as this. For one thing, she does not make the usual mistake of presupposing that humanity is the goal of evolution. A fanciful speaking plant or a more plausible hearing spider are likewise steps towards the perfection of the creation. More crucially, her God's eye view gives her a dual perspective on evolution, both from within time and from beyond it. Viewed from within time, evolution moves only towards greater adaptation to current environments, not to any more specific goal. But while Rogers's God does not know the precise goal of evolution, he knows that it has one.

Only God, with his perspective from beyond time, knows that his creatures are unfinished. And yet curiously, since Darwin, we too share this knowledge, as time does not stand still and natural selection is ongoing. While we have no grounds to believe that they ever will or can be finished, that natural selection can ever stop, like Tennyson, Rogers chooses to imagine that God may know better. Even then, this may be merely because his view of creation is split, half in time and half beyond it. In contrast with Tennyson's 'The Making of Man', for example, there is nothing in Rogers's poem to suggest that 'the duration / Of the creation' is finite, even if, at some point, God may find 'solace' within it.

Rogers's vision in 'The Possible Suffering of a God during Creation' is compelling, partly because, unlike the moonfish, we are able to feel our own imprisonment within time. Rogers puts before us a God whose perspective paradoxically allows us to step outside that prison as he joins us within it, and whose compassion for his creation is both a consolation and an invitation towards a compassion of our own.

How does this Christian compassion square with the Job-like theology of 'Against the Ethereal'? One answer is that they do not have to square at all. A poet is under no obligation to be consistent. She may not even be writing in the same voice. But Rogers does not often write in overtly dramatic voices, and her commitments to both science and spirituality are genuine. When contrasted with the open speculation of the earlier poem, the conviction of 'Against the Ethereal' might suggest that she has changed her mind. But Rogers does not let that conviction go unchallenged even within that poem itself, so it seems more likely that it marks rather a change of mood, an alternative view but still a provisional one, from within the same overall mindset. The echoes of and parallels with 'The Possible Suffering of a God during Creation' are an implicit invitation to read the two poems alongside one another, to see them as complementary rather than contradictory visions. Through their different perspectives and tones, Rogers allows herself to comprehend God in a Darwinian universe as at once the God of Christ and the God of Job.

Like the Bible itself, Rogers's poems present God in ways that appear to be, or even are, contradictory, but that unite nonetheless in a sensitive spirituality and a tentative theology. Whether their vision of God is true is, of course, another matter. Rogers is in a minority among Darwinian poets in finding a God that Christians can recognise at large in the world. But her honesty in facing up to the darker implications of Darwinism is no less genuine on this account. For all their theological differences, the service she does us through her poetry is not unlike Hardy's. Neither poet denies the problem of suffering or pretends that Darwinism is untroubling. But they both offer us solidarity in the face of the Darwinian condition. In Hardy's poems, that solidarity is occasioned by the absence of God. In Rogers's, God himself stands alongside us, suffering our suffering in 'The Possible Suffering of a God during Creation', alive in our life in 'Against the Ethereal'. Whether we choose Hardy's hand or Rogers's – whether we resolve to do without God or to rediscover Him – we are steeled for the experience of life in a Darwinian universe.

4

Death

DARWINISM, DEATH AND IMMORTALITY

In the conclusion to *The Descent of Man*, Darwin wrote 'He who believes in the advancement of man from some low organised form, will naturally ask how does this bear on the belief in the immortality of the soul' ([1871] 2004: 682). Darwinism poses a problem for our belief in immortality because, where evolution is a gradual process, the distinction between being mortal and being immortal is a stark one. As John Dupré notes, 'it is not that evolution cannot endow an organism with a radically new capacity. This happens throughout the history of life. But evolution does so by gradual steps and continuous change' (2003: 65). It is hard to imagine a sliding scale of immortality. The belief that human beings and human beings alone have immortal souls is easy to maintain if all species of animals, people included, were separately created. But it is much harder to maintain if we evolved from other, non-human animals, as Darwinism shows that we did.

If we accept that our immortal souls cannot have evolved gradually, we have three options to choose from. The first is to suppose that all life is immortal: that immortality is, in effect, a property of life itself. This is superficially appealing. It has the spirit of generosity on its side. But it is not philosophically very satisfying, and it does not ultimately solve our problem. Traditionally, immortality is pegged to individuality. It is an individual soul that survives into an afterlife or migrates from one body to another. That is all very well if you are a person, or a cow, or a crab. But what if you are a fungus, where is it impossible to say where one individual stops and another begins? And what would it mean for a (presumably) unconscious fungus to be immortal anyway? This problem does not go away if we limit immortality to animal life, or even to conscious life, as there are no firm lines between animals and non-animals, nor between conscious organisms and unconscious ones. Unlike immortality, we can imagine consciousness existing with different degrees of definition or complexity, as the study of animal behaviour and our own experiences of being intoxicated or

— 102 —

half-asleep suggest it does. (I will return to the subject of animal consciousness in Chapter 6.)

The second option is to suppose that God gifted humanity with immortal souls at some particular point in our physical evolution. On this view, human beings have what the Victorian Catholic evolutionist St George Mivart called a 'double nature'. In his critique of Darwin's theory, defiantly titled *On the Genesis of Species*, Mivart drew a line in the sand. Our bodies may be the product of evolution, but our souls were given to us by an act of 'direct and immediate creation' (1871: 331). On this point Darwin himself was inclined, if not to agree, then at least to be accommodating. In *The Descent of Man* he remarked that, as few people worry overmuch about when exactly a human embryo becomes immortal, 'there is no greater cause for anxiety because the period cannot possibly be determined in the gradually ascending organic scale' ([1871] 2004: 683).

Changes to abortion laws have turned the souls of embryos into an urgent ethical concern for many. The polite entente between Darwinism and Christianity papers over some equally unsettling cracks. Darwin's willingness to leave the question of when we got our souls unanswerable is an evasion of the fact that there must presumably be an answer, assuming we have immortal souls at all. Looked at on a geological scale, it may seem plausible that, as the Anglican ornithologist and evolutionist David Lack postulated, 'a supernatural event took place at the time of man's first appearance, before which our ancestors were proto-human mammals and after which, through the divine gift of a soul, they were truly human' (1957: 89). We cannot of course know exactly which human species was the first to have a soul. Did the Neanderthals have souls, for example, or the so-called 'hobbits', *Homo floresiensis*? Are souls the property of all hominids, of the different species and subspecies which make up the genus *Homo*, or just of *Homo sapiens*?

We do not know the answers to these questions, but it is possible to imagine a taxonomy in which there are answers. But this is a Linnaean approach, not a Darwinian one. In the light of Darwinism, the divisions between species are an artefact of time and classification. There was a time when those hominids whose descendents were going to become *Homo neanderthalensis* and those whose were to become *Homo sapiens* were the same people, whatever we might call them. Looked at minutely, the accommodation between Darwinism and Christianity implies that the gift of immortality came not between species, but between generations. As Michael Ruse asks, 'are Darwinian Christians to believe that one generation had no souls at all and the next did, even though, intellectually, they were virtually identical?' (2003: 345) Logically, this is not impossible. Nor is it impossible that a key aspect of what we recognise as the human intellect is the gift of the soul. After all, the archaeology of the human mind is tentative at best. But either way, this divide between two generations remains at the very least oddly arbitrary.

Aside from an attachment to doctrine, one of the main motives that drives people to take this second option is that they cannot bring themselves to face the third: that our deaths, and those of all other organisms, are final. It is not pure coincidence that the enthusiasm for psychical research among English intellectuals took off in the 1860s in the aftermath of *The Origin of Species*, nor that many of the leading lights of English Spiritualism were evolutionists, including the poets Frederic Myers and George Barlow as well as Wallace. In his recent book *Is Nature Enough?* the theologian John Haught comes close to admitting that it is his 'instinctive revolt against' the prospect that 'anything as luminously real and palpable as consciousness could end up in the pit of final nothingness' which compels him to believe in immortality (2006: 199).

Tennyson once told a story about a Parisian who went into a restaurant, ordered an excellent dinner, ate it, and promptly killed himself with a chloroformed handkerchief. Tennyson's gloss on the story was, 'That's what I should do if I thought there was no future life' (Lyell 1902: 137). The anecdote is darkly comic, but Tennyson was in earnest. Time and again in his later poems we hear voices telling us that without immortality life can have neither hope, nor meaning, nor moral purpose. As well as Tennyson's self-portrait as Jeremiah in 'Vastness' and the sensuous and embittered materialist in 'By an Evolutionist', there is the young poet reproached by his master in 'The Ancient Sage', the atheist in 'Despair' (the survivor of a half-successful suicide pact between himself and his wife) and the eponymous hero in 'Lucretius' (to whom I will return in Chapter 8). Speaking in his own voice, Tennyson demands in 'Wages' 'if the wages of Virtue be dust, / Would she have heart to endure for the life of the worm and the fly?' (ll. 6–7). In 'A Voice Spake out of the Skies' he sets out an allegorical equivalent to the story of the Parisian's dinner, asking whether there could be any good grounds for charity or even self-preservation 'If the world and all within it / Were nothing the next minute' (ll. 9–10) – an analogy for the individual's death in a purely material universe.

The most poignant of these late poems is 'Frater Ave atque Vale', written in 1880, a year after Tennyson's brother Charles Tennyson Turner's death:

Row us out from Desenzano, to your Sirmione row!
So they rowed, and there we landed – 'O venusta Sirmio!'

There to me through all the groves of olive in the summer glow,
There beneath the Roman ruin where the purple flowers grow,
Came that 'Ave atque Vale' of the Poet's hopeless woe,
Tenderest of Roman poets nineteen-hundred years ago,
'Frater Ave atque Vale' – as we wandered to and fro
Gazing at the Lydian laughter of the Garda Lake below
Sweet Catullus's all-but-island, olive-silvery Sirmio!

Tennyson's brief elegy for his brother is a tissue of allusions to the Roman poet Catullus and his lament for his own brother, which famously ends 'Brother, hail and farewell'. The imagery of the lake and the peninsula are drawn from another of Catullus's poems, as well as from Tennyson's own visit to them. Along with the lilting alliteration in 's' and the single doleful but soothing rhyme, they give this short poem a prevailing sense of calm which compensates for Tennyson's grief. But crucially that consolation is only possible for Tennyson because his own woe, unlike that of the pagan Roman, is not 'hopeless'. And yet the poem would not be so profoundly moving were it not for Tennyson's sense that hopelessness is once again a very real prospect. Tied to faith, hope for Tennyson is essential but always provisional, and so precarious.

For Tennyson, as for Haught and the Spiritualists, the absence of an afterlife makes even this life intolerably pointless. One of the most vital services Darwinian poetry can perform is to help us confront what Pattiann Rogers calls – recalling both the ghastly whiteness of Frost's 'Design' and the 'blanker whiteness' of his 'Desert Places' (l. 11) – 'the white stare, the smothering fog, the albino terror, / The blankness of death' ('White Prayer', ll. 28–9). One approach is to make life look worse so that death looks a little better. In *The City of Dreadful Night*, James Thomson offers us 'The certitude of Death' as our 'One anodyne for torture and despair' (I, ll. 80–1). Confirming Tennyson's worst fears, he assures us, through the character of a preacher:

But if you would not this poor life fulfil,
Lo, you are free to end it when you will,
    Without the fear of waking after death.
                    (XIV, ll. 82–4)

For Thomson, death is a blessing rather than a curse because, like Browning's Caliban, he believes that 'with the life, the pain shall stop'.

For the forgotten Victorian poet and evolutionist Thomas Gordon Hake, by contrast, the very experience of life is so wonderful that even the briefest of lives is infinitely better than no life at all. Near the end of his sonnet sequence *The New Day*, published in 1890, Hake cries out:

> Think what a boon is life, however short!
>   To be, though in an hour to but have been;
> To know, or to have known, of wonders wrought;
>   To see the vast existence, or have seen,
> As it rolls round in spheres, and deluges
> The soul's perceptions!
>
> (LXXXIV, ll. 1–6)

Hake's verse may be awkward but his enthusiasm is infectious as he seeks to persuade us that a short life is not necessarily a sad one. But though his jubilation is a tonic, it is also deceptive. If life is this wonderful, who would willingly lose it? Hake deals with death by setting it aside, not facing it, at least not in this sonnet, and when he does face it in the very last sonnet of his sequence he cannot bring himself to rule out the faint hope of immortality. On the other side, Thomson's pessimism is equally partial. It is so lugubrious that it is hard to take it at face value, and if life is better than Thomson suggests, then the promise of a release from it is worth correspondingly less.

In his short poem 'One must recall as one mourns the dead', A. R. Ammons suggests that we ought not to lie to ourselves about death being a longed-for release any more than we should pretend that it is not final. Robert Pack makes the same point in his poem 'The Long and the Short of What's Good and What's Bad', declaring 'I want to even out the odds / that favour bad hope since hope causes // us to lie – as if good-byes really were good; / they're not' (ll. 59–62). This same note (Pack calls it the 'heroic ring of disenchantment' (1991: 23)) is sounded by many Darwinian poets facing up to death. We hear it in Rogers's refusal to forgive death at the end of 'Against the Ethereal', for example, and in Edna St Vincent Millay's dogged repetitions of 'I am not resigned' (ll. 1, 4, 16) and 'I know. But I do not approve' (ll. 11, 16) in 'Dirge Without Music'. Pack himself even goes so far as to denounce consciousness itself in 'Stellar Thanksgiving', switching mid-line from a hymn to evolution to a stark reminder of the inevitability of death, as he remarks that 'rousing consolation might aspire / to praise this curse of consciousness' (ll. 38–9) which confronts us with 'the emptying of all we cherish, / waste of all we sow' (ll. 43–4).

These poets offer us a solidarity akin to that which Hardy holds up in 'Hap' and 'A Plaint to Man' – 'the brotherhood of sharing what we lose', as Pack calls it in 'The First Word at Last' (l. 51). We can find in them the courage we too need to face mortality. But poetry can also take us beyond this face-off with death. In his long poem *Garbage*, Ammons remarks 'I want to get // around to where I can say I'm glad I was here, / even if I must go' (1993: xiv, ll. 2–4). In this chapter, I shall look at poems by three of the major poets of the Darwinian world view, George Meredith, Robinson Jeffers and Hardy, each of whom seeks to bring us to that point by reaching his own distinctive accommodation with death and loss without denying their finality. In the process, they give us a rich sense of the different roles poetry can play in equipping us to live and die in a Darwinian universe.

'IN THE WOODS': GEORGE MEREDITH

Meredith shared Hake's love of life, but combined it with a genuine openness to death. One of his most compelling expressions of this openness is 'In the Woods', a short sequence of nine lyrics published in the *Fortnightly Review* in 1870. Meredith did not reprint it, although he published revised versions of three of the lyrics as poems in their own right as 'Whimper of Sympathy', 'Woodland Peace' and 'Dirge in Woods'. 'In the Woods' is a difficult poem to pin down. It is a series of lyrics, but many of the lyrics in question are more didactic than lyrical in tone. It shifts too between an allegorical mode in which the woods are a symbolic landscape representing the journey of life, and a more personal one as Meredith meditates for himself on real features of a real wood.

The beginnings of this complex interplay of tones and modes are already apparent in the opening lyric:

> Hill-sides are dark,
> And hill-tops reach the star,
>   And down is the lark,
>   And I from my mark
>   Am far.
> Unlighted I foot the ways.
> I know that a dawn is before me,
> And behind me many days;
>   Not what is o'er me.

Like Robert Frost's famous poems 'The Road Not Taken' and 'Stopping by Woods on a Snowy Evening', this beautifully economical lyric takes the allegorical motif of a journey through dark woods (the *selva oscura* of Dante's *Inferno*) and recasts it in lyric form. In these poems, the journey and the woods remain archetypal images of life at large, but they acquire a new significance as well.

When Meredith and Frost invoke this old motif in their lyrics, they refresh it, suggesting that it is true not just within their philosophies but to their own experience of life. By abstracting the woods from any specific narrative they give them a new symbolic power too. In a modern lyric, woods suggest a range of resonances, drawing on Christian allegory but also on myths, legends and indeed on the actual experience of being in woods. So the woods that Meredith takes us into in his poem are at once an allegorical space through which we are all journeying; a symbol which encapsulates Meredith's own journey through life as he experiences it; and a real environment in which Meredith himself has wandered at night.

Meredith's opening lyric captures perfectly the weariness of a long, dark walk at night. The first five lines have two different rhymes, but they are so close to one another that we hear one insistent tread. The metre varies, as Meredith switches between iambs and the faster anapaests, with two not one unstressed syllables before each stressed one. The underlying rhythm is consistent, however, with two beats per line in the first four lines, again echoing the walker's alternating paces. The rhyme words are all stressed, so the long '-ar-' sound becomes an oppressive echo – all the more so as its first associations in this poem are with darkness. Aside from 'tops', the stressed syllables in the first five lines ('sides', 'down', 'I' and the rhyme words) all sound long vowels, compounding this sense of weariness. This leads in turn to a falling away to one stress, one step, in the fifth line.

In the closing lines of this lyric, however, Meredith gathers his resolve. The next three lines are longer, with three stresses not two. His pace has quickened. He is covering more ground. His feet fall more nimbly, less insistently, with the last words of the seventh and ninth lines ('me' in both) unstressed. That oppressive '-ar-' has gone, and been replaced by the more muted '-or-' sound of 'dawn', 'before' and 'o'er'. This sound is softer in itself, it is repeated less interminably, and its associations within the poem are more hopeful.

Between them, these two sounds draw out the allegorical associations of Meredith's journey through the woods which underlie 'In the Woods' as a whole. The '-ar-' sounds suggest darkness but also (although it is 'down' at first) the lark. Within the poem, the dark wood and living creatures are emblems of this life. The '-or-' sounds, on the other hand, look forward to a 'dawn' and up to that which is overhead. Allegorically, these unite to suggest a Christian revelation of heaven through death. And yet while the 'dawn' seems certain, Meredith juxtaposes this certainty with his frank ignorance of 'what is o'er me'.

The allegorical significance of the woods is developed in Meredith's second lyric:

I am in deep woods,
   Between the two twilights.

Whatsoever I am and may be,
Write it down to the light in me;
I am I, and it is my deed;
For I know that paths are dark
   Between the two twilights:

My foot on the nodding weed,
My hand on the wrinkled bark,
I have made my choice to proceed
By the light I have within;
And the issue rests with me,
Who might sleep in a chrysalis,
In the fold of a simple prayer,
   Between the two twilights.

Flying safe from even to morn:
Not stumbling abroad in air
That shudders to touch and to kiss,
And is unfraternal and thin:
Self-hunted in it, forlorn,
Unloved, unresting, bare,
   Between the two twilights:

Having nought but the light in me,
Which I take for my soul in arms,
Resolved to go unto the wells
For water, rejecting spells,
And mouthings of magic for charms,
And the cup that does not flow.

I am in deep woods
   Between the two twilights:

Over valley and hill
I hear the woodland wave,
Like the voice of Time, as slow,
The voice of Life, as grave,
The voice of Death, as still.

Here the known quantities of the first lyric – the past days and the future dawn – have faded to 'twilights'. The only clear light in this second lyric comes from Meredith himself. When he declares 'I am I, and it is my deed' he speaks for himself, but the implication is that we are all what we make of ourselves. It is up to us whether or not 'to proceed'.

For Meredith, the decision to continue walking the dark paths takes moral and intellectual courage, especially as he can no longer be sure that they will lead him out of the woods and into the daylight. The alternative – to 'sleep in a chrysalis' – sounds enticingly comfortable, anticipating Frost's famous lines from the end of 'Stopping by Woods on a Snowy Evening':

> The woods are lovely, dark, and deep,
> But I have promises to keep,
> And miles to go before I sleep,
> And miles to go before I sleep.
>
> (ll. 13–16)

But Meredith's woods are not 'lovely, dark, and deep'. In place of this invit-ing, if sinister, Romantic ideal, we have the reality of weeds and 'wrinkled bark'. And, while Frost's rhymes suggest that the woods are tempting him to sleep there and then, Meredith's image of sleeping in a chrysalis suggests shutting himself away from the woods, not losing himself in them.

Meredith identifies this shutting out of reality with the comfort of religious faith, 'the fold of a simple prayer'. He associates it with Christian ritual too, specifically the Eucharist, as he resolves 'to go unto the wells / For water', rather than looking to what he dismisses as 'mouthings of magic for charms, / And the cup that does not flow'. As Meredith sees it, faith in immortality is an evasion of our duty to face the realities and uncertainties of life, and to judge them by the light of our own intelligence and experience.

Over the next five sections of his poem Meredith builds on this contrast between a self-sufficient acceptance of nature as it really is and a depend-ence on the unrealistic otherworldliness of Christian faith. His third lyric substitutes a joyful 'song' for the 'grave' 'voice of Life', while a solemn, silent song reiterates the stillness of death:

> Take up thy song from woods and fields
> Whilst thou hast heart, and living yields
>   Delight: let that expire –
> Let thy delight in living die,
> Take thou thy song from star and sky,
>   And join the silent quire.

At first, the fourth lyric seems to follow this advice, picking up too on the image of the chrysalis from the second lyric, after its metamorphosis into a butterfly:

With the butterfly roaming abroad
    On the sunny March day,
The pine-cones opened and blew
Winged seeds, and aloft they flew
Butterfly-like in the ray,
    And hung to the breeze:
Spinning they fell to the sod.
    Ask you my rhyme
    Which shall be trees?
    They have had their time.

By this point in the sequence Meredith has set aside the allegorical image of the walk in dark woods at night. Instead he revisits the woods in daylight. Two details in particular stand out. One is the butterfly itself. Implicitly, the image of the chrysalis allows for a rebirth, a metamorphosis, while conventionally the butterfly is an image of the soul. By associating the chrysalis with faith in the second lyric, Meredith appears to hint that the butterfly itself might represent the soul liberated from the body after death. But here the same image is reclaimed for Meredith's 'delight' in this life. By explicit or implied analogies, the butterfly is united with the pine trees and the poet 'roaming abroad' in the woods. The other significant detail is Meredith's choice of the word 'sod' for the soil onto which the pine-seeds fall. Unlike 'soil' or 'ground', 'sod' has specific associations with the grave. By choosing that word, Meredith gestures to the wider human relevance of his closing moral.

In his classic study of Meredith, *A Troubled Eden*, Norman Kelvin points out the significance of the falling seeds in this lyric. As Kelvin observes, Meredith's remark that 'They have had their time' is a reply to Tennyson's charge against nature that 'of fifty seeds / She often brings but one to bear' (*In Memoriam*, LV, ll. 11–12). Where for Tennyson nature's profligacy is a disturbing sign of her disregard for individual life, for Meredith it is simply, in Kelvin's words, 'another of nature's nontragic processes' (1961: 138–9). Natural selection, which determines 'which shall be trees' and which shall return 'to the sod', does nothing to undo Meredith's calm delight in watching the seeds fall. Yet these sombre phrases force natural selection and its bearing on our own mortality upon us as we read, while Meredith's direct address to us as readers of his 'rhyme' challenges us to agree with his judgement.

Meredith challenges us again two lyrics further on. Like Frost's 'Design', the sixth lyric of 'In the Woods' is a sardonic commentary on natural selection encapsulated in an act of predation:

Hawk or shrike has done this deed
Of downy feathers, a cruel sight.
Sweet sentimentalist, intercede
With Providence: it is not right!

Complain, revolt; say heaven is wrong,
Say nature is vile, that can allow
The innocent to be torn, the strong
To tower and govern – witness how!

O it were pleasant with you
To fly from this struggle of foes,
The shambles, the charnel, the wrinkle:
To be housed in the drop of dew
That hangs on the cheek of the rose,
And lives the life of a twinkle.

When Meredith revised this lyric for republication in 1887 he called it 'Whimper of Sympathy'. The revised poem has fashionable sentimental poetry in its sights. In this original text, the 'sweet sentimentalist' is rather a spokesman for a naïve natural theology which expects to find benevolence in nature. Meredith's caricature of his contemporaries in the second verse is clumsy. But the third verse (the sestet, taking this lyric to be a sonnet of sorts) is more powerful. After the inflated rhetoric of the octet, Meredith changes his tone, suggesting that it would be genuinely enviable to be able to believe that nature was benevolent. At the same time, he shows a barely muted contempt for anyone who uses this belief to hide from themselves the reality that nature is a 'shambles' or slaughterhouse in which organisms 'struggle' to survive.

Meredith is divided between his hard-nosed commitment to facing reality and his humane understanding of those for whom reality is too much. The contrast he draws between his own Darwinian truth to nature and a sentimental Christianity appalled at its own disillusionment mirrors the choice he faces in the woods at night in his second lyric. The 'sweet sentimentalist' would prefer to 'sleep in a chrysalis', and Meredith jibes at him for it, but not out of bitterness. At the beginning of *The City of Dreadful Night*, Thomson claims to be motivated by 'a cold rage . . . To show the bitter old and wrinkled truth' (PROEM, ll. 8–9). Thomson is determined to disillusion us, even though he knows the pain of disillusionment himself all too well. Meredith, by contrast, wants to jolt us out of our sentimental self-deceptions because he believes that we are genuinely better off without them. The process may be painful, but in the end we will be stronger, better, even happier for it.

A life lived under illusions may be pleasanter than one exposed to the truth, but that very word 'pleasant' sounds feeble when set against the 'delight' Meredith urges us to take in nature in his third lyric. Meredith is no self-mortifying puritan. We have a duty to confront the truth, and to do so is a mark of moral courage. By the same token, to choose a 'pleasant' life over honesty is a failing and a weakness. But for those with the strength to choose it, honesty leads to a more robust joy.

Meredith affirms the joy of honest Darwinism again in his seventh lyric:

Sweet as Eden is the air,
    And Eden-sweet the ray.
No Paradise is lost for them
That foot by branching root and stem,
And lightly with the woodland share
    The change of night and day.

      Here all things say,
      'We know not,' even as I.
      'We brood, we strive to sky,
      We gaze upon decay,
      We wot of life through death.
      We are patient: what is dumb
      We question not, nor ask
      The hidden to unmask,
      The distant to draw near.'

    And this the woodland saith:
    'I know not hope nor fear:
    I take whate'er shall come;
I raise my head to all things fair,
    From foul I turn away.'

Sweet as Eden is the air,
And Eden-sweet the ray.

Meredith's re-evaluation of the Christian faith in immortality in the light of Darwinism culminates in these lines. Identifying the woods themselves with Paradise, he repudiates the doctrine of the Fall and the need for a redemptive Heaven after death. In the Romantic mode, the poet himself, the doubting but courageous walker through the woods at night, has become the model of the unfallen man untroubled by an unfallen nature. The oppressive darkness of that night has been absorbed within the cycle of night and day, and the menacing allegorical landscape with which the poem began has been transformed into an earthly Paradise.

Meredith's last two lyrics offer further complementary conclusions to the sequence as a whole. The eighth lyric is an exegesis, drawing out from the poem a contrast between 'the lover of life', who represents Meredith himself, and 'lust after life', which again he repudiates:

> The lover of life holds life in his hand,
>   Like a ring for the bride.
> The lover of life is free of dread:
> The lover of life holds life in his hand,
>   As the hills hold the day.
>
> But lust after life waves life like a brand,
>   For an ensign of pride.
> The lust after life is life half-dead:
> Yea, lust after life hugs life like a brand,
>   Dreading air and the ray.
>
>   For the sake of life,
>   For that life is dear,
>   The lust after life
>   Clings to it fast.
>   For the sake of life,
>   For that life is fair,
>   The lover of life
>   Flings it broadcast.
>
> The lover of life knows his labour divine,
>   And therein is at peace.
> The lust after life craves a touch and a sign
>   That the life shall increase.

The lust after life in the chills of its lust
   Claims a passport of death.
The lover of life sees the flame in our dust
   And a gift in our breath.

These lines have the gnomic appeal of a set of proverbs. Meredith's fine balance between repetition and variation gives them an engaging poise which sugars the pill of his didacticism. The patterning is complex but regular. The metre and syntax of the verses are mirrored in pairs, while the anapaestic rhythms and alternating four- and two-stress lines of the last two stanzas encourage us to anticipate the completion of each proverb.

Meredith's didactic message itself is bold and original. To condemn the desire for an afterlife as 'lust' is uncompromising, even shocking – so much so that it can take some time to realise that that is exactly what he is saying. To cling to life because it is dear does not seem a sin. But Meredith sees that this desire for life can lead to a craving for an afterlife and a fear of death which 'chill' life itself. In their desperation for a revelation of immortality, those who 'lust after life' forget the value of the 'gift in our breath'. They are not 'at peace'. Ultimately, Meredith implies, they are not even true to their own faith. It is the 'lover of life', untroubled by death, who sees life as a 'gift', not those whose piety requires the quid pro quo of a life after death.

Though its style is very different, and Meredith's verse more accomplished than Hake's, the eighth lyric of 'In the Woods' chimes with the eighty-fourth sonnet of *The New Day*. But, on Meredith's terms, Hake reveals his love of life to be lust after life in his last sonnet. For his part, Meredith does not flinch in the face of death in his last lyric:

A wind sways the pines,
   And below
Not a breath of wild air:
All still as the mosses that glow
On the flooring and over the lines
   Of the roots here and there.
The pine-tree drops its dead:
They are quiet as under the sea.
   Overhead, overhead,
   Rushes life in a race,
   As the clouds the clouds chase:
     And we go,
And we drop like the fruits of the tree,

Even we,
Even so.

In this last section of his poem, Meredith returns to the lyric mode with which he began. He returns too to the falling pine-seeds of section IV, except that here it is no longer the seeds but the empty cones that are falling, in autumn, not spring. Meredith achieves this poem's wistful, elegiac tone substantially through his metre. Once again, he uses mainly anapaests. With twice as many unstressed syllables as stressed ones, anapaests tend to speed up the pace of a poem. Here Meredith counteracts that tendency by end-stopping most of the lines and weaving between lines of one, two or three stresses, so the metre never has the chance to gather speed. Instead, the anapaests here create a calm, unemphatic verse. The varying line-lengths generate both a sense of the continuity of life and a recurrent dying fall as longer lines give way to shorter ones. At the very end of the poem, this dying fall comes to represent our own deaths. As the rhythms repeat they reaffirm Meredith's point that our deaths are merely another part of the natural process.

When Meredith republished the ninth section of 'In the Woods' in *A Reading of Earth* he retitled it 'Dirge in Woods'. It was barely revised at all, but the change in the title changes how we read the lines. Meredith's decision to call this poem a dirge after the fact directs us to hear in it a dominant note of regret. In its original context, however, this lyric sounds rather a note of quiet acceptance. There is none of Millay's refusal to be resigned, none of her withholding of approval. Ultimately the woods are a place of death for Meredith. There is, it seems, no 'dawn' beyond them after all. But this is only because they are also the place of life. Where Hake cannot bring himself to accept death at the last, and Thomson's promise of death as release degrades life itself, Meredith shows us that it is indeed possible to love life and accept death, if we accept that death is merely life played out and that we, like the pine-seeds, have our time.

DEATH AND DYING: ROBINSON JEFFERS

The Californian poet Robinson Jeffers shares Meredith's equanimity in the face of death. Here is Jeffers considering his own death in 'Vulture', written in his late sixties:

I had walked since dawn and lay down to rest on a bare hillside
Above the ocean. I saw through half-shut eyelids a vulture wheeling
    high up in heaven,

And presently it passed again, but lower and nearer, its orbit narrowing,
    I understood then
That I was under inspection. I lay death-still and heard the flight-
    feathers
Whistle above me and make their circle and come nearer. I could see
    the naked red head between the great wings
Beak downward staring. I said, 'My dear bird we are wasting time here.
These old bones will still work; they are not for you.' But how beautiful
    he'd looked, gliding down
On those great sails; how beautiful he looked, veering away in the sea-
    light over the precipice. I tell you solemnly
That I was sorry to have disappointed him. To be eaten by that beak
    and become part of him, to share those wings and those eyes –
What a sublime end of one's body, what an enskyment; what a life after
    death.

In 'Vulture' Jeffers turns Meredith's abstract idea of death as part of the cycle of life into a vivid material reality. For all his professed solemnity, Jeffers contemplates the prospect of being eaten by a turkey vulture with remarkable good humour. The genius of his poem lies in uniting these two conflicting tones: solemn or, better, awed, and wry or good-humoured.

The first sign that this poem is going to depart from Jeffers's more usual tendency to take himself seriously comes when he remarks that he is 'under inspection'. But the incongruousness of this phrase does not change the tone of the poem on its own. Jeffers's narrative style remains predominantly sombre, even frightening, with the emphasis placed on the vulture's 'naked red head' by internal rhymes and on its 'Beak downward staring' by its position at the beginning of a line and the caesura straight after. That is, until Jeffers tells us what he said to the vulture. "'My dear bird. . .'" is charmingly affectionate and ridiculously polite. Jeffers claims the vulture as a friend. From now on it is not menacing but beautiful.

We are able to enter into Jeffers's rapture at the prospect of becoming part of this magnificent bird because he so clearly enjoys contemplating it himself, above all in his masterful last line. Here Jeffers uses parallel syntax and internal rhyme to tie together the 'sublime', 'enskyment' and 'life after death'. The very word 'enskyment' places his ecstasy beyond the reach of everyday language. Like Hardy in 'Hap', Jeffers is driven to coin a new word to capture what he wants to convey, while the act of coining such a richly evocative word testifies to the originality of his vision.

Even the punctuation in this line is carefully judged, giving us a faint pause and a realignment of the syntax before we come to 'what a life after death'. Jeffers wants us to register the significance of this claim. He means to substitute his vision of a life after death for the more familiar Christian one. But he also wants us to think about what it means to describe having-been-eaten as 'life after death' at all. Jeffers's vision of an afterlife looks transcendental to the living poet as he imagines sharing the vulture's form, because in his imagination he shares its consciousness as well. But Jeffers knows that this is merely his aesthetics as a living poet admiring the beauty of nature. In reality, the life after death that he promises us is the bird's life, not our own. Jeffers does not seek personal immortality any more than Meredith does. Instead, through his magnificent vulture, he invites us to enjoy imaginatively today the material fact that we will be eaten tomorrow.

By focussing on something that would have happened after death and not before, Jeffers skirts round the material reality of death itself in 'Vulture'. But he is not shy of imagining death elsewhere. In *Cawdor*, one of the long narrative poems that made him famous in the 1920s, Jeffers uses the death of one of his characters (old Martial, the father of the poem's anti-heroine Fera) to explore how a purely material consciousness might experience death. This episode stands alone as a unique exercise in imagining how death may feel according to the logic of Darwinian materialist biology.

Old Martial has been dying since the beginning of the poem forty pages before. When he finally dies, Fera briefly confronts the 'pitiful' prospect that 'the mind / Goes working on', before reassuring herself that while she is 'between the teeth still' he is 'not troubled', for all that he cannot '*feel* the salvation'. At this point the narrator interjects:

> She was mistaken. Sleep and delirium are full of dreams;
> The locked-up coma had trailed its clue of dream across the crippled
>   passages; now death continued
> Unbroken the delusions of the shadow before. If these had been
>   relative to any movement outside
> They'd have grown slower as the life ebbed and stagnated as it ceased,
>   but the only measure of the dream's
> Time was the dreamer, who geared in the same change could feel none;
>   in his private dream, out of the pulses
> Of breath and blood, as every dreamer is out of the hour-notched arch
>   of the sky. The brain growing cold
> The dream hung in suspense and no one knew that it did. Gently with
>   delicate mindless fingers
> Decomposition began to pick and caress the unstable chemistry

Of the cells of the brain; Oh very gently, as the first weak breath of
    wind in a wood: the storm is still far,
The leaves are stirred faintly to a gentle whispering: the nerve-cells, by
    what would soon destroy them, were stirred
To a gentle whispering. Or one might say the brain began to glow, with
    its own light, in the starless
Darkness under the dead bone sky; like bits of rotting wood on the floor
    of the night forest
Warm rains have soaked, you see them beside the path shine like vague
    eyes. So gently the dead man's brain
Glowing by itself made and enjoyed its dream . . .

Out of time, undistracted by the nudging pulse-beat, perfectly real to
    itself being insulated
From all touch of reality the dream triumphed, building from past
    experience present paradise
More intense as the decay quickened, but ever more primitive as it
    proceeded, until the ecstasy
Soared through a flighty carnival of wines and women to the simple
    delight of eating flesh, and tended
Even higher, to an unconditional delight. But then the
    interconnections between the groups of the brain
Failing, the dreamer and the dream split into multitude. Soon the
    altered cells became unfit to express
Any human or at all describable form of consciousness.

(2001: 221–4)

In this extraordinary passage Jeffers models the experience of death on the
experience of dreaming. His logic is this: in dreams, the automatic unconscious processes of the brain generate a form of consciousness. This is more
a simulacrum of consciousness than consciousness proper, however, as we
are not conscious of anything external. Indeed, we are cut off from external
stimuli altogether. Instead, the worlds that we inhabit when dreaming exist
only within our own minds, and our conscious selves exist only to themselves. And yet it remains we who are conscious of them nonetheless, to
some degree and in whatever altered form.

To a materialist like Jeffers, this is not because the dreams are being
played out before some non-material spirit or soul sat in the seat of consciousness. It is because our consciousness at such times is the dream
itself. In effect, we dream our dream-selves into existence. Yet because the
brains that produce our dream-selves are the same brains that produce our

conscious selves in their interaction with the outside world, and because those brains continue to interpret to themselves the worlds that their own processes create, our dream-selves share a sense of identity with our conscious selves. We have relatively little control over them, and the worlds they inhabit may be grotesque and incoherent, but we experience them as ourselves nonetheless.

If we can experience these products of unconscious physiological processes within the brain consciously as though they are ourselves, then other such processes taking place in the brain could presumably generate similar experiences. Jeffers hypothesises that the chemical processes of decomposition after death might effectively mimic dreams, as individual neurons in the brain are triggered by their own collapse. Decay for Jeffers is simply another material process taking place within a material organ, but because that material organ is the brain, and the brain generates consciousness automatically, consciousness does not end with death but persists as the brain decays. There is a brief hiatus before decay sets in as the brain grows 'cold' and stops working for itself. But the consciousness that is resumed once it begins to break down is still the product of the same brain, so it is essentially the same as the dead man's dream-self before death. Over time, Jeffers imagines, as the brain breaks down, the dream-self reverts to more and more primitive states, generating more primitive urges which the dream, as wish fulfilment, satisfies. In the end, the brain is broken down to such an extent that it no longer sustains a unified consciousness at all, and the parallel processes of decay and evolutionary reversion are complete. (In a reprise of this motif later in the poem, Jeffers imagines the sudden transformation of a unified consciousness into dispersed 'fragments of consciousness' when the hero Hood Cawdor's skull is 'burst open' and the 'gray and white jellies' of his brain are spilt 'like liquor from a broken flask' after he falls headlong from a cliff – see 2001: 252–3.)

Jeffers's achievement in this passage is to set before us an imaginatively compelling and at the same time logically self-consistent picture of what it might be like for a purely material being to die. This combination of imagination and rationality defines the poetics of the passage. On the one hand, there are epic similes, as the decomposing brain is likened first to a forest gently stirred by the onset of a storm, then to a piece of rotting wood on the forest floor, as it glows under 'the dead bone sky' that is the skull. On the other, there is the scientific vocabulary of the 'unstable chemistry' of 'decomposition' itself. Jeffers's long but measured free-verse lines too are equally well-suited to the stately Homeric tone of his similes and to prosaic discussions of neurology, while his attention to dreams fits with the preoccupations of both poetry and psychology.

This marriage of poetry and science encourages us to consider Jeffers's hypothesis about death as a scientific proposition, for all that *Cawdor* is a poem, not a medical treatise. The trope of evolutionary regression seems more fanciful now than it would have done eighty years ago. This aside, Jeffers's account of what it is to die appears plausible enough. Jeffers invites us to probe imaginatively the nature of death as science understands it. When he does this himself, he finds it to be a more gradual process and a less appalling prospect than his materialism might lead him to expect. It is even oddly timeless, as dreams are, for all that time ticks by at the usual pace outside us as we sleep. In this timelessness above all, Jeffers offers us a fresh consolation, even as we recognise that, like the dream of immortality itself, it may be merely another wish fulfilment.

LOVE AND LOSS: THOMAS HARDY

Meredith and Jeffers face their own extinction with equanimity. But what about the extinction of others? Even if our own deaths lose their sting, how are we to cope with the loss of those we love? One of the most poignant expressions of loss within a Darwinian universe is a sequence of four sonnets by the minor Victorian poet William Canton. 'The Latter Law' was first published in 1879. Over the course of the first three sonnets, Canton tells us how, 'schooled to resignation' (i, l. 1), he had accepted that there was no God and no afterlife. Instead he adopted a new 'creed' (l. 5) founded on the Darwinian revelation of natural law and our kinship with nature. Like most of his poetry, Canton's account of his Darwinian 'creed' in these sonnets is derivative and unremarkable, as well as being in Bowler's terms non-Darwinian. When his hope that nature can substitute for faith is shattered in the fourth sonnet, however, Canton achieves a powerful and original truthfulness:

> But when my child, my one girl-babe lay dead –
>   The blossom of me, my dream and my desire –
>   And unshed tears burned in my eyes like fire,
> And when my wife subdued her sobs, and said –
> *Oh! husband, do not grieve, be comforted,*
>   *She is with Christ!* – I laughed in my despair.
>   With Christ! O God! and where is Christ, and where
> My poor dead babe? And where the countless dead?
>
> The great glad Earth – my kin! – is glad as though
>   No child had ever died; the heaven of May

Leans like a laughing face above my grief.
Is *she* clean lost for ever? How shall I know?
O Christ! art Thou still Christ? And shall I pray
For fulness of belief or unbelief?

This sonnet is so moving because in it Canton speaks what he feels, not what he ought to say. There is nothing in his Darwinian creed that can console him for his appalling loss. The promise that his daughter is 'with Christ' now seems a taunt as Christ too is nowhere, while kinship with nature counts for nothing when nature does not care. Even the beauty of spring becomes a horrible mockery. Canton is left paralysed by his loss, unable to accept it but equally unable to disbelieve it. He has nothing to lean on but the sonnet form itself, with its tradition of knotted perplexity over love and grief going back to Dante and Petrarch. Canton makes this tradition his own in the image of 'unshed tears' burning his eyes, an image which reworks a classic Petrarchan paradox to capture perfectly the pain of struggling to cry.

'The Latter Law' epitomises the problem of bereavement in a Darwinian materialist world, but it offers no solution to that problem. It captures the moment of loss, but Canton as we see him is powerless to pass beyond that moment. The only balm he can find for grief is its expression through poetry. Other Darwinian poets manage to pass beyond this stage, however. Meredith, Jeffers and Hardy were all widowed. Each explored his grief and its implications in poetry: Meredith in 'A Faith on Trial', Jeffers in *Hungerfield*, Hardy in the elegiac lyrics collected under the non-descript title 'Poems of 1912–13'. Meredith's and Jeffers's poems are substantial, but they cannot match the power or subtlety of Hardy's lyrics. Among the finest poems of personal grief in English, they are one of the crowning achievements of Darwinian poetry.

Hardy's Darwinism shapes his outlook on mortality in all twenty-one of the 'Poems of 1912–13', and in many other poems besides. But three in particular stand out as engaging directly with the problem of loss in a Darwinian universe. The first of these, 'Your Last Drive', was written in December 1912, in the first weeks after Emma Hardy's death:

Here by the moorway you returned,
And saw the borough lights ahead
That lit your face – all undiscerned
To be in a week the face of the dead,
And you told of the charm of that haloed view
That never again would beam on you.

And on your left you passed the spot
Where eight days later you were to lie,
And be spoken of as one who was not;
Beholding it with a heedless eye
As alien from you, though under its tree
You soon would halt everlastingly.

I drove not with you . . . Yet had I sat
At your side that eve I should not have seen
That the countenance I was glancing at
Had a last-time look in the flickering sheen,
Nor have read the writing upon your face,
'I go hence soon to my resting-place;

'You may miss me then. But I shall not know
How many times you visit me there,
Or what your thoughts are, or if you go
There never at all. And I shall not care.
Should you censure me I shall take no heed,
And even your praises no more shall need.'

True: never you'll know. And you will not mind.
But shall I then slight you because of such?
Dear ghost, in the past did you ever find
The thought 'What profit,' move me much?
Yet abides the fact, indeed, the same, –
You are past love, praise, indifference, blame.

In this poem Hardy concentrates his mind on the irrevocability of death
and loss, the abrupt transition as someone we love comes to 'be spoken of
as one who was not'. Fittingly, 'Your Last Drive' is riddled with negatives.
As in 'Hap', Hardy coins a fresh negative, 'undiscerned', to call attention
to the peculiarity of his thought: that it might be possible to discern from
the face of an apparently healthy woman that in a week she would be
dead. Two stanzas later, Hardy discounts this – even he would have seen
no trace of her death on her face – but by raising it first he draws out both
the unpredictability of death and its finality. Hardy uses the future historic
tense 'would' and 'were to' to affirm that that which was not known was no
less definitely to come to pass, and that that which might have been has
become that which 'never again' will be.

Emma herself has passed in this poem from someone who does things for herself in the active voice to one who exists purely passively if at all. She no longer speaks, she is 'spoken of'. She no longer is, she is 'not', and even that is said in the past tense. When she appears to speak in her own voice, it is only a voice from the past that was not heard. Indeed, it is not even that, but rather a text written on her face to be read by another, written almost entirely in the negative voice, and itself unread.

Aside from the conventional reference to 'my resting-place', there is nothing in this poem to suggest that Emma exists at all as herself any longer. Except, that is, her palpable presence within the poem itself. Hardy writes about her absence, but in so doing he sets her vividly before us, even to the extent of laying bare their marriage. For all that he attributes the words he gives Emma to her unread face, they are still spoken in her voice. In her petulance and his indifference to it, we hear the tones of their life together rehearsed after her death. In the last stanza Hardy sounds a new note too, of tenderness rediscovered through loss, even drawing attention to his own perversity in bestowing this tenderness and care on Emma only once she herself is past caring.

This stanza distils other paradoxes of the poem too. He refuses to 'slight' her, and yet she defiantly anticipates his 'censure' and the last word of the poem is 'blame'. He addresses her as 'Dear ghost', a touching and affection-ate phrase which implies her disembodied presence, but the literal context affirms not presence but absence. Emma is often seen as a ghost in these poems, but she is a ghost conjured by Hardy's past memories and present regret, never a spirit in her own right. He insists that he is not motivated by 'profit', for himself nor for her. Yet the poem is surely profoundly valuable, to him but also to us, as it fixes our eyes firmly on the finality of death while defiantly maintaining the right to live within our own minds as if death were not final after all.

In poetry, Hardy implies, we can and may suspend our disbelief in an afterlife, providing we do so knowingly. Poetry, for Hardy, is a sustaining fiction that enables us to face 'the fact' that the dead are indeed 'past love, praise, indifference, blame'. The sustaining power of poetry is embodied too in 'Rain on a Grave', dated 31 January 1913:

Clouds spout upon her
  Their waters amain
  In ruthless disdain, –
Her who but lately
  Had shivered with pain
As at touch of dishonour
If there had lit on her

So coldly, so straightly
    Such arrows of rain.

One who to shelter
    Her delicate head
Would quicken and quicken
    Each tentative tread
If drops chanced to pelt her
    That summertime spills
    In dust-paven rills
When thunder-clouds thicken
    And birds close their bills.

Would that I lay there
    And she were housed here!
Or better, together
Were folded away there
Exposed to one weather
We both, – who would stray there
When sunny the day there,
    Or evening was clear
    At the prime of the year.

Soon will be growing
    Green blades from her mound,
And daisies be showing
    Like stars on the ground,
Till she form part of them –
Ay – the sweet heart of them,
Loved beyond measure
With a child's pleasure
    All her life's round.

Hardy begins this poem with an irony in keeping with 'Your Last Drive'. Emma, who used to hurry away from the rain when she was alive, now suffers it unmoved in her grave. As before, Hardy draws out the distance between Emma alive and Emma dead. Again too we have an affectionate but not idealised portrait of her. Her touchiness and Hardy's disregard for it are both neatly caught in the faintly absurd sight of her reacting to rain as if it were a personal affront – a description in which Hardy is not ashamed to show her mild 'dishonour' himself. But where in 'Your Last Drive' his affection only becomes clear in his closing address to her 'dear ghost', in 'Rain on a Grave' it animates the whole poem. We do not need to be told that Emma is 'Loved beyond measure / With a child's pleasure', as the poem itself bears witness to this throughout.

For a poem about death and loss, 'Rain on a Grave' is extraordinarily playful. In it, Hardy takes 'a child's pleasure' in the joy of verse which revels in going 'beyond measure' for its own sake. Each of the four verses begins in the same way. The first two lines each have five syllables, and in each pair, the first and fourth syllables of the first line are stressed, as are the second and last syllables of the second line. This sets up an expectation of regularity which Hardy takes delight in flouting. As the first line of each verse ends with an unstressed syllable, we listen for and are rewarded with virtuoso polysyllabic rhymes, often comically stretched over two words. Hardy delights in light but exuberant alliteration too, and in the short, rapid, rarely end-stopped, anapaestic lines themselves.

Hardy's elegies are predominantly explorations of those memories that give the most vivid sense of the continued presence in our lives of those whom death has taken away. 'Rain on the Grave' is dominated by such memories. The irony of Emma being rained upon recalls to Hardy's mind walks she took when she was alive. In the first two verses he remembers her walking as if alone, with himself merely watching and not accompanying her. In the third verse his wish to be reunited with her leads him to remember their walking more truly together in the 'prime of the year', suggesting too the prime of their marriage. Hardy's death-wish is encapsulated in another paradoxical image, as he imagines himself and Emma at once 'folded away' and 'exposed'. Like those in 'Your Last Drive', this paradox embodies the breaking down through poetry of the unbreachable walls between life and death.

In the final verse of this poem Hardy recalls Meredith and anticipates Jeffers by suggesting that those walls are not unbreachable after all, as in death we become part of other non-human lives. This is a motif that recurs in others of his poems. The 'homely Northern breast and brain' of a drummer killed in the Boer War 'Grow to some Southern tree' in 'Drummer Hodge' (ll. 15–16), while in 'Transformations' the dead of a Wessex village live on in the yew tree, grass and roses of a churchyard. But, as in 'Vulture', this is an imaginative indulgence more than a reality of which we could ever be conscious. For all that life is a cycle, the dead individual still remains dead. It is only in Hardy's affectionate imagination that Emma's individuality persists in the daisies.

But then Hardy's delight in nature uncompromised by death is calculat-edly naïve. Hardy's model here is Wordsworth's equally deliberate naïvety in many of his poems. The context of a meditation on a grave suggests that

Hardy had in mind 'We are Seven' in particular. In this poem, Wordsworth draws a contrast between the urbane adult narrator and an eight-year old country girl. When the narrator asks the girl how many brothers and sisters she has, she tells him that there are seven of them altogether: two living in Conway, two at sea, two buried in the church-yard and herself. The narrator insists repeatedly that if two are dead that leaves only five, while the girl equally tenaciously insists 'we are seven' nonetheless. In setting up this contrast between his narrator's rationality and the girl's imagination – the one insisting that her brother and sister are dead, the other persisting as if they were alive – Wordsworth invites us to judge each of them, philosophically and morally. The implication is that rationality on its own is incomplete and even inhumane. When Hardy describes his own joy in loving the dead Emma as 'a child's pleasure' he has in mind children as Wordsworth paints them, unconcerned with the bald rationality of facts, and healthily free in their imaginations. Indulging his own imagination and enjoying his craft, Hardy assumes the role of the Wordsworthian child for himself, taking comfort and pleasure in the thought of Emma living on in the flowers on her grave.

In 'Rain on a Grave', the grave which was alienated from Emma while she was alive in 'Your Last Drive' becomes the site of her continuing life after her death. In 'At Castle Boterel', Hardy returns rather to the image of Emma as a 'dear ghost':

As I drive to the junction of lane and highway,
    And the drizzle bedrenches the waggonette,
I look behind at the fading byway,
    And see on its slope, now glistening wet,
        Distinctly yet

Myself and a girlish form benighted
    In dry March weather. We climb the road
Beside a chaise. We had just alighted
    To ease the sturdy pony's load
        When he sighed and slowed.

What we did as we climbed, and what we talked of
    Matters not much, nor to what it led, –
Something that life will not be balked of
    Without rude reason till hope is dead,
        And feeling fled.

It filled but a minute. But was there ever
    A time of such quality, since or before,

In that hill's story? To one mind never,
　　Though it has been climbed, foot-swift, foot-sore,
　　　By thousands more.

Primaeval rocks form the road's steep border,
　　And much have they faced there, first and last,
Of the transitory in Earth's long order;
　　But what they record in colour and cast
　　　Is – that we two passed.

And to me, though Time's unflinching rigour,
　　In mindless rote, has ruled from sight
The substance now, one phantom figure
　　Remains on the slope, as when that night
　　　Saw us alight.

I look and see it there, shrinking, shrinking,
　　I look back at it amid the rain
For the very last time; for my sand is sinking,
　　And I shall traverse old love's domain
　　　Never again.

Hardy wrote this poem in March 1913, during a tour of the district in Cornwall where he and Emma first met. Castle Boterel is the name for the coastal town of Boscastle in the parallel universe of Hardy's Wessex – 'called a town, though merely a large village', as Parson Swancourt remarks in Hardy's early novel A Pair of Blue Eyes ([1873] 2005: 15). A Pair of Blue Eyes is in part a fictionalisation of Hardy's romance with Emma. It is also one of the novels in which he alludes most directly to Darwinism, as the literary reviewer Henry Knight finds himself hanging half-way down a cliff, face-to-face with a fossilised trilobite (ibid.: 199–202). This same conjunction of ideas – Emma, youthful romance, Cornwall, geology and Darwinism – recur forty years on in 'At Castle Boterel'.

　　This poem again testifies to the versatility of anapaestic metre. Changing freely between iambic and anapaestic feet, sometimes end-stopping his lines, sometimes breaking them with a caesura in the middle of a line, and keeping up a regular rhyme-scheme throughout, Hardy is able to achieve an effect that is both conversational and soberly measured. As in 'Rain on a Grave', he alternates polysyllabic rhymes with simpler monosyllabic rhymes on stressed final syllables. But because of the longer four-beat lines and the regular stanza-form the effect is utterly different. There is nothing playful about 'At Castle Boterel'. Hardy only once spreads the rhyme over more than one word, and then in phrases that are so similar that there is nothing incongruous or comic about it.

That double-stressed, four-word rhyme ('what we talked of' / 'not be balked of') calls attention to the most crucial moment in the poem, however. Hardy is evasive. He speaks only of '*something* that life will not be balked of'. But whatever we read this 'something' as being – love, romance, companionship, desire – it is allied to 'hope' and 'feeling' and opposed to 'reason'. Reason, like loss, is a 'rude' awakening, and Hardy again resists it through poetry, frankly avowing a subjective vision in which the only true significance the hill at Boscastle has is its significance to him. The rocks no longer bear witness to the Darwinian reality of 'transitory' life but to the persistence of his memory of Emma. Time may have eroded all trace of her 'substance', but the scene nonetheless keeps her 'dear ghost' alive. Appropriately, even Boscastle itself has become Hardy's own version of it: Castle Boterel.

And yet, as in 'Your Last Drive' and 'Rain on a Grave', Hardy's dogged resistance to 'reason' is premised on an honest admission of where reason leads. Hardy openly admits that his marriage to Emma hardly 'matters' from the perspective of 'Earth's long order'. Boscastle might keep Emma's 'phantom' alive in his memory, but he is an old man himself, and he does not expect to return there again. In all three poems, Hardy's poetic imagination allows him to evade for a time 'Time's unflinching rigour' – the finality of death in the Darwinian universe revealed by 'reason'. But he never denies it. Emma is dwindling, even in his memory, and his own 'sand is sinking'.

The role poetry plays in facing death after Darwin differs from poet to poet. For Meredith and Jeffers it is a vehicle for speaking the truth, a lens through which we can examine death honestly and see it clearly. For Hardy, it is almost exactly the opposite, an imaginative space into which we can escape, knowingly, from death's grim finality. What it offers, in Hardy's own words, is 'an Idealism of Fancy' to replace 'the old transcendental ideals', 'an idealism in which fancy is no longer tricked out and made to masquerade as belief, but is frankly and honestly accepted as an imaginative solace in the lack of any substantial solace to be found in life' (1962: 310). This ultimately pessimistic vision differs radically from the qualified optimism of Meredith and Jeffers. Yet all three poets demonstrate the power of poetry to ameliorate the bitterness of death in a strictly material universe without denying that, as the last words of 'At Castle Boterel' remind us, once dead, we are 'Never again'.

5

Humanity's Place in Nature

In 1863, Darwin's friend and ally T. H. Huxley published a short book entitled *Man's Place in Nature*. In the aftermath of the *Origin of Species* Huxley had challenged Richard Owen, the doyen of British palaeontologists, over the biological classification of humanity. Following the French school of comparative anatomy founded by Georges Cuvier, Owen and other leading biologists classified human beings as a distinct mammalian order. Humans comprised the two-handed Bimanes, while the other primates were all members of the four-handed Quadrumana. This taxonomy cemented the judgement that, in the words of T. R. Jones, then Professor of Natural History and Comparative Anatomy at King's College, London, 'placed above the brute creation, Man forms the culminating point of the great scheme of Nature here below, while his intellectual superiority, and, much more, his immortal destiny, ally him closely with higher and unseen existences' (1865: 445).

Huxley countered that, because we are closer to the apes in our physiology than they are to other primates, we ought to be classified merely as a distinct family within the same order, not as an order apart (1893–4: VII, 145). Huxley's aim was to restore an older taxonomy, devised by Linnaeus in the eighteenth century, but with a Darwinian twist. We were not only 'in substance and in structure, one with the brutes', but almost certainly born of them too (ibid.: 155). Darwin himself was inclined to push these conclusions further. As Huxley vacillated between classifying humanity as a family or a sub-order, Darwin mooted that we should perhaps be thought of as only a sub-family ([1871] 2004: 179). Biologists still dispute how far Huxley's conclusions should be taken: whether humans and the extinct hominids deserve a family of their own, or whether it is more appropriate to think of ourselves as just another lineage of chimpanzees. Either way, since Huxley we have remained firmly ensconced within the order Primates.

This debate over human classification is not mere scholasticism, however. It is symbolic of how we see ourselves in relation to the rest of the natural world. As Huxley wrote in an uncharacteristically baroque sentence, 'It is as if nature herself had foreseen the arrogance of man, and with Roman severity had provided that his intellect, by its very triumphs, should call into prominence the slaves, admonishing the conqueror that he is but dust' (1893–4: VII, 146). The reclassification of human beings first as primates, then as apes and, lastly, in the words of the evolutionary anthropologist Robert Foley, as 'just another type of African ape' (1995: 65) is a vivid illustration of the implications of Darwinian theory for our place in the natural world at large.

Human beings seem to be uniquely preoccupied with the question of their place in nature. In his poem 'Wodwo', Ted Hughes imagines a proto-human exploring its environment. Hughes borrows the figure of the 'wodwo' or wild man of the woods from the Middle English poem *Sir Gawain and the Green Knight*. J. R. R. Tolkien revived this same figure at much the same time in *The Lord of the Rings*, but where Tolkien's Woses or Wild Men are closely modelled on their medieval antecedents, Hughes's wodwo is a different beast. His poem was first published in 1961, a year after Sir Alistair Hardy, then Professor of Zoology at Oxford University, announced his hypothesis that human beings had gone through an aquatic phase in their evolution. In the poem, Hughes imagines just such an aquatic ape. At the same time, he gives it the symbolic resonance of the medieval wild man.

Hughes's wodwo is another kind of human, one we can imagine meeting, if not today then at least within the half-remembered past of folklore. Unlike the aquatic ape or the medieval wild man, however, it is intensely self-conscious. The poem begins with the question 'What am I?'. Thereafter every aspect of its behaviour and environment prompts a new question, and each question is ultimately about itself. Hughes captures this never-ending process by piling questions on top of one another. Before the wodwo has finished one it is on to the next, as the poem progressively abandons punctuation and keeps up a rolling enjambment with not one of its twenty-eight lines end-stopped.

The wodwo is aware of its physical limitations. These are conceived in terms not of the space it fills, but rather of the point of exhaustion:

> if I go
> to the end on this way past these trees and past these trees
> till I get tired that's touching one wall of me
>
> (ll. 21–3)

This brilliantly original image is deftly matched by the challenge of reading Hughes's poem aloud without getting out of breath. Aside from affirming its limitations, however, the wodwo gives no definite answers to any of the questions it asks. But the questions themselves and the suppositions on which they are based are nonetheless revealing. Inevitably framed within language, they presuppose that that language is real and absolute, rather than relative:

> But what shall I be called am I the first
> have I an owner what shape am I what
> shape am I am I huge . . .
>> (ll. 19–21)

The wodwo's questioning presumes that there are final answers, that it is something specific and that naming it will tell it what, that it is a particular shape and size, that things can be definitively 'huge' or 'first' or, as it tentatively concludes, 'the exact centre' (l. 25).

Hughes's wodwo sees itself as unique, distinct from the rest of the living world, 'not rooted but dropped / out of nothing' (ll. 11–12). From this starting point, the natural world itself seems utterly puzzling. Roots and water in particular seem to imply continuities that the wodwo simply cannot comprehend. Indeed, the wodwo does not even seem continuous with itself. It is so utterly cerebral that it is alienated from its own body and actions. Nothing it does seems motivated, only scrutinised. Even the interest that it takes in opening up and eating a frog is interrogated, as if by someone else. As it remarks after picking bark off a rotten tree stump, 'me and doing that have coincided very queerly' (l. 18).

The wodwo's predicament is at once comic, touching and unsettling. Like Morgan in 'The Archaeopteryx's Song', Hughes shows us ourselves in a distorting mirror. What we see is a creature at odds with its environment and unable to understand it, largely because of preconceived assumptions about its own difference. These lead the wodwo further and further away from the idea it entertains briefly at the beginning of the poem that different creatures may have different points of view. More than this, Hughes suggests that the very process of interrogating our relationship to the rest of nature alienates us from it. By asking questions about ourselves, questions that we imagine can have definite answers, we reinforce our sense of our own uniqueness, for all that this process is self-sustaining and has no bearing on whether we are truly special and distinct or not.

When the wodwo turns its attention to the natural world it begins to doubt its supposition that it is 'the exact centre'. As I argued in the last two chapters, Darwinian natural history calls God into question and undermines our belief in immortality. It strikes a third blow at our existential self-confidence too, dislodging us from our privileged place in the universe.

In Jeffers's controversial poem 'The Inhumanist', published in 1948, the eponymous hero builds a cairn as a landmark. Imagining it as 'his little pyramid', he asks himself:

'To whom this monument: Jesus or Caesar or Mother Eve?
No,' he said, 'to Copernicus: Nicky Kupernick: who first pushed man
Out of his insane self-importance and the world's navel, and taught him his
place.
    And the next one to Darwin.'

(2001: 610)

Copernicus 'taught [man] his place' by replacing a geocentric cosmology, in which the universe revolved around our Earth, with a heliocentric one, in which the Earth and the other planets revolve around the Sun. Since then, astronomy has further decentred us from any spatial position of significance within the universe, leaving our solar system as one of billions near the edge of one galaxy among billions. Darwinism compounds this effect by reminding us that we are one twig on the tree of life among millions, that we have existed at all only for a minute fraction of the four billion years during which life has lived on this planet, and that even this existence was not a foregone conclusion.

Since the late nineteenth century, poets have taken our position in the Darwinian universe as their starting point in exploring our relationship to the cosmos, the Earth and each other. In this chapter, I will begin with the cosmic perspective, considering how a number of Victorian poets responded to the decentring of humanity, before homing in on Jeffers, in particular on his poem 'Night', which brings astronomy and Darwinism together in its meditation on our insignificance in the universe at large. I will then move on to look at poems by three contemporary American poets, A. R. Ammons, Philip Appleman and Robert Pack, who extrapolate from a Darwinian world view towards an environmental ethic on the one hand and the humane solidarity epitomised by Hardy in 'The Plaint to Man' on the other.

'AN IDIOT ON A CRUMBLING THRONE': THE COSMIC PERSPECTIVE

The impact of Darwin's discoveries on our self-image as a species was felt acutely by his fellow Victorians. Tennyson was appalled by the 'Vastness' of the universe and 'the deeps of a meaningless Past', which seemed to reduce our species and its history to nothing 'but a trouble of ants in the gleam of a million million of suns' ('Vastness', ll. 4, 34). For Hopkins, the fact

— 133 —

that Darwinism taught that life was in a permanent state of flux suggested that we too were but burning on 'nature's bonfire' and would end up 'in an enormous dark / Drowned' ('That Nature is a Heraclitean Fire and of the comfort of the Resurrection', ll. 9, 12–13). For Bernard Shaw, Darwinism had 'a hideous fatalism about it', implying 'a ghastly and damnable reduction of beauty and intelligence, of strength and purpose, of honor and aspiration, to such casually picturesque changes as an avalanche may make in a mountain landscape, or a railway accident in a human figure' ([1921] 1939: xxxii).

Tennyson was sustained by his faith in immortality, Hopkins by his belief in Christ's redemptive mission, Shaw by his conviction that Neo-Lamarckian Vitalism, not Darwinism, was the correct theory of evolution. Their contemporary, the essayist and poet John Addington Symonds, had no such convictions. This sonnet, from Symonds's sequence 'An Old Gordian Knot', first published in 1880, pithily sums up his, and our, predicament:

Part of the whole that never can be known,
   Is this poor atom that we call our world;
   Part of this part amid confusion hurled
   Is man, an idiot on a crumbling throne:
Yea, and each separate soul that works alone,
   Striving to pierce the clouds around him curled,
   Gasps but one moment in the tempest whirled,
   And what he builds strong Death hath overthrown.
How shall this fragment of a waif, this scape
   In the oblivion of unreckoned years,
   This momentary guest of time, this ape
That grins and chatters amid smiles and tears, –
   How shall he seize the skirts of God and shape
   To solid form the truth that disappears?

                                 (VII)

Symonds spares himself and his readers nothing in this sonnet, using repetition and rhyme to pinpoint the case against what Huxley called 'the arrogance of man'. Sticking within the strict parameters of a Petrarchan sonnet, he nevertheless allows himself to depart from the usual iambic pentameter line in two ways, each to subtle but powerful effect. Firstly, he starts a number of his lines on a stress, replacing the unstress/stress pattern of the iambic foot with the opposite stress/unstress pattern, called a trochee. This is most noticeable in the first and third lines, where Symonds uses his metre to reinforce the diminishing parallels between the Earth as 'Part of the whole' and man as merely 'Part of this part'. Symonds's other device is to break a number of his lines off-centre. These unexpected caesurae emphasise the phrases that follow them. We are made to pay particular attention as our species is scorned as an 'idiot' and – reinforced by rhyme and with a clear allusion to Darwin – a grinning, chattering 'ape'. Faced with the universe's justified contempt, what grounds have we to claim privileged knowledge of nature or an exalted position within it?

The American poet and novelist Stephen Crane made a similar point in this bald epigram, published in 1899:

> A man said to the universe:
> "Sir, I exist!"
> "However," replied the universe,
> "The fact has not created in me
> A sense of obligation."

Crane's epigram is so dry that it resists further comment. Like Symonds's sonnet, it brings us face-to-face with the preposterousness of our collective self-importance. As with the confrontation with death, however, poetry can take us beyond the stoical admission that, as James Thomson wittily rhymes in *The City of Dreadful Night*, 'We bow down to the universal laws, / Which never had for man a special clause' (xiv, ll. 61–2).

It is Jeffers who affirms the insignificance of humanity on the cosmic scale most persistently within his poetry. In his preface to *The Double Axe and Other Poems* (the collection which included 'The Inhumanist', and in which he torpedoed his own reputation by condemning America's victorious intervention in the Second World War) Jeffers declares that his volume 'presents, more explicitly than previous poems of mine, a new attitude, a new manner of thought and feeling, which came to me at the end of the war of 1914'. This attitude is 'based on a recognition of the astonishing beauty of things and their living wholeness, and on a rational acceptance of the fact that mankind is neither central nor important in the universe' (2001: 719). In fact, Jeffers's world view did not remain constant, and his increasingly abrasive poetry is not simply a testimony to his growing lack of self-censorship. It was only as the catastrophe of the 1930s and 1940s unfolded that Jeffers's detached disregard for human vanity grew into loathing for humanity as a whole as 'a botched experiment that has run wild and ought to be stopped' ('Orca', l. 23).

Confronting the horror of war, Jeffers turned what was originally an outlook into a philosophy, much as George Meredith did in his later poetry. Alongside his Inhumanism, the vague transcendentalism of Jeffers's earlier poetry was recast in 'The Inhumanist' as a pantheistic celebration of 'one energy, / One existence, one music, one organism, one life, one God' (2001: 592–3). To gain a sense of Jeffers's power and insight as a prophet of the Darwinian condition, we need to peel away these nihilistic and pantheistic accretions that were built up around his original vision by factors other than Darwinism itself. This means returning for the most part to the poetry that Jeffers wrote in the early 1920s, before the long run-up to the Second World War was obviously underway. For all the changes to his world view, these poems do indeed fit the description he gives of them twenty years on in the preface to *The Double Axe*.

In Chapter 1, I quoted Jeffers's insistence that poetry should deal with 'permanent things'. This requires the poet to distinguish those things which truly are permanent from those which are ephemeral. In his 1923 preface to *Tamar*, for example, Jeffers insists that, while a railroad 'is actual, in its fantastic way, for a century or two', it is 'not real', on the grounds that 'in most of the human past and most of the human future it is not existent'. An aeroplane, on the other hand, is 'as poetic as a plow or a ship' because, even though 'it is not existent in the human past except as a most ancient of dreams', it 'is existent, in some form or other, in all the human future' (2001: 708). Here, Jeffers's realistic attitude to technological change seems temporarily spellbound by his excitement at the prospect of flight. Most of the distinctions Jeffers draws in his early poems themselves are less arbitrary, however. In 'Point Joe', Jeffers explicitly (and prosaically) declares that 'Permanent things are what is needful in a poem, things temporally / Of great dimension, things continually renewed or always present' (ll. 11–12). As in Hardy's famous war lyric, 'In Time of "The Breaking of Nations"', the struggle to win food from the land is seen as a timeless activity, set against the circumstantial details of 'fashionable and momentary things' (l. 14). Elsewhere, as Jeffers pans back to look at the present in the context of human history and even of prehistory as a whole, the contrast between the timeless and the ephemeral becomes ever more stark.

For Jeffers, human history itself is but a series of passing events and preoccupations which diminish to insignificance beside the ongoing processes of nature. In poems such as 'The Cycle' and 'Shine, Perishing Republic', animal migrations, the fruiting of plants, the sea, cliffs and mountains all become symbols of a permanence that puts the growing political power of America, 'heavily thickening into empire' ('Shine, Perishing Republic', l. 1), into perspective. In 'Continent's End', even the sea itself (both the mother and the symbol of life in the poem) is young beside the 'tides of fire' (l. 16) that first formed and still underlie 'the beds of granite' (l. 2). In 'The Treasure', Jeffers pans back further still, taking the Copernican turn to heart, as he declares 'the earth too's an ephemerid', while even the stars are 'short-lived as grass' (ll. 1–2). It is not 'the flash of activity' but 'the incredible depths' on either side of it, the 'enormous repose after, enormous repose before', which form the 'treasure' of the poem's title (ll. 6–7).

The most ambitious of these early lyrics is 'Night'. Helen Vendler has remarked that Jeffers's lyric poems are not lyrics at all, but oratory (1995: 58). But 'Night' is undoubtedly a lyric poem. In fact, it is a subtle hybrid of different lyric forms. In this poem, short verses of seven short lines alternate with longer verses of twelve longer lines. Even the longer lines are short for Jeffers, and while they remain free rather than strictly metrical, the echoes of regular accentual verse are more distinct. The lines in the shorter verses have three, four or occasionally two stresses, like most popular idiomatic poetry in English. Those in the longer verses have five or six stresses, recalling both the iambic pentameter and the hexameter line dominant in classical Greek and Roman poetry. These contrasting models reflect the different roles the different verses play within Jeffers's poem. The shorter verses sound a typically lyrical or elegiac note. They are gentle and meas-ured, dwelling on otherwise unobtrusive details of the natural landscape as night falls. The longer verses are episodes from a more formal hymn in praise of Night. In them, Jeffers takes the Romantic ode of Wordsworth, Shelley or Keats and restores to it the austerity and the public voice of a Greek chorus. But the alternation between the long and short verses gives a respite from the intensity of this more declamatory voice, allowing us time to assimilate its pronouncements and take stock of them.

As 'Night' begins, we find ourselves watching a particular wave draw back from a particular rock. Over the first two verses our vision expands to include more rocks, 'the prone ocean' covered by 'the low cloud' (ll. 7–8), then the mountain, pinewood and river behind us. These concrete realities draw us into the poem. They seem to fix us in time and space, yet in con-trast with many of his other poems, Jeffers does not identify the landscape expressly with the Big Sur coastline in northern California, at least not until he resolves the pines into 'old redwoods' (l. 23) in the third verse. Instead he allows us, as we read the poem, to construct the landscape for ourselves from our own memories and impressions of rocky shores, pine-woods, narrow valleys and so on.

The experience we are invited to share in 'Night' is thus both particular and universal. But Jeffers's vision is idiosyncratic, giving rise to original and surprising turns of phrase and image, as in this description of the encroach-ing night:

> Over the dark mountain, over the dark pinewood,
> Down the long dark valley along the shrunken river,
> Returns the splendor without rays, the shining of shadow,
> Peace-bringer, the matrix of all shining and quieter of shining.
>
> (ll. 8–11)

The paradoxes of 'the splendor without rays, the shining of shadow' invite us to think about night in a fresh way as the positive antitype of light. The alliteration picks out these images, while the repetition of 'dark' three times in the previous two lines allows this paradoxical 'shining', itself repeated three times, to stand out all the more.

'Night' is a lyric, but Vendler is right that it is also oratory. Jeffers's use of alliteration and assonance is subtly suggestive throughout his poem. Never overdoing the repetition of a single sound, he uses shifting sounds to build up patterns among related words or concepts, or to establish relationships between seemingly dissociated ones. In the opening verse he evokes the scene by echoing the sound of the retreating wave in long 'o's and 'ou's and in a series of changing initial and final 's' sounds. There the effect is clearly onomatopoeic, but more often Jeffers is after more abstract associations. At the end of the first long verse, repeated 'l's unobtrusively link together the 'lights', 'laughter', 'labor, lust and delight' sponsored by the 'blond favorite' of the 'sun-lovers' (the sun itself) as 'blemishes' (ll. 16–18). In the second long verse, Jeffers weaves a tissue of 'f's, 'l's, 'k's, 'd's and long and short 'i's to draw us into his image of the star Antares as nothing more than a 'flicker of a spark in the faint far glimmer / Of a lost fire dying in the desert, dim coals of a sand-pit the Bedouins / Wandered from at dawn' (ll. 34–6). The third long verse is brimful of these associational alliterations, bridging the gaps between contrasting concepts such as passion and peace, song and silence, men and moths. They seem to confirm that, 'as a sailor loves the sea', so even those who love life 'heartily' will be content to steer the 'helm' for 'harbor' (l. 57). They knit memory, motherhood, mating and the womb inextricably together too with the 'primal' 'quietness' and 'silences' symbolised by the 'Night' itself (ll. 53–4).

'Night' embodies the rhetorical power of poetry to persuade us that it speaks truth and to accept the truth that it speaks. The overall effect of all these alliterations and internal rhymes is to assure us that these things are right – not merely factually correct, but proper, as it should be. The night, the darkness, will consume each star in its time. Reading Jeffers's poem, this can seem not appalling but fitting, even comforting. In the closing words of the poem, 'Life is grown sweeter and lonelier, / And death is no evil' (ll. 63–4). Like Meredith in 'In the Woods', Jeffers invites us to accept our place as a mortal part of nature, apart and alone within the universe, but nothing in its eyes.

In all these early poems, Jeffers aspires to a detachment akin to permanence himself. In 'Continent's End', he tells the sea,

> The tides are in our veins, we still mirror the stars, life is your child, but
>   there is in me
> Older and harder than life and more impartial, the eye that watched
>   before there was an ocean.
>
> (ll. 11–12)

In 'Night', he generalises from this powerfully elemental portrait of himself to life at large:

> And life, the flicker of men and moths and the wolf on the hill,
> Though furious for continuance, passionately feeding, passionately
> Remaking itself upon its mates, remembers deep inward
> The calm mother, the quietness of the womb and the egg,
> The primal and the latter silences: dear Night it is memory
> Prophesies, prophecy that remembers, the charm of the dark.
>
> (ll. 50–5)

Both these poems strike a prophetic note typical of Jeffers. The fiercely 'impartial' gaze of the first and the death-wish of the second are both characteristic too. But within 'Night' at least, Jeffers offers a complementary perspective to set against this fatalistic nihilism. Through the personification of Antares, Arcturus and Orion, he invites us to feel a fellowship with the stars. The stars and constellations are raised into mythic archetypes, emblems of our own transient existence writ large. Through this analogy, Jeffers calls on us to see ourselves in relative terms. Where Symonds's sonnet diminishes us absolutely, 'Night' allows that we too, like the stars, have significance to ourselves by our own measure. It is only relative to the stars that we are insignificant, as the stars themselves are relative to the eternal Night. In 'Night', Jeffers encourages us not to forget our own scale in space and time, but to remember the universal scale too, and to accept it, in order that we may 'love the four-score years / Heartily' ourselves (ll. 56–7).

'EARTH'S CATASTROPHE': THE PLANETARY PERSPECTIVE

As the poet William Everson, Jeffers's disciple and foremost interpreter, has observed 'The ecological crisis has driven home with great force the pertinence of Jeffers' insistence that man divorced from nature is a monstrosity' (Jeffers 1977: xiv). Other recent American poets have reached the same conclusion. In his essay 'Taking Dominion over the Wilderness', Robert Pack argues forcefully that we need to rid ourselves of 'our species-centred self-idolatry' and replace it with a 'reverence for a world of diverse forms of life'. For Pack, however, this imperative is born not from an awareness of humanity's insignificance within a vast universe but from our new knowledge of just how significant we are in the ecology of our own 'small planet'. As he writes in his essay, 'the immemorial idea of the vastness and inexhaustibility of nature needs to be replaced with the idea of the finiteness and vulnerability of nature' (1993b: 272).

Jeffers looks out to the stars, but he also takes heart in 'The beauty of things' here on Earth, declaring movingly in 'Credo' that 'the heartbreaking beauty / Will remain when there is no heart to break for it' (ll. 11–12) – no human heart, that is. Three-quarters of a century later, it seems less certain that we can depend on this reassurance. Instead, as Pack remarks, there may be a real danger that 'nature's evolutionary plenitude' may be 'superseded by human creation', leaving us with 'nothing outside ourselves worthy of reverence and awe' (1993b: 272). In such circumstances, Jeffers's 'Night' would prove a barren consolation indeed.

Ammons shares Pack's fear in his poetry. His long poem *Sphere* is a complex and constantly shifting meditation on life on Earth. Like Jeffers, Ammons suggests that it is in our own best interests 'to confront nothingness' as 'to be saved is here, local and mortal: // everything else is a glassworks of flight: a crystal/ hankering after the unlikely: futures on the next illusion' (1974: xxxiii, ll. 4, 6–8). Where Jeffers uses an analogy between human beings and stars to restore meaning to human life within a cosmic perspective, Ammons places 'each of us' individually 'in the peak and center / of perception', a 'cone of ages' (xlvii, ll. 4–5). This image is at once radically subjectivist and scrupulously scientific. Invoking the concept of space-time, Ammons substitutes relativity for relativism, binding us in to the existence of the entire universe as it passes through our individual perceptions.

Yet the consolation Ammons finds in this idea is cut across by a ghastly irony he finds in another scientific theory, evolution. As Ammons sees it,

> man waited
> 75,000 years in a single cave (cold, hunger, inexplicable
> visitation of disease) only to rise to the bright, complex
>
> knowledge of his destruction!
>
> (xlv, l.10–xlvi, l.1)

Like Browning's Caliban and Hughes's wodwo, the solitary man waiting in the one cave is at once an archetypal evolutionary prototype (the caveman, in place of the savage or the aquatic ape) and a half-comic caricature of him. But Ammons's primary point, that the end point of our evolution is the knowledge of our extinction, is one he takes seriously enough to reinforce a few lines further on, asking 'when we have made the sufficient mirror will // it have been only to show how things will break: know thyself / and vanish!' (xlvi, ll. 9–11) As Ammons sees it, it is not only our evolution that will end in extinction, but our quest for understanding going back to the adage 'know thyself', borrowed by ancient Greek philosophers and poets from the Delphic oracle.

The 'destruction' learnt at last by the caveman has many facets, including his own death. Among them is the environmental realisation that 'it may / be the mind can wear out the earth', conjuring up the prospect of 'an empty mind on a / bleached planet' (xxiii, 4–5) as another implied end of evolution. As the environmental crisis deepened in the 1980s and 1990s this possibility became a central concern of Ammons's poetry. In *Garbage*, a poem whose dominant image comes to stand at once for pollution and for the joyful proliferation and recycling of life and language, Ammons admits regretfully that 'since words were // introduced here things have gone poorly for the / planet' (1993: xii, ll. 2–4). He goes on to set the current ecological crisis in the context of evolution, as he does more pointedly in his short poem 'Questionable Procedures':

A bit of the universe's
business slopped
over and, strung
out of the way,
cooled and lode-slow
gave rise
here and there to
a quickness like
shade, protoplasm,
a see-through
coming and going of
dots and pulsing veils
that soon enough filled
the bit seas:
the veils and cauls
toughened, curled
into rolls, centralized

backbone: taking to
the land and coming up
into us, our agency,
they milled the
green continents white.

The strength of this poem lies in its ability to shock. The nonchalant opening diminishes life, as Symonds and Crane do in their poems. But Ammons restores our sense of life's beauty and worth, only to knock us back with the stark warning that our own life is destroying them.

Like Jeffers, Ammons begins with the assumption that life on Earth is unintended and trivial. But over the course of the poem he shifts from this cosmic perspective to a geocentric one. Evolutionary history is telescoped into twenty-two short lines and only five events: the origin of life, the formation of multicellular life-forms, the emergence of vertebrates, their colonisation of the land, and our own ecological impact on the rest of life. Ammons chooses Blake's 'dark Satanic mills', the archetypal image of the industrial revolution, to symbolise the damage we are doing. But in the forefront of his mind he has a more ubiquitous milling: the grinding of corn into flour.

Life in this poem may be unconscious and incidental, but it is also varied and vividly alive with movement. This variety and beauty is crushed out by mechanistic utilitarianism. The myths of progress and purposive evolution into which generations have sought to subsume Darwinism are not merely aesthetically 'questionable', as Ammons's sardonic title implies, they are hopelessly deluded. Deliberate 'agency' is introduced into life only at the latest moment and is fatal to it. All that remains is a dead, corpse-white ugliness, from which, like the hero of the Welsh poet John Barnie's futuristic verse-novel *Ice*, Ammons is 'looking to some long past world / to which there is no way back' (2001: 150). Like Barnie, Ammons realises that, after Darwin, extinction is absolute, including the extinctions we cause. Whatever we destroy is irretrievable, and its destruction impacts back on the destroyer, leaving our world depleted and our own species exposed. As Ammons comments in *Garbage*, with a hint of gallows humour, 'here we are at // last, last, probably' (1993: xii, ll. 42–3).

Like James Lovelock in *Gaia* (2000: xii), Ammons takes 'the view from space' and sees the scar humanity is leaving on the planet as a whole. Appleman has a similarly acute sense of the global threat posed by humanity. His first book, *The Silent Explosion*, sounded a note of warning over overpopulation as early as 1965, and he has kept up his campaign by editing Malthus alongside Darwin for the Norton Critical Editions. In his poetry,

however, he focuses more closely on indicative instances of the human
blight on nature, while still retaining the long Darwinian view. One of the
most sophisticated of these ecological poems is 'How Evolution Came to
Indiana', published in *Darwin's Ark*:

> In Indianapolis they drive
> five hundred miles and end up
> where they started: survival
> of the fittest. In the swamps
> of Auburn and Elkhart,
> in the jungles of South Bend,
> one-cylinder chain-driven runabouts fall
> to air-cooled V-4's, 2-speed gearboxes,
> 16-horse flat-twin midships engines –
> carcasses left behind
> by monobloc motors, electric starters,
> 3-speed gears, six cylinders, 2-chain drive,
> overhead cams, supercharged
> to 88 miles an hour in second gear, the age
> of Leviathan . . .
> > *There is grandeur in this view of life,*
> > *as endless forms*
> > *most beautiful and wonderful*
> > *are being evolved.*
> And then
> the drying up, the panic,
> the monsters dying: Elcar, Cord,
> Auburn, Duesenberg, Stutz – somewhere
> out there, the chassis of Studebakers,
> Marmons, Lafayettes, Bendixes, all
> rusting in high-octane smog,
> ashes to ashes, they
> end up where they started.

The central conceit of this poem is straightforward. Appleman likens the
superseding of one generation of automobiles by the next to the extinction
of the dinosaurs. The cars are listed baldly through names and statistics
which sound like they have been lifted from a trade magazine. These are
interwoven with passing evocations of the age of the dinosaurs as it is exists
in the popular imagination. Appleman keeps these allusions sufficiently
consistent with his account of the automobile industry that they do not

seem forced, although the presence of 'swamps' and 'jungles' in modern Indiana is clearly playful. Rather less subtly, Appleman drives a wedge into the middle of his poem with a quotation from the last and most famous sentence of *The Origin of Species*. Like Darwin's contemporary and would-be nemesis, Samuel Butler, in his satirical utopia *Erewhon*, Appleman suggests that even the evolution of machines is a process of the survival of the fittest.

'How Evolution Came to Indiana' is a much richer poem than this simple summary suggests. It is not merely an account of the car industry in general. It is very specifically an account of that industry in Indiana. The automobiles named in the last lines are all classic cars of the 1920s and 1930s, all made in Indiana, most of them in the northern towns of Auburn, Elkhart and South Bend. Appleman's analogy takes the post-war economic decline of these cities as an illustration of the principles of Darwinian evolution. The irony is that Indiana is one of many mid-West states where the theory of evolution has been publicly challenged by creationism in schools, law courts and the legislature.

Appleman confronts the creationists of Indiana with an illustration of Darwin's theory from their own recent history. He even taunts them with a quotation from Darwin himself, pared down to remove any trace of Darwin's accommodating reference to life 'having been originally breathed' into the first organisms ([1859] 2003: 398). As usual, Appleman has no interest in such an accommodation, although his reference to Leviathan is another hint that the God of the Book of Job might be a fitting model for the cosmic order. As the 'carcasses' and 'monsters' are at once the cars themselves and the dinosaurs they are likened to, so 'Leviathan' is both a word from the argot of the 1960s motor trade and a symbol, from Job 41, of the power of nature beyond the control or comprehension of humanity.

The allusion to Job and the quotation from Darwin both gesture towards a third layer of significance which Appleman develops at the end of his poem. The 'age / of Leviathan' does indeed suggest 'grandeur', but it is hard not to read Appleman's appropriation of Darwin's phrase 'most beautiful and wonderful' ironically. Classic cars can be beautiful objects, but Appleman's account of them here is studiedly functional, not aesthetic. Darwin's poetic prose sets off Appleman's anti-poetic verse. The names Studebaker and Duesenberg are evocative, calling up a bygone age. But the 'forms' Appleman describes for us, in the form in which he describes them, are ugly and mechanistic, not 'beautiful and wonderful' at all. This ugliness prefigures the pollution that will further disfigure them, as they rust in the 'high-octane smog' of their own making.

'How Evolution Came to Indiana' is not only a clever comment on and intervention in the evolution–creation debate, drawing on the economics of the automobile industry in the mid-West. It is an epitome of humanity's impact on the environment, exemplified once again through the car. For the centenary of *The Origin of Species* in 1959, Appleman co-edited a collection of essays entitled *1859: Entering an Age of Crisis*. In his introduction to this collection, the magisterial critic Howard Mumford Jones drew together the major political and cultural events that happened in that year, including the publication of John Stuart Mill's essay *On Liberty*, Edward FitzGerald's translation of the *Rubáiyát of Omar Khayyám* and Meredith's novel *The Ordeal of Richard Feverel* alongside the *Origin*. At the end of his essay, however, Jones suggested that, more significant than any of these books, even Darwin's, was what a 'forty-year old railway conductor' discovered when 'boring holes in the earth at Titusville, Pennsylvania, on 27 August 1859'. At 'a depth of sixty-nine feet' he 'struck oil at its source and proved for the first time the existence of reservoirs of petroleum within the surface of the earth' (1959: 28). For Jones, the significance of this event was that, as petrol came to eclipse coal, so cars and planes replaced trains and ships, and America superseded Britain as the dominant world power.

Like Jones, Appleman sets the theory of evolution and the car economy alongside one another. Rather than choosing which is the more significant, however, he brings them into conjunction. Darwin's theory is derived in part from economics itself, and gives us in turn a rudimentary model for the evolution of the car industry. But it also helps us to comprehend the damage that that industry – and industry at large – is doing. Ecologically, Darwinism reminds us of the dependence of an organism on its environment. As a historical science, it can point to other occasions when rapid changes to the environment have had a drastic impact on living creatures, the most famous if not quite the most grievous being the meteor strike that led to the extinction of the dinosaurs. Leading palaeontologists such as Michael Benton (2003) and Richard Leakey (Leakey and Lewin 1995) have likened our own impact on biodiversity to these catastrophic events in prehistory. Appleman draws the same analogy implicitly in his poem. It is not only the cars that will corrode in the smog. As the echo of the funeral service suggests, we too shall return to 'ashes', ending up, as the poem itself does, where we started: beyond the evolutionary process – not because we were specially created by God, but because we will be unable to survive in the alien atmosphere we ourselves will have created.

Returning to Pack, he too sees human beings as the agent of mass extinction. In his essay 'Naming the Animals' he names us as 'the earth's preeminent catastrophe', worse even than the meteorite that killed off the dinosaurs (1997: 196). This essay was written as a gloss on his poem 'The

Trees Will Die', itself a meditation on Bill McKibben's injunction in *The End of Nature* to consider that, with climate change, the very trees will die. In this poem, Pack enumerates and describes the different kinds of trees that he has known over the last thirty years living in Vermont.

'The Trees Will Die' begins slowly, dwelling on the colours and shapes of different oaks and maples as Pack or his speaker describes them to an unnamed listener, perhaps, from the tender and domestic relationship between them, his wife. He pauses here and there to consider their origins in 'an indifferent force – / just evolutionary randomness, / yet so like old divinity' (ll. 47–9), and also their place in our own evolution. The trees, Pack reminds us, are part of our natural environment. As a key source of fuel they have been crucial to our survival. They are intimately bound to our imaginations through the symbols we have made of them and the names they have elicited from us. And yet, they are dying off, unable to adapt to the rapidity of climate change, because young trees and any favourable mutations they may contain take a long time to reach maturity, and because they cannot migrate as quickly as animals.

Towards its close, Pack's poem moves more rapidly, listing trees with ever more urgency, culminating in:

> of course
> the cornucopia of fruits –
> apple and cherry, pear and plum and peach –
> each with a tang that suits
>
> the palate of whatever taste
> one might have dreamt of ripened paradise.
> (ll. 73–7)

Characteristically, Pack writes in steady but not insistent iambics, retaining enough formal metrics to give the sense that we are listening to measured, careful, considered speech, but not so much that the verse draws attention to itself. The more conspicuous poetic effect here is alliteration. The climax of his list of trees moves from 'of course' to 'cornucopia' and from there on to the 'pear and plum and peach'. With their plosive initial 'p's, these 'fruits' (echoed in the rhyme with 'suits') burst on our 'palate' as we read aloud. This tactile sensation created by Pack's verse complements and enhances the imaginative appeal of his language, conjuring just for a moment the sense of 'ripened paradise' itself. The rich internal rhyme in this phrase is the last lingering of this dream before the most definite full stop in the whole poem.

For the last sentence of his poem, Pack abruptly changes his register, from the luxuriating to the austerely scientific blended with the Biblical:

When I consider how
a man-made shift in climate of a few degrees
    reveals the rebel power we now

       have learned to cultivate
in order to subdue the animals
    and take dominion, like a curse,
over the fields, the forests, and the atmosphere –
    as if the universe

       belonged to us alone – I wonder
if consideration of the family of trees
    might give us pause
and let us once again obey the sun,
    whose light commands all human laws.

                    (ll. 78–90)

In his essays, Pack argues that the ecological crisis is a product of the attitude encapsulated in God's commandment to Adam and Eve in Genesis 1: 28 to 'subdue' the Earth and take 'dominion' over all other living things (1993b: 271; 1997: 193). He makes the same point in this poem by appropriating God's language and calling it a 'curse'. Like Satan's, ours is a 'rebel power' born of arrogance.

In 'Naming the Animals', Pack is unequivocal, writing that:

We as a species need to change ourselves radically through an act of reasoned will – a change no species has ever been called upon to accomplish. The power of naming, therefore, that poets must summon today, more urgently than ever before, is to name ourselves as devourers gone berserk, as the scourge of the earth, and, perhaps, in the realization of that naming, to reinvigorate our commitment as preservers and our role as celebrators. (1997: 198–9)

In 'The Trees Will Die' itself, Pack backs off from this Swiftian role as the scourge of humanity – a role Jeffers, Ammons and Appleman all play with more conviction. Instead, he coaxes us back to dwell as he has done in his poem on the life-giving beauty of nature.

To 'obey the sun' is a hard injunction to interpret, let alone follow, but

Pack presumably means much what he means in 'Taking Dominion over the Wilderness', where he argues that 'without wilderness, our humanity is diminished because we fail to perceive the beauty inherent in our ephemerality; we fail to acknowledge ourselves as creatures among other creatures, among other evolving and vanishing forms' (1993b: 281). By contemplating the family of trees, we can come to realise and accept that 'we drop like the fruits of the tree, / Even we, / Even so', as Meredith puts it at the end of 'In the Woods'. But more than that, we can steep ourselves in their beauty, and rise with a renewed urge to sustain it. As Pack says in the closing paragraph of 'Naming the Animals':

> Without a sense of beauty that derives from otherness, from nature's independent existence, a prior world on which our fabricated cultural world depends, the capacity for taking delight in our surroundings will have withered away. Even before the planet becomes inhospitable to the human species, we will have died in spirit. (1997: 200)

Recalling our place on Earth as well as our place in the universe, the Darwinian poet today has a calling, even a duty, to remind us that, in ruining our planet, we are wrecking ourselves as well.

'ALL WE'VE GOT': THE HUMAN PERSPECTIVE

Along with astronomy, Darwinism has subverted, even inverted, our view of our place in the universe. Viewed astronomically, our significance dwindles to something infinitesimal. Through palaeontology, Darwinism teaches the same lesson on the planetary scale. Through ecology, it has called this inference into question, but only with the grim analysis that our power for blind destruction has far outstripped that of the wider life on Earth from which we were born. But there is a third scale on which we can view humanity from the perspective of Darwinism. This is the human scale itself. On this scale, human beings are individuals who remain meaningful, even in a meaningless universe.

As Hardy realises in 'The Plaint to Man', the more the universe is emptied of meaning, the more we are thrown back on our relationships with one another. This renewed if chastened humanism is the other value besides environmentalism that is most characteristic of modern Darwinian poetry. It is implicit, for example, in the speaker's intimacy with his wife in 'The Trees Will Die'. Their shared experience and outlook is integral to the value he places on the trees themselves. In 'Naming the Animals', Pack calls our twin impulses to dominate and to celebrate nature (both, he notes, enshrined in Genesis) 'the tragedy of our species' (1997: 198). His poem trusts to celebration as a way to counter the 'curse' of 'dominion', but in so doing it reminds us too that we celebrate nature to and for each other – something that is implicit in the very act of writing a poem to be read by other human beings.

The Darwinian humanism implicit in Pack's poem is brought out explicitly in Appleman's 'Waldorf-Astoria Euphoria, The Joy of Big Cities', the first of two poems from *Darwin's Ark* grouped together as 'Euphorias'. Appleman prefaces these poems with quotations from Darwin's *The Expression of the Emotions in Man and Animals*. The first quotation, introducing both poems together, reads, 'I heard a child, a little under four years old, when asked what was meant by being in good spirits, answer, "It is laughing, talking, and kissing."' The second, introducing 'Waldorf-Astoria Euphoria' itself reads, 'Joy, when intense, leads to various purposeless movements – to dancing about, clapping the hands, stamping, etc.' Then Appleman launches into his poem:

> You feel so good, you stop walking:
> they swirl around you, racing the 6:15.
> You bless them all with a smile
> you cannot explain: they are suddenly
> precious. You look around, with your alien eyes,
> at forty floors of windows where
> they are laughing, talking, and kissing: you realize
> they are priceless. You feel them
> under the pavement, riding the uptown express,
> straphanging bodies waving
> like kelp, and you know
> they are irreplaceable; you think of them
> all over town, bursting
> with unused happiness, and you clap,
> and clap again, and clapping, you sing
> a song you thought you'd forgotten, and your waist
> moves gently, like jonquils, and your hand
> catches her fingertips, and she smiles, her arms
> moving like willows,
> and the fruitseller dances with apples,
> crying a musical language, and a girl
> with a bongo comes on with rhythm,
> her hips moving like wheatfields, and
> the hardhats coming up from the manholes,

their bodies moving like jackhammers,
and Chinese voices like windchimes
sing to the women from San Juan
who gather around like palm trees, and the cops
have cordoned the street and are dancing
with women from Minnesota,
their thighs as seductive as seaweed;
and you know that sooner or later
this had to happen: that somehow
it would all break out, all that pent-up
joy, and people would sing and hold hands,
their bodies swerving like taxis,
and the music inside their heads
would fill the streets with dancing,
clapping hands, and stamping;
and you sing another chorus
of we,
hey, we,
yes, we,
I said we
are all
we've got.

'Waldorf-Astoria Euphoria' is gloriously inclusive. At first the title might
lead us to expect a picture of privilege and exclusivity. The Waldorf=Astoria
(as it prefers to call itself) is one of New York's most famous and plushest
hotels, the one-time home of debutantes and gangsters. The gangsters may
be gone, but the debs are representative of those we see 'laughing, talking,
and kissing' in the hotel's forty-odd stories of plate-glass windows. But the
title opens out to 'The Joy of Big Cities' at large, and so does the poem. The
Waldorf's residents are 'priceless', genuinely, not comically or sarcastically.
So are the commuters running for the 6:15 or strap-hanging on the subway,
the workmen in the drains, the market traders, indeed the entire cosmopolitan population of New York City, drawn from and representing the whole
world from China to Puerto Rico. Even the NYPD get to be included in
this celebration of humanity, in the carnivalesque scene of them 'dancing
/ with women from Minnesota' whose thighs – or is it the cops'? – are 'as
seductive as seaweed'.

Thrust into the very centre of this whirl of spontaneous exuberance are
you, the reader. 'Waldorf-Astoria Euphoria' is written in the second person
and the present tense. Twelve of the first sixteen lines address us directly as

'you'. This is not obtrusive, once we have entered into the poem's conceit and accepted our role as its central character. But it does keep us imaginatively onsite, participating in the scene in our minds and not merely observing it, as we might if this were a first- or third-person narrative. Only once Appleman has got us dancing (inside the poem and through its rhythms and instructions as we read) does he start to spread that movement, first to the willowy woman or girl who may or may not have been with us all along, and then on round the rest of the city.

Like Pattiann Rogers in 'Against the Ethereal', Appleman sustains this movement with present participles, borrowed from the little child who told Darwin that being in good spirits meant 'laughing, talking, and kissing', and from Darwin's own account of joy resulting in 'dancing', 'clapping' and 'stamping'. But Appleman's participles have none of the urgency of Rogers's. They do not embody deliberate intent, the pursuit of a goal, but movement that is, as Darwin himself says, purely 'purposeless'. At the same time, Appleman's simple and regular phrasing eases the poem along, the easy, familiar word 'like' repeating itself in eight out of nine similes, all within one long sentence.

'Waldorf-Astoria Euphoria' is a celebration of human life for its own sake. But, like 'Bildad' and 'How Evolution Came to Indiana', it has a punch-line that packs a punch. In the last six lines our role within the poem changes. We are no longer simply celebrating our common humanity with the rest of New York. We are interpreting that celebration. The poem moves from the second person to the first person as Appleman puts words into our mouths. Even over the first four of these short final lines, we seem to be still simply affirming our collective identity, repeating and rhyming 'we' at the end of each line. Then, in the last two lines, we realise that we are affirming something else too: Appleman's belief that there is no God, and that 'we', living here and now, are the only source of love and joy that we have.

Appleman's poem is a joyful incitement to love one another. But it comes with the stark warning that if we do not, we lose everything. As Ammons remarks towards the end of *Garbage*, 'if there is to be any regard for // human life, it will have to be ours' (1993: xviii, ll.104–5). How we take these warnings depends on our preconceptions. Even for an atheist humanist like Appleman himself, 'Waldorf-Astoria Euphoria' ends on a deliberately dark note, a kind of black bathos. But a memento mori is also a carpe diem, and the atheist reader can return to the carnival atmosphere of the rest of the poem with an undiminished if altered enthusiasm. For a Christian reader, on the other hand, the last six lines throw down a challenge. The question the poem poses is, whether its insistence that we are all we've got compromises the joy it so vibrantly expresses. Appleman assures us it does not. After all, 'you' are only singing another chorus of a song 'you' have been singing all along, and it has not stopped 'you' from dancing. But then, after reading the last lines you may no longer be so ready to accept the role that Appleman thrusts upon you.

In *Sphere*, Ammons offers us a choice:

> what we can celebrate
> is the condition we are in, or we can renounce the condition
> we are in and celebrate a condition we might be in or ought
>
> to be in:
>
> (1974: xcii, ll. 7–10)

For Hardy, Darwin throws us back on each other because he takes away any basis we have for trusting to transcendental hope. In 'The Plaint to Man', 'loving-kindness' is the best response to 'dependence', not a cause for celebration in itself. For Appleman, Darwin's books hold out a positive promise which is well worth celebrating in itself. Darwinism, as Appleman experiences it, can be as joyous as a revivalist church meeting. His fantasy of dancing in the city streets is extrapolated from Darwin's own 'good spirits', but also from those of the little Victorian child. By quoting Darwin quoting this little child, Appleman reminds us that this is not merely the godless Darwin speaking, but an innocent three-year-old. Laughing, talking and kissing in this poem are thus joyfully innocent as well as joyful. The dancing may be sexy but it too is not openly sexual, seductive, sea-weedy thighs aside.

And yet, the values implied by Appleman's openness and inclusiveness are quintessentially liberal values. 'Waldorf-Astoria Euphoria' calls up an image of Woodstock transposed to New York City, an image that would surely appear debauched to moral conservatives, who could easily read the poem as implying that sex itself is innocent, even among total strangers who gather dancing on the streets. After all, we do not know whether that touch between your fingertips and hers has any warrant in past relations or not, nor where it might lead. As far as Appleman is concerned, it does not appear to matter either way, so long as there is spontaneous love and joy in the moment itself.

For all its innocence and joy, 'Waldorf-Astoria Euphoria', typically for Appleman, drives a wedge between those who share his atheism and his liberal values and those who do not. The further a reader stands from Appleman's own position on either account, the more disconcerting or

displeasing the poem is likely to be. But for a reader facing up to the implications of Darwinism for our place in the universe – and willing to accept
the innocence of joy – Appleman's poem is a tonic, a jubilant affirmation of
humanity's due importance to ourselves, even in the void. Few things could
be further from Jeffers's Inhumanism, with its desire for human extinction,
yet they share the same roots. We value each other not less but all the more
when we know no other guarantee of value, because the value that we have
is our value to ourselves, as to the universe at large, wonderful as it seems,
we are nothing.

6

Humans and Other Animals

More than kin and less than kind

As Huxley observed in *Man's Place in Nature*, Darwinism fundamentally alters our relationship with the rest of the natural world. To say that, after Darwin, we are animals does not make this transformation quite clear enough. Pre-Darwinian thinkers from Aristotle to Linnaeus said the same. For them, it was a matter of taxonomy. After Darwin, it is a matter of kinship. Focussing narrowly on us, on human beings, we are now properly animals by nature as well as by kind. This is widely recognised.

What is not so widely appreciated are the implications for how we should think about them, that is, about other animals. Since Darwin, that category (nonhuman animals) has ceased to be a natural kind at all. Chimpanzees are more closely related to humans than they are to gorillas or orang-utans, let alone to fish. The six million years and a quarter of a million generations that have passed since our bloodlines parted company is as nothing to the close-on 400 million years and millions of generations that have gone by since any ancestor of ours could reasonably be called a fish. Even so, we (humans and chimpanzees) are more closely related to some of the animals we call 'fish' than those fish (specifically lungfish and coelacanths) are to any other fish currently alive. We can go on and on, expanding the category 'ourselves' to include each new set of cousins we encounter as we trace our genealogy back in time. Richard Dawkins does just that in his richest book, *The Ancestor's Tale*, taking us back to the ever-more-approximate moments when our ancestors diverged from those of other fishes, of starfish and sea urchins, of worms, snails and spiders, of jellyfish, of sponges, of mushrooms, of plants, ultimately even of bacteria.

Like the repositioning of humans within the order Primates, this is not merely an academic exercise. It has a profound bearing on how we think about other creatures, in particular animals. Not least, it raises important ethical questions. Writing to the Secretary of the Humanitarian League in 1910, Hardy remarked that:

Few people seem to perceive fully as yet that the most far-reaching consequence of the establishment of the common origin of all species is ethical . . . While man was deemed to be a creation apart from all other creations, a secondary or tertiary morality was considered good enough towards the 'inferior' races; but no person who reasons nowadays can escape the trying conclusion that this is not maintainable. (1962: 349)

This conclusion is not 'maintainable' partly because, as Ammons insists in *Garbage*, our kinship with other organisms strongly suggests that 'right regard / for human life' includes 'all other forms of life' too (1993: xviii, ll. 105–6).

More crucially, Darwinian zoology has transformed, albeit haltingly, the entire framework for our understanding of animal psychology. In *The Descent of Man* and *The Expression of the Emotions in Man and Animals*, Darwin identified a continuity between the behaviour and emotions of human beings and those of other animals, particularly social animals. His work in this area was dismissed as naïvely anthropomorphic for much of the twentieth century. In 1894, the pioneering psychologist C. Lloyd Morgan insisted that studies of animal behaviour should not invoke higher mental states such as consciousness or complex intelligence to explain actions that could be explained as readily by simpler processes. Morgan's canon had the advantage of parsimony. It fitted too with the developmental models of evolution then in vogue. But as the primatologist Frans de Waal (1996: 64–5) and the philosopher Elliott Sober both point out, it neglects alternative forms of parsimony and evolutionary logic which emphasise the shared evolutionary origins of humans and other primates or indeed other mammals. Following this logic, Sober sets out his own alternative canon that 'if two derived behaviours are homologous, then the hypothesis that they are produced by the same proximate mechanism is more parsimonious than the hypothesis that they are produced by different proximate mechanisms' (2005: 96).

As Mary Midgley observes, evolution makes the 'arbitrary, groundless dogma' that animals are so different from us that extrapolations from human psychology to animal psychology should be ruled out of court 'most implausible' (1983: 128). This a priori deduction from Darwinian theory has been borne out by research in ethology, which has demonstrated in great detail the complex social relations between nonhuman animals, and in neurology, which has shown no marked difference between our own nervous systems and those of other, closely related animals. As Marian Stamp Dawkins concludes in her scrupulous account of the evidence for consciousness from animal behaviour, if we accept the argument from analogy to infer consciousness in other people on the grounds that they are like us in certain key ways, then it is going to be very difficult to maintain that consciousness should not be attributed to other species if they have at least some of those same key features. (1998: 176)

Arguably, Darwin's anthropomorphism is not strictly anthropomorphism at all. In *Darwin Loves You*, George Levine suggests that it is rather a form of 'zoomorphism': one animal mind imagining another to be like itself. Levine sees Darwin's approach as following the logic that 'humans are animals, and therefore one can – as an animal oneself – understand non-human behavior simply by imagining one's way into the animal's mind' (2006: 197). Ammons makes the same point in *Garbage*. Noting that 'our cousins the birds talk in the morning', he affirms 'I know some of their "words" / because I know, share with them, their states / of being and feeling' (1993: vii, ll. 137, 139–41).

As well as reminding us of our likeness to other animals, however, Darwinism reminds us too of the distances between us and them, both genealogically and ecologically. As Levine himself observes in his essay 'The heartbeat of the squirrel', the philosopher Thomas Nagel's famous question 'What is it like to be a bat?' remains a genuine problem (Levine 2008: 245–60; Nagel 1979: 165–80). In Sandra Mitchell's formulation, 'similarity between humans and nonhuman animals is just what we should expect on the basis of an evolutionary account of the origin and diversification of life on the planet – but not any willy-nilly similarity' (2005: 102).

Darwinism leads us to expect that the minds of less closely related creatures would tend to diverge more than those of more closely related creatures. But it also leads us to expect more dramatic divergence between the minds of equally closely related creatures that occupy very different niches. We are at least as closely related to bats as we are to dogs, but we can guess at a dog's mind more plausibly than a bat's, and not merely because we have long-standing social relations of our own with dogs. By the same logic, a coelacanth may be more closely related to me than it is to a sea trout, but I would wager that its experience of life is more like the trout's. Yet none of this overturns the basic expectation that it is indeed like *something* to be a bat, or a dog, or a fish, or indeed an octopus or a bee – that animals which are like us in having complex sensory and nervous systems have some form of conscious awareness as well.

Hardy captures this realization neatly in his poem 'An August Midnight', written in 1899:

A shaded lamp and a waving blind,
And the beat of a clock from a distant floor:
On this scene enter – winged, horned, and spined –
A longlegs, a moth, and a dumbledore;
While 'mid my page there idly stands
A sleepy fly, that rubs its hands. . .

Thus meet we five, in this still place,
At this point of time, at this point in space.
– My guests besmear my new-penned line,
Or bang at the lamp and fall supine.
'God's humblest, they!' I muse. Yet why?
They know Earth-secrets that know not I.

The first thing that strikes Hardy about these four insects is how alien they seem. They are 'winged, horned, and spined', like devils in a medieval fresco. But even before the end of the first stanza he has started to identify with them. The fly, he imagines, is 'sleepy', like he is himself (or would perhaps like to be), it being midnight and warm enough that the windows are still open, letting in the breeze and the insects. The fly is rubbing its 'hands' together too, not the first of its three pairs of feet, while by the second verse, the insects have all become his 'guests'.

Like Darwin's, Hardy's anthropomorphism in 'An August Midnight' is affectionate. It appears whimsical too, even sentimental, until the closing couplet. Hardy's impersonation of conventional piety here is calculatedly hollow. Instead of affirming the pre-Darwinian hierarchy, with humanity as the least humble of God's humble creatures, Hardy exposes it as a failure of the imagination. Like Morgan's trilobites, Hardy's insects have their own senses and environments, giving them privileged access to realms of experience and consciousness that – limited as they may be – will always remain beyond us. As Robert Frost remarks in a poem on the same theme, 'A Considerable Speck', 'I have a mind myself and recognize / Mind when I meet with it in any guise' (ll. 30–1). The considerable speck itself (a mite running purposefully across Frost's page) betrays its agency more directly than the insects in Hardy's study, but Frost's empirical conclusion ('Plainly with an intelligence I dealt' (l. 15)) is reached by Hardy too, as an a priori deduction from Darwinism.

Darwin's zoomorphism is rich, morally and psychologically as well as scientifically. As Levine remarks, it sets us on a path towards 'an enchantment that depends not on anthropocentric imaginations of the world but on anthropomorphic, imaginatively metaphorical impulses to understand it and love it' (2006: 251). Hardy's poem is testimony to this. In moving from a pious, sentimental platitude to a Darwinian philosophy of mind, his speaker makes a moral as well as an intellectual advance. The conventional piety may be benevolent, but only as an indulgence – 'a secondary or tertiary morality', as Hardy puts it in his letter. The Darwinian view, by contrast, is egalitarian, respectful and open-minded. As George Meredith promises in 'The Woods of Westermain', this fellow-feeling itself is ample consolation for abandoning 'Your proud title of elect' (IV, l. 32):

> Drink the sense the notes infuse,
> You a larger self will find:
> Sweetest fellowship ensues
> With the creatures of your kind.
> (III, ll. 93–6)

After Darwin, our 'kind' is an almost infinitely elastic category. As Darwinians, we can love nature without sentimentalising or underestimating it. The world beyond us remains morally unchanged, but our relationship to it is changed profoundly through this act of imagination.

As Darwinism has become the foundation of biology, it has inevitably had a marked impact on how poets write about animals. Conventionally, as the poet George MacBeth remarked, 'All good poems about animals are about something else as well' (1965: 7). Like earlier poets, a Darwinian poet can take an animal as a conduit to something else, a means of writing about the nature of a Darwinian universe at large. On the other hand, unlike many earlier poets, he or she is also confronted with the challenge of how to imagine, and how far to try to represent, the 'Earth-secrets' of other animals. Hardy's sense of their different experiences of the world and Meredith's exhortation to expand ourselves through 'fellowship' both lead poets in this direction, for all that, as the ecocritic Lawrence Buell has pointed out, 'self-evidently no human can speak *as* the environment, *as* nature, *as* a nonhuman animal' (2005: 7).

Darwinism and its poetics have permeated poetry about animals more thoroughly than they have the wider poetic tradition at large. Any modern poem that raises an animal's evolutionary history, its ecology, even its behaviour, is almost by definition a Darwinian poem. Clearly it would not be possible to cover even a representative selection of such poems in a single chapter. To give a sense of the range and scope of Darwinian animal poetry, whilst keeping the focus on poems which probe the wider implications of Darwinism, I am going to look at three types of animal in particular in this chapter. Each has its own specific significance within Darwinian poetry. The first is the hawk, which has been adopted by a number of poets from Robinson Jeffers onwards as an emblem of Darwinian nature as predatory and inhuman. The second is the songbird. Darwinian poets have been drawn to larks and thrushes not by Darwinism itself but by the model of Romantic poetry. In responding to the Romantics, however, they have reinterpreted the songbirds and their songs in the light of Darwin's vision of nature. The third is the deer. From roe-deer to moose, these are the largest unthreatening wild animals English or American poets and readers are likely to encounter in their own countries. As such, they provide the best opportunity for meditations on the divide between ourselves and other intelligent creatures.

At 'the master-fulcrum of violence': Hawks and falcons

Nothing in modern poetry bears witness to Darwin's influence more directly than the way poets write about birds of prey. Before the twentieth century, raptors, particularly eagles and falcons, were the noblest of birds. Socially, they were aristocrats – fittingly, given their association with the elite sport of falconry. Spiritually, they were close to the gods, like Jove's eagle or Gerard Manley Hopkins's windhover, a kestrel taken as a symbol of Christ's chivalry. Since Darwinism has taken hold, however, falcons have been folded into the more disreputable category of hawks, for poets if not for ornithologists. To the Darwinian poet, the hawk is the archetype of predatory nature. It is utterly inhuman, but also patently intelligent. It is efficient and heartless, but not cruel. Above all, it is unsentimental, the bane of Meredith's 'sweet sentimentalist' appalled at its kill in 'In the Woods'.

Hawks play this role again and again in modern British and American poetry. In Ted Hughes's 'The Hawk in the Rain' 'the hawk hangs still' at 'the master-/ Fulcrum of violence' (ll. 14–15). In Dylan Thomas's 'Over Sir John's Hill' he 'pulls to his claws / And gallows, up the rays of his eyes the small birds' (ll. 3–4). In Robert Penn Warren's 'Evening Hawk' 'his motion / Is that of a honed steel-edge' and his eye is 'unforgiving' (ll. 7–8, 13), while in Warren's 'Mortal Limit' he is associated with the mountains' 'gray jags / Of mercilessness' (ll. 2–3). Even when August Kleinzahler points out the touching vulnerability and companionship of hawks in his recent poem 'Anniversary', the hawk as the symbol of Darwinian nature remains his point of reference.

The poet primarily responsible for this transformation in the symbolic associations of birds of prey is Jeffers. Throughout the 1920s and 1930s, Jeffers took the hawk (falcons and even eagles included) as the overriding symbol of his vision of nature. In long narrative poems such as *Cawdor* and *Give Your Heart to the Hawks*, and in lyric after lyric ('Hurt Hawks', 'The Cruel Falcon', 'Rock and Hawk', 'The Beaks of Eagles' and so on) he returns obsessively to this image. It is as if Jeffers fancied himself as a hawk, or at least aspired to become one. If there is a touch of bravado to this pose (as in his infamous and surely disingenuous remark that 'I'd sooner, except the penalties, kill a man than a hawk' ('Hurt Hawks', l. 18)) Jeffers returns to his hawks too because they seem to him truly emblematic of nature as Darwin reveals it.

The poem that encapsulates this most clearly is 'Rock and Hawk':

Here is a symbol in which
Many high tragic thoughts
Watch their own eyes.

This gray rock, standing tall
On the headland, where the sea-wind
Lets no tree grow,

Earthquake-proved, and signatured
By ages of storms: on its peak
A falcon has perched.

I think, here is your emblem
To hang in the future sky;
Not the cross, not the hive,

But this; bright power, dark peace;
Fierce consciousness joined with final
Disinterestedness;

Life with calm death; the falcon's
Realist eyes and act
Married to the massive

Mysticism of stone,
Which failure cannot cast down
Nor success make proud.

In 'Rock and Hawk', the hawk – a falcon – is identified with the first term in each of the pairs set out in the last three verses. It represents 'bright power', 'Fierce consciousness' and life, as against peace, disinterest and death. The last of these pairs needs a gloss, as the falcon's very power and fierceness would seem to associate it with death rather than life. But like Rogers in 'Against the Ethereal', Jeffers celebrates the hawk for its life, regardless of its merciless predation. The fact that the hawk kills is subordinated to the fact that it is alive. Its killing is simply a 'Realist . . . act'. Yet Jeffers keeps the idea of predation in our minds even as he downplays it. Where Meredith focuses on the kill in 'In the Woods', Jeffers personifies killing itself.

Like the image it describes, 'Rock and Hawk' is monumental. The hawk is held up as a symbol without the direct ethical, political or aesthetic exegesis that distracts from it in many of Jeffers's other hawk poems. Jeffers uses a much shorter line than usual, and a sparse poetic technique with few overt effects aside from a light touch of alliteration and the balanced pairings which make up the second half of the poem. But the poem's stark directness is also its weakness. Jeffers's voice in 'Rock and Hawk' is portentous, even deliberately so, especially in the obscure opening verse. His messianic tendency, which he both parades and mocks in 'The Inhumanist', is acted out in earnest here, as he offers up his hawk as a new symbol for a new religion.

Jeffers's poetry is the most obsessive iteration of the image of the hawk as a symbol of Darwinian nature. The fullest single exposition of this symbol is Hughes's famous poem, 'Hawk Roosting', first published in 1959. This visceral, violent poem splits its critics down the middle. In an interview, Hughes remarked that 'That bird is accused of being a fascist . . . the symbol of some horrible totalitarian genocidal dictator. Actually what I had in mind was that in this hawk Nature is thinking' (Faas 1980: 199). The key question is how far Hughes succeeds in realising his aim to represent Nature thinking through the hawk – how well, in other words, he rises to Buell's challenge to speak 'as nature, as a nonhuman animal'. For Alan Bold, Hughes achieves 'a remarkable feat of empathy' with the hawk, even though the result is misanthropic, as indeed it is in much of Jeffers's poetry (1976: 61). Ekbert Faas goes further, calling the hawk a 'startlingly autonomous product' which 'invades our consciousness' through 'its numinous force' (1980: 67). For Herbert Lomas and Keith Sagar, on the other hand, the poem is unconvincing. As Lomas sees it, the hawk is 'heavily anthropomorphized' and 'thinks as no bird could' (1987: 413–14). Sagar agrees, making the more subtle point too that 'Hughes cannot yet get behind the fallen nature of our tradition, and therefore cannot render the hawk's vision other than in terms of deranged human vision' (2006: 116).

Like 'Rock and Hawk', 'Hawk Roosting' is a self-consciously Darwinian poem. Darwinism gives Hughes a warrant for his anthropomorphism, but it also reminds us that we remain blind to the 'Earth-secrets' of other species. Neither Jeffers nor Hughes realise the ultimate unknowability of the hawk's mind. In presuming to comprehend its 'fierce consciousness', they project on to it their own preconceived and selective idea of nature after Darwin, rather than presenting the hawk in and for itself. To paraphrase Nagel, Hughes has gone beyond asking what it would be like for him to be a hawk himself, but he has not gone so far as to depict persuasively what it might be like for the hawk itself to be a hawk. Hughes's hawk remarks that 'It took the whole of Creation / To produce my foot, my each feather' (ll. 10–11), yet it is not clear why a hawk should think about nature teleologically merely because humans have made the same mistake. When the hawk declares that 'No arguments assert my right [to kill]' (l. 20), this assertion itself presupposes distinctively human concepts of rights and justification even as it denies them. And why should a hawk – or Nature, for that matter – insist 'Nothing has changed since I began. / My eye has permitted no change' (ll. 22–3)? These quirks make sense if we read 'Hawk Roosting' – like Morgan's 'Archaeopteryx's Song' or Hughes's own 'Wodwo' – as a satire on human arrogance through the device of the anthropomorphic animal. But that is not the poem Hughes meant to write.

While 'Hawk Roosting' is typical of Hughes's animal poems in its preoccupation with predation, it is atypical in generalising from a single animal to nature as a whole. In poems such as 'Jaguar', 'Pike' and 'Wolfwatching', Hughes again meditates on the exterior and interior worlds of fierce, predatory animals. But where Hughes's jaguar, pike and wolves bear witness to Darwinian nature, they are not required to embody it. They remain animals, not symbols. On the other hand, when Hughes transforms an animal into a myth in *Crow*, it comes to embody a dark and highly personal vision of life which incorporates Darwinism but at the same time moves beyond it. By contrast, the hawk in 'Hawk Roosting' is neither itself nor a living myth embodying Hughes's own vision but rather a received idea.

Both Jeffers and Hughes strong-arm the hawk into a predetermined role. For a poem to bring out the hawk's full power as a symbol of Darwinian nature, the encounter with the hawk has to come as a genuine revelation. One poem which achieves this is 'Sea-Hawk' by the American poet Richard Eberhart, published two years before Hughes's poem in his collection *Great Praises*:

The six-foot nest of the sea-hawk,
Almost inaccessible,
Surveys from the headland the lonely, the violent waters.

I have driven him off,
Somewhat foolhardily,
And look into the fierce eye of the offspring.

It is an eye of fire,
An eye of icy crystal,
A threat of ancient purity,

Power of an immense reserve,
An agate-well of purpose,
Life before man, and maybe after.

How many centuries of sight
In this piercing, inhuman perfection
Stretch the gaze off the rocky promontory,

To make the mind exult
At the eye of a sea-hawk,
A blaze of grandeur, permanence of the impersonal.

The hawk (here an osprey chick) has broadly the same set of meanings for Eberhart as it does for Jeffers and Hughes. It symbolises the inhuman power of nonhuman nature. It is 'fierce', with a 'piercing' gaze and the will to fulfil its own 'purpose'. Like Jeffers, Eberhart associates his hawk with the 'permanence' of rock, and sees it as emblematic of life before and after humankind.

The difference between Eberhart's poem and Jeffers's lies not in the symbolic significance of the hawk, but in the way that significance is communicated. In 'Sea-Hawk', the poet encounters the symbolic bird as if for the first time, and the encounter carries the conviction of a personal revelation. The first two verses of 'Sea-Hawk' set the scene. The 'lonely, violent' sea, the 'inaccessible' cliff and the huge nest build up an impression of a suitably wild landscape, much like that of so many of Jeffers's own poems. Unlike Jeffers, however, who identifies himself with the rugged landscape in poems like 'Continent's End', Eberhart has 'somewhat foolhardily' trespassed on this scene. Even on its own, this two-word description of his behaviour gives a sense of his character. He knows he is taking a risk, but knows too that it is not as great a risk as all that. This poet is an amateur adventurer, not a self-appointed seer. He is a curious but also self-deprecating everyman, looking into the hawk's eye as we read. This persona gives his reactions to the hawk an authenticity and an immediacy that Jeffers's lack in 'Rock and Hawk', even though Eberhart's language is more conventionally poetic than Jeffers's, for example in its Petrarchan juxtaposition of fire and ice.

In 'Rock and Hawk', Jeffers describes his symbols in abstract terms: 'power' and 'peace', 'consciousness' and 'disinterestedness', realism and mysticism. In 'Sea-Hawk', Eberhart explores the symbolic meaning of his hawk through further symbols: the 'fire', reignited (in an echo of Darwin himself) as a 'blaze of grandeur', the 'icy crystal', the 'agate-well'. Together these different images for the hawk's eye capture the experience of trying to comprehend its gaze by drawing it into analogy with other phenomena. Yet as the chosen analogies suggest, for Eberhart the hawk is an ultimately incomprehensible elemental force, a 'threat of ancient purity'. Eberhart is able to use abstract phrases like this more effectively than Jeffers does, partly because his poem has its leavening of imagery and partly because his repeated formulation – an x of y – suggests a greater depth of field than Jeffers's monumental pairings.

Above all, Eberhart gives the impression of time as a perspective in his poem. He stares down the 'centuries of sight' with the hatchling hawk as he gazes into the 'agate-well' of its eye. Jeffers too insists on the 'permanence of the impersonal', but he gives us no vantage point from which to see it. We are told about it, but we experience none of the vertigo which in Eberhart's poem makes us realise it for ourselves. In 'Continent's End', Jeffers succeeds in turning himself into an embodiment of the raw elemental force underlying life, but it is Eberhart rather than Jeffers or Hughes who best succeeds in remaking a hawk into a symbol of a specifically Darwinian nature.

'A diminished thing': Songbirds and birdsong

As ruthless and efficient predators, raptors are obvious candidates to be turned into symbols of Darwinian nature, although the very fact that they seem so fitting makes it all too easy for poets to project onto them their own vision of nature red in beak and claw. Unlike birds of prey, songbirds are not such vivid emblems of Darwinism. Many of them are predators, but that goes largely unnoticed; the death of a worm or a snail does not trouble even the sweetest sentimentalist very greatly. Instead, Darwinian poets are drawn to these songbirds by their place in the poetic tradition, above all by the model of such famous Romantic poems as Shelley's 'To a Skylark' and Keats's 'Ode to a Nightingale'.

Darwinian poetry about songbirds directly answers these Romantic poems, so they share many of the same motifs. In both, the poem rehearses the poet's experience of hearing a bird singing in distinctive circumstances. It records the mood that the song stimulates, seeking to explain or interpret its meaning. But Darwinian poetry undermines the ecstasies of the Romantics. The typical Darwinian songbird is undistinguished. In place of skylarks and nightingales, both of which are genuinely remarkable in their songs and behaviour, we are shown thrushes and wood warblers. Where the Romantic songbird is ethereal, even mythic – a 'blithe spirit' ('To a Skylark', l. 1) or a 'dryad' ('Ode to a Nightingale', l. 7) – the Darwinian songbird is simply a bird. Where the song of the Romantic songbird is transcendent, that of the Darwinian songbird is earthbound, with the promise of 'rapture so divine' ('To a Skylark', l. 65) distinctly muted.

Three well-known poems which span the twentieth century form the core of the Darwinian tradition of songbird poetry, answering each other as well as their Romantic forebears. These are Hardy's 'The Darkling Thrush', first published in *The Graphic* in December 1900; Robert Frost's 'The Oven Bird', from his collection *Mountain Interval*, published in 1916; and Amy Clampitt's 'A Hermit Thrush', from her collection *Archaic Figure*, published in 1987. Here is Hardy's poem:

> I leant upon a coppice gate
>   When Frost was spectre-gray,
> And Winter's dregs made desolate
>   The weakening eye of day.
> The tangled bine-stems scored the sky
>   Like strings of broken lyres,
> And all mankind that haunted nigh
>   Had sought their household fires.
>
> The land's sharp features seemed to be
>   The Century's corpse outleant,
> His crypt the cloudy canopy,
>   The wind his death-lament.
> The ancient pulse of germ and birth
>   Was shrunken hard and dry,
> And every spirit upon earth
>   Seemed fervourless as I.
>
> At once a voice arose among
>   The bleak twigs overhead
> In a full-hearted evensong
>   Of joy illimited;

An aged thrush, frail, gaunt, and small,
    In blast-beruffled plume,
Had chosen thus to fling his soul
    Upon the growing gloom.

So little cause for carolings
    Of such ecstatic sound
Was written on terrestrial things
    Afar or nigh around,
That I could think there trembled through
    His happy good-night air
Some blessed Hope, whereof he knew
    And I was unaware.

Here is Frost's:

There is a singer everyone has heard,
Loud, a mid-summer and a mid-wood bird,
Who makes the solid tree trunks sound again.
He says that leaves are old and that for flowers
Mid-summer is to spring as one to ten.
He says the early petal-fall is past,
When pear and cherry bloom went down in showers
On sunny days a moment overcast;
And comes that other fall we name the fall.
He says the highway dust is over all.
The bird would cease and be as other birds
But that he knows in singing not to sing.
The question that he frames in all but words
Is what to make of a diminished thing.

And here is the encounter with the hermit thrush from the end of Clampitt's:

Watching
the longest day take cover under
a monk's-cowl overcast,

with thunder, rain and wind, then waiting,
we drop everything to listen as a
hermit thrush distills its fragmentary,
hesitant, in the end

unbroken music. From what source (beyond us, or
the wells within?) such links perceived arrive –
diminished sequences so uninsistingly
not even human – there's

hardly a vocabulary left to wonder, uncertain
as we are of so much in this existence, this
botched, cumbersome, much-mended,
not unsatisfactory thing.

(ll. 62–76)

The theme of all three of these poems is disenchantment, 'what to make
of a diminished thing'. Where the hawks in Darwinian poetry symbolize
predatory nature, these birds call attention to and address the dearth of
spiritual meaning in a material universe.

On the face of it, Hardy's poem seems close to the Romantic model. For
all that it is 'frail, gaunt, and small', his thrush sings beautifully with an
ecstasy that the poet cannot match but that nonetheless inspires him. By
contrast, Frost's oven bird – a wood warbler – 'is prosaic; he says rather than
sings', as John Cunningham observes (2001: 266), and 'knows . . . not to
sing'. To begin with, Clampitt's hermit thrush too can only manage a 'fragmentary' and 'hesitant' song. Even once its song has become 'unbroken', it
remains, in a direct echo of Frost, 'diminished'.

Yet this contrast between Hardy on the one side and Frost and Clampitt
on the other is more a matter of style or technique than substance. Shelley
and Keats write rapturously about the transcendent beauty of the skylark's
and the nightingale's songs. They voice directly the heightened state of
mind into which they are transported, even as they allow that that state
of mind is unsustainable and can never reach the birds' own ecstasy. But
Hardy remains untransported. The thrush's ecstasy is beyond his comprehension. He confidently attributes its song to 'joy illimited', but he cannot
ascertain the cause of that joy at all, and nor can he fully share it.

Some of Hardy's critics have charged him with cynicism in 'The Darkling
Thrush'. The poet Donald Davie suggested that he wrote it as an anthology
piece, deliberately engineering it to be ambiguous in order to cater both
to the disillusioned (like himself) and to those who would prefer a more
upbeat message to greet the new century (1973: 38; see also Mallett 2000:
331). For all that it is couched in Christian terms of 'evensong' and bless-
ings, the consolation offered by 'The Darkling Thrush' is surely very faint.
Even in the moment of 'Hope', all Hardy gives us is a possibility without
conviction ('I could think') that there may be 'Some' vague hope of which

he himself remains 'unaware'. These closing lines identify hope as a form of faith, but in their very hesitancy they reduce that faith to a broken parody of faith itself, making Hardy's projection of hope onto the bird seem little more than a wish-fulfilment driven by his own inability to find any other grounds for hope.

Yet Hardy's poem is consolatory nonetheless. In spite of the irony of resting hope on such a fragile base as birdsong out of season, in spite even of the grotesque morbidity which sees the Earth itself as a corpse, 'The Darkling Thrush' is a comforting poem, even to the disillusioned. What Hardy gives us, as in his poems to Emma, is the consolation of poetry itself. Strikingly – and unusually for Hardy – 'The Darkling Thrush' is written in an entirely regular iambic metre. Measured out over a consistent alternation of four- and three-beat lines this regularity is reassuring. It is this comfort – the comfort deriving from the poetic form itself – that sustains the impression that the old thrush's song might be a comfort in its own right.

The mood Hardy's metre creates does not belie his Darwinian pessimism, in which even 'The ancient pulse of germ and birth' seems bereft of purpose or meaning. But it does assuage it, recreating something of the easy happiness that the thrush genuinely appears to feel. In this, it offers us a surrogate for a hope that the poem suggests may be too faint to be sustained in itself. Furthermore, the regular pulse of the verse recalls, even revives, the 'pulse of germ and birth' itself. As in 'Rain on a Grave' and 'Drummer Hodge', Hardy reminds us, if only faintly, that fresh life grows from death, just as the end of one century is the birth of the next.

The irony of Hardy's poem lies in the disjunction between the birdsong itself and the weight of significance placed upon it, a disjunction he himself draws out when he emphasises how 'little cause' there is in the external world for trusting to that significance at all. The same irony underlies Frost's poem. Cunningham suggests that the claim 'that the bird "knows" and "says"', that is, 'understands, interprets', is given the lie because 'we know in Frost that unself-conscious birds cannot do so' (2001: 267). But this reading seems over-determined, given that Frost recognises mind even in a mite in 'A Considerable Speck'. It is not so much that the oven bird cannot think like this as that we have no grounds for thinking it would.

Robert Pack makes this point in an illuminating reading of 'The Oven Bird' in his study *Belief and Uncertainty in the Poetry of Robert Frost*. Pack points out that Frost begins the poem with the 'playful and strategic lie' that everyone has heard the oven bird sing. As Pack notes, 'Frost knows perfectly well that not every reader has heard the call of an oven bird' (I haven't, for one). What is more, 'surely no one has heard an oven bird that says "leaves are old" or that "the early petal-fall is past'" (Pack 2004b: 137). It is not the bird's understanding or even interpretation that is at issue, but the claim that we can know that understanding – its 'Earth-secret' – for ourselves. This is all to the point because, as Pack brilliantly observes, 'Frost is playing a game with the reader's credulity, for the question of what we can believe on the basis of the little that we know is precisely the problem Frost is exploring here', precisely the question Hardy raises too in 'The Darkling Thrush' (ibid.: 138).

Like Hughes's hawk, Frost's oven bird sounds like a person, not a bird. In Hughes's poem, this is a problem, because it is supposedly the bird itself who is speaking. But in Frost's poem we only ever hear what the speaker tells us it says. So 'The Oven Bird' is not a portrait of the bird itself at all, but rather of the speaker. His view of life, like Hardy's, is morose. Frost does not copy Hardy's ghoulish imagery, but he intimates that he shares his preoccupation with death in the image of the 'highway dust' that 'is over all'. He shares too his vision of nature as somehow lessened – 'shrunken' in Hardy, 'diminished' in Frost.

Where Hardy conventionally sets that vision in winter, Frost goes further, telling us that even mid-summer itself is a diminishment. This is pessimism taken to the point of perversity. It would be shocking, had Frost not skilfully set up his poem to be familiar and homely. Again, metre plays a part here. Frost uses the iambic pentameter as his basic metre, varying it enough to create his characteristic conversational effect without undermining its measured authority. He teases us too with a pun in the third line, hinting that the oven bird (and the poem) may have a healing gift, making the trees 'sound', that is healthy, not merely resonant. This note of optimism is soon drowned out, but even as the poem's elegiac tone becomes established that tone itself continues to hold out that promise that we too may become 'sound again'. Frost works to achieve this by reconciling us to the disillusionment that he smuggles into the poem, both through a confrontation with it – typically for Frost, indirectly, as that disillusionment is projected onto the bird – and through the soothing power of elegy itself.

Frost's perverse insistence that even summer is a diminishment is a step too far for Clampitt. Instead she reinstates the longest day as the moment at which 'the months-long exhalation of diminishment' (l. 30) begins. But the landscape in which her poem's speaker and its addressee make their picnic already seems diminished itself, bearing the scars of 'yet another winter' (l. 11) even in the height of summer. Throughout her poem Clampitt repeats certain key-words which knit her diffuse meditations together. She repeats four times the idea that very little in life is 'certain' (ll. 1, 28, 57,

73). The poem is shot through with Hardyesque negatives prefixed with 'un-' and with negative clauses too: 'Nothing's certain' (l. 1), 'there's no knowing' (l. 10), 'there's no use' (l. 19), 'there's nothing here' (l. 20), 'that no point is fixed, that there's no foothold' (l. 37) and so on. Even when these clauses and words are themselves neutral – 'the low-tide-uncovered isthmus' (l. 2), for example – they combine to create an impression of a mind trapped in its own pessimism.

But, like Hardy and Frost, Clampitt seeks to make something of this diminished thing. She does so by easing herself out of this pessimism, using the same device of repetition that she uses to create it. Alongside the insistent negatives, from a little over half-way through her poem she begins also to repeat the idea of mending, as 'from / year to year the earth's sore surface / mends and rebinds itself' (ll. 45–7). The poem's overarching concern is with another repeated term, 'attachment' (ll. 17, 43, 61), to places and, less overtly but more poignantly, to people. By the beginning of the end of the poem, Clampitt has achieved a hesitant equilibrium whereby 'all attachment may prove at best, perhaps, / a broken, a much-mended thing' (ll. 61–2). She is neither sure of this claim nor satisfied by it, but this oscillation of breaking and mending appears to be the best that can be hoped for.

This is her state of mind, mirrored in the unseasonable weather, when the hermit thrush begins to sing 'its fragmentary, / hesitant, in the end // unbroken music'. The syntax of Clampitt's last sentence, as she responds to the bird's song, is so tortuous that it is hard to decipher. She appears to be asking directly a question Hardy and Frost raise through their ironies: whether the significance we give to birdsong comes from 'beyond us, or / the wells within?' She poses this question by focussing on the 'links' which make the song appear 'unbroken' to us. In effect, she asks whether the 'not even human' 'sequences' of the bird's song mean something in themselves, that is to the bird, or only to us. She gives no answer to this question, but the birdsong has an impact on her all the same. As with Hardy and Frost, it is this impact that is key, not the unknowable meaning inherent in the song. In the poem's closing line, after repeating the motifs of uncertainty and mending, she resolves her pessimism through a double negative, again stating directly what Hardy and Frost suggest through their use of verse. 'Botched' and 'cumbersome' as it is, 'much-mended' as it needs to be, life is 'not unsatisfactory' after all.

'The Darkling Thrush', 'The Oven Bird' and 'A Hermit Thrush' form a unified tradition of Darwinian poems about songbirds in the twentieth century. There are two earlier poems which reply to the Romantic tradition from a Darwinian perspective to very different effect. Meredith's

'The Lark Ascending' was published in the *Fortnightly Review* in 1881 and reprinted alongside 'The Woods of Westermain' in *Poems and Lyrics of the Joy of Earth* in 1883. Hardy's 'Shelley's Skylark' was published in 1901 in the same collection as 'The Darkling Thrush', but a headnote to the poem traces its origin back to Hardy's tour of Italy in the Spring of 1887. Both of these poems are inspired more directly by Shelley than the poems I have discussed so far, and they share in his uplifted and uplifting response to the skylark. But while they do not confront either the violence of natural selection nor the disenchantment of materialism each remains a distinctively Darwinian poem.

Structurally, 'The Lark Ascending' follows 'To a Skylark' closely. In each poem the poet listens to and meditates on the sound of a skylark singing in a field. Each begins with a description of the birdsong itself (Shelley, ll. 1–60; Meredith, ll. 1–64). Both go on to ponder what the song might be about (Shelley, ll. 61–85; Meredith, ll. 65–84) and to contrast the lark's uninhibited joy with human constraints and grief (Shelley, ll. 86–100; Meredith, ll. 85–98). Finally, each poet takes the lark and its song as an ideal for the poet himself (Shelley, ll. 101–5; Meredith, ll. 99–122).

Turning from the structure of the two poems to their form and language, however, we see the contrasts between them straightaway. This is the first sentence (or two, depending on how you read the punctuation) of Shelley's poem, which is also its first verse:

> Hail to thee, blithe Spirit!
>   Bird thou never wert,
> That from Heaven, or near it,
>   Pourest thy full heart
> In profuse strains of unpremeditated art.
>   (ll. 1–5)

This is the first half of Meredith's first sentence:

> He rises and begins to round,
> He drops the silver chain of sound,
> Of many links without a break,
> In chirrup, whistle, slur and shake,
> All intervolved and spreading wide,
> Like water-dimples down a tide
> Where ripple ripple overcurls
> And eddy into eddy whirls;

A press of hurried notes that run
So fleet they scarce are more than one,
Yet changeingly the trills repeat
And linger ringing while they fleet,
Sweet to the quick o' the ear, and dear
To her beyond the handmaid ear,
Who sits beside our inner springs,
Too often dry for this he brings,
Which seems the very jet of earth
At sight of sun, her music's mirth,
As up he wings the spiral stair,
A song of light, and pierces air
With fountain ardour, fountain play,
To reach the shining tops of day,
And drink in everything discerned
An ecstasy to music turned,
Impelled by what his happy bill
Disperses; drinking, showering still,
Unthinking save that he may give
His voice the outlet, there to live
Renewed in endless notes of glee,
So thirsty of his voice is he,
For all to hear and all to know
That he is joy, awake, aglow,
The tumult of the heart to hear
Through pureness filtered crystal-clear,
And know the pleasure sprinkled bright
By simple singing of delight . . .

(ll. 1–36)

The contrast is glaring. Shelley's stanza is five lines long. Meredith goes on without a full stop for sixty-four lines in total. Yet both poets derive their verse form from their subject: the skylark itself. Shelley's stanza reproduces in the ear and (horizontally) on the page the lark's (vertically) undulating flight. Meredith chooses rather to imitate its song. The terms used by standard bird guides to describe the skylark's song – a 'long aerial song' with 'sweet liquid notes' (Robbins et al. 1983: 218), 'an apparently endless warbling song' (Watson and Campbell 1980: 122), a 'high-pitched, slightly jangled but brilliantly musical outpouring' (Peterson et al. 1993: 163) – match the poem almost exactly. Meredith uses a raft of techniques to create this effect. There is direct onomatopoeia, as he names the bird's chirrup, whistle, trill and so on. There is indirect onomatopoeia too, as he imitates these sounds in other phrases such as 'Where ripple ripple overcurls / And eddy into eddy whirls' and 'Yet changeingly the trills repeat / And linger ringing while they fleet', echoing respectively the 'liquid' quality of the lark's song, alluded to too in the pattern of imagery built up around moving water, and its high-pitched jangling. The regular flow of the metre and the unwavering rhyming couplets recall these two patterns of sound as well, while Meredith's immensely long sentence simulates the lark's 'apparently endless' song made up of 'links without a break'.

The difference in form between Shelley's poem and Meredith's is matched by a difference in idiom. Where Shelley uses a complex five-line stanza form, Meredith uses the most familiar and popular English metre, the four-beat iambic rhyming couplet. Where Shelley's style is self-consciously poetic, Meredith's is plainly popular or demotic. Even his coinages such as 'water-dimples' and 'overcurls' are made up of familiar words brought together. These different forms and idioms are appropriate to each poet's vision. Shelley's skylark is otherworldly. His conceit, that the bird is a 'blithe spirit', is matched with a poetic form and style that is removed from everyday language. Meredith's lark, on the other hand, is very much of this Earth, so he writes about it in familiar idiomatic English.

In 'To a Skylark', Shelley places his lark beyond knowledge, and so beyond science. Having declared 'What thou art we know not', all he can seek to answer is the question 'What is most like thee?' (ll. 31–2) His poem is therefore a tissue of similes, for the bird itself, not just for its song. Meredith too uses similes, likening the song to water rippling, dew trembling, rain on a wind-blown aspen tree, and so on. But the bird itself is never in doubt. It is a fellow creature. It lives in the pastoral, arable, partly wooded landscape that is its typical English habitat, and its song awakens 'The best in us to him akin' (l. 56).

Grounded as it is in this ecological and evolutionary reality, Meredith's poem nevertheless offers a Romantic transcendence of its own. The promise of 'unbodied joy' (l. 15) held out by Shelley's skylark remains forever out of reach. Even Shelley himself can only hope to learn 'half the gladness / That thy brain must know' (ll. 101–2). By contrast, the 'joy, awake, aglow' embodied in Meredith's lark is available to us all:

And you shall hear the herb and tree,
The better heart of men shall see,
Shall feel celestially, as long
As you crave nothing save the song.
(ll. 81–4)

Meredith's lark itself does indeed 'crave' its song. It is 'thirsty' to 'drink' its own voice. This impulse aside, it is 'unthinking' in its 'ecstasy'. Because of this it is able to sing a 'song seraphically free / Of taint of personality' (ll. 93–4). In these lines Meredith holds out the promise that we too can attain the same impersonal, celestial, seraphic state as the lark, if we can only achieve the 'self-forgetfulness divine' (l. 114) which occurs 'In the brain's reflex of yon bird' (l. 112).

To do this, we must lose ourselves as the lark itself does in the 'love of Earth' – a phrase Meredith repeats to ensure that we grasp its full importance (ll. 66, 108). As he sings, the lark takes in and becomes one with what he witnesses: 'The woods and brooks, the sheep and kine, / He is, the hills, the human line, / The meadows green, the fallows brown', even 'The dreams of labour in the town' (ll. 71–4). This is a transcendent experience, not merely for the lark itself, but for all those who are transformed by its song, as they enter imaginatively into it.

In the closing lines of his poem, Meredith draws a parallel between the lark and men 'whom we revere, / Now names, and men still housing here' (ll. 99–100). Like the lark's, their 'love of Earth is deep' (l. 108), so the lark's song puts Meredith in mind of them. In the process, the boundary between Meredith himself and these sages – men like Thomas Carlyle, whose recent death Meredith alludes to here, and perhaps Darwin himself – collapses:

> Wherefore their soul in me, or mine,
> Through self-forgetfulness divine,
> In them, that song aloft maintains,
> To fill the sky and thrill the plains
> With showerings drawn from human stores,
> As he [the lark] to silence nearer soars,
> Extends the world at wings and dome,
> More spacious making more our home,
> Till lost on his aërial rings
> In light, and then the fancy sings.
>
> (ll. 113–22)

The process by which Meredith's 'soul' becomes indistinguishable from theirs – and from the lark's – recalls the process of reading itself, as readers subsume themselves, if only partially and temporarily, in the minds of others. The more we lose ourselves in Meredith's poem, the more we fulfil his aim and the closer we come to the state of mind he identifies with the lark. In these closing lines, the poem itself vanishes in its transcendent reverie, first nearing 'silence' like the lark, then disappearing out of sight and into pure 'fancy' at the very moment the bird itself does.

'The Lark Ascending' is the longest and most ambitious of the Darwinian songbird poems. It aims not just to compensate us for the disenchantment that comes with Darwinism but to overturn it with a Darwinian re-enchantment of its own. The state of mind that Meredith embodies in 'The Lark Ascending' is mystical, but it does not need a non-material cosmology to sustain it. Instead, the bird's example – the sound of its song and its joy in its natural environment – is sufficient, assisted and imitated by the mantra-like rhythms of the poem itself. But Meredith's ambition nonetheless leads to a paradox. The poem's regular rhythms and rhymes may indeed help to bring about the mystical state of mind that it advocates. Yet the more they do so, the harder it is to concentrate on the words themselves. In creating a form that approximates to birdsong Meredith runs the risk that we will only hear its sounds and not its meaning. But then, if that happens, the poem has already succeeded in bringing about the very abstraction from thought and personal preoccupations that it promises.

Meredith's Darwinian Romanticism is attractive, and I will return to it again in Chapter 8. His playful exuberance and metrical wizardry remain enchanting too, for all that his overt didacticism is out of fashion. Hardy's response to 'To a Skylark', 'Shelley's Skylark', is playful and exuberant without being didactic. It too remains fresh 100 years on:

Somewhere afield here something lies
In Earth's oblivious eyeless trust
That moved a poet to prophecies –
A pinch of unseen, unguarded dust:

The dust of the lark that Shelley heard,
And made immortal through times to be; –
Though it only lived like another bird,
And knew not its immortality:

Lived its meek life; then, one day, fell –
A little ball of feather and bone;
And how it perished, when piped farewell,
And where it wastes, are alike unknown.

Maybe it rests in the loam I view,
Maybe it throbs in a myrtle's green,

Maybe it sleeps in the coming hue
Of a grape on the slopes of yon inland scene.

Go find it, faeries, go and find
That tiny pinch of priceless dust,
And bring a casket silver-lined,
And framed of gold that gems encrust;

And we will lay it safe therein,
And consecrate it to endless time;
For it inspired a bard to win
Ecstatic heights in thought and rhyme.

Like 'The Darkling Thrush' and Hardy's elegies for Emma, 'Shelley's Skylark' is an exploration of the power of poetry in a world where nature is strictly material. Its first three stanzas establish its terms of reference. On the one side is a Darwinian, materialist view of nature, in which 'Earth' is 'oblivious' and the lark just 'another bird', a 'little ball of feather and bone'. On the other is Shelley's poetry, through which, unbeknown to itself, the lark is given 'its immortality'.

As Hardy seeks to bridge this divide in his poem, he sets in train a series of playful paradoxes. His image of the bird as a poetic relic, to be preserved in a mock-reliquary, is a fanciful parody of Italian Roman Catholicism, reinforced by Hardy's decision to include 'Shelley's Skylark', set in the countryside around Livorno, in the section of *Poems of the Past and Present* headed 'Poems of Pilgrimage'. But this particular relic is strictly material. It is just 'dust'. This dust is priceless, however, because when it was alive it inspired Shelley. Yet its pricelessness inheres not in the dust itself at all, but in Shelley's poem, which already guarantees its immortality and will persist regardless. Again, though the dust is clearly material, it can only be found by invoking supernatural 'faeries', like those in *A Midsummer Night's Dream* – reasonably enough, as only impossible agents can perform impossible tasks. Finally, by laying the bird's venerable dust safe in its reliquary, the poet and his faeries would in fact be depriving it of the actual life after death that it already has (albeit equally unknowingly) since being absorbed back into the vibrant, anapaestic cycle of living nature, as Emma Hardy is in 'Rain on a Grave'.

'Shelley's Skylark' conjures up supernatural agencies within a material world. These agencies, the 'faeries', do not represent the supernatural itself, but the supernatural or transcendent power of poetry. Poetry, Hardy suggests, is a kind of magic. It can bestow immortality and conjure faeries to perform further impossible but charmingly trivial tasks. It can even make the trivial seem wonderful, as Hardy does here. The skylark heard by Shelley was nothing but a bird, but in the 'ecstatic heights' of his poetry it becomes something immortal. In a whimsical parallel, Hardy's own skylark has been turned from a pinch of dust into a gorgeous sacred relic. Yet it remains dust throughout. Like magic, poetry transforms the world by transforming how we see it, not the thing itself. For Hardy, unlike Meredith, the idealism of 'fancy' is only ever an illusionist's trick, never a path to enlightenment. In 'Shelley's Skylark', the Darwinian world is transformed into something sublime in Shelley's poem and something delightfully ridiculous in Hardy's own. But nature itself is still strictly material, dust is still dust, and the Earth remains oblivious.

'SOMEONE ELSE ADDITIONAL TO HIM': DEER IN MODERN POETRY

One of the central tenets of modern ecocriticism is that writers and artists should let other animals be. That is, animals should be 'celebrated in and for themselves rather than being subjugated to human purposes' (Pinkney 1999: 414; see also Buell 2005: 55; Garrard 2004: 31–2). Applying this test to the poems I have discussed so far in this chapter, both the hawk poems and the songbird poems tend to fall short. Jeffers and Hughes impose their own meanings on their hawks when they take them to be symbols of a Darwinian vision of nature. Frost does the same with his oven bird, albeit knowingly. Eberhart's osprey chick is transformed into an elemental force, while Hardy imagines his thrush as a seer and celebrates his lark not for itself but because it inspired Shelley. As for Clampitt's hermit thrush, it has little more than a cameo in the poem named after it. Only Meredith enters into the mind of his lark in its own right and for its own sake, and then only initially.

There is one strand of Darwinian animal poetry in particular, however, that addresses the implications of our evolutionary and ecological relationship to other animals by letting them be. These are poems about deer. As the only large and largely unthreatening wild animals that still exist in any numbers in Britain, and among the few still at large in America, deer lend themselves to poems which consider animals as fellow creatures inhabiting a wild natural world of which we ourselves are no longer a part. From *Sir Gawain and the Green Knight* to John Davidson's 'A Runnable Stag', the occasion for earlier poetry about deer in English tended to be the hunt. This tradition has not died out entirely – witness Hughes's powerful poem 'The Stag' – but it is increasingly anachronistic, particularly in England. No longer coloured by predation, the relationship between humans and deer need not be bound by preconceived notions of nature red in tooth and claw. Instead, the incidental encounter between human being and deer has become a recurrent motif, as our different worlds come fleetingly into contact with one another.

Like 'An August Midnight', Darwinian poems about deer tend to be structured by the twin Darwinian realisations of our kinship to animals and of the ultimately unbridgeable distance between us. Hardy's 'The Fallow Deer at the Lonely House', published in 1922, is an early example. An apparently slight poem, it nonetheless establishes the central themes of the genre:

> One without looks in to-night
>   Through the curtain-chink
> From the sheet of glistening white;
> One without looks in to-night
>   As we sit and think
>   By the fender-brink.
>
> We do not discern those eyes
>   Watching in the snow;
> Lit by lamps of rosy dyes
> We do not discern those eyes
>   Wondering, aglow,
>   Fourfooted, tiptoe.

The domestic scenario in this poem is unusual for a poem about a wild animal, but the sense of a divide between the poet and the deer is typical. Hardy uses the window, the curtain and the walls of the house as physical markers of this separation between the human sphere and nature. But there is a further divide too. As Susan Miller has pointed out, Hardy's speaker knows and at the same time does not know that the deer is there (2007: 102–4). We can resolve this paradox if we choose to. Perhaps Hardy knows in his mind that the deer is there, even though he cannot see it. But a visionary imagination does not square with the emphasis Hardy places on his unawareness of the deer's presence in the second stanza. A more satisfactory resolution might be to read Hardy as re-imagining a scene he experienced perhaps the night before, in the light of the discovery that there was a deer standing outside his window, though he did not know it at the time. Perhaps the deer left footprints. After all, Hardy tells us twice that there was snow on the ground.

These speculations may seem extraneous to the poem itself, but they help to identify the source of the paradox, which is Hardy's decision to write his poem in the present tense. Through the disparity between what the speaker knows in the present moment of the poem and what he knows as he narrates it in the present tense, Hardy both registers and transcends the barrier of time between himself and the deer. By the time he knows the deer was there, it has gone. But by writing in the present tense, Hardy recovers the encounter with the deer within his imagination even as he affirms that that encounter did not in fact happen. The immediacy of the present tense carries with it a sense of possibility. The speaker might yet twitch the curtain and meet the deer's gaze. If he were to, he would see that it is a creature capable of 'wondering' – being curious, or perhaps marvelling – as he is himself. Hardy establishes the possibility of reciprocal curiosity and wonder here, but walls and time obstruct it, and the deer is left alone to wonder to itself about humankind.

This motif of a thwarted encounter between human and deer is reworked by Edna St Vincent Millay in her poem 'The Fawn', from 1934:

There it was I saw what I shall never forget
And never retrieve.
Monstrous and beautiful to human eyes, hard to believe,
He lay, yet there he lay,
Asleep on the moss, his head on his polished cleft small ebony hooves,
The child of the doe, the dappled child of the deer.

Surely his mother had never said, "Lie here
Till I return," so spotty and plain to see
On the green moss lay he.
His eyes had opened; he considered me.

I would have given more than I care to say
To thrifty ears, might I have had him for my friend
One moment only of that forest day:

Might I have had the acceptance, not the love
Of those clear eyes;
Might I have been for him the bough above
Or the root beneath his forest bed,
A part of the forest, seen without surprise.

Was it alarm, or was it the wind of my fear lest he depart
That jerked him to his jointy knees,

And sent him crashing off, leaping and stumbling
On his new legs, between the stems of the white trees?

In some ways, Millay's poem is an inversion of Hardy's. Here it is the human who has entered the deer's environment, rather than the other way round. Where Hardy writes in the present tense, Millay emphasises the fact that she can 'never retrieve' her encounter by writing about it in the past tense. And where Hardy never meets his fallow deer, Millay and the fawn do indeed encounter one another face to face. Yet the awareness that the deer is a conscious being, with thoughts as well as feelings, is the same: Hardy's deer wonders, Millay's considers. So too is the divide between them, symbolised in the physical walls of Hardy's house in 'The Fallow Deer at the Lonely House'.

This divide is the more absolute in Millay's poem because it is confirmed by the meeting itself. Hardy hints that the deer is alien to us by reminding us that these watching eyes belong to a mind that is 'fourfooted'. Millay registers the fawn's otherness immediately and more dramatically in the word 'monstrous'. This is an extraordinary way to describe a young deer. It would be perplexing, even grotesque, were it not followed by the description of it as 'beautiful' and 'hard to believe'. Unlike Hardy, Millay is predominantly an urban poet. For her, the natural world is both wonderful and fearful because she is alienated from it, as the fawn's response to her painfully reminds her. She has no hope of being 'a part of the forest' because her own response to it is so self-conscious. Her very desire for the fawn's 'acceptance' is so intense that she suspects he may have got wind of it. She longs to be 'seen without surprise', and yet she is palpably surprised herself when she sees the fawn.

In 'The Woods of Westermain', Meredith counsels:

You must love the light so well
That no darkness will seem fell.
Love it so you could accost
Fellowly a livid ghost.
Whish! the phantom wisps away,
Owns him smoke to cocks of day.

(IV, ll. 1–6)

As in 'The Lark Ascending', Meredith's self-conscious teaching is to abandon self-consciousness and do as nature does. 'The Fawn' encapsulates the difficulty of acting on this advice. Millay does indeed move beyond her first, disturbed response to the fawn, accepting and reaching out to it as a young, perhaps orphaned animal, not a monster. Yet the fawn itself will not accept her. No matter how much she longs that it were not, the barrier between the two of them seems impassable.

Other poems of the same period capture the same sense of an impassable barrier between humans and animals in different ways. In Jeffers's 'Night', the 'slender / Flocks of the mountain forest' (ll. 20–1) are creatures of the night itself, by contrast with the diurnal, sun-loving humans. They are met with by the reader in the poem, but their 'shy / Wild muzzles' (ll. 24–5) remind us that they would startle at an actual encounter. In 'Earthy Anecdote', the first poem of Wallace Stevens's landmark collection *Harmonium*, published in 1923, there is no direct human encounter with nature either. Instead, nature exists on its own, separate from any human engagement. But, as the poem's title reveals, that is the point.

The word 'anecdote' is never incidental in Stevens's poetry. In one of the most famous poems in *Harmonium*, 'Anecdote of the Jar', the speaker gives an otherwise 'slovenly wilderness' (l. 4) form and focus by placing a jar on the top of a hill. The account he gives of placing the jar is the anecdote, but the jar is also the human point of reference on which any anecdote depends. In 'Earthy Anecdote', there is no single or singular event that can constitute an anecdote. All we have is repeated patterns of activity which in turn generate repeated patterns of phrasing within the poem itself, as the 'bucks' (ll. 1, 14) go 'clattering' (ll. 1, 5) across Oklahoma and swerve 'In a swift, circular line' (ll. 7, 11) right and left to avoid the predatory 'firecat' (ll. 3, 9, 13, 15, 19). It seems that Darwinian nature, with its turbulent but repetitive migrations, predations and escapes, resists our attempts to draw meaning from it. It resists interpretation, as the poem itself does, or would, were it not for the disjuncture between it and its title.

For Stevens, an earthy anecdote – an anecdote derived exclusively from the natural word – is a contradiction in terms. But Stevens's own 'Earthy Anecdote' does not quite fit this description. As with the jar, he has made one singular alteration to nature in the telling. The bucks in this poem are presumably pronghorn, rather than deer, though it hardly matters. But the animal preying on them is not a puma, for instance, but a 'firecat'. By substituting a quasi-mythical predator for a real one (or alternatively a feline personification of fire for fire itself) Stevens gives these events a semblance of significance. Yet it is only a semblance, and the real significance they might have for the animals themselves is never touched on. Unlike Hardy and Millay, Stevens does not attribute consciousness to the animals in his poem. Indeed, their movements seem mechanical and predictable. But then, Stevens's point is at least partly that, whatever awareness of their lives bucks and wild cats may have, we have no access to it. We cannot tell their stories for them; we can only turn them into anecdotes, imposing our own meanings and myths upon them.

The tradition of Darwinian poetry on deer initiated by Hardy, Millay, Jeffers and Stevens still thrives. From Hughes's 'Roe-deer' to Warren's 'Caribou' to Pack's characteristically sophisticated 'Elk in Winter' and Elizabeth Bishop's much-admired 'The Moose' an encounter between human and deer leads the poet to ask how and how far our kinship with wild animals allows us to cross the divide between us and them. The poem that addresses this question most directly and powerfully, and to which all these later poems implicitly reply, is Frost's 'The Most of It', first published in 1942:

He thought he kept the universe alone;
For all the voice in answer he could wake
Was but the mocking echo of his own
From some tree-hidden cliff across the lake.
Some morning from the boulder-broken beach
He would cry out on life, that what it wants
Is not its own love back in copy speech,
But counter-love, original response.
And nothing ever came of what he cried
Unless it was the embodiment that crashed
In the cliff's talus on the other side,
And then in the far-distant water splashed,
But after a time allowed for it to swim,
Instead of proving human when it neared
And someone else additional to him,
As a great buck it powerfully appeared,
Pushing the crumpled water up ahead,
And landed pouring like a waterfall,
And stumbled through the rocks with horny tread,
And forced the underbrush – and that was all.

For many critics, this poem is an allegory of humanity's isolation in the universe. As Cunningham puts it, 'the naive cryer does indeed "ke[ep] the universe alone." He only is the locus of values, love, original response in it' (2001: 264). In this reading, the buck itself becomes, like Jeffers's hawks, a symbol, representing in William Doreski's words 'the attributes of the nonhuman world – bestial power, monumentality, and a certain unrelenting purpose' (1995: 25), or in Robert Faggen's more theological reading (citing Job), 'a vast creaturely world of struggle culminating in the vision of behemoth and leviathan' (1997: 79). Pack gives a more nuanced reading of the poem, but even for him the buck is wholly symbolic, with Frost typically leaving the reader unable to resolve whether or not it is a revelation, proof of 'God's "voice in answer"', or 'merely a physical event', an indicator, 'according to the principles of Darwinian evolution, of nature as indifferent to human hopes and aspirations' (2004b: 141).

These readings parallel my reading of 'Earthy Anecdote'. But setting 'The Most of It' alongside 'The Fallow Deer at the Lonely House' and 'The Fawn', together with Frost's own poems 'The Oven Bird' and 'A Considerable Speck', leads to a very different insight. Read ecologically and in the light of Darwinism, the overriding irony of 'The Most of It' is that the buck is indeed 'someone else additional to him'. The human protagonist cannot see this, however, because he is trapped – like Frost's critics – within humanity's characteristic species-solipsism. He thinks he wants an 'original response' from nature, yet when nature presents him with something that is not just a 'mocking echo' of himself he loses interest. This irony is close to tragic. The man's wish for 'counter-love' (a strikingly ambiguous phrase) is both brave and generous. In his unconscious identification of his own life with life at large ('He would cry out on life, that what it wants. . .') he comes near to the attitude that Meredith teaches in his poetry and Millay aspires to in 'The Fawn'. Yet for all that he yearns for some source of meaning beyond humanity, when he meets it he cannot see it.

Like Millay, Frost is less ready than Meredith or even Hardy to believe that there is really scope for the barrier between humans and other animals to be broken down. By showing us a perspective beyond that of the protagonist himself he suggests that it is, at least in principle, possible for human beings to reach across the divide if they realise that there is 'someone else additional' on the other side. But it remains an open question whether the other animals themselves will respond. Even more than the fallow deer peering into Hardy's window, Frost's buck crosses a symbolic physical divide between nature and man, represented here by the lake. But where Hardy's deer is curious about human beings, Frost's buck takes no more interest in the protagonist than he does in it. Instead, like Millay's fawn, it 'stumbles' on its way, but without even the recognition involved in alarm.

Frost's final comment, 'and that was all', is typically open. It could be the protagonist's thought voiced by the narrator. As at the end of 'Design', the use of a dash to frame the closing remark invites the possibility that there is a change of voice here, or at least of perspective. But the narrator himself

has been far from unequivocal that the buck's appearance has as much significance as the man wanted to find in nature. Here Frost's critics are surely
right. Yet if nature itself, in particular animal nature, is the only source of
meaning beyond ourselves, as the only other 'original response', then – as
Frost's own title implies – we should surely make the most of it.

7

Love and Sex

DARWINISM AND SEX

Since Darwin, sex has been at the very heart of biology. Within Darwinian theory, the winnowing effect of natural selection drives evolution. But natural selection only operates at all because of the variations between organisms thrown up during the processes of reproduction. One source of these variations is the mutation or miscopying of genetic material. Another is the random selection and recombination of genes through sexual reproduction. Sex enables variations that arise in individuals to spread across populations, ultimately shaping whole species.

Sex also introduces a new element of competition into the process of evolution, or rather two. In intrasexual selection, as a rule, male animals – stags, for example, or bull elephant seals – battle it out between themselves for the right to breed. Natural selection thus becomes no longer simply a matter of survival but also of dominance. More remarkably, sex introduces an element of deliberate choice into evolution through intersexual or mate selection. It is still debated whether mate choice acts as a surrogate for natural selection, as Wallace suggested, or a supplement to it, as Darwin argued.

According to Wallace, even this kind of sexual selection is essentially natural selection by proxy, as female and, less frequently, male animals choose their mates on the basis of indicators of their general fitness in the struggle for life. The astonishing results of research on black grouse in Sweden, where the only variable that correlated with the choices made by the females was whether or not the male was still alive six months after mating, lend dramatic support to this hypothesis (Stamp Dawkins 1998: 32–4). According to Darwin, on the other hand, sexual selection really is a matter of aesthetic preferences. Ultimately, these two models are complementary. Wallace reminds us that natural selection always has the last word. Only peacocks that are already very fit could survive with their extraordinary tails. But where Wallace explains differences and trends within a given species, Darwin can also explain the differences between species. Glossy and colourful feathers may be an indicator of fitness in male ducks, but on its own this cannot explain the distinct patterns of these feathers in the drakes of such closely related species as mallards, pintails, gadwalls, garganeys and teals, the females of which are all but indistinguishable to the untrained eye. It seems that certain ancestral ducks simply preferred certain drakes. Together, inherited (or perhaps learnt) preferences and inherited patterns became a force for speciation.

Sex is not only at the heart of Darwinian biology. It has been central to Darwinian social and psychological theorising ever since Darwin himself. It is a familiar critique of Darwinism that it repeats and reinforces gender stereotypes. But like other ideological disputes, the debates over gender roles and homosexuality have seen Darwinism invoked by both sides. There have been Darwinian feminists as well as Darwinian chauvinists, just as there have been Darwinian socialists and social liberals as well as Darwinian economic liberals and Darwinian fascists. Often the Darwinian feminists and socialists have been one and the same, as in the cases of Olive Schreiner, Mathilde Blind and Wallace himself. On the other hand, as George Levine has shown (2006: 169–201), even Darwin – seemingly the epitome of the bearded Victorian patriarch seeing his own values reflected back at him in nature – found himself making a radical case for female choice, not as a mere political ideal, but as an engine of evolution itself. More recently, the tendency of evolutionary psychologists to find confirmation of established gender roles in the mating preferences and habits of American undergraduates and others has met with sustained criticism from men and women whose Darwinian credentials are as impeccable as their own.

The current debate over the implications of Darwinism for our understanding of sexuality and gender concerns the question of how far it is legitimate to reify norms of human behaviour into something called 'human nature'. For all that they are generally careful to insist that biology is a description of nature, not a prescription for it, evolutionary psychologists tend to presume that it is possible to make assertions about human nature on the basis of statistical analyses. Although many of the leading figures who have contributed to this movement have been at pains to declare themselves social liberals – mainly to rebut unfair assumptions and allegations made about them by their opponents – it remains true that these assertions tend to reinforce the status quo, or worse to give the supposed imprimatur of 'nature' to an ideological reaction against sexual and social freedoms.

Many Darwinians who are concerned by this danger have argued that current evolutionary psychologists make the same mistake as Victorian Social Darwinists, ignoring the cultural and ideological factors that shape human behaviour (and their own expectations) and so make a biological analysis of human behaviour invariably inadequate and partial. In arguing that it is impossible to distinguish 'human nature' from culture, modern Darwinists like Stephen Jay Gould, Steven Rose and John Dupré in effect debar Darwinism from having anything more than a physiological relevance to sex and gender.

It is possible, however, to argue that Darwinism itself reinforces the socially liberal position. Alfred Kinsey, the architect and lead author of the famous Kinsey reports on human sexual behaviour, was a Darwinist. Kinsey has been largely written out of the history of evolutionary thought. He is not mentioned in the standard history of evolutionary thought, nor in the most comprehensive survey of Social Darwinism, nor in the leading philosophical companion to Darwin, nor in the best recent textbook on evolutionary psychology (Bowler, 2003; Hawkins, 1997; Hodge and Radick, 2003; Cartwright, 2008). Yet he has at least a fair claim to be the most influential Darwinist of the post-war period. Kinsey's biographer has identified 'Darwin and his hypothesis' as 'the single most important intellectual influence' on Kinsey's life and work (Gathorne-Hardy 2005: 14). The evolutionary framework of Kinsey's thinking is clear in the reports themselves, for example, in the sections of the second report, *Sexual Behaviour in the Human Female*, devoted to the 'Phylogenetic Origins' of pre-marital petting and the 'Mammalian Background' to homosexual responses and contacts (Kinsey et al. 1953: 228–31, 448–51).

Superficially, the socio-political arguments Kinsey makes in his reports seem to be classic examples of Social Darwinist logic, just from a liberal rather than a conservative perspective. Kinsey finds countless examples of heterosexual 'petting' and homosexual sexual activity among both human and non-human mammals. He concludes that these activities are natural, and declares that they are therefore healthy and (implicitly) good. In fact, Kinsey's arguments are much more sophisticated than this. Firstly, the terms of the moral and legal argument were set not by Kinsey himself, but by those who declared such activities to be contrary to nature. In staking this claim to natural law, the social conservatives played into Kinsey's hands. Secondly, and more crucially, Kinsey's argument is not that nature sanctions any given sexual or social practice, but that it sanctions all practices equally. Although this certainly tallies with his own libertarian ideology, it involves a different process of reasoning from that of Social Darwinism or evolutionary psychology, grounded in a different – and more properly Darwinian – approach to taxonomy.

In one of the introductory chapters setting out their first report, *Sexual Behaviour in the Human Male*, Kinsey and his co-authors remark that 'Modern taxonomy is the product of an increasing awareness among biologists of the uniqueness of individuals, and of the wide range of variation which may occur in any population of individuals' (Kinsey et al. 1948: 17). For Kinsey, as for Darwin, a species is not some abstract Platonic type that can be finally described but rather a population of individuals who share a common descent and certain common features across a range of variations. Kinsey gets to the heart of Darwinian natural history when he declares that 'It is a fundamental of taxonomy that nature rarely deals with discrete categories. Only the human mind invents categories and tries to force facts into separated pigeon-holes' (Kinsey et al. 1948: 639).

The implications of this principle become clear if we compare Kinsey's account of male homosexuality with Wilson's proposal that homosexuality may have a genetic element passed down through kin selection. Kinsey argues from his data that there is a spectrum of desire and behaviour among men and women, skewed towards heterosexuality, but covering the complete range from full heterosexuality (0 on the famous Kinsey scale, including around a third of men) to full homosexuality (6 on the scale, including around 4 per cent). Wilson takes the same data and homes in on the 4 per cent, arguing that this 'truly homophile' minority only occurs among humans, while the 'potential for bisexuality in the brain' is common to humans and other mammals (2004: 144).

For Kinsey, homosexuality among men or women at point 6 on his scale is the same biological phenomenon as it is among those at points 1 to 5, merely manifested more fully and to the exclusion of heterosexuality. For Wilson, human homosexuality becomes distinct from human and animal bisexuality. It therefore requires its own evolutionary explanation. This Wilson provides by arguing that, in the absence of children of their own, homosexuals would have been more likely to look out for the well-being of their siblings and other relatives. Furthermore, their relatives may have benefited if homosexuals, 'freed from the special obligations of parental duties', had assumed 'the roles of seers, shamans, artists, and keepers of tribal knowledge' (2004: 144–5; see also 2000: 555). Although Wilson does not make this case explicitly, it is presumably this that gives a putative homosexual gene an advantage in a human population that it would not have in a non-human one.

Wilson and Kinsey share the same liberal agenda, the social and moral rehabilitation of homosexuality. But where Wilson aspires to give a definite account of 'human nature', for Kinsey such an account is not only unachievable, it is meaningless. Some people are closer to the norm than others in their behaviour or desires, but this is a statistical analysis. To reify such results by using the language of 'human nature', rather than Kinsey's own language of averages and variations, is to misrepresent them. In selecting homosexuality from the more complete picture of variations that Kinsey sets out in describing what humans do, Wilson attempts to squeeze the variety of a Darwinian species into a series of Linnaean pigeon-holes.

By contrast, Kinsey's account of human sexuality in all its multiplicity is based on a genuinely Darwinian understanding of natural history. Kinsey's insistence that what is is natural runs counter to the entrenched assumption that the only natural function of sex is reproduction, and that sex that is not, at least in principle, reproductive is perverse and unnatural. Darwinism exposes this assumption as ideological, not scientific. As well as Kinsey's natural history of human sexuality, studies in comparative primatology, particularly Frans de Waal's work on the social and sexual behaviour of bonobos (the less familiar of the two species of chimpanzee), strongly suggest that, in de Waal's words, 'very few human sexual practices can be dismissed as "unnatural"' (de Waal and Lanting 1997: 5).

Like Kinsey and de Waal, George Meredith, Edna St Vincent Millay and Thom Gunn see love as an aspect of our biology, not our spirituality. This has subtle but profound implications. Where a Cartesian divide between the mind or soul and the body can lead to an idea of love as essentially higher than and in conflict with desire, a Darwinian realisation that love and desire in all their forms are expressions of biological impulses and imperatives leads to a different analysis of the tensions between them. Where an emphasis on the differences between men and women and heterosexuals and homosexuals – whether it calls itself Darwinian or not, and whatever its own motivation – can lead to stereotyping or a failure of sympathy, a properly Darwinian awareness of our animal biology leads to a broadening and deepening of our human sympathy. As with non-human animals, the Darwinian poetry of the human animal yields a new and profound sense of our common condition.

A DARWINIAN SEX COMEDY: CONSTANCE NADEN'S 'EVOLUTIONAL EROTICS'

For most of the twentieth century, Darwin's account of human sexuality was eclipsed by Freud's. With the rise of evolutionary psychology and cognitive science, however, Darwinian biology is once again routinely cited as central to our understanding of sexuality and sexual difference, as it was in the decades after Darwin himself published *The Descent of Man*. With the rediscovery of this quasi-Darwinian psychology, the comic poems in which the late Victorian poet and evolutionist Constance Naden satirised and probed the evolutionary psychology of her own day have regained their piquancy. In discussing Edwin Morgan's poems in Chapter 1, I drew a distinction between poems that engage with Darwinism as a discourse and those that accept it as the scientific truth. Later in this chapter, I will turn to three poets whose love poetry is shaped by Darwinism not merely as a discourse but also as a fact. First, however, I want to look at Naden's satirical examination of Darwinian discourses of love and desire.

Constance Naden was born in 1858, the year that the theory of natural selection was first aired in public in a joint paper to the Linnaean Society by Darwin and Wallace. A generation younger than Hardy or Meredith, Naden grew up in an England already largely convinced that life had evolved. Tennyson may have been widely regarded by his contemporaries as having the best grasp of science, but of all the Victorian poets it was Naden who had the most comprehensive and up-to-date scientific education. In her twenties she took courses in botany at the Birmingham and Midland Institute and in organic chemistry, physiology, geology and physics at the newly opened Mason Science College (later the University of Birmingham). She was awarded first-class certificates in every one of these sciences. To her French and German teacher at the BMI she was 'the most brilliant pupil' of his career (cited Hughes 1890: 18); to William Tilden, the Professor of Chemistry at Mason College, she was 'the most brilliant student' to have attended the College (ibid.: 67–8). The President of the Birmingham Natural History and Microscopical Society, William Hughes, even remarked that 'it was impossible to be in Miss Naden's company without the unmistakable feeling that one was in the presence of a superior intelligence' (ibid.: 58). She was, in his eyes, Birmingham's 'most gifted daughter' (ibid.: 3).

Naden's brilliance was manifold. While a student, she published many articles on materialism and evolution in the *Journal of Science* and *Knowledge*. She was only thirty-one when she died, following an operation to remove an ovarian cyst, but she had already established herself as a significant evolutionary theorist in her own right. Herbert Spencer, whose influence on Victorian evolutionism was second only to Darwin's, asked her to write a response to one of his critics in the *Fortnightly Review*. After her death, he would pay tribute to her as the most gifted woman he had known, George Eliot alone aside (Hughes 1890: 89–91; Lewins 1894: 1). As well as being a philosopher of science, Naden was an energetic social and political reformer who campaigned for a wide range of progressive causes, including votes for women, Irish Home Rule and the provision of medical aid to women in India (Hughes 1890: 51; Daniell 1890: xvii; Lewins 1894: 22).

Naden was also a poet. Her poetry is informed throughout by her scientific education. Some of her more earnest poems flirt with the cosmic evolutionism typical of much late Victorian poetry, although as a rule they hold back from committing to it. These poems won the praise of no less eminent a Victorian than Gladstone (Hughes 1890: 32; Lewins 1894: 3–4), but like many of the poems I discussed in Chapter 2, their interest today is largely historical. Naden's comic poetry, on the other hand, is not only still funny, but it remains pertinent to how we think about evolution and sex today.

Naden's finest achievement as a comic poet is the series of four poems grouped together under the title 'Evolutional Erotics', published in her collection *A Modern Apostle* in 1887. These four poems both parody and probe the evolutionary accounts of sexual desire given by Darwin and others. In the first poem, 'Scientific Wooing', a young male scientist who has fallen in love with Mary Maud Trevylyan sets out to woo her with scientific analogies and the force of argument. In 'The New Orthodoxy', the tables are turned as Amy Merton, a student at Girton College, Cambridge, writes a letter to her sweetheart Fred, rebuking him for his flippancy and doubts about modern science. In 'Natural Selection', a geologist with a study full of fossils loses his beloved Chloe to 'an idealess lad' (l. 17) who dances and sings better than he can. Finally, in 'Solomon Redivivus, 1886', a self-appointed 'modern Sage' (l. 2) attempts to charm his very own Queen of Sheba by telling her the story of their shared evolutionary history, from when they first split apart as amoebae to their reunion as human beings.

In all of these poems, the power of sexual selection is in the hands of the women. This is most immediately apparent in 'Natural Selection', spoken by the disappointed geologist:

I had found out a gift for my fair,
    I had found where the cave-men were laid;
Skull, femur, and pelvis were there,
    And spears, that of silex they made.

But he ne'er could be true, she averred,
    Who would dig up an ancestor's grave –
And I loved her the more when I heard
    Such filial regard for the Cave.

My shelves, they are furnished with stones
    All sorted and labelled with care,

And a splendid collection of bones,
    Each one of them ancient and rare;

One would think she might like to retire
    To my study – she calls it a 'hole!'
Not a fossil I heard her admire,
    But I begged it, or borrowed, or stole.

But there comes an idealess lad,
    With a strut, and a stare, and a smirk;
And I watch, scientific though sad,
    The Law of Selection at work.

Of Science he hasn't a trace,
    He seeks not the How and the Why,
But he sings with an amateur's grace,
    And he dances much better than I.

And we know the more dandified males
    By dance and by song win their wives –
'Tis a law that with *Aves* prevails,
    And even in *Homo* survives.

Shall I rage as they whirl in the valse?
    Shall I sneer as they carol and coo?
Ah no! for since Chloe is false,
    I'm certain that Darwin is true!

With its buoyant anapaestic rhythms and exuberant delight in rhyme, 'Natural Selection' is engaging and funny. It is also a deft exposé of key flaws in the method and the logic of much Darwinian writing about sex, then and now.

Does Chloe's choice of the 'idealess lad' bear out Darwin's theory of sexual selection, as the geologist in Naden's poem believes? On the face of it, it seems to. The contrast between the gauche scientist and the graceful dandy is obvious, even clichéd. The flagrantly forced rhymes in the last verse invite us to revel in this cliché, even as Naden's speaker resigns himself to it with a stoical empiricism. But the same rhymes prevent us from taking his conclusion at face value. Naden's speaker jumps too readily from a single observation to the 'certain' knowledge that 'Darwin is true'. Like Amy Merton, he has taken up Darwinism as the new orthodoxy. But

Amy's own example shows that he cannot simply conclude on the basis of his own experience that women are bound to prefer elegant intellectual lightweights over serious men well-versed in science.

Comic clichés apart, this may seem obvious, but Naden's point is that even the most eminent Darwinians move all too readily from anecdotal evidence to familiar stereotypes when describing sexual behaviour. They presume, that is, that sexual choice is species-typical (natural), an elision that Naden draws out by calling her poem on sexual selection 'Natural Selection' instead. In her own essay on sexual selection, 'The Evolution of the Sense of Beauty', published in *Knowledge* in 1885, Naden calls Darwin himself to account. In particular, she teases him for his use of the language of Victorian social mores in describing the 'courtship' of birds:

> How did the birds obtain their fine feathers? They obtained them by *courtship*. How the *Rupicola Crocea* [cock-of-the-rock] capers about, spreads his beautiful orange wings and his tail like an orange fan, that so he may win him a bride; how the gold pheasants 'expand and raise their splendid frills,' and even 'twist them obliquely towards the female on whichever side she may be standing,' at the same time turning 'their beautiful tails and tail-coverts a little toward the same side'; how the peacock shows similar good judgment in displaying to the best advantage, not only his train, but his rich blue throat and breast; is it not written in the book of Darwin, in the book of the Chronicles of the Descent of Man? (1891: 79–80)

In this passage, as in her poems, Naden pokes fun at those who treat Darwin as an authority, as if he were a biblical prophet or a prehistoric chronicler who had witnessed the descent of man in person. But she also pokes fun at Darwin himself.

Naden's quibble is not with Darwin's anthropomorphism so much as with the form that anthropomorphism takes. Her prose blends direct quotation from *The Descent of Man* ([1871] 2004: 446) and a close paraphrase of Darwin's own language and his sources with touches of parody. Where Darwin himself is scrupulous to refer to 'females', for example, Naden extends his analogy between people and birds by calling them 'brides'. This selective reading and judicious exaggeration draws attention to Darwin's unselfconsciousness in describing the mating behaviour of birds as if it took place in a Victorian ballroom. The problem is not that Darwin's account is inaccurate, or even that there is a better language he could have used for describing the birds' behaviour. It is rather that all language carries with it connotations to which we need to be alert. The analogy between human and bird 'courtship' is descriptively invaluable, but we ought not to get carried away into thinking that birds think of or experience their own courtship in the same way that we do, whoever 'we' may be.

Naden's telling critique of Darwin and his followers in 'Natural Selection' and 'The Evolution of the Sense of Beauty' is apt to modern Darwinians too. Gould warned repeatedly against taking adaptationism as an article of faith backed by the authority of Darwin instead of examining each case of supposed adaptation on its own merits. On the other side, the heated debate over the 'selfish gene' is testimony to the unruliness of connotations, for all that Dawkins has tried hard to control them. The risk of misrepresentation is worse still when writers are unaware that there might be a disjunction between their language and what they are describing, as Naden implies Darwin is in his account of sexual selection in birds.

A current case in point is the tendency of evolutionary psychologists to identify human universals without realising that the words they use to name them carry with them connotations that call into question their universality. John Dupré gives as an example the claim that 'marriage' is universal when anthropologists use the term to refer to a vast range of institutions, some voluntary, some forced; some monogamous, some polygamous, a few polyandrous; most between men and women, but some between people of the same sex; all shaped by the particular rules of a given culture, and all freighted with complex meanings within that culture. Dupré remains open to 'the possibility that these various social institutions may nevertheless reflect the same underlying universal psychology', but he rightly insists 'that evidence about marriage in diverse societies offered in support of such a hypothesis cannot, on pain of blatant question-begging, start with the assumption that these different forms of marriage are fundamentally the same thing' (2001: 59).

Naden's 'Evolutional Erotics' demonstrate that poetry can play a part in holding scientists to account for flaws in their methods. But as prose like Dupré's or her own can perform this function too, what does Naden gain by writing in verse? What is distinctive about poetry as a critical and satirical tool? The comedy in 'Natural Selection' is both more immediate than that in 'The Evolution of the Sense of Beauty' and less obvious in its implications. We are invited to laugh at her speaker and his response to his own predicament, but beyond that, it is up to us what conclusions we draw. As a result the poem works on two levels at once, as a piece of broad comedy mocking the supposed social ineptitude of scientists and their unflinching commitment to science, and as a witty critique of scientific practice aimed at scientists themselves and their readers.

This applies to the other three poems in 'Evolutional Erotics' too, especially in combination with one another. 'Scientific Wooing', 'Natural Selection' and 'Solomon Redivivus' are all spoken by men who make themselves ridiculous by using science as a form of sexual display. 'The New Orthodoxy' reminds us not to generalise from such anecdotes, but at the same time it borders on self-mockery, suggesting that Naden has her own enthusiasms and image in mind. Early in the poem, Amy Merton reassures her fiancé,

> Trust me, Fred, beneath the curls
> Of the most 'advanced' of girls,
> Many a foolish fancy whirls,
>   Bidding Fact defiance,
> And the simplest village maid
> Needs not to be much afraid
> Of her sister, sage and staid,
>   Bachelor of Science.
>   (ll. 9–16)

Of the four speakers of 'Evolutional Erotics', Amy is the most winning. She is affectionate and playful. As if to mirror both her 'foolish fancy' and her intellectual ambition, Naden has given her the most exuberant and demanding rhyme-scheme of all her speakers.

Amy is indeed 'advanced', in her education, her casual frankness and her liking for new technology. Unlike the advanced men in Naden's poems, however, she is not self-important or alienated. As Amy reproaches Fred for his doubts about modern science, Naden teases her for her unquestioning faith in it and her dogmatic insistence that her future husband share this faith. At the same time, she makes it clear that Amy has read and understood a wide range of scientific literature for herself:

> Oh, the wicked tales I hear!
> Not that you at Ruskin jeer,
> Nor that at Carlyle you sneer,
>   With his growls dyspeptic:
> But that, having read in vain
> Huxley, Tyndall, Clifford, Bain,
> All the scientific train –
>   You're a hardened sceptic!
>
> Things with fin, and claw, and hoof
> Join to give us perfect proof

That our being's warp and woof
   We from near and far win;
Yet your flippant doubts you vaunt,
And – to please a maiden aunt –
You've been heard to say you can't
   Pin your faith to Darwin!

Then you jest, because Laplace
Said this Earth was nought but gas
Till the vast rotating mass
   Denser grew and denser:
Something worse they whisper too,
But I'm sure it *can't* be true –
For they tell me, Fred, that you
   Scoff at Herbert Spencer!
          (ll. 33–56)

Amy's reproaches to Fred imply that she too has read the physicist John Tyndall, the mathematician and atheist W. K. Clifford and the philosopher Alexander Bain, as well as Huxley, Spencer and Darwin. She is also familiar with the work of the French astronomer Laplace, either directly or at second-hand. This is an impressive curriculum, hardly narrower than Naden's own. Amy may tend to take science on trust, but she has pursued it with commitment, and her paraphrase of Darwin's argument that the homologous bones in the limbs of different vertebrates point to their common evolutionary origins suggests she has worked through the arguments and been persuaded by them. Furthermore, she is clearly no mere follower, as she is quite capable of resisting the cultural authority and rhetorical powers of Ruskin and Carlyle.

Amy Merton's sin of trusting too much in the 'new orthodoxy' of science is an error of degree rather than kind. Her earnest 'faith' – a resonant and ironic word in this context – in Darwin, Spencer and company is an only marginally distorted mirror of Naden's own intellectual allegiances. In 'The New Orthodoxy' and the other 'Evolutional Erotics', Naden reminds herself as well as us of the temptations of the mind. Her speakers are at once too cerebral, too invested in the mind at the expense of their own and others' bodies, and not sufficiently rational, not sceptical enough towards their intellectual masters.

In an editorial for the *Mason College Magazine*, Naden argued that an education that promoted the mind above the body would be detrimental to the health of the nation, physiologically but also socially, as 'excessive specialization' would narrow the range of each individual's sympathies for others. 'The heart,' she wrote, 'will revenge itself upon the brain. A nation, which has forgotten how to enjoy, will soon forget how to think – and the sooner the better' (cited in Hughes 1890: 69). For Naden, thought without enjoyment, the brain without the heart, science without play and romance, are not worth having. Naden's 'Evolutional Erotics' are a reminder to take pleasure in both science and love. They succeed because, through comedy, they give pleasure themselves, a pleasure that is both palpable and intellectual at the same time.

THE DARWINIAN LOVE SONNET:
GEORGE MEREDITH AND EDNA ST VINCENT MILLAY

In 'Evolutional Erotics', Naden gives us a spoof of what a Darwinian love poetry might look like. The model for her poems is not love poetry at all, but the comic lyrics published in *Punch* and other Victorian satirical magazines. For an authentic Darwinian love poetry, we need to look to a more authentic form of love poetry itself. In the sixteenth century the sonnet became the most conventional form for love poetry in English and across Europe. Even by the mid-1600s, however, the love sonnet's conventionality weighed against its versatility. All the mastery and wit of the most brilliant sonneteers – Shakespeare among them – could not cancel out the tawdriness of the ever more derivative sonnet sequences produced on a near-industrial scale in the 1590s and after. After Shakespeare, the English love sonnet lay in eclipse for nearly two centuries until it was revived by the so-called Della Cruscan poets in the late eighteenth century and then by some of the finest love poets of the nineteenth century, from John Keats and Elizabeth Barrett Browning to Dante Gabriel and Christina Rossetti.

More than any other American poet, Edna St Vincent Millay belongs to this revived tradition. Her sonnets allude to and engage with, among others, Petrarch, Sidney, Shakespeare, Donne, both Rossettis and Yeats. But they also embody a distinctively Darwinian vision. This is clearest in this famous sonnet, from her 1920 collection, *A Few Figs from Thistles*:

I shall forget you presently, my dear,
So make the most of this, your little day,
Your little month, your little half a year,
Ere I forget, or die, or move away,
And we are done forever; by and by
I shall forget you, as I said, but now,
If you entreat me with your loveliest lie

I will protest you with my favourite vow.
I would indeed that love were longer-lived,
And oaths were not so brittle as they are,
But so it is, and nature has contrived
To struggle on without a break thus far, –
Whether or not we find what we are seeking
Is idle, biologically speaking.

Millay's voice in this sonnet is typically knowing, even cynical. Conventionally, sonneteers profess a love that will endure even after death, but Millay admits openly that this is a fiction, a lovely lie. In reality, she suggests, love is transitory. Rather than lasting forever, there comes a time when it is 'done forever', a point she underlines with the only clear caesura in the poem. Lovers, herself included, maintain the pretence that vows are made to last. But this is only a performance, and one which is repeated with each new love affair, until so many vows have been tried and tested that she at least has a particular 'favourite' among them.

Millay's sonnet draws attention to the discrepancy between the idealistic language of love and the reality that romantic relationships are prone to the vicissitudes of everyday life. Her Elizabethan predecessors enjoyed the same paradox. By the 1590s, the sonnet had become a self-sustaining performance of love with little reference to real relationships, bar the occasional sly admission that the one did not reflect the other. For all that they professed to look in their hearts and write, Philip Sidney and his successors worked with what they knew to be a received idea of love, not the thing itself. As Giles Fletcher wrote in the dedicatory epistle to his sonnet sequence *Licia*, 'a man may write of love, and not be in love, as well as of husbandry and not go to plough: or of witches and be none: or of holiness and be flat profane' (1593). With the characteristic wit of the age, the test for the Elizabethan sonneteer was to give a performance of love that was plausible on its own terms whilst artfully exposing the artificiality of those very terms themselves.

Where the Victorian sonneteers and critics reacted against their Elizabethan predecessors, putting a premium not on wit but on sincerity, Millay returns to this more artful model of love poetry, and of love itself. Unlike the Elizabethans, however, Millay views the reality of love through the lens of Darwinism, as signalled here by her pun on nature's famous 'struggle' for existence. As Millay sees it, we should not expect our ideals of love to be realised, because our desires are driven by biological processes to which our own sense of fulfilment is immaterial. The closer she comes to saying this outright in the sestet of this sonnet, the more detached her voice becomes. The alliteration implicitly identified with the false ideal of undying love, with its 'loveliest lie' and its 'favourite vow', persists as far as her forlorn wish that 'love were longer-lived', but no further. Instead, the 'brittle' oaths remind us how 'little' time is given to love in the opening lines. Millay's voice becomes first briskly dismissive – 'But so it is' – then archly sardonic, in its contrived remark about 'nature' having 'contrived' to 'struggle on . . . thus far' itself. Finally, in her closing couplet, Millay relaxes into nonchalant so-called double rhymes, with their final unstressed syllables, as she casually uses the language of science to dismiss the language of love.

Millay's manner in this sonnet implies that there is little more to say on the subject. But this is more a reflection of her manner in her stand-alone sonnets in general, than a reflection on Darwinism and love poetry *per se*. For fuller and richer accounts of love from this same biological perspective, we need to look at Millay's sonnet sequence *Fatal Interview*, published in 1931, and at its closest model, structurally and intellectually, if not stylistically: George Meredith's agonising analysis of the collapse of a marriage, *Modern Love*, published as early as 1862 and reissued with minor revisions thirty years later.

The two poems have similar plots, although Meredith's is the more developed. Both centre on a married woman's adultery. In *Modern Love*, the story is told partly by a narrator and partly by the husband, with these two voices at times blending into one another. In *Fatal Interview*, it is told by the wife. Meredith's poem, which is also a sonnet sequence, opens with the image of the husband and the wife lying in bed together, their marriage already effectively over:

> Like sculptured effigies they might be seen
> Upon their marriage-tomb, the sword between;
> Each wishing for the sword that severs all.
>
> (i, ll. 14–16)

In a direct allusion, Millay repeats this image at the beginning of her sequence, as the wife, dwelling on her burgeoning relationship, remarks 'The scar of this encounter like a sword / Will lie between me and my troubled lord' (ii, ll. 13–14). *Modern Love* thus starts at a later stage than *Fatal Interview*, with the bond of marriage already severed by adultery.

The two poems take different vantage points too. *Fatal Interview* is concerned almost entirely with the affair, *Modern Love* with the marriage that it tears apart. By the tenth sonnet of *Fatal Interview*, the lover has kissed her male beloved. By the twelfth, they have slept together. They continue unsteadily as lovers, until eventually he makes his excuses and she tells him to leave. In *Modern Love*, we never find out the full extent of the wife's infidelity. Her husband convinces himself that she has been only emotionally, not sexually, unfaithful, but her own sense of sin in the poem's closing sonnets suggests that he may be mistaken. His own indiscretions, on the other hand, are set down with remarkable frankness for a poem of the early 1860s, particularly one that identifies itself so boldly with 'modern' life.

On the advice of his doctor – 'Distraction is the panacea, Sir!' (XXVII, l. 1) – the husband in *Modern Love* tries sex with other women as the cure for an ailing marriage. After dalliances, probably with prostitutes, he embarks on an affair of his own with a woman he addresses, in true Petrarchan style, as his 'Lady' (his wife is addressed as 'Madam'). Just after this affair has been consummated, however, he catches sight of his wife walking hand-in-hand with her own lover. This reduces him to a kind of paralysis. His wife proposes that they resume their marriage. With a heavy heart, he agrees. Finally, just as he thinks their old love may be recovering, she leaves him, apparently so he can resume his relationship with his Lady, which she has only now found out about. The husband tracks her down, only to lose her for good that same night as she poisons herself.

Both Millay and Meredith invoke the model of Petrarchism in their sonnets, and both of them transform it. As John Addington Symonds argued in his essay 'The Dantesque and Platonic Ideals of Love', Dantesque or Petrarchan love, like Platonic love or homosexuality, had always been an extramarital desire (1893: 55–86). Dante's Beatrice, Petrarch's Laura, Astrophil's Stella (in Sidney's *Astrophil and Stella*), are all the wives of other men. But where the Renaissance sonneteers wrote about unrequited desire from the male lover's perspective, Millay and Meredith write about consummated adultery from the woman's side and the cuckolded husband's respectively – appropriately enough, as Millay was a married woman who had a number of lovers, while Meredith wrote *Modern Love* soon after his wife Mary left him for the painter Henry Wallis. (A few years earlier Wallis had painted the most famous image of Meredith, as the poet Chatterton self-poisoned in a garret).

Fatal Interview and *Modern Love* are both sonnet sequences; both tell the semi-autobiographical story of an adulterous affair through self-contained vignettes (the sonnets themselves); and both invoke the conventions of Renaissance love poetry. The styles of the two poems are nonetheless very different. Here is one of the early sonnets from *Fatal Interview*, where the speaker is trying to persuade her beloved to give in to her sexual advances:

Since I cannot persuade you from this mood
Of pale preoccupation with the dead,
Not for my comfort nor for your own good
Shift your concern to living bones instead;
Since that which Helen did and ended Troy
Is more than I can do though I be warm,
Have up your buried girls, egregious boy,
And stand with them against the unburied storm.
When you lie wasted and your blood runs thin,
And what's to do must with dispatch be done,
Call Cressid, call Elaine, call Isolt in! –
More bland the ichor of a ghost should run
Along your dubious veins than the rude sea
Of passion pounding all day long in me.

(vi)

This sonnet encapsulates Millay's mastery of her Petrarchan form and idiom. She matches her syntax impeccably to the form, seamlessly merging the rhyme-scheme of the Shakespearean sonnet (with three quatrains and a final couplet) and the structure of the Petrarchan sonnet (an octet followed by a sestet). Her first sentence forms the octet, and is divided at the mid-point at the end of the first quatrain. At the *volta* or turn marked by the end of the octet, Millay moves from the present moment to an imagined future, and the two sentences that remain divide the sestet neatly into two tercets. Almost all the lines are end-stopped, either formally with punctuation or at a natural pause within a phrase. The only exceptions are the last three lines, which run on like the running blood they describe. All the lines are built on a regular pentameter meter too, with ten syllables in each line, allowing for an appropriately old-fashioned elision in 'the unburied storm' (half way to 'th'unburied storm') when that line is read aloud.

Like so many Elizabethan sonnets, this sonnet is an exercise in persuasion. The lover calls to mind classical and Arthurian legends as she tries to persuade her beloved to sleep with her. Her conceit is that he is too preoccupied with the ideal women of myth to appreciate the flesh and blood woman before him. The particular women she alludes to are themselves famous for their illicit and ill-fated love affairs, so it is a further irony that his own ideal of love matches neatly the reality she is offering him. Millay's rhetoric itself is appropriately Petrarchan too. There are direct echoes of a number of famous Elizabethan sonnets, including Michael Drayton's 'Since there's no help, come, let us kiss and part!' and Shakespeare's 'When in the chronicle of wasted time'. There is the familiar Petrarchan opposition between warmth and cold, and another Petrarchan paradox in the image of 'living bones'. Word-for-word Millay's vocabulary is not especially archaic, but her elliptical and euphemistic style has a similar effect. It can take a number of readings before it becomes clear that the governing image in the sestet – 'what's to do' – is the very modern procedure of a blood transfusion. It is a characteristically Petrarchan irony too that the beloved should be reproached for his preoccupation with literature in a poem that is itself so self-consciously literary.

The elegance of Millay's sonnet contrasts markedly with the tortured violence of this early sonnet from *Modern Love*:

> This was the woman; what now of the man?
> But pass him. If he comes beneath a heel,
> He shall be crushed until he cannot feel,
> Or, being callous, haply till he can.
> But he is nothing: – nothing? Only mark
> The rich light striking out from her on him!
> Ha! what a sense it is when her eyes swim
> Across the man she singles, leaving dark
> All else! Lord God, who mad'st the thing so fair,
> See that I am drawn to her even now!
> It cannot be such harm on her cool brow
> To put a kiss? Yet if I meet him there!
> But she is mine! Ah, no! I know too well
> I claim a star whose light is overcast:
> I claim a phantom-woman in the Past.
> The hour has struck, though I heard not the bell!
>
> (III)

Meredith's lines, like Millay's, are each ten syllables long. But the varied patterns of stresses, the frequent enjambments running on from one line to the next, the even more frequent caesurae – sometimes two in a single line – make it almost impossible to hear the regular metre that underpins his verse. Uniquely, Meredith's sonnets have sixteen lines each, divided into four quatrains, so there is no direct equivalent to either the Petrarchan *volta* or the deft Shakespearean couplet. Instead, Meredith gives us a form that barely contains the suspicion, the fury, the sheer emotional confusion of his characters, in particular the husband. In place of a single elegant turn, what we see is a rage of reversals, the poetic equivalent of an animal pacing ever more frantically in its cage, with the caesurae marking the bars.

These two sonnets are central to how each of these sequences works as a Darwinian love poem. In Millay's poem the conventions of Petrarchism come to stand for biological impulses. For all its artifice, Petrarchism is well-suited to this kind of biological poetry because its introspection is already tied to the body. Petrarch's famous icy fire is as much a bodily sensation as an image of mental and emotional paralysis. Millay takes this bodily introspection and makes it visceral. Where the Petrarchan tradition concentrates on the heart, she adds the flesh (iv), the bones (vi), the blood (viii) with its pulses (xviii) and veins (xxviii), even the lungs (xxii). The personified Love becomes 'This beast that rends me in the sight of all, / This love' (ii, ll. 1–2). The icy fire itself becomes 'the desirous body's heat and sweat' (viii, l. 10), while in the sonnet quoted above, the contrast between her living body and her beloved's dead books is mirrored in her warmth and his pallor – itself an ironic allusion to the pale beauty of the conventional Petrarchan beloved.

Fatal Interview articulates a biological understanding of love from the beginning. In *Modern Love*, the same understanding needs to be learnt. Sonnet iii is the first sonnet in which we hear the husband's voice directly. It is hard to say exactly where the narrator leaves off and the husband begins. It is even unclear who the 'man' is, until the husband identifies him as his wife's lover, 'the man she singles'. At this point we can look back and hear the husband's voice more distinctly in the dismissal of the man as 'nothing', and then further back in what may be an avowal of his own callousness, or a callous wish to punish his wife's callous lover. The replacement of the narrator's voice with the husband's comes to seem more a process than an event – a process which may even go into reverse as the second 'nothing?' in the fifth line can equally well be the husband's internal question of himself or the narrator's ironic counter-observation.

Regardless of the voice, the imagery of this sonnet grounds the husband's perceptions not in modern biology but in the second and third chapters of Genesis. His wife's lover is cast as the serpent, cursed by God to be crushed underfoot but also – although this slips the husband's mind – empowered to bruise the heel that bruises his head. His wife herself is created by God and, like Eve, tempts him against his better judgement. As the husband sees it, marriage is itself properly a matter of possession, in accordance with God's curse on Eve in Genesis 3.16 that 'thy desire shall be to thy husband, and he shall rule over thee'. Her own actions give this ideal the lie, as he realises, but still it sets the pattern for how he thinks about her, here and in other early sonnets of the sequence. Throughout the first ten or so sonnets he sees her as responsible for the collapse of their marriage, and as falsely tempting him into ignoring this by manipulating his desire for her.

In these early sonnets Meredith grounds the husband's misogyny not only in his experience, as his wife conducts an affair with another man, but also in the biblical world view through which he interprets that experience. Over the course of the poem, however, he puts that world view behind him, along with the misogyny that feeds on it. This process begins in sonnet XIII, where Meredith introduces a Darwinian concept of nature defined not by God's will but by the 'laws of growth':

'I play for Seasons; not Eternities!'
Says Nature, laughing on her way. 'So must
All those whose stake is nothing more than dust!'
And lo, she wins, and of her harmonies
She is full sure! Upon her dying rose
She drops a look of fondness, and goes by,
Scarce any retrospection in her eye;
For she the laws of growth most deeply knows,
Whose hands bear, here, a seed-bag – there, an urn.
Pledged she herself to aught, 'twould mark her end!
This lesson of our only visible friend,
Can we not teach our foolish hearts to learn?
Yes! yes! – but, oh, our human rose is fair
Surpassingly! Lose calmly Love's great bliss,
When the renewed for ever of a kiss
Whirls life within the shower of loosened hair!

(XIII)

This complex sonnet changes its meaning depending on whether we hear it in the husband's voice or in Meredith's own. It changes its significance as we read on too as it represents an early stage in Meredith's thinking about the implications of evolution for how we understand ourselves, a hypothesis which he tests by watching how the husband in his poem responds to the same idea.

The first twelve lines of this sonnet are an exercise in Social Darwinism. In naming nature as 'our only visible friend', Meredith and the husband turn their backs on the invisible God as a source of moral wisdom. Instead, they turn to our understanding of the natural world. For Meredith, as for Darwin, nature has no long-term objectives, no grand plan. It is simply the processes of birth, growth and death, which together create the persisting 'harmonies' of the natural world. Meredith's account of nature in this sonnet is not entirely unsentimental. He allows it 'a look of fondness' at the 'dying rose', embodying the fondness that some at least of nature's creatures undoubtedly feel for one another. Nonetheless, nature as Meredith presents it here accepts that everything in life is transitory, as Meredith himself does in 'In the Woods'. This 'lesson' is reinforced through rhyme, which covertly insists that we 'must' accept that we are 'dust' and so 'learn' the lesson of the 'urn'.

Meredith uses the flexibility of his sixteen-line form to reinstate a *volta* after the first three quatrains. It is not clear whether the last four lines are the husband's reply to Meredith or to himself. Either way, he first accepts and then rejects nature's 'lesson'. What is curious is how he interprets that lesson in the first place. In 'In the Woods', 'The Woods of Westermain' and 'The Lark Ascending', Meredith urges us to accept nature on its own terms and to realise that we ourselves are part of the natural world. Here the husband considers nature's 'lesson' to be rather that we should imitate nature's processes in our own lives. If nature accepts that things pass, we should do the same. For the husband, this means he should accept that his marriage is over.

The logic that the husband both employs and resists is the logic of Social Darwinism. But mortality (nature's 'urn') is not the same as the passing of relationships. The husband's resistance to his own Social Darwinist arguments is driven by love and erotic desire, encapsulated in the rhymes of 'fair' and 'hair' and 'bliss' and 'kiss', and in the intoxicating image of life whirled 'within the shower of loosened hair'. He is not moved by the idea of nature's urn but by nature's 'seed-bag', or more literally his own. Meredith exposes two flaws at the heart of Social Darwinism: any imitation of 'Nature' will be selective, and any theory of nature that runs counter to our own natural impulses is inevitably a partial one. Sex is, after all, as natural as death.

As *Modern Love* unfolds, the husband refines his understanding of the 'lesson' of nature. In one direction, this leads to a distinctly cynical attitude to sex, embodied in this sonnet, spoken soon after he has begun courting his new Lady:

> What are we first? First, animals; and next
> Intelligences at a leap; on whom
> Pale lies the distant shadow of the tomb,
> And all that draweth on the tomb for text.
> Into which state comes Love, the crowning sun:
> Beneath whose light the shadow loses form.
> We are the lords of life, and life is warm.
> Intelligence and instinct now are one.
> But Nature says: 'My children most they seem
> When they least know me: therefore I decree

That they shall suffer.' Swift doth young Love flee,
And we stand wakened, shivering from our dream.
Then if we study Nature we are wise.
Thus do the few who live but with the day:
The scientific animals are they. –
Lady, this is my sonnet to your eyes.

(xxx)

The final line of this sonnet comes as a shock, an extraordinary twist of the knife, as Meredith reminds us that his poem is modelled on the idealising Elizabethan sonnet sequence: that this disquisition on our animal natures is supposedly a love poem. The poem that Meredith alludes to most directly is Shakespeare's famous sonnet 130, 'My mistress' eyes are nothing like the sun', itself a satirical recapitulation and rebuttal of the Petrarchan tradition. The husband's cold evocation of the same tradition appears to claim that Social Darwinist theorising is apt to a love poem. But his argument is the opposite. Nature in this sonnet runs wholly counter to the ideal of Love. Lovers seem to be nature's 'children', living for the moment and no doubt impelled by sex, but they forget her own insistence on transience. The 'scientific' position is rather to accept that we are animals and to live as such, from day to day.

In his own mind, the husband has found a way of combining the lesson of the 'urn' with that of the 'seed-bag', claiming a license for an unrestrained and egocentric hedonism in the Darwinian view of nature. So far Meredith has given little reason to prefer Darwinism over Genesis, at least not morally. Nature may have the advantage of being more 'visible' than the God who curses Eve, but her morality is no better, at least not as the husband interprets it. In the sonnets which tell the story of his affair with the Lady, Darwinism seems to be allied to a cynicism and sexual self-indulgence which pays no heed to the feelings of anyone else involved. As Isobel Armstrong writes, 'the violent jealousy and anger so adeptly disclosed in *Modern Love*' seem to epitomise 'the predatory cruelties of a post-Darwinian understanding of sexuality' (1993: 455–6).

But Darwinism is also integral to the process by which the husband is disillusioned of the morally enfeebling and misogynistic world view that he holds at the beginning of the poem. Crucially, an understanding of love as biologically driven paves the way for a more egalitarian view of men's and women's sexuality. The first tentative sign of this moral development occurs in sonnet xx, where the husband takes responsibility for his own sexual indiscretions, past and future, rather than blaming them on the devil (whether in the person of his wife or of her lover). As he remarks, 'That man I do suspect / A coward, who would burden the poor deuce / With what ensues from his own slipperiness' (ll. 8–10). In owning up to a 'slipperiness' of his own, he hints that the image of the snake is not only apt to others. He goes on to own up to the reason why:

> I have just found a wanton-scented tress
> In an old desk, dusty for lack of use.
> Of days and nights it is demonstrative,
> That, like some aged star, gleam luridly.
> If for those times I must ask charity,
> Have I not any charity to give?
>
> (ll. 11–16)

Here the husband – and Meredith through him – affirm the equivalence of male and female sexual indiscretion in the face of the notorious double-standard of Victorian sexual morality, personified in the doctor who prescribes prostitutes as a tonic for a married man. The implication of the 'wanton-scented tress' is that the husband has frequented prostitutes or perhaps kept a courtesan in the past, although whether before or after his marriage is unspecified. That queasy phrase 'dusty for lack of use' suggests an old habit – hers of seduction or his own of masturbation – that he (like the doctor) sees as functional. This distasteful revelation reveals his cynical attitude to sex. At the same time, his admission that he is not subject to a different standard of sexual morality from his wife merely because he is a man remains a necessary stage in his moral growth.

Unsurprisingly, the husband's affair with his Lady stunts this moral growth rather than advancing it. In spite of his claim that he would not 'burden the poor deuce' with his own moral failings, that is exactly what he does when he begins this affair, declaring 'I feel the promptings of Satanic power' (xxviii, l. 15) and claiming not to care 'if the devil snare me, body and mind' (xxvii, l. 10). In fact, it is not until after the crisis of sonnet xxxix that he truly begins to appreciate the moral implications of his behaviour, and of Darwinism. In this sonnet, he glories in the sexual conquest of his Lady, in a grotesquely exaggerated parody of Romantic love poetry, before the sight of his wife and her lover reduces him once again to an impotent rage.

As he and his wife decide to pick up their marriage, the full moral implications of his actions dawn on him. 'We two have taken up a lifeless vow / To rob a living passion', he declares, 'We have struck despair / Into two hearts' (xli, ll. 11–12, 14–15). In resuming his marriage, the husband sees his affair with his Lady from her point of view for the first time. In so doing, he realises the moral bankruptcy of his pursuit of sexual power and gratification for its own sake. At last, he admits responsibility for the misery he has caused through his seductions, as he had said he would some twenty sonnets before. But he realises too that for him and his wife to deprive their lovers of happiness by carrying on with their dead marriage is no less a moral fault than their adultery itself.

Neither the poem's readers nor the wife herself yet know that her renunciation of her own affair was premised on her ignorance of his. At first, her fault seems greater than her husband's, because it is her priggish self-denial that commands them to take up their 'lifeless vow'. In his words, she is 'bent on martyrdom' (XLII, l. 2). But it is only the husband who knows how much pain this will cause, and he does nothing to stop it. His sympathy has grown dramatically, reaching out even to his wife's rejected lover, yet he remains morally weak and irresolute. Ultimately, however, it is his admission of his own weakness that enables him to hold back from judging others:

If I the death of Love had deeply planned,
I never could have made it half so sure,
As by the unblest kisses which upbraid
The full-waked sense; or failing that, degrade!
'Tis morning: but no morning can restore
What we have forfeited. I see no sin;
The wrong is mixed. In tragic life, God wot,
No villain need be! Passions spin the plot:
We are betrayed by what is false within.
(XLIII, ll. 8–16)

On the one hand, this sonnet marks yet another step towards the husband's admission of his moral culpability. He may not have set out to destroy love through the 'unblest kisses' of adultery, but he realises now that that is what he did, and that those kisses remain a reproach and a shame to him. On the other hand, it marks a move too towards forgiveness. He blames himself as much as his wife for the adultery they both committed. Ultimately, neither of them is the 'villain'. The concept of 'sin', he suggests, is misplaced. Instead it is our biological passions – love, desire, jealousy – that betray us, men and women alike.

Grounded in Darwinian biology, Meredith's egalitarian understanding of gender and sexual morality in *Modern Love* is one of the very few redemptive possibilities this bleak poem offers us. It is the wife's final tragedy that she does not take this offer up. Just as their relationship seems to be moving towards a new if diminished intimacy, predicated on openness and forgiveness, she misinterprets his admission of his affair as implying that he would rather resume it than be tied down in marriage to her. At least, that is what the husband believes she does. But this too may be a misinterpretation. At the end of sonnet XLVIII, he asks 'Will the hard world my sentience of her share?', declaring 'I feel the truth; so let the world surmise' (ll. 15–16). As he suspects, we ('the world') have good grounds to doubt his judgement.

At the beginning of the next sonnet, we are told by the narrator that 'He found her by the ocean's moaning verge, / Nor any wicked change in her discerned' (XLIX, ll. 1–2). This unspotted 'wicked change' presages her suicide at the end of this sonnet, glossed with the cryptic remark that 'That night he learned how silence best can speak / The awful things when Pity pleads for Sin' (ll. 11–12). Unlike her husband, the wife has not passed through the moral crucible of Darwinism. His understanding of himself and others as biological beings eventually leads him to a new moral perspective. The canon against self-slaughter notwithstanding, the self-loathing prompted by her pre-Darwinian conviction of sin drives her to suicide.

Modern Love is one of the most agonising poems in English. Arthur Symons captured Meredith's method perfectly when he described it as 'an astonishing feat in the vivisection of the heart' (1916: 143). Reading purely for the plot, we might be tempted to see Modern Love and Meredith with it as brutishly misogynistic and brutally Darwinian in equal measure, with the poem itself a cruel act of literary revenge taken by the poet on his (by then dead) ex-wife. But Meredith's real victim in his poem is not the wife but the husband. As his biographer Mervyn Jones notes, he deliberately evens out the moral stakes in the marriage by making the husband guilty of sexual infidelities of his own (1999: 93). More than this, the entire poem is a merciless excoriation of his weaknesses, cruelties and stupidities, misogyny included.

Through the moral education of the husband in Modern Love, Meredith takes the side of his own wife who deserted him. As Jones remarks with only mild exaggeration,

> For almost any other Victorian male, the effect of Meredith's experience would have been to induce a righteous misogyny . . . Remarkably – let us say, astonishingly – the effect on Meredith was to deepen the sympathy for women that resounds as a *leitmotiv* through all his novels [and indeed many of his poems]. (ibid.: 94)

At the same time, unlike some of the merciless husbands of Victorian fiction – Henleigh Grandcourt in George Eliot's *Daniel Deronda*, for example, or Gilbert Osmond in Henry James's *The Portrait of a Lady* – the husband in *Modern Love* is not cast beyond the reach of sympathy. Seeing the collapse of his marriage from within his own disordered mind, we are all too well aware of his pain. We are aware too of his powerlessness, again in stark contrast with Grandcourt or Osmond and with received expectations of marriage in patriarchal mid-Victorian England. And over the course of the poem we see his moral growth, including his acceptance of his redefined role as a man in the age of 'modern love', with its realigned and more egalitarian expectations of men and women.

Modern Love is an indictment of misogyny, the doctrine of sin and the tyranny of miserable marriages over both men and women. To put these behind us, Meredith suggests, we must also put behind us the moral tradition grounded in Genesis which underpins them. In a letter to his friend Frederick Maxse in 1861, he wrote that 'Our great error has been (the error of all religion, as I fancy) to raise a spiritual system in antagonism to Nature' (1970: I, 93). Over the course of his poem, he pares down the ethical implications of nature to the realisation that we are biological beings with only a partial responsibility for our desires and emotions. Moral codes and practices which seek to contain these Darwinian impulses are not in themselves wrong nor futile. The husband has no more doubt than his wife does that their adultery was immoral. But these moral codes can nonetheless become a source of profound pain and misery, indeed of tragedy. With its sarcastic title and darkly ironic appropriation of the sonnet sequence, *Modern Love* seems at first a bitter indictment of the mores of a 'modern', mid-Victorian England in which the edifice of the happy marriage is only sustained by a pervasive hypocrisy. But Meredith's poem holds out too the promise of a more genuine modernity founded on a sympathetic moral and psychological understanding, itself grounded in the secular biology of Darwinism.

Through the form of the sonnet sequence (a unique fusion of lyric, dramatic, and narrative poetry) Meredith is able to anatomise a mind in process, charting the emergence of an egalitarian sexual morality in an unpromising individual in an equally unpromising set of circumstances. Millay takes a similar view of sexuality, particularly female sexuality, as grounded in biology. But as she holds this position from the start of her sequence, so she takes it further. For Meredith, biology mitigates the offence of adultery, but it does not excuse it. For Millay, the biological basis of sex warrants, even appears to demand, free love. The biological understanding of love is superior to any ideal, she suggests, because it is true. This is not a Social Darwinist argument that what is, is right. Instead, it is an argument about honesty. To acknowledge the truth of one's own biology is to be honest to oneself and to others. It is a form of integrity.

Millay articulates this view most directly in sonnet XXII:

Now by this moon, before this moon shall wane
I shall be dead or I shall be with you!
No moral concept can outweigh the pain
Past rack and wheel this absence puts me through;
Faith, honour, pride, endurance, what the tongues
Of tedious men will say, or what the law –
For which of these do I fill up my lungs
With brine and fire at every breath I draw?
Time, and to spare, for patience by and by,
Time to be cold and time to sleep alone;
Let me no more until the hour I die
Defraud my innocent senses of their own.
Before this moon shall darken, say of me:
She's in her grave, or where she wants to be.

Here Millay juxtaposes abstract moral concepts and conventional opinions against the fleshly reality of the body. Her poetry heightens that reality, invoking instruments of torture and Petrarchan paradoxes to express the pain of longing. It heightens too the contrast between morality and biology. Internal rhymes set the 'moral concept' against the 'pain' it cannot 'outweigh', while the wagging 'tongues' of censorious old men are contrasted with her own vital 'lungs', the gratuitous, man-made 'law' with the natural need to 'draw' breath. Towards the end of her sonnet, however, Millay moves away from drawing contrasts between moral codes and bodily needs and towards identifying the two. Her 'senses', she insists, are 'innocent'. Our evolved bodies are not guilty in and of themselves. Neither we nor they are compromised by original sin.

To affirm an abstract moral ideal, Millay suggests, is dishonestly to deny the natural and legitimate impulses of our bodies. Does this mean that for Millay we should always act upon our desires? Not necessarily. Overall, it is a moot point whether *Fatal Interview* endorses the affair it records or not. The lover herself never disavows her love, but the pain she experiences as a result of it is, she suggests, barely endurable:

There is a word I dare not speak again,
A face I never again must call to mind;
I was not craven ever nor blenched at pain,

But pain to such degree and of such kind
As I must suffer if I think of you,
Not in my senses will I undergo.

(XLIX, ll. 9–14)

If the pain of desire is unequivocally bodily, so too is the pain of memory. Now the affair is over, it is the memory of her beloved rather than the desire for him that threatens barbarously to tear her body apart. Arguably, this is the same pain of absence that she felt before, only in a more final form. And yet she makes no effort to overturn this finality. In another late sonnet, she tells her estranged beloved 'unto my inmost core / I do desire your kiss upon my mouth' (XLV, ll. 9f), but she makes no further attempt to gain that kiss.

It is up to us whether we find against the adulterous lover in *Fatal Interview*, as the husband finds against himself (in part) in *Modern Love*. But in giving these adulterous lovers voices, Millay and Meredith allow us to understand them from within, not merely to judge them from without. In her essay 'The Natural History of German Life', George Eliot remarked that 'the greatest benefit we owe to the artist, whether painter, poet, or novelist, is the extension of our sympathies' (1992: 263). Millay and Meredith do indeed extend our sympathies in these poems, drawing us into the agonised minds and tormented bodies of their speakers: their 'senses', as Millay deftly suggests, in both senses of that word. As we feel for them, so we are drawn to reflect on our own minds and bodies in love. The implication of both poems is that we too ought to own up to our desires, and give them their due as we decide who to love, how to love and how to judge our own and other lovers' behaviour. For both poets, this means that the restrictive codes which have regulated love and sex – and through which men in particular have circumscribed the conduct of women – need to change. In giving a poetic voice to the moral and psychological implications of Darwinian biology, Millay and Meredith use their poetry to call too for sexual equality and the social liberation of women.

METAMORPHOSIS: THOM GUNN AND THE HUMAN ANIMAL

In drawing attention to our biology in their love sonnets, Millay and Meredith draw attention too to the fact that we are animals. In her late sonnet 'I too beneath your moon, almighty Sex', sexual desire leaves Millay 'crying like a cat' (l. 2). In *Modern Love*, the husband feels 'the wild beast in him' (IX, l. 1), for all that his wife treats him 'as something that is tame' (V, l. 4). Hardy makes the same point too in *Tess of the d'Urbervilles*. Pregnant out of wedlock, Tess feels herself to be 'out of harmony' with the natural world, 'a figure of Guilt intruding

— 212 —

into the haunts of Innocence' peopled by 'sleeping birds' and 'skipping rabbits'. 'But', Hardy writes, 'all the while she was making a distinction where there was no difference. Feeling herself in antagonism she was quite in accord. She had been made to break an accepted social law, but no law known to the environment in which she fancied herself such an anomaly' ([1891] 1978: 135).

These reminders that humans are animals are developed in the poetry of one of the best and bravest English (and adoptively American) poets of the post-war era: Thom Gunn. For Gunn, as for Millay and Meredith, human animality is revealed above all in sex. This is clear in 'Adultery', a poem which rehearses in miniature the plot of *Fatal Interview* and *Modern Love*:

Hot beautiful furless animals
played in a clearing opened by their desire
play climaxing to a transparent rage
that raised them above desire itself
– glimpses of clearing after clearing.

Leaving, she recomposed her face
to look as if she had just come
from the new Bergman movie
(which she had in fact seen before).
By the time she was home she'd done it
and her face was all grown over with expression.
Dedicated to her husband, showing
how interesting it had been, how
innovative, a real breakthrough
(you know how I love you, darling?)
he should see it too it would
change his entire outlook.

She played this little drama. And
she half believed it as she shaped it,
having played it before in the interest
of preserving the lovely house,
its rooms airy with freedoms,
the children going to a progressive school,
grass smoked when there were guests,
and philodendrons growing in slow trust.

Her husband looked at her silently,
she seemed, for a moment, an objective matter,

and in his thoughts he reviewed the drama:
a thicket of good-natured fictions,
not interesting, not
innovative, a real throwback
(you know how bored we are, darling?)
she should see it too it would
change her entire outlook.

This poem works with a series of contrasts. The first lies in the account of the adulterous lovers' experience of sex in the opening paragraph. These first five lines paint a picture of sex that is realistic but also metaphorical, natural but also transcendental. In the second line of the poem, reality and metaphor are elided. The forest clearing in which the animals are playing becomes not a literal clearing but a space inside their own lives 'opened by their desire'. Looking back from this moment – when an apparently real description segues into metaphor – it becomes clear that the metaphor and the reality coexist from the outset. The lovers are literally 'furless animals', but their behaviour is also figuratively animalistic as they abandon themselves to sensual pleasure. The title directs us to over-interpret this opening line in this way, reading 'hot' as sexually charged and 'furless' as naked. Yet on its own, the image of animals at 'play' is innocent, and this sense of innocence persists, in spite of the lovers' adultery. As well as opening a 'clearing' in each of their lives, their desire for one another opens them up to each other. Their emotions become 'transparent'. They are 'beautiful' too, with the natural, unselfconscious beauty of animals.

As well as their beauty, Gunn celebrates the lovers' desire. Like sex itself, Gunn's vocabulary in these lines is at once repetitive and increasingly ecstatic. Both 'play' and 'desire' are reinforced through repetition. The lovers' 'rage' – an unexplained burst of fury at the moment of orgasm – 'raises' them to a state beyond desire. In this moment, the apparent contradiction between 'hot' animalistic desire and the image of innocent animals at play is resolved. Sex takes the lovers to an ecstasy that is at once sexual and beyond sex. Gunn captures this process in a cycle of words and ideas bound together by subtle echoes. The opening up of a 'clearing' through desire enables a 'climaxing' which in turn provides 'glimpses of clearing after clearing' beyond. In each climax, desire is transcended, while each new clearing holds the promise of a new climax, born once again of desire.

The second contrast that Gunn sets out in his poem is between the honest ecstasy of the woman's affair and the mundane deceptions of her marriage. As the poem moves into its second paragraph, the intense echoes and repetitions come to an end, and with them the rich ambiguities of metaphor and reality, illicit desire and innocent play. Instead, Gunn reverts to a largely prosaic idiom as the woman herself re-enters the banality of her everyday life and the lies that maintain it. Where the opening lines enact a repetition that leads to transcendence, the next two paragraphs merely record the repetitive habits of deception, with the narrator distorting the record only slightly through his sad, sardonic description of her 'recomposed' face 'grown over with expression'. This image apart, Gunn chooses bathos as the effect best placed to bring home the abrupt transition from ecstasy to the mundane.

As the poem unfolds, further contrasts emerge: between the genuine and tangible if pedestrian benefits of the woman's marriage and the elusive and intangible heights of her adulterous affair; between how she sees her deception and how her husband sees (through) it; and, most directly but also most suggestively, between her account of 'the new Bergman movie' and his 'review' of her 'drama'. Their life together is at once affluent and liberal. On one level, her affair seems in keeping with their shared 'freedoms', their casually antiestablishment grass-smoking hedonism. Yet unlike her affair, their bohemianism is somehow self-conscious, self-satisfied too. The 'slow trust' that the philodendrons need in order to grow is a smug illusion. With their heart-shaped but poisonous leaves, these houseplants are an apt if unobtrusive symbol of their marriage.

The contrasts round which 'Adultery' is built foster ironies. One of these is the fact that the wife believes her own deception more than her husband does. She lives both her lives subjectively, if separately. He sees her performance objectively and as a whole. Gunn does not specify, but it seems likely that 'the new Bergman movie' is (or refers back to) *Scenes from a Marriage*, itself a study in adultery. Watching his wife's deceptions, the husband sees a scene from his own marriage as it might appear to an outsider. The judgements he passes on her performance are ostensibly aesthetic, not moral. But how we interpret them depends on what exactly we think it is he is judging. Is the 'little drama' her performance of the role of a loving wife, when she is actually an adulteress ('you know how I love you, darling?')? Or is it her adultery itself? In having the husband call her performance a 'throwback', Gunn recalls his portrait of the adulterous lovers themselves as 'animals'. For a self-consciously 'progressive' couple, is it an evolutionary regression for one of them to abandon herself to sexual desire? Or is it rather a 'breakthrough'?

The evolutionary language of a 'throwback' raises in turn the moral questions that haunt this poem. With remarkable charity and insight, the husband realises that his wife's lies are ultimately 'good-natured', not malign. She does genuinely value their life together, and she wants to protect him as well as herself from pain. But for all his forgiveness, these last lines remain perhaps bitter and certainly deeply sad. The boredom that he owns up to masks a desperate yearning for things to change, to get better. The impression the poem leaves is that this is a forlorn hope. His objectivity may only be momentary, but it suggests nonetheless that they are too far gone, too estranged, too alienated from one another, to be reunited.

'Adultery' is morally compelling because, for all the contrasts it sets up, it does not prejudice one perspective over another. The husband's view of his wife's affair as a 'thicket' of lies does not efface her experience of it as 'clearing after clearing'. Nonetheless, each view qualifies the other. Gunn implies that, just as there are no absolute aesthetic standards, there can be no absolute moral judgements where consensual sex is concerned. He is as frank as Meredith in admitting that adultery is a source of tragedy, as one impetus conflicts inevitably with another. But both poets realise that to apportion blame a priori is to impose judgements that are at best partial. It is to seal off, too, rich seams of human nature that may lead a given individual to a space in their lives where they might indeed be able to regain the authenticity of a hot, beautiful, furless animal.

When John Addington Symonds pointed out the parallel between Dantesque and Platonic love, he had a hidden agenda. If Victorian England could accept that adultery could be idealistic, it might be able to get over its abhorrence of homosexuality. Gunn, like Symonds, was homosexual. 'Adultery' is not a well-disguised poem about a homosexual affair. The details of the marriage and the characterisation are too concrete for that to be plausible. But undoubtedly Gunn's awareness of the conflict between his own sexuality and social expectations made him more acutely aware of the more comprehensive opposition between sex and the social codes that regulate it. For Gunn, as for Meredith and Millay, this is a conflict between biology and what Hardy calls 'accepted social law', between our animal natures and our strictly human moralities. Of the three, Gunn is the most enthusiastic advocate of living our lives, particularly our sex lives, according to our nature. And for Gunn, as for Kinsey, our nature includes – for some of us at least – homosexuality.

In 'Adultery', the adulterous lovers are described as animals as they have sex. The transformation of a human being into an animal is a recurrent symbol of human sexuality within Gunn's poetry. An early example is 'The Allegory of the Wolf Boy'. In this poem an adolescent boy inhabits an upper-middle-class world of tennis and tea in the daytime but seeks out the moon, sprouts 'close dark hair' and 'Drops on four feet' at night (ll. 21, 24). There are hints that the boy may be homosexual, as the moon's 'infertile light / Shall loose desires hoarded against his will' (ll. 15–16).

But Gunn himself warned against presupposing that his poems are about homosexuality (1982: 187–8). In an interview given shortly before his death, he remarked that he saw the werewolf as 'a marvelous allegory of sexuality – all sexuality', with 'desire, the wolf, coming over the person who is very reluctant to acknowledge but can't help acknowledging it'. While this is, as Gunn noted, the experience of 'being in the closet', it is also a more universal phenomenon (Hennessy 2005).

Over time, Gunn would become more open about his own sexuality in his poetry. But homosexual desire remains an emblem for sexuality at large, as well as for homosexuality itself. Gunn praised his friend and fellow poet Robert Duncan for transforming American poetry so that it could accommodate homosexual material 'not as something perverse or eccentric or morbid, but as evidence of the many available ways in which people live their lives, of the many available ways in which people love or fail to love' (1982: 134). Gunn's words here are revealingly ambiguous. Homosexuality for Gunn is both one (or some) of these many ways and a symbol for them all. It is both a specific type of sexuality, and the archetype of sexuality as a whole.

The double meaning of homosexuality within Gunn's poetry can be seen in 'Tom-Dobbin', from his 1971 collection *Moly*. The transition from man to animal occurs many times in this collection. The epigraph and the title are taken from the *Odyssey*, where Odysseus is given the herb moly as an antidote to Circe's magic, which has turned his sailors into animals. In the first poem, 'Rites of Passage', Gunn reimagines the transformation into a horned animal in Oedipal terms, recasting the picture of adolescence in 'The Allegory of the Wolf Boy' in a more specifically confrontational form. In the next, the title poem 'Moly', the quest for the moly itself is presented as a desperate and implicitly hopeless bid to cure the bestiality within. Neither of these poems presents animal sexuality as a positive condition, although both could be said to record the rage and misery of the unwilling animal rather than necessarily condemning animality itself.

This interpretation gains some credence from the progression of the five so-called centaur poems that comprise 'Tom-Dobbin'. In 'The Allegory of the Wolf Boy', the blond boy grows dark hair when he transforms into a wolf. In the first section of 'Tom-Dobbin', instead of a radical transformation from one state into another, Gunn traces an 'imperceptible transition' (l. 8) as the downy blond human skin melts into a chestnut brown horse's hide. The wolf boy is described half-ironically as an 'exception to the natural laws' (l. 22). The centaur, by contrast, is an unironic symbol of the 'seamless' (l. 7) divide between humans and animals in a Darwinian world. The division between body and mind is porous too, as light coming in at the eye becomes light 'in the mind' (l. 3). Even the familiar idea that the move from the animal to the human is 'a beginning upward' (l. 18) – literalized in the body of the centaur itself – is complicated by this seamlessness. Human qualities may be higher, but they have animal beginnings, and 'the one . . . is also the other' (ll. 11–12).

Gunn's centaur recalls the Roman poet Ovid's mythological epic *Metamorphoses*. Hughes too revives the poetry of metamorphosis in his vibrant *Tales from Ovid*. Hughes's Ovidian world is superficially apt to a Darwinian age. In it, humans and animals live at the mercy of the amoral violence of the natural order. But in Hughes, following Ovid, metamorphoses entail the transformation of a person into something utterly different. There is often an ironic analogy between the two (for example, between Arachne the spinner and the spider she becomes) but in their nature they are presumed to be wholly different. Hence a human being may become a constellation of stars or a spring as readily as a deer or a bear. In Gunn's Darwinian metamorphoses, by contrast, the human becomes something he or she already is: an animal. To become an animal in Gunn's poetry is to realize one's own animal nature.

Gunn introduces the idea of seamlessness into the form of his first centaur poem as well its content, the broken lines making the move from one line to another a gradual rather than an absolute transition. For the second poem, Gunn chooses a very different verse form, combining the highly conventional heroic couplet with crudely demotic language. His opening couplet is studiedly inelegant:

Hot in his mind, Tom watches Dobbin fuck,
Watches, and smiles with pleasure, oh what luck.
(ll. 1–2)

Gunn's use of 'fuck' is the most obvious challenge to the reader here, but it is not the only one. The rhyme with 'oh what luck' deliberately draws attention to Tom's (and perhaps Thom's) voyeurism. Gunn's punctuation highlights Tom's pedestrian imagination too. Instead of 'oh what luck!' Gunn gives us 'oh what luck.' Tom may be pleased, but he is not fired up. The sight of the horses fucking is pornographic but also banal, essentially because Tom's mind is banal itself. There is no 'poetic' idealisation here. In 'Roan Stallion', one of his most powerful narrative poems, Robinson Jeffers gives us a magnificent stallion as a symbol of native sexuality. Gunn's Tom gives us Dobbin.

Gunn takes the couplet as a form flexible and versatile enough for him to switch from one register into another in the middle of a poem. In some ways, the most shocking thing about this poem is not the bald account of Tom watching Dobbin fuck, nor even the fact that he masturbates as he does it, but the extraordinary image of his ejaculated semen 'shooting like a star, / In which all colours of the spectrum are' (ll. 9–10). Suddenly the poem is transformed from an obscene spectacle into a celebration of beauty. It moves from a literal into a symbolic mode. This move is signalled by the collapse of the distinction between Tom and Dobbin, as they come simultaneously. Their union (at a distance) prefigures the union of 'all colours' in the pure white light of the star, an image which suggests that all life is encapsulated in the semen, all experience fused and transcended in orgasm.

This image, together with the bold, at times surprising, colours of the landscape in this second poem, hint at another of the sources for Gunn's idea of seamlessness. *Moly* was written under the influence of LSD. Like many of his generation, Gunn saw the experience of acid as revelatory, not merely illusory. In an essay written in 1973 Gunn characterised poetry as 'reaching out into the unexplained areas of the mind, in which the air is too thickly primitive or too fine for us to live continually' (1982: 152). In 'Tom-Dobbin', the acid trip, poetry and sex all fulfil the same function. The distinction between human and animal is transcended, both in that the two animals – Tom and Dobbin, human and horse – 'join to one' (l. 7), and in that Tom himself becomes momentarily purely animal. Gregory Woods has observed that in Gunn's poetry becoming an animal typically 'involves becoming more human, more humane', not less (1987: 225). As Gunn's remark in his essay implies, this is a condition that is at once 'primitive' and a refinement, an improvement, if an unsustainable one, of day-to-day life. It is both a 'throwback' and a 'breakthrough', as he writes in 'Adultery'.

The third poem in the cycle reinforces this hedonism as Gunn records how, through an orgy, a man (who may or may not be Tom) transcends his own identity, becoming part of a mingling community of lovers. This poem fulfils the promise of seamlessness set out in the first poem, in part by going over to prose in place of verse. In the fourth poem, Gunn returns more directly to the theme of biology. Where the first poem posits the centaur as a symbol of the human animal, the fourth reflects on another centaurine animal in an expressly evolutionary context. Like the centaur, the platypus is an improbable combination of creatures. In the poem, its 'crisp perfected outline' is belied by its anatomical mix of 'webs, fur, beak' (l. 3). A mammal that lays eggs and has a duck's bill and webbed feet, the platypus is a living embodiment of the blurred lines of Darwinian evolution. Indeed, along with the lungfish, it was Darwin's favourite example of a missing link, for all that Gunn's poetic account of its evolution is on the face of it more

Lamarckian than Darwinian, invoking 'mixed habits' (l. 2) which both are and create its nature.

Unlike other mammals, the mother platypus does not lactate from teats but from its skin. This gives Gunn another image of blurred lines, and a further opportunity to multiply the categories into which we might place her. She seems as much a moist, ripe fruit as an animal. The most significant image of blurring in this poem, however, is the blurring of the mother and child within 'One breaking outline that includes the two' (l. 10). Gunn invites us to see this outline 'through darkness' (l. 9), again combining the literal with the figurative. The platypus is in 'her cave' (l. 4), so to see the outline of her and her son we would need to see through the dark. But we would also need to see in a new way.

The cave itself suggests this. Gunn's decision to call the platypus's small burrow a 'cave' is sufficiently odd that it must be more than merely picturesque. In Plato's *Republic*, humanity's inability to see the truth is famously represented as our seeing only the shadow of the ideal cast on the wall of a cave. Like the men in Plato's cave, Gunn suggests, we need to learn to 'see through darkness', to see things as they really are. The image of the platypus suckling its young within a single outline suggests that, for all that we too are each 'hatched into separation' (l. 8), we remain part of a single whole.

In his second and third centaur poems, Gunn presents the union between individuals as something that takes place through sex. In the fourth, he sees it as an corollary of motherhood. Mammals become one with one another through gestation and suckling as well as through sex. In both cases, Gunn implies, we attain a state of mind in which we do not distinguish ourselves from others. As in the first poem, we reach 'upward' towards this state of mind, like the platypus rising to her cave. But we are also returning to our 'beginning', to a time before we are born or give birth, before a mother's child rises from 'her close tunnel' (l. 4) into its own individual existence. And we are returning too to the 'thickly primitive' world of purely animal existence. In this sense, to see through darkness is to see back in time. At the same time, it is to see reality in a new, ideal light: to see life comprised not of distinct individuals, but a single whole.

The broadening of Gunn's idea of how animals transcend their individuality through biology in the fourth of his centaur poems impacts on how he thinks about sex too, when he returns to it in the fifth and last of them. Where the other centaur poems observe their subjects from a third-person perspective, here one of the lovers speaks the poem himself. As they close in together, even the distinction between the lovers themselves is washed away. 'Me' and 'him' become genuinely, indistinguishably 'we'. The water through which the two are moving becomes their 'one flesh' in which their 'selves' are imagined 'floating' (ll. 5–6). The image of people floating in water that is also flesh calls to mind the womb. These lovers are brothers *in utero*. Like the hot, furless animals in 'Adultery', they have achieved 'the trust, the brotherhood, the repossession of innocence, the nakedness of spirit' that Gunn felt were characteristic of the 'acid years' (1982: 184). For Gunn, sex is as intoxicating and as revelatory as a drug. But it is also a means by which we can recapture our authentic human nature – our nature as mammals, for whom the relationships between lovers and between parents and children transcend the needs and identities of individuals.

In 1979 Gunn wrote that the utopian vision of the acid years was 'still a possibility' (1982: 184). Over the next decade, the onset of AIDS turned Gunn's adopted hometown of San Francisco into the first epicentre of a worldwide catastrophe. Gunn himself became its great poet. His response to the epidemic which killed so many of his close friends and devastated the gay community came in *The Man with Night Sweats*, published in 1992. Gunn does not reject the values of *Moly* in *The Man with Night Sweats*, but he does qualify them. After AIDS, it is even more vital for Gunn that homosexuality should be accepted as a part of human nature, not a flouting of it. At the same time, once known, AIDS transforms the psychological and ethical landscape. There are no boys turning into wolves, no men masturbating at the sight of mating horses in *The Man with Night Sweats*. Instead, there are people dying, others acutely aware of their vulnerability to death, and all sustained by a love more characterised by friendship than sex. This is not a disavowal of the pan-sexual promiscuity celebrated in Gunn's earlier poems, so much as a guarded elegy for it.

Instead of representing the human animal directly through symbolic myths of werewolves and centaurs in *The Man with Night Sweats* Gunn takes a more indirect approach. In the middle of a collection of poems devoted to human relationships the reader encounters a poem called 'The Life of the Otter'. As it appears on the page, this poem recalls the first poem of 'Tom-Dobbin'. There the shift from half-line to half-line mirrors the centaur's seamless transition from man to horse. Here a similar typographical form shows us the otter's liquid movement through water, with its parabolas, loops and downward curves depicted as well as described. Aurally, however, the two poems are distinct. Where the earlier poem is freeform, 'The Life of the Otter' is closely based on blank verse. This is clearest in lines such as 'Of which the speed contains its own repose' (l. 33), but the structure of the iambic pentameter is clearly audible too in phrases that reach over two or even three typographical lines, such as 'Now / while he flows / out of a downward curve' (ll. 20–2). The rhythms of the underlying metre nudge us towards becoming 'half lost / In the exuberance of dip and wheel' (ll. 11–12), like the otter itself, as the patterning of sounds comes to transcend their meaning. At the same time, the metre exercises its control over the poem as a whole, so that like the otter itself we are only 'half lost', not utterly distracted, as we might be by the more insistent rhythms of 'The Lark Ascending', for example.

In 'The Life of the Otter', Gunn returns to the image of an animal at play. For the otter, 'play' (repeated four times in as many lines, ll. 13–16) is 'all there is' (l. 17). In its purely animal existence, Gunn resolves the contrast he sets out in 'Adultery' between the erotic 'play' of the lovers and the day-to-day regularities of the married couple. The otter is perpetually in the same transcendent state the lovers experience through sex. But for the otter this state of 'play' is 'Functional but as if gratuitous' (l. 19). Gunn's thinking here is expressly adaptationist, but with a twist. He does not deny that the otter's activity serves a function ('hunt, procreation, feeding' (l. 18)) but he insists that it remains 'play' nonetheless. Furthermore, this 'play' is not a surrogate for real activity, not 'practice', nor a recreational 'relaxation' or 'escape' (ll. 16–17). In other words, it does not have its own function, it is rather the condition of performing functional activity itself. In neo-Darwinian terms, it is the reward or incentive set up by natural selection to persuade the otter to survive and reproduce. The same activity that appears as 'functional' from one perspective appears as 'play' from another.

For the otter, everything is play. Gunn invites us to think about life at large, and our own lives, in the same terms. Everything in life, no matter how functional, can carry with it the pleasure of play. This pleasure may seem 'gratuitous', but it is part of our adaptation to life, part of what it is to live life healthily and fully. In another sense, the pleasure of play is indeed 'gratuitous', because it comes to us for free, but only if we can abandon the self-conscious pursuit of meaning that characterises another semi-aquatic creature, Hughes's wodwo. As Naden remarks, we have to relearn how to enjoy ourselves.

In the otter, Gunn gives us a model of hedonism free from the tragedy of conflicting perspectives and motivations that dogs the lovers in *Modern Love*, *Fatal Interview* and 'Adultery', free too from the unfolding horror of AIDS. He can do this partly because the otter as we see it exists and plays on its own. In effect, its state of 'play' is an ideal, abstracted from conflicts and obligations. It is a purely solipsistic pleasure, a point reinforced by the otter's solitude. But in the pleasure Gunn himself takes in the otter's play, it takes on another dimension. Like the lovers in his fifth centaur poem, Gunn's pleasure is both self-gratifying and sympathetic. Through the medium of the poem he provides us too with both kinds of pleasure.

Gunn does not state it explicitly in this poem, but he nonetheless suggests that this double pleasure in our own play and the play of others has a particular bearing on sex. He draws our attention to the otter's 'genitals' (l. 24), its 'Potency / set in fur / like an ornament' (ll. 34–6). As play and function coexist, so function coexists with aesthetics. The pleasure Gunn takes in the otter's genitals is not purely aesthetic, however, or at least not disinterestedly so. In the context of a collection of poems largely about homosexual love, the closing description of the otter's 'firm muscular trunk' (l. 31) as it dives into the water suggests a human swimmer as much as an animal. The otter's genitals lead Gunn towards an implied reverie about a man's 'Potency / set in fur'.

In these closing lines, the otter undergoes a metamorphosis in Gunn's mind's eye, becoming human even as it is at its most animal. As it does so, its genitals become the focus of his determination to collapse function and play into one. A man's genitals, like the otter's, serve the purpose of procreation. But their needs are fulfilled not through procreation itself but through play. Indeed, by choosing play as the method and pleasure as the reward, natural selection has ensured that it is play rather than procreation that brings sexual satisfaction. Play prioritises the immediate ends (satisfaction) over the ultimate end (procreation), and the means to those immediate ends include homosexual as well as heterosexual sex. For Gunn, the pleasure he takes in another man's genitals is thus as natural and as healthy as the pleasure he takes in admiring the otter, and as the otter's play itself.

In 'The Life of the Otter', Gunn reaffirms his view that both animalistic play and homosexual desire are natural and healthy in themselves. Nonetheless, AIDS constrains them both. Gunn's regret at this loss is captured in his masterful poem 'The Missing', written in 1987 and published towards the end of *The Man with Night Sweats*. In an autobiographical essay, Gunn remarks that in metrical verse 'the nature of the control being exercised' becomes 'part of the life being spoken about' (1982: 179). In this heart-wrenching poem Gunn exercises a meticulous control to stop himself from falling apart. This parallels the transformation within the poem of his own body into a statue, another metamorphosis, except here Gunn becomes less not more human, as his friends die and their intimacies are withdrawn. Instead of becoming animal, he becomes stone, reversing the famous metamorphosis of Pygmalion's image, the statue brought to life by its sculptor's erotic desire.

The stages of Gunn's transformation represent a progressive withdrawal in the face of 'the plague' (l. 1). At first, he feels himself changing into the statue 'with a sculpted skin' (l. 4). His aside that he does not like this coldness 'nowadays' (l. 5) refers back to his earlier poetry. Before the liberation of *Moly*, Gunn's poetry tended to be characterised by a celebration of seemingly impregnable, leather-clad, hyper-masculinity. Woods argues that this motif is a pose, suggesting that in 'Tom-Dobbin' the process of becoming an animal is 'a means of release from pose, an emancipation of the poseur' (1987: 225). In 'The Missing', Gunn endorses this reading of his own poetry. The 'warmth' (l. 6) born of and expressed through an apparently 'unlimited embrace' (l. 12) had melted his own earlier reserve.

As in 'Tom-Dobbin', Gunn draws out the biological vitality of sex and particularly gay sex. As well as 'warmth', the 'living mass' (l. 10) demonstrates 'ceaseless movement' (l. 15) and a 'pulsing presence' (l. 18). Like the natural world itself, sex is characterised by aggression as well as ease, recalling the sudden unexplained 'rage' of the lovers in 'Adultery'. It is at once solipsistic and generous, and above all playful. It is also akin to both friendship and family love. Indeed, for Gunn, sex itself and an openness to the desires of others extend our sense of family without end, as dance does for Appleman in 'Waldorf-Astoria Euphoria'.

Yet this erotic and social ideal cannot survive AIDS. The collective life of love that was self-supporting becomes 'unsupported' (l. 20) for those who are left. In the absence of 'support' (l. 16), Gunn is thrown back on his earlier 'pose' (l. 21). As the poem draws to a close, it becomes clear that he has regressed even beyond the statue, part-way to the uncarved rock. The end of the life around him has left him frozen, incomplete, fossilized. Here again he confronts the tragedy of love in a Darwinian age: the irresolvable conflict between a biological impulse and a conscious social and personal imperative. Gunn cannot live according to his biology because to do so would be to kill himself and others in the process. But without the playful love that is born of that biology life becomes a living death and the human animal turns to stone.

Ultimately, all three of the major Darwinian love poets find tragedy in sexual desire. But for all of them it is also a source of hope, of authentic self-fulfilment and collective happiness. For Meredith, Millay and Gunn it is a fundamental implication of Darwinism that all human desire falls by definition within the scope of human nature. As Kinsey and de Waal rightly insist, there are no preordained rules for what is or is not natural for the human species, only the empirical, natural-historical facts of what human beings collectively and individually feel and do. Given this premise, these poets insist that the sexual desires of all people deserve the same consideration, whether they are men or women, married or single, straight or gay.

Even so, all three have their doubts as to how far the free play of those desires is itself desirable. In *Modern Love*, the possibility is tantalising that had they only been able to emancipate themselves from convention and end their marriage the husband and wife might have been happy and their lovers along with them. But, as Meredith shows us, convention itself is internalised, and has its own hold on us as a part of us. In *Fatal Interview*, Millay acknowledges that even an offer of love freely accepted may come to be painfully rebuffed in time. Even Gunn, the most unrestrained advocate of free love, accepts that one woman's 'clearing' is another man's 'thicket', and that, even if social constraint were overcome, the prospect of death would always force us back into our carapaces. Yet for all this, there remains the hope in their poems that if people accept their own natures and the desires that manifest them they may yet rediscover the joy of their 'innocent senses', the delight of 'beautiful furless animals' at play, and not strike despair into the hearts of others through their insensitivity, intolerance and intransigence.

8

On Balance

Fᴏʀ ʙᴇᴛᴛᴇʀ ᴏʀ ꜰᴏʀ ᴡᴏʀꜱᴇ

In his recent poem 'Darwin in the Galapagos' from his sequence 'Planet Wave', Edwin Morgan conjures up the image of the air bright with Darwin's finches – 'well, bright and dark' (l. 9). For Morgan himself, Darwin's revelation of life as a gorgeous evolutionary process is indeed bright. As his Darwin remarks,

> 'I can hardly sleep for excitement!
> Nothing is immutable, life changes, we evolve.
> Process is gorgeous, is it not!
> Process is progress, don't you see!'
>
> (ll. 29–32)

For others, however, Darwin is the prophet of nothing more than 'the universe's grand indifference', as Amy Clampitt puts it in 'A Curfew' (l. 42). In 'Camouflage', Clampitt asks herself why a killdeer (a common North American plover) tries to distract her away from its eggs by feigning injury. Her reply is telling:

> We have
> no answer except accident,
> the trillion-times-over-again
> repeated predicament
>
> sifted with so spendthrift
> a disregard for casualties
> we can hardly bear to think of
> a system so heartless, so shiftless
> as being in charge here.
>
> (ll. 33–41)

'It's / too much like us' (ll. 41–2), Clampitt adds, in a wry inversion of the argument that it is God who is a projection of human characteristics onto an inhuman nature. Whether Darwinism disturbs us because the nature it reveals is too like us or too alien – whether, to borrow from Wilde, we suffer from the rage of Caliban seeing his own face in the glass, or the rage of Caliban not seeing his own face in the glass – either way, it can seem appalling (1966: 16).

Even for those accustomed to it, Darwinism can spell the end of God, the finality of death, the insignificance of humanity, the nightmare of environmental collapse, the violence of nature and the tragedy of desire. The need many people feel to resist this dispiriting vision is neatly captured in 'My Father Shaving Charles Darwin', by the current British poet Neil Rollinson:

As he sinks his backside into the domed
seat of the barber's shop, my father
tips him back like a spaceman to gaze

at the cobwebs whiskered with shavings.
He strokes his fingers through Mr Darwin's
facial hair and tugs, as you might

an implausible stick-on beard.
Well what's it to be, lad?
Only a trim, a bit of a tidy up, says Darwin

settling into the chair.
My father pulls the clippers
out of their box and flicks the switch.

We'll have you looking like a man in next
to no time, my father mutters over the Brylcreem,
can't have you looking like a monkey.

His beard comes off like sparks on a foundry floor.
Need a pair of goggles for this job, he shouts
above the din. He dreams of shaving

the world's heretics clean of their facial hair,
Sigmund Freud, Karl Marx, Fidel Castro; doing his
own little bit for God and for moral decency.

He strops the blade, it runs in furrows
across the man's face, leaving the glass-like purity
that makes my father want to weep.

When the transformation is complete
he takes off the cape and brushes Mr Darwin's neck.
My father's eyes are filled with tears.

He's done a good job, he's humming now,
the tune of 'Jerusalem', stroking the shaven jaws
of Charles Darwin, who sits in his chair, petrified.

Like Morgan, Rollinson uses Darwin himself as a symbol of the Darwinian vision. The portrait of the 'petrified' Darwin, transformed from a monkey into a man, is splendidly comic, but it is the barber himself who is the more intriguing and ultimately the more touching character. Rollinson identifies him as his father, a member of an older generation, puritanical and hidebound, by contrast with Rollinson himself, who was a child of the 1960s (just: he was born in 1960) and who is best known as an explicitly erotic poet. Within this poem, the barber seems older even than Darwin himself, addressing the famous bearded patriarch as 'lad'. As he begins the process of shearing off Darwin's beard, he too is transformed, from a resentful mutterer into a spectacular grotesque, a secularist's nightmare, the godly equivalent of Sweeny Todd. But this barber does not want to slit Darwin's throat, only to reimpose upon him the 'glass-like purity' of clean-shaven orthodoxy.

Rollinson's surreal imagination transforms Darwin's magnificent entangled bank of a beard into the perfect symbol of the unruliness, the indecency, of his ideas. But his poem also realises the terror that those ideas hold for a man like his father, whose sense of God and moral decency is premised on assumptions that Darwinism – like psychoanalysis and communism, and indeed intellectual enquiry in general – will not let be. The tears that well up in the barber's eyes reveal the relief he would feel if these ideas could be erased, but also the desperation that he feels when faced with them. Darwin may end his ordeal terrified of the barber, but in the long run the barber himself is the more vulnerable.

The poets who grapple with Darwinism are not champions of orthodoxy like Rollinson's barber. But they are aware, as he is, of the distress that facing up to Darwinism can entail. Some, like Morgan, admit that others feel this pain but are so far from feeling it themselves that they pay heed to it only briefly. Others, like James Thomson in *The City of Dreadful Night*, feel it acutely, even absolutely, precisely because, unlike the barber, they see no alternative but to accept that Darwin's vision is correct. For Thomson, this translates into

> The sense that every struggle brings defeat
> > Because Fate holds no prize to crown success;
> That all the oracles are dumb or cheat
> > Because they have no secret to express;
> That none can pierce the vast black veil uncertain
> Because there is no light beyond the curtain;
> > That all is vanity and nothingness.
>
> (xxi, ll. 64–70)

In *In Memoriam*, the 'hope of answer, or redress' which lies 'behind the veil' consoles Tennyson for his sense that, even before Darwin, geology and natural history paint a picture of life that is 'futile' and 'frail' (lvi, ll. 25–8). Appropriating both Tennyson's image and the language of Ecclesiastes, Thomson refuses this consolation because for him it has no foundation. Science has lifted the veil, only to show that there is nothing behind it. In Thomson's poem, his master Shelley's warning 'Lift not the painted veil' takes on a new and grim significance. In Shelley's sonnet, the poet's gift of seeing beyond the veil leaves him disillusioned, because he has been inspired with Fear and Hope beyond the scope of the material world. For Thomson, the hope that Shelley found and that Tennyson hoped to find behind the veil is not to be found even there, let alone here. The result is a double-disillusionment, for which Thomson can offer no consolation beside 'iron endurance' (l. 82), solidarity and the grisly pleasure of the Gothic black humour with which he laces his poem.

From Hardy and Meredith onwards, the leading Darwinian poets have felt bound to answer the pessimism that Thomson deduced from Darwinism. They differ widely in where they stand on the spectrum from Thomson to Morgan, but each has taken on the same task, more or less self-consciously, of drawing out for their readers what it is that makes life in a Darwinian universe at worst tolerable, at best joyful. In so doing, they have weighed up the good and the bad, passing their judgement on the Darwinian condition as a whole. In this chapter I will draw out some of their conclusions, and their impact as poetry. First, I will look at how Frost, Ammons and Rogers expressly weigh up the Darwinian condition. Each bites on the grit of Darwinism but finds all the same that there is something to counterbalance the view that 'all is vanity and nothingness'. Next, I will explore how Hardy, Clampitt and Gunn use poetry itself to revive the sense of enchantment seemingly worn away by Darwin's materialist view of nature. Finally, I will weigh up the opposing reactions to Darwin implicit in two of the earliest, fullest and most compelling poems to respond to his ideas: Meredith's celebratory 'Ode to the Spirit of Earth in Autumn' and Tennyson's deeply unsettled and unsettling 'Lucretius'.

'THE JUST PROPORTION OF GOOD TO ILL': WEIGHING UP EVOLUTION

In the late 1930s, Robert Frost began issuing a poem as a booklet each Christmas. It was a tradition he would sustain off and on until 1960. One of the earliest of these poems is 'Our Hold on the Planet', printed in 1940 and revised for inclusion in Frost's next collection, A *Witness Tree*, in 1942. In this poem, Frost weighs up the 'proportion of good to ill' in nature in the light of natural selection:

> We asked for rain. It didn't flash and roar.
> It didn't lose its temper at our demand
> And blow a gale. It didn't misunderstand
> And give us more than our spokesman bargained for;
> And just because we owned to a wish for rain,
> Send us a flood and bid us be damned and drown.
> It gently threw us a glittering shower down.
> And when we had taken that into the roots of grain,
> It threw us another and then another still,
> Till the spongy soil again was natal wet.
> We may doubt the just proportion of good to ill.
> There is much in nature against us. But we forget:
> Take nature altogether since time began,
> Including human nature, in peace and war,
> And it must be a little more in favor of man,
> Say a fraction of one percent at the very least,
> Or our number living wouldn't be steadily more,
> Our hold on the planet wouldn't have so increased.

Frost's poem is an extended sonnet, with an extra quatrain between the octet and the sestet. Like Meredith's sixteen-line sonnets in *Modern Love*, Frost's reshaping of this traditional form gives him the freedom to relax within his poem. This relaxation shows itself in his stretching out the narrative component of his poem from eight lines to ten, in keeping with slow saturation by the gentle rain.

Constrained neither by human wishes nor by its own rage, the weather happens to give Frost and his fellow farmers exactly what they need. In the first line, 'It' could refer to the rain itself, or simply to a state of affairs, as in the phrase 'it is raining'. Over the next few lines, however, 'It' becomes more anthropomorphic, a weather god capable of negotiating with a 'spokesman'. If 'It' chose, 'It' might damn the farmers with too much rain. As it happens, however, 'It' is not capricious, but benign, giving the farmers just enough rain to take 'into the roots of grain'; it is an oddly active image: we tend to think of plants 'taking' water in themselves by their own roots.

Frost's increasingly concrete personification of the weather and of human agency has the paradoxical effect of drawing out how utterly impersonal these forces really are. His description of rural life is oddly pagan for a Christmas poem, although his 'It' recalls the biblical God both in the farmers' fear that it might send a flood and damn them, and in its actual benevolence. The poem returns to a point of subsistence, where what pagans and Christians alike most need from their gods is good weather. In these circumstances, any religion looks like – and looks to – superstition.

As Frost enacts the *volta* within his poem, however, he switches from a superstitious to a scientific register which renders our guesses about what 'It' is – God, Fortune, the vicissitudes of the weather – irrelevant. Using the freedom of his modified sonnet form, Frost creates a two-stage *volta*. The two spare lines left at the end of the third quatrain set up a change of perspective in preparation for the statistical thesis set out in the sestet. These two lines belong both to the superstitious discourse and to the scientific one. They weigh up the 'proportion' of good and ill mathematically, and they speak in terms of 'nature' in the abstract, not anthropomorphically. On the other hand, they still cast natural things as 'against us', and the very word 'ill' suggests ill will or malicious intent, rather than the arbitrary unconcern for humanity encapsulated in Hardy's 'Hap'. In the sestet itself, however, Frost sets this ambiguity aside, making the case that (whether or not nature is purely material) the very fact that the human population has been increasing is proof that nature is more favourable to humanity than not. There may be things 'in nature against us', but there must be more that supports us, otherwise 'nature' would not provide the fertile 'natal' soil in which we thrive. As Frost remarks of another animal in another modified sonnet, 'On a Bird Singing in Its Sleep', 'It could not have come down to us so far . . . If singing out of sleep and dream that way / Had made it much more easily a prey' (ll. 9, 13–14).

Frost wrote 'Our Hold on the Planet' as the United States was inching towards war. In returning to the seemingly timeless processes of agriculture in such a time, Frost offers his readers a long-term hope in place of a short-term fear, as Hardy did before him in 'In Time of "The Breaking of Nations"'. It is, of course, a qualified hope. Frost's poetry never lets us lose sight of the dark, and it is hardly a cause for jubilation that nature is, all told, 'a fraction of one percent' in our favour. Human beings can hardly call themselves a chosen race on those terms. On the other hand, Frost reminds us that even our own wars – intra-specific competition at its most brutal – have not tipped the balance against us. With the world descending into another world war, 'human nature' must be included within the balance of 'nature' as a whole, lest the bloody brutality that turned Jeffers against humanity should outweigh the hopes offered by the fruitful environment of nature at large.

Over time, Frost's poem has acquired an ironic cast that it did not have when it was first written. It now looks, paradoxically, as though the tightening grip of our hold on the planet is precisely what will undo us. A. R. Ammons predicts this in *Sphere*, *Garbage* and 'Questionable Procedures'. In his earlier poem, 'The City Limits', he sees Darwinism in a different, more optimistic, light. Like Pattiann Rogers in 'The Possible Suffering of a God during Creation', Ammons uses a long, slow, free-verse line, alliteration, internal rhymes and a polysyllabic, Latinate vocabulary in this poem to suggest an authoritative, patient voice. Like the light that defines the symbolism of his poem, the underlying form of the poem is not disturbed by the particular details of each phrase as he sustains a single sentence over six verses, each of the same length. The syntax too is constant, as each new clause repeats the opening phrase 'when you consider' (ll. 1, 3, 5, 8, 12), always after a caesura and always at the end of a line.

In 'The Possible Suffering', Rogers includes commonplace words alongside the elevated diction of science and theology. Ammons does the same in 'The City Limits'. This colloquial idiom and imagery deepens into a frank account of the bodily processes of death and decay. Ammons skips all euphemisms, challenging us directly not to feel disgust at the sight of 'flies swarming the dumped / guts of a natural slaughter or the coil of shit' (ll. 10–11). The colours of the flies, their 'glow-blue // bodies and gold-skeined wings' (ll. 9–10), reflect the impartiality of the light, again challenging us to feel the same impartiality and to recognise the beauty of these colours even on flies which are themselves feeding on carrion or faeces. Ammons's coinage 'glow-blue' makes this harder still, with its spooneristic echoes of blow-flies and bloated, suggesting the same repulsive associations as the 'bloated odors' in Rogers's poem.

As well as challenging us, however, Ammons leads us towards the 'generosity' (l. 12) symbolised by light. Having taken us into the middle of a fly-blown corpse he pulls back once again towards the serenity suggested by the tone of the first half of his poem, epitomised in the echoing of 'radiance' (l. 1) in 'abundance' (l. 2). There is still a hint of horror at the purposeless 'slaughter' that characterises the Darwinian world – the world beyond the city limits, perhaps, although Ammons's title is ambiguous – even as, in the last line of the poem, 'fear lit by the breadth of such calmly turns to praise' (l. 24). In using this word 'praise', Ammons invokes Christianity and the praise of God and his creation. At the same time, he recalls a more earthly pleasure at springtime economically suggested by the image of 'May bushes' (l. 23). Ammons's choice of light as a model of impartial benevolence towards all nature itself recalls both Christian symbolism and physical science. Like Frost, Ammons offers both Christian and non-Christian readers a basis for judging nature to be on balance for the good, blow-flies and 'dumped guts' notwithstanding.

In another poem, 'Shit List; or, Omnium-gatherum of Diversity into Unity', Ammons uses the playfully disgusting comedy of a catalogue of excrement to invite us to revel in the diversity of nature. Rogers does something not dissimilar if more elegant in the title poem of her collection *Geocentric*:

> Indecent, self-soiled, bilious
> reek of turnip and toadstool
> decay, dribbling the black oil
> of wilted succulents, the brown
> fester of rotting orchids,
> in plain view, that stain
> of stinkhorn down your front,
> that leaking roil of bracket
> fungi down your back, you
> purple-haired, grainy-fuzzed
> smolder of refuse, fathering
> fumes and boils and powdery
> mildews, enduring the constant
> interruption of sink-mire
> flatulence, contagious
> with ear wax, corn smut,
> blister rust, backwash
> and graveyard debris, rich
> with manure bog and dry-rot
> harbouring not only egg-addled
> garbage and wrinkled lip
> of orange-peel mold but also
> the clotted breath of overripe
> radish and burnt leek, bearing

every dank, malodorous rut
and scarp, all sulphur fissures
and fetid hillside seepages, old,
old, dependable, engendering
forever the stench and stretch
and warm seeth of inevitable
putrefaction, nobody
loves you as I do.

In this poem, Rogers weighs up the filth and misery of the Darwinian condition, not with any explicit reference to theology but simply to acknowledge them for herself. As she has remarked, she wrote it to force herself to confront the more unpleasant side of nature, in case her habit of celebrating nature in her poetry should lull her into a naïvely one-sided optimism (1999: 34). To counter this tendency, she adapts her usual style to invective. She shortens both words and lines, steps up the alliteration, and runs all the natural-historical examples that we would expect to find in one of her poems into a single sentence, leaving the main verb till the very last line. Aside from a brief lapse into her characteristic Latinate idiom in the phrase 'enduring the constant / interruption of. . .', Rogers keeps her vocabulary terse, to the point and largely commonplace and Anglo-Saxon.

Rogers's technique of naming in her poetry is easily adapted to name-calling. Her comprehensive knowledge of zoology and botany extends here into mycology, or the study of funguses. There are no animals in this poem, only rotting plants and an assortment of mushrooms and moulds. In titling her poem 'Geocentric', Rogers chooses them to stand in for all the natural processes of the Earth as a whole. Their names and descriptions thus become insults applied to nature as a whole. And yet the pace of Rogers's verse means that this poem about decay is full of life and vigour, while this liveliness and the relish with which she names ensure that this one-sided flyting or poem of insult is at the same time a celebration of the grotesque processes it records.

For the first half of Rogers's poem, its inventiveness is felt mainly in her choice of examples and in her vivid descriptions of them. These are enhanced by alliteration and occasional internal echoes, as when the 'black oil' recurs as a 'leaking roil' and then as 'boils', or when 'smut' leads on to 'rust'. In the second half of her poem, however, the examples themselves become alternately more extravagant and more pedestrian. The 'sulphur fissures' and 'fetid hillside seepages' suggest an entire landscape in decay – a creation not of the natural world itself but of the disgust Rogers has chosen to impersonate. On the other hand, the detail of the mouldy orange peel and the bathos of 'the clotted breath of overripe / radish' have the same effect, not through their extravagance, but through their very pettiness. Just as the God's-eye view that Rogers adopts in 'The Possible Suffering' misses no detail, so the jaded perspective of her speaker in this poem spots even the most trivial blemish on the face of the planet.

Rogers herself is of course far from disgusted by nature. Her impersonation is a mask which she removes with a flourish in the last line. The word 'dependable', casually slipped in a few lines before the end of the poem, hints at a change of direction, a change which seems to carry on into the description of the Earth as 'engendering / forever. . .'. The 'stench and stretch / and warm seeth' of decay belie this change, yet the first impression remains, qualifying the reappearance of 'inevitable / putrefaction' so that it seems a less disgusting, more neutral process, the inevitable corollary of 'engendering forever'. Rogers's declaration of love in the last line is not truly surprising, especially not to any reader who knows her poetry. Her invective is clearly comic, not bitter, and her persona is a performance, not a character in its own right. Even so, through her performance, Rogers like Ammons confronts us with a distasteful side of material nature. Where Ammons challenges us to assume his own serene outlook in 'The City Limits', Rogers uses comedy and the rapidity of her verse to inspire the same exuberance in the face of decay that she feels herself. Her poem stands as a testimony to her own love of nature, warm seeth and all. But it is also a model of a geocentric, or Earth-centred, vision within which it is possible to love even a world full of ugliness and 'inevitable putrefaction'.

DISENCHANTMENT AND RE-ENCHANTMENT: THE POWER OF PARADOX

In the summer of 1905, Thomas Hardy paid George Meredith a visit at his house on Box Hill. The two men had known each since 1869, when Meredith, as a reader for the publishers Chapman & Hall, had advised Hardy against publishing his confrontational and now lost first novel *The Poor Man and the Lady* in case hostile reviews should bury his reputation before it could be born. Since then, they had corresponded and occasionally met. A few days after Hardy's visit, Meredith remarked in a letter to Edmund Gosse, 'I am always glad to see him, and have regrets at his going; for the double reason, that I like him, and am afflicted by his twilight view of life' (1970: III, 1529). Some months later, Hardy joked to Gosse that he was worried in case he had shaken Meredith's optimism, as 'G.M. converted to pessimism by me is too terrible a catastrophe to think of' (1978–88: III, 187). It is characteristic of both men that Meredith should have welcomed the chance to wrestle with Hardy's darker vision, even at a cost to his own mental comfort, and that Hardy should have found the spectacle of his own pessimism bleakly amusing.

The contrast between Meredith's outlook and Hardy's is clear in Hardy's poem 'To Outer Nature', from his first collection of poetry, *Wessex Poems and Other Verses*, published in 1898:

> Show thee as I thought thee
> When I early sought thee,
>   Omen-scouting,
>   All undoubting
> Love alone had wrought thee –
>
> Wrought thee for my pleasure,
> Planned thee as a measure
>   For expounding
>   And resounding
> Glad things that men treasure.
>
> O for but a moment
> Of that old endowment –
>   Light to gaily
>   See thy daily
> Iris-hued embowment!
>
> But such re-adorning
> Time forbids with scorning –
>   Makes me see things
>   Cease to be things
> They were in my morning.
>
> Fad'st thou, glow-forsaken,
> Darkness-overtaken!
>   Thy first sweetness,
>   Radiance, meetness,
> None shall re-awaken.
>
> Why not sempiternal
> Thou and I? Our vernal
>   Brightness keeping,
>   Time outleaping;
> Passed the hodiernal!

Like 'Hap', which was published in the same collection, 'To Outer Nature' depends for its effect on the idiosyncrasy of Hardy's language. Its particular blend of striking coinages, elliptical and at times perplexing syntax, and rapid, trochaic rhythms, makes this poem more reminiscent of Meredith's poetry than is usual for Hardy. But Hardy's outlook remains markedly different from Meredith's. His is indeed a 'twilight view of life', as the 'light' of 'morning' – the 'radiance' praised by Ammons – has been 'darkness-overtaken', we are told, forever.

In the lost world view of Hardy's 'morning', nature was made for man as part of a divine plan. This was a world of design, not happenstance. Hardy reinforces this point by repeating the word 'wrought', and by presenting his younger self as 'Omen-scouting, / All undoubting'. Within this world view, natural phenomena have symbolic meaning. The most potent of these symbols (the symbol that underwrites the entire project of reading nature symbolically) is the rainbow, the sign of God's covenant with mankind after the Flood. Hence the central image of the rainbow in this poem, described with a rococo indulgence in florid circumlocution as an 'Iris-hued embowment'. The fading of the light in 'To Outer Nature' is also the fading of the rainbow, as the belief in the 'old endowment' – God's bequest of a nature specially made for man – becomes untenable.

The first five stanzas of 'To Outer Nature' are self-consistent. Hardy still longs for the pre-Darwinian trust in a benevolent and ordered nature, but the passing of time has denied him it, and it is now irrecoverable. This motif of disillusionment is so common in Hardy's poetry that it becomes self-referential in poems such as 'The Problem' and his last published poem, 'He Resolves to Say No More'. In these poems, Hardy ostensibly refuses to disabuse others of beliefs he has already undermined by declaring his own disenchantment.

Every now and again, Hardy suggests that there is some compensation for the loss of our illusions. In 'He Resolves to Say No More', for example, he describes himself as 'By truth made free' (l. 18), while in 'To Sincerity', written in February 1899, he entertains the possibility that

> Yet, would men look at true things,
> And unilluded view things,
> And count to bear undue things,
>
> The real might mend the seeming,
> Facts better their foredeeming,
> And Life its disesteeming.
>
> (ll. 13–18)

This tentative step towards Meredith's optimism is not typical, however. 'On a Fine Morning', written in the same month as 'To Sincerity', is more representative:

> Whence comes Solace? – Not from seeing
> What is doing, suffering, being,
> Not from noting Life's conditions,
> Nor from heeding Time's monitions;
>   But in cleaving to the Dream,
>   And in gazing at the gleam
>   Whereby gray things golden seem.
>
> Thus do I this heyday, holding
> Shadows but as lights unfolding,
> As no specious show this moment
> With its iris-hued embowment;
>   But as nothing other than
>   Part of a benignant plan;
>   Proof that earth was made for man.

This poem revives the theme and imagery of 'To Outer Nature', even to the point of repeating that unlikely phrase 'iris-hued embowment'. Like 'The Problem' and 'He Resolves to Say No More', it works through an obvious irony, affirming in the second verse beliefs that it has already declared to be false in the first. The 'benignant plan' by which 'earth was made for man' is 'the Dream', not the reality of 'Life's conditions'. Having spelt this out in the first verse, Hardy leaves no doubt that his assertion of 'proof' in the second verse is a calculated suspension of disbelief, not a belief proper. As he says at the end of another poem, 'To Life',

>   I'll tune me to the mood,
>   And mumm with thee till eve;
>   And maybe what as interlude
>   I feign, I shall believe!
>   (ll. 13–16)

Hardy's explicit disingenuousness in these poems ensures that, whatever he imagines he might believe, we know that he does not truly believe it.

'To Outer Nature' does not quite conform to this pattern. The last verse marks a sudden change of direction, but it is not clear how we are to take it. Hardy seems to defy his own insistence that 'None shall re-awaken' the glow of the old world view. Certainly, he imagines sustaining a 'brightness' of some kind, whether or not it is founded on the same beliefs. It is possible to read this ending as foreshadowing the more openly disingenuous endings of 'To Life' and 'On a Fine Morning', with the radical switch in perspectives showing that the speaker is deceiving himself. But the celebratory, forward-looking tenor of this last stanza does not steer us towards reading it ironically, nor as expressing a desperate and forlorn hope. Rather, it suggests we should see it as an inspiring and revivifying aspiration, whether or not it is attainable.

At the same time, Hardy's language keeps us puzzling over exactly what he means. The entire poem is riddled with coinages and compound words. Outlandish as these may seem, for the most part they are made up of familiar English words, in keeping with the principles set down by Hardy's old master, the Dorset dialect poet William Barnes (1878; 1880). Even the pseudo-Latinate neologism 'embowment' has the steady English word 'bow' at its heart. In his last verse, however, Hardy jettisons this attachment to English in favour of Latin. Furthermore, his syntax makes it tricky to decipher these cumbersome Latinate words even if we understand the words themselves. 'Sempiternal' is an adjective meaning 'everlasting', but here Hardy seems to use it as a verb, or at least omitting a verb, so his question appears to mean 'Why should Nature and I not be everlasting?' 'Vernal' too is an adjective, and a more familiar one, meaning 'pertaining to the Spring'. Here Hardy uses the word in its usual capacity, to set a year alongside the existing parallel between a day and a lifetime. 'Hodiernal' on the other hand – another adjective, meaning 'pertaining to today' – is reified into a noun, 'the hodiernal', 'that which is of today', which, Hardy imagines, we can transcend.

This transcendence itself is a mystery. What might it mean to outleap Time, to pass beyond that which is of today? A superficial reading might see Hardy as imagining a future moment in which, once he has reached it, he will be disabused of his disillusionment. But 'the hodiernal' does not only suggest 'today' in the specific sense of the current moment. Instead, the reification of that moment implies the perpetual present, that condition of time within which (at any given time) we exist. Passing the hodiernal in the temporal sense of getting to the future is thus as much an impossibility as outleaping, or overleaping, time itself. The only way to outleap time is to step outside the temporal dimension entirely, by entering knowingly into the paradoxical world of poetry, where a wife can be both dead and alive, a thrush's song at once disillusioning and comforting, a dead skylark both immortal and mere dust.

Unlike more starkly ironic poems such as 'On a Fine Morning' and 'To

Life', where the performance of poetry is all too obviously mummery, 'To Outer Nature' gives its readers an entrée into this transcendent world through the pleasure of the verse itself. It shares with 'Rain on a Grave' both a frank delight in polysyllabic rhymes – including the same rhyme of 'pleasure' with 'measure' – and a lively, rapid rhythm. Of the two poems, 'To Outer Nature' is metrically far more regular, but although Hardy keeps consistently to a trochaic metre, his touch is light enough that it does not seem repetitive or insistent. At the same time, the verse is regular enough that it raises and fulfils the pleasure of expectation.

Then there are the pleasures of Hardy's language itself: the blend of novelty and familiarity in his coinages, the surprise at their ingenuity and originality, even the mild puzzlement that follows from their peculiarity and that of his syntax. For a poem about the loss of enchantment, 'To Outer Nature' is itself strangely, even delightfully, enchanting. And because its language is so unusual, it repays rereading, becoming itself a space outside time to which we can return, passing beyond the hodiernal realities in the same moment as we confront them.

Hardy's promise that poetry can provide re-enchantment within the disenchanted Darwinian world anticipates the use that Ammons and Rogers make of poetry in their poems, as does his use of verse to recreate in us an apt mood for responding to this enchantment. Even so, there are a number of differences between them. The later poets are more explicit in itemising both what is good and what is bad about the Darwinian world as they find it, setting light and love against natural slaughter and putrefaction. Furthermore, they draw attention to the good that still exists within nature itself. While all three set up an opposition between the same conflicting judgements (that after Darwin nature is brutal, ugly, disenchanted, or that it remains nonetheless beautiful, loveable and marvellous) Ammons and Rogers follow Frost in resolving those oppositions by deciding that, all told, the good in nature outweighs the bad. Hardy, on the other hand, remains – to use his own word in the opposite context – 'undoubting' that, after Darwin, nature can no longer give us solace. Where for Ammons and Rogers, poetry leads us back to a sense of the wonder of nature, for Hardy, it is a substitute for a wonder that truly is lost. To re-awaken this wonder at all, even within the poem, Hardy must open up a paradoxical realm in which the good can persist regardless: the realm of poetry itself.

Hardy's play with paradox foreshadows Amy Clampitt's response to Darwinism in her famous debut poem, 'The Sun Underfoot among the Sundews', first published in the *New Yorker* in 1978. Sundews ('insectivorous plants of the genus *Drosera*', as Clampitt explains in a note to her poem (1997: 435)) are the main subject of Darwin's late study *Insectivorous*

Plants, published in 1875. With her sundews, Clampitt traps us into considering Darwin's theory of evolution.

Although it is never made explicit, this poem works with a single dominant parallel, between the reader of the poem and the gnats fed on by the sundews. Addressing us directly as 'you', Clampitt involves her readers in the action of her poem, much as Appleman does in 'Waldorf-Astoria Euphoria', but to very different effect. The poem opens with the suggestion that the teacup-shaped bog brimming with sundews infront of us is 'An ingenuity too astonishing / to be quite fortuitous' (ll. 1–2). Clampitt then has us step into the bog ourselves, up to our shoulders. As we become enmired in the beautiful but menacing scene, we become trapped too within the poem, bound up in repeated patterns of phrasing and perplexing contortions of syntax as dazzling as the sundews themselves. Once she has caught us, Clampitt forces us to return to the question of cause and meaning hinted at in her opening phrase. She offers us the alternatives of a First Cause and Natural Selection (both capitalised within the poem, ll. 26, 31) to explain the existence of these beautiful and predatory plants. Wryly irreverent towards both theology and Darwinism, she leaves us with only a dazzling perplexity rather than any clear answer one way or the other.

Clampitt's poem requires us to ask both whether natural selection is a sufficient cause to explain organisms as bizarre and beautiful as the sundews and whether it conflicts with faith, either in itself or in the nature it reveals. Like Frost, Clampitt dodges any attempt to pin down her own position on these questions. The closing paragraph of 'The Sun Underfoot among the Sundews' gives the impression of simplicity, as it first repeats phrases from earlier in her poem and then concludes with the poem's slowest, shortest lines and simplest vocabulary. In the last line of the poem, however, Clampitt rounds off her poem with a paradox, telling us that, literally dazzled by the light relected off the sundews, 'you start to fall upward' (l. 37).

By definition, it is impossible to fall upwards, so we cannot take this image at face value. In the poem, we fall upward because of the light reflected off the bog full of sundews. This light, like the poem itself, is dizzying. But as we are disoriented, are we actually falling upward, even within the poem, or are we rather falling down into the reflected sunlight? In other words, do we move 'upward' or do we 'fall', given that the two are mutually exclusive? And if we imagine that we truly are falling upward, what should we make of this ascension in the light of our doubts as to whether to invoke a First Cause or Natural Selection (or neither) as the explanation for the sundews? In this image, Clampitt may be suggesting that the wonder of nature corroborates Christian theology, but she may equally be suggesting that it substitutes for it. Even if we knew which of these was true, we still cannot know for certain whether we are falling or rising, moving downward into a hellish, predatory pit, or upward into a heaven of light.

Clampitt takes Hardy's concept of poetry as a paradoxical space in which contradictory truths may exist alongside one another to a new level of paradox. In 'The Sun Underfoot among the Sundews', the paradoxes are at once a trap and an escape, a knotty and irresolvable intellectual puzzle and an imaginative leap beyond it. In this imaginative leap (the promise of falling upwards, born like Ammons's radiance of so much light) Clampitt restores the enchantment of nature. At the same time, her poetic technique imitates the beguiling effect of the carnivorous plants, implying that that enchantment itself may be deceptive, even deadly.

Both Hardy and Clampitt are ambivalent towards the re-enchantment of nature that they effect in their poems. In 'The Garden of the Gods', Thom Gunn is more wholehearted:

All plants grow here; the most minute,
    Glowing from the turf, is in its place.
    The constant vision of the race:
Lawned orchard deep with flower and fruit.

So bright, that some who see it near,
    Think there is lapis on the stems,
    And think green, blue, and crimson gems
Hang from the vines and briars here.

They follow path to path in wonder
    Through the intense undazzling light.
    Nowhere does blossom flare so white!
Nowhere so black is earthmould under!

It goes, though it may come again.
    But if at last they try to tell,
    They search for trope or parallel,
And cannot, after all, explain.

It was sufficient, there, to be,
    And meaning, thus, was superseded.
    – Night circles it, it has receded,
Distant and difficult to see.

Where my foot rests, I hear the creak
  From generations of my kin,
  Layer on layer, pressed leaf-thin.
They merely are. They cannot speak.

This was the garden's place of birth:
  I trace it downward from my mind,
  Through breast and calf I feel it vined,
And rooted in the death-rich earth.

This poem is taken from *Moly*, the same collection as 'Tom-Dobbin'. The occasional inversions in its syntax, poetic elisions such as 'lapis' for 'lapis lazuli', and coinages such as 'lawn' used as a verb, contribute to the sense that we are being led into a magical and unreal realm. This realm has no direct equivalent in 'Tom-Dobbin', but it shares the same origins as the transcendence promised by Gunn in that poem. Both poems bear the hallmark of LSD in their mind-bending visions or experiences, set beyond the reach of everyday understanding, and both trace these transcendent experiences to the evolutionary roots of human nature. The fusion of individuals in 'Tom-Dobbin' and the vision of the garden in 'The Garden of the Gods' may be prompted by drugs, but they stem from the core of our natural history.

Like Hardy, Ammons and Clampitt, Gunn takes light to be the overarching sign of the wonder in nature. His garden is a dreamscape in which all colours are preternaturally distinct, like a painting by Burne-Jones. Yet, unlike Clampitt's sundews, they are nonetheless 'undazzling'. What we see in Gunn's poem, we see clearly. As in 'The City Limits' and 'Geocentric', this includes the black 'earthmould' as well as the white blossom. But whereas Ammons and Rogers set the white against the black, Gunn's vision does not judge between these polarities. Instead, it accepts them both. The point is not to judge, nor to interpret, but simply to experience: 'It was sufficient, there, to be, / And meaning, thus, was superseded'. The deliberate, qualifying pauses in the middle of these lines invite us to dwell on them as we read. Where Clampitt challenges us to unriddle the implications of her poem for how we should think about nature, Gunn tells us instead not to concern ourselves with meanings beyond the experience captured within and relayed through the poem itself.

Gunn's claim that the vision is 'Distant and difficult to see', that it cannot be captured in 'trope or parallel', gives rise to a paradox, as the garden itself is precisely such a trope which Gunn sets vividly before our minds' eyes. His elevation of existence over significance is again paradoxical, as the medium of poetry itself binds together meaning and experience. Gunn's poem is loaded with meaning, and the evaluation of meaning, even in its very disavowal of it.

This becomes vividly apparent in the last two stanzas, where Gunn seeks to account for the vision which it is supposedly sufficient simply to experience. Gunn imagines his dead ancestors underfoot, layered like geological strata. Where Hardy imagines Emma grown into flowers and grass at the end of 'Rain on a Grave', and Jeffers contemplates his own 'enskyment' in the flesh of a vulture, Gunn imagines the dead lying forever where they are buried, enriching the soil. Their existence – 'They merely are. They cannot speak' – recalls the visionaries in the garden and after. As the poet voices the unvoiceable impressions of the visionaries, so he speaks for the speechless dead.

Gunn can speak for the dead in his poem because he and his vision are born of them. In the last verse of 'The Garden of the Gods' he undergoes another, extraordinary metamorphosis, changing from a human mind, inside a human but also animal body, into a plant. The vision of the garden itself is no longer found only in the mind, but in the blood and then, as the hinted veins become 'vines', in the roots and stems of the plant. Like the ecstasies in 'Tom-Dobbin', the garden is both a revelation of and a revelling in our kinship with the rest of life. We are not rootless, as Hughes's wodwo feels himself to be, but rooted. What we are rooted in is the rich remains of our dead, reaching down through the strata, back to our non-human and even non-animal ancestry. Gunn's garden thus combines ideals of human thought and myth – Arcadia, the Earthly Paradise, the Garden of Eden – with the fact of lived existence going back far deeper.

For Gunn to choose a garden for his image of nature after Darwin may seem wrongheaded. In *Evolution and Ethics*, Huxley takes the garden to be rather the ideal image of humanity's resistance to nature, particularly to the brutalities of natural selection. But Gunn is not showing us the garden as a realistic image of nature itself. Rather, like Hardy's promise of 'vernal / Brightness', it is a model for how to look on nature, concentrating not on meaning but on being, not on the process of interpretation that leaves us like the wodwo perpetually alienated from the rest of nature, but on the fact of lived experience which we share with it.

For Hardy and Gunn, the re-enchantment of nature after the disenchantment of Darwinism depends upon how we look at nature, not on nature itself. Where Frost and Ammons look to nature itself for grounds to praise it, Hardy and Gunn look into themselves. Where Gunn differs from Hardy is in attributing his patently unreal vision of nature as a whole to his own human nature itself. In 'The Garden of the Gods', he squares the circle, tracing even our delusions about the wonder of nature to nature, valuing them as our nature, and finally leading us to see that they are not delusions at all, as the wonder of nature is not a matter of reality but of perception, not a fact but a judgement – one that follows, paradoxically but naturally, from the suspension of judgement itself.

DARWIN'S PAGANS: MEREDITH'S 'ODE' AND TENNYSON'S 'LUCRETIUS'

Four of the fullest and most incisive poetic responses to Darwin's ideas were published within a decade of *The Origin of Species* itself. I discussed Browning's 'Caliban upon Setebos' and Meredith's *Modern Love* in earlier chapters. Of the other two, Meredith's 'Ode to the Spirit of Earth in Autumn' appeared alongside *Modern Love* in 1862, while Tennyson's 'Lucretius' was begun in the mid-1860s and first published in *Macmillan's Magazine* in 1868. Early as they are, these two poems engage with almost all the questions I have discussed so far, how Darwinism impacts on belief in God, what it implies about death, where it leaves the human animal as a human and as an animal, how it changes our understanding of our desires and so on. Like the other poems discussed in this chapter, each of them also implicitly passes judgement on the Darwinian condition.

In earlier chapters I argued that Darwinism poses some grave if not necessarily insoluble problems for Christianity. For both Meredith and Tennyson, the Darwinian world view seemed closer to that of classical paganism. In his poem, Tennyson explores the implications of Darwinism by impersonating the pre-Christian poet and philosopher Lucretius. In his didactic epic *De Rerum Natura* (*On the Nature of the Universe*), Lucretius argued that there was no need to appeal to the supernatural to explain the world around us. His unflinching empiricism and his atomic theory of matter led many Victorian scientists, secularists, theologians and poets to find parallels between his thinking and current science. Like Keats in his 'Ode to Psyche', Meredith encounters the divinities of pre-Christian Greece and Rome himself in his poem. Unlike Keats, however, he does not lament that he has come 'too late for antique vows, / Too, too late for the fond believing lyre' (ll. 36–7). Instead he joins dryads, satyrs and other 'revel-gathering spirits' in 'a night of Pagan glee' that took place only 'last night' (ll. 1, 29, 88).

The difference between Tennyson's approach to Darwinism and Meredith's maps onto the famous distinction drawn by Browning between objective and subjective poets. The objective poet, typified by Shakespeare (and implicitly by Browning himself), is concerned with human subjectivity. The subjective poet on the other hand, typified by Shelley, seeks out objective truths, 'the *Ideas* of Plato, seeds of creation lying burningly on the Divine Hand'. The objectivity of the objective poet and the subjectivity of the subjective poet do not refer to their concerns, therefore, but to their methods. The objective poet observes other people with sympathy and insight, and records 'the manifested action of the human heart and brain'. The subjective poet is concerned rather with 'the primal elements of humanity' within himself, and seeks to realise his own vision of them in his poetry (1981: 1, 1001–2).

In Browning's terms, Tennyson approaches Darwinism as an objective poet, Meredith as a subjective poet. This is reflected in the genres of their two poems. Aside from a short framing narrative, 'Lucretius' is a dramatic monologue spoken in Lucretius's voice. In a dramatic monologue, readers are invited less to share the speaker's visions than to scrutinise them. Tennyson asks us to understand and sympathise with Lucretius as he confronts the implications of his quasi-Darwinian materialist world view, but he does not seek to win us over to that world view. Instead, the dramatic monologue as a form and the story of Lucretius's suicide enable Tennyson to stage a predicament that he sees as following from Darwinism.

Tennyson's portrait of Lucretius derives substantially from *De Rerum Natura* itself, but the plot of his poem is taken from a legend, perpetuated by St Jerome, that Lucretius killed himself after being driven mad by a love potion given to him by his jealous wife. In Tennyson's poem, the effects of this potion are physiological, as it 'Confused the chemic labour of the blood, / And tickling the brute brain within the man's / Made havock among those tender cells' (ll. 20–2). For Lucretius himself, the origin of species was best explained by a series of unrelated moments of spontaneous generation (1999: 159–63). In his reference to 'the brute brain within the man's', however, Tennyson implicitly traces the origins of humanity to animals. In this evolutionary view of psychology, animal urges which we have partly outgrown remain latent within us. Lucretius's mind has been disordered by being returned to something closer to its animal origins. The mental effects of the poison within the poem are thus an objective correlative for the subjective impact of accepting a Darwinian psychology within a purely materialist philosophy. Through Lucretius, Tennyson pathologises Darwinism, presenting the Darwinian world view as misguided even to the point of madness.

Where 'Lucretius' is essentially a dramatic monologue, Meredith's 'Ode to the Spirit of Earth in Autumn' is, as the title implies, a Romantic ode. In a Romantic ode, the poet within the poem is at once the witness to the truth of his vision and the prophet who can realise that vision through the poem itself. Through its imagery and rhythms the poem synthesises for the reader a transcendent experience that ostensibly cannot be recovered, like Gunn's visit to the Garden of the Gods. The experience of reading the poem thus stands as testimony to the truth of the vision itself. For Meredith, as for Wordsworth, Coleridge, Shelley and Keats, the poetic imagination is a mode of perception which enables the poet, if only fleetingly, to glimpse truths that transcend our everyday life. The pagan spirits he discerns in the 'Ode' and the presiding spirit of Earth herself are the symbolic embodiment of these truths. They are, in effect, subjective correlatives for the objective fact of Darwinian nature.

In Romantic poetry, the poet typically records transcendent experiences at one remove, finding them in dreams or half-forgotten memories, or attributing them to others whose wisdom he himself only half comprehends, such as children or animals. Meredith mimics this effect in his 'Ode' through a distinction between seeing and hearing. Echoing the husband in sonnet XIII of *Modern Love*, the poet within the poem identifies Mother Earth as 'our only visible friend':

> There is a curtain o'er us.
> For once, good souls, we'll not pretend
> To be aught better than her who bore us,
> And is our only visible friend.
>   (ll. 89–92)

Meredith's curtain is both the darkness of the stormy night itself and the Romantic veil. The veil stands, as it does for Tennyson, as a symbol of the post-Romantic condition: the poet cannot see behind it. Instead, all he can see to put his trust in is the Earth itself. Yet as the poet himself is denied any transcendent vision, his poem sets it before our eyes in the vividly, even startlingly, physical image of a spirit bursting out from a tree, like Ariel freed by Prospero at the end of *The Tempest*:

> Could I be sole there not to see
> The life within the life awake;
> The spirit bursting from the tree,
> And rising from the troubled lake?
>   (ll. 80–3)

Through his visual imagination, Meredith can describe the transcendent vision he cannot see. Within the poem itself, however, he gains his knowledge of the unknowable not through sight but through sound. He hears the 'Dryad voices' in the wind and 'a low swell that noised / Of far-off ocean'

in the massive pine trees (ll. 49, 68–9). He invites us too to listen to the
Earth herself, urging 'Hark to her laughter! who laughs like this, / Can
she be dead, or rooted in pain?' (ll. 93–4) By separating the senses of sight
and hearing, Meredith is able paradoxically both to insist that we have
no access to anything beyond visible nature and to affirm the reality of a
transcendent realm within it. He replaces the promise of something 'o'er us'
(Tennyson's deferred 'hope', forever 'behind the veil') with an immediate
joy in 'her who bore us'.

All the same, Meredith agrees with Hardy that the old Edenic idyll of
nature – the 'Iris-hued embowment' – is no longer sustainable. His 'Ode'
begins with this remarkable evocation of a sunset:

> Fair Mother Earth lay on her back last night,
> To gaze her fill on Autumn's sunset skies,
> When at a waving of the fallen light,
> Sprang realms of rosy fruitage o'er her eyes.
> A lustrous heavenly orchard hung the West,
> Wherein the blood of Eden bloomed again:
> Red were the myriad cherub-mouths that pressed,
> Among the clusters, rich with song, full fain,
> But dumb, because that overmastering spell
> Of rapture held them dumb: then, here and there,
> A golden harp lost strings; a crimson shell
> Burnt grey; and sheaves of lustre fell to air.
> The illimitable eagerness of hue
> Bronzed, and the beamy winged bloom that flew
> 'Mid those bunched fruits and thronging figures failed.
> A green-edged lake of saffron touched the blue,
> With isles of fireless purple lying through:
> And Fancy on that lake to seek lost treasures sailed.
>
> (ll. 1–18)

The fecundity of Meredith's visual imagination in this passage is extraordinary. In the opening lines he gives new life to the hackneyed personification
of Mother Earth. She acts and feels, as if she has a real embodied presence
on Earth as well as being the Earth herself. The surprising vividness of
this opening sets the tone for Meredith's unfolding of the sunset through
unexpected images that shift and transform before our eyes. One image
or colour leads to another. The pink of the evening sky suggests an apple
orchard, which in turn suggests Eden before the Fall. This prelapsarian scene
is first peopled with enraptured cherubim, then transformed into a more

generalised idyll in the near-perfect image of the rays of the dropping sun bound together as 'sheaves of lustre'. As the light fails, the colours change with extraordinary rapidity, from rose to gold to crimson to grey to bronze to green, saffron and purple, all alongside traces of the initial blue. The bold simplicity with which Meredith names these colours contrasts with the extravagant complexity of his imagery, capturing the startling brilliance of the sunset itself.

Eden cannot last, however. In its metre and rhyme-scheme Meredith's opening passage recalls a Petrarchan sonnet, with an extra quatrain slipped in before the closing sestet as in 'Our Hold on the Planet'. The *volta* between the quatrains and the sestet marks the point at which the brilliant light begins to fade. As it fails, so the Edenic idyll of the first twelve lines vanishes with it. What remains is Fancy, the poetic imagination at its freest and least self-regarding. In closing this passage with a hexameter, Meredith signals his allegiance to the younger Romantic poets Shelley, Keats and Byron, who themselves borrowed the same device from Edmund Spenser's Renaissance romance *The Faerie Queene*. Foreshadowing Hardy, Meredith implies that the lost treasures of rapture and the original state of innocence can be regained in this fallen world through poetry itself.

But the world to which Meredith's own poetry leads us looks very different from the Eden glimpsed at the outset. As the light fades, so the wind gathers. The silence is replaced with a noise as of 'A thousand horns from some far vale / In ambush sounding on the gale' (ll. 26–7), then:

> Forth from the cloven sky came bands
> Of revel-gathering spirits; trooping down,
> Some rode the tree-tops; some on torn cloud-strips,
>   Burst screaming thro' the lighted town:
> And scudding seaward, some fell on big ships:
>   Or mounting the sea-horses blew
>   Bright foam-flakes on the black review
>   Of heaving hulls and burying beaks.
>
>   (ll. 28–35)

In place of the regular metre of a sonnet, we are faced with a chaos of unpredictable rhythms and rhymes and tumultuous patterns of alliteration. In place of Eden, the 'glorious South-west' wind (l. 21) brings something that looks at first like Hell, peopled with daemonic spirits bent on the violent pleasure of disruption.

Yet this dangerous revel, associated at first with pain, darkness and even death, increasingly commands approval. In place of the 'disenchanted harmony' of 'heaven', we are invited to join in 'earth's laughter' (ll. 38–9). The wind brings death to the landscape, but it also brings the landscape to life:

> Night on the rolling foliage fell:
> But I, who love old hymning night,
> And know the Dryad voices well,
> Discerned them as their leaves took flight,
> Like souls to wander after death:
> Great armies in imperial dyes,
> And mad to tread the air and rise,
> The savage freedom of the skies
> To taste before they rot. (ll. 47–55)

This passage is again extraordinary for the richness and vividness of Meredith's imagination and for the density and originality of his ideas. Again, he begins by revivifying an old cliché, in this case the idea of nightfall. Night does not just fall in this poem. It falls on the leaves with the physical force of the wind and the biological finality of death, both evoked through booming assonance and abrupt alliteration as 'Night on the rolling foliage fell'.

Bearding and interpreting this night is the poet himself, who like Keats in his famous 'Ode to a Nightingale' seems half in love with death. But for Meredith, unlike Keats, death is not easeful but revivifying. In likening the falling leaves to undying souls, he claims the value of immortality for the ephemeral freedom of mortal life. Like Thomas Gordon Hake in *The New Day*, Meredith revels in the experience of life for its own sake, made all the more vibrant and life-like through the fact of death. That experience is for Meredith both 'imperial' and 'savage', majestic and unfettered. It is profoundly bodily and not wholly sane, but commanding and invigorating nonetheless.

Meredith does not blind himself to the destructive violence of nature. Through his pagan mythology, he distils an idea of nature that is at once exultant and frankly dangerous, dispelling any misguided trust in its benevolence. His Mother Nature is a 'Bacchante Mother' (ll. 158). Like Agave in Euripides's *Bacchae*, she unknowingly tears her own children to pieces. And yet, seen from another angle, she is the 'mother of kindness' (l. 128). Like Shelley's west wind, Darwinian nature is both 'destroyer and preserver' ('Ode to the West Wind', l. 14).

As in his later poems, Meredith is careful to distinguish beneficence from benevolence. Darwinian biology is true, but it does not require us to see Earth as 'rooted in pain' (l. 94). Meredith welcomes Darwinian science in his 'Ode', because he denies the pessimistic conclusions that other poets would derive from it. Nature may have 'been slain by the narrow brain, / But for us who love her she lives again' (ll. 95–6). As his rhymes stress, to emphasise 'pain' over pleasure is the act of a 'narrow brain'. Meredith does not repudiate the harshness associated with Darwinism, but he incorporates it into a wider but no less Darwinian perspective. It is this breadth of vision grounded in love that allows 'slain' nature to live 'again'. Meredith rejects outright materialism too in the 'Ode'. Insisting that 'Life thoroughly lived is a fact in the brain' (l. 184), he reminds us that, whether the causes of life are material or not, life itself remains an empirical but non-material fact.

In *In Memoriam*, Tennyson is profoundly unsettled by a nature for whom 'The spirit does but mean the breath' (LVI, l. 7). Meredith joyfully celebrates that breath as spirit in its own right. His vision of nature may seem a far cry from Darwin's, but his poem illustrates how apt Romantic visions and pagan myths are to a Darwinian world, providing we distinguish Fancy from fact and symbols from the underlying realities they symbolise, and providing too that we seek for these transcendent 'lost treasures' not in an ideal realm which is by definition unknowable, but within the spheres of phenomenal nature and poetry itself.

How does Tennyson himself respond to Meredith's pagan ideals? After the brief narrative introduction to his poem, Lucretius awakes to recall three nightmares. A man of his time, his dreams are haunted by Helen of Troy and the 'mulberry-faced Dictator', Sulla (l. 54), who ruled Rome from 82 to 79 BC. Alongside these classical allusions, however, Lucretius's dreams, visions and thinking in Tennyson's poem all carry resonances of Meredith's neo-pagan 'Ode'. The occasion for Lucretius's dreaming is a violent storm, like the windy night Meredith celebrates in his poem. His dreams project both his materialist philosophy and the erotic desires stimulated by the love potion. Within his philosophy as he expounds it in Tennyson's poem, the goddess Venus stands, like Meredith's Mother Earth, for 'The all-generating powers and genial heat / Of Nature' in living things which only 'appear' to be 'the work of mighty Gods' (ll. 97–8, 102). Both poets – Meredith himself and Tennyson's Lucretius – interpret nature in organic terms, rejecting divine intervention and the argument from design. For both, these organic processes are both maternal and sexual.

Although Lucretius shares many of Meredith's ideas and images, his interpretation of and responses to them are markedly different. The dominant note of Tennyson's poem is self-loathing. Lucretius is unconsciously appalled by his own theories of nature and disgusted at his animal desires.

His dreams bring these unconscious reactions to the fore. The first of them calls up a fearful image of a purposeless universe:

> for it seemed
> A void was made in Nature; all her bonds
> Cracked; and I saw the flaring atom-streams
> And torrents of her myriad universe,
> Ruining along the illimitable inane,
> Fly on to clash together again, and make
> Another and another frame of things
> For ever.
>
> (ll. 36–43)

Within Lucretius's atomism, the forms we see around us are the circumstantial products of random gatherings of atoms, easily cracked apart. In Darwinism too there is no steady state, as the processes of evolution are continually remaking the living world with no guarantee of permanency. Through this first dream, Tennyson suggests that the idea of a purely material universe in perpetual flux remains unconsciously appalling even to those who consciously accept it without a qualm.

Meredith's identification of the spirit with the life is not enough to satisfy Tennyson's need for the universe to have a moral purpose and for life to continue after death. Like Meredith, Lucretius may have renounced these needs consciously, but unconsciously they still grip him. As he himself observes, he still prays to the gods, even though his own philosophy tells him this is pointless. He prides himself on his insistence on the finality of death which 'plucks / The mortal soul from out immortal hell' (ll. 261–2), yet the price he pays is a philosophy in which the extinction not only of the individual but of humanity as a whole is all but certain. With 'careless' gods (ll. 150, 208) and no hope of an afterlife, there is nothing to bind him to morality nor deter him from suicide. Lucretius's desperation suggests that he is not resigned to this 'void . . . in Nature' after all.

Lucretius's materialist philosophy is at least his own. As he says, 'that was mine, my dream, I knew it' (l. 43). As his wife's potion begins to take effect, however, his unconscious mind reveals to him erotic desires and fears which he does not at first recognise. In his second dream, 'all the blood by Sylla shed' rains from the sky (l. 47) turning into prostitutes, 'girls, Hetairai, curious in their art' (l. 52), who crowd around him until he wakes 'Half-suffocated' (l. 58). In his third dream, Lucretius sees the breasts of Helen of Troy illuminated in 'utter gloom' (l. 60). A sword hovers to pierce them, but '[sinks] down shamed / At all that beauty' (ll. 63–4). 'The fire that left the roofless Ilion' shoots out of Helen's breasts, and Lucretius wakes as if 'scorched' himself (ll. 65–6).

These dreams anticipate and invite Freudian readings. Lucretius's repressed sexuality, released by the potion, has come back to haunt him. His apparent disregard for women, including his young and sexually confident wife whom he patronises and neglects, is betrayed as a morbid fear of his own desire. On the other hand, he has been poisoned and his mind may be chemically unbalanced. Perhaps these dreams really are alien to Lucretius's unpoisoned self. Tennyson's own interpretation, however, is that they manifest an evolutionary regression. In the image of 'the brute brain within the man's', Tennyson implies that the effect of the poison is to draw up to the surface something already there within the human mind, and not just within the mind of the individual human but within us all. According to the models of progressive evolution that Tennyson himself preferred it was at least in theory possible 'to let the ape and tiger die', raising ourselves up from and out of our animal condition. Within Darwinism, this makes little sense, as we are animals. The 'brute brain' will continue to haunt us because it is part of our nature.

Unrestrained sexual desire seems essentially brutish to Tennyson. In his disgust, Lucretius too insistently identifies sexual urges with the condition of being an animal. He dismisses the prostitutes in his dream as 'Hired animalisms' (l. 53). Later, recalling his dreams, he raves against 'These prodigies of myriad nakednesses / And twisted shapes of lust . . . blasting the long quiet of my breast/ With animal heat and dire insanity' (ll. 156–63). As he at last comes to admit that these fantasies are his own, he berates himself for his 'monkey-spite' (l. 211) and, in a deleted variant from the manuscript of the poem, his 'monkey-filth' (l. 206 var.). Lucretius is horrified at being turned into an animal, both by his desires themselves and by his incontrollable fear of them.

Lucretius's disgust at sexuality may suggest an individual neurosis rather than anything more universal. Its wider relevance becomes more apparent, however, in an extraordinary scene in which Tennyson restages an erotic encounter between a nymph and a satyr from Meredith's 'Ode'. In the opening paragraph of Man's Place in Nature, Huxley suggested that centaurs and satyrs are the mythic equivalents, perhaps even folk-memories, of the anthropoid apes, 'creatures approaching man more nearly than they in their essential structure, and yet as thoroughly brutal as the goat's or horse's half of the mythical compound' (1893–4: vii, 1; see also Amigoni 2007: 121–2). The satyrs in Meredith's and Tennyson's poems (like the centaurs in Gunn's) are cast in this mould, as enduring symbols of our animal origins and persistent animal nature.

Here is the scene in Meredith's poem:

The crimson-footed nymph is panting up the glade,
With the wine-jar at her arm-pit, and the drunken ivy-braid
Round her forehead, breasts, and thighs: starts a Satyr, and they speed:
Hear the crushing of the leaves: hear the cracking of the bough!
And the whistling of the bramble, the piping of the weed!

(ll. 98–102)

The exuberant erotic play in these lines is given an exhilarating immediacy, as events of 'last night' are described in the present tense. The metre,
established as iambic hexameter in the first line, is already a foot longer
than blank verse, while the substitution of two or even three anapaests per
line thereafter further enhances its energy and rapidity. As the sounds of
the chase give way to notes of pleasure, which resonate through the glade
and onomatopoeically through the poem itself, we are invited to 'hear'
these sounds for ourselves, witnessing and enjoying the unrestrained eroticism of the natural world which they embody.

In the equivalent scene in Tennyson's poem, Lucretius watches as the
mountain landscape behind his country villa transforms itself in front of his
eyes into a scene of mythic eroticism:

For look! what is it? there? yon arbutus
Totters; a noiseless riot underneath
Strikes through the wood, sets all the tops quivering –
The mountain quickens into Nymph and Faun;
And here an Oread – how the sun delights
To glance and shift about her slippery sides,
And rosy knees and supple roundedness,
And budded bosom-peaks – who this way runs
Before the rest – A satyr, a satyr, see,
Follows; but him I proved impossible;
Twy-natured is no nature: yet he draws
Nearer and nearer, and I scan him now
Beastlier than any phantom of his kind
That ever butted his rough brother-brute
For lust or lusty blood or provender:
I hate, abhor, spit, sicken at him; and she
Loathes him as well; such a precipitate heel,
Fledged as it were with Mercury's ankle-wing,
Whirls her to me: but will she fling herself,

Shameless upon me? Catch her, goat-foot: nay,
Hide, hide them, million-myrtled wilderness,
And cavern-shadowing laurels, hide! do I wish –
What? – that the bush were leafless? or to whelm
All of them in one massacre?

(ll. 184–207)

This passage is profoundly disturbing. Step by step, Lucretius's unconscious mind is set out before him, exposing him as hateful to himself. The first figment of his imagination to appear as the 'quivering' mountain 'quickens' into life is an Oread, a mountain nymph. Lucretius lingers over her naked body, even as he displaces his own desire for her onto the sun, whose light picks out alliteratively the details of her form, tempting us to join him in his prurient fascination with her. If the Oread embodies Lucretius's ideal object of desire, the satyr personifies that desire itself. At first Lucretius identifies with the Oread, as he insistently asserts his loathing for the satyr. When it looks as though the naked nymph might throw herself upon him, however, even for protection, he reacts as he did to the hetairai in his dream. In a perverse moment of moral purity, born of a claustrophobic panic at the prospect of an erotic encounter, Lucretius gives her over to the satyr, again displacing his own desires.

In classical art, satyrs are typically represented as half man, half goat, priapic and leering. In *De Rerum Natura*, Lucretius argues that centaurs and other 'creatures of a double nature / Composed of alien limbs and twofold body' cannot possibly exist because the physiology of the two parts would be incompatible (1999: 162). He is, of course, right. The satyr does not really exist on the mountainside, only in (Tennyson's) Lucretius's own mind. And yet as a projection of his desires, the satyr shows that Lucretius himself is 'twy-natured'. Lucretius's underlying identification with the satyr is betrayed by his voyeuristic wish 'that the bush were leafless'. At the same time, his self-loathing manifests itself in the contrary impulse towards a 'massacre' of these mythic creatures, the oread and the other nymphs as well as the satyr.

This combination of voyeurism and violence in Tennyson's poem exposes impulses that may be seen to underlie Meredith's 'Ode' too. I suggested that the encounter between the nymph and the satyr in Meredith's poem was a scene of erotic play, but as Tennyson reminds us, sex between satyrs and nymphs in classical myths is rarely consensual. Furthermore, as Tennyson again makes clear, we are invited to take a vicarious pleasure in others' animalistic or at best 'twy-natured' sex. Meredith's poem is not pornographic, but the impulse he is encouraging seems to be – all the more so if we are indeed being invited to 'peer behind the bushes' (as Tennyson wrote in his manuscript, l. 206 var.) at a rape. Isobel Armstrong detects what she takes to be a 'self-indulgent eroticism' and a disturbing 'fascination with the rape of vulnerable women' in Meredith's early poems 'The Rape of Aurora' and 'Daphne' (1993: 457). As I read them, this 'fascination' in these early poems is deliberately rather than inadvertently disturbing. By contrast, if the eroticism of this scene from the 'Ode' is disturbing, it is not because it betrays a fascination with rape, but because it does not consider it. We are not told whether the nymph receives the satyr's advances willingly or not, because in his enthusiasm for 'life thoroughly lived' Meredith does not think to raise the question.

As Tennyson observes, the Darwinian nature that Meredith asks us to exult in is a world of violent struggles for 'lust or lusty blood or provender'. 'Life thoroughly lived' needs the counterbalance of moral restraint. And yet Lucretius's last words in Tennyson's poem, spoken to his wife when she accuses herself of 'having failed in duty to him' (l. 277), are 'Thy duty? What is duty? Fare thee well!' (l. 280). For Tennyson, Darwinism, like Lucretius's materialism, renders the concept of moral duty incoherent, as a morality that is merely evolved instinct lacks any solid foundation.

When Lucretius asks 'Why should I, beastlike as I find myself, / Not manlike end myself?' (ll. 231–2) he is asking Tennyson's own question of a purely material universe in which humans are merely another species of animal. The realisation that he is 'beastlike' is neither reversible nor tolerable for Lucretius, and he prefers suicide to the shame of being at the mercy of the 'unseen monster' (l. 219) of his own primitive desires. Indeed, with no gods to intervene or direct him, the act of suicide seems to Lucretius the only way for him to regain his full humanity, as 'What beast has heart to do it?' (l. 233) Yet in committing it he moves from one moral disaster to another.

Tennyson's poem poses a moral and psychological challenge to its Darwinian readers, who must either dispute his assessment of Darwinism or despair. Tennyson saves himself from this fate by declining to believe that Darwinism is the full truth. Yet in Lucretius, he allows himself to imagine how Darwinism might affect him if he came to believe that its materialist account of the universe and our place in it were comprehensively correct. The poem's power lies not in Tennyson's judgements on Lucretius, but in his profound sympathy for him. Lucretius may loathe himself, but Tennyson still respects his moral integrity, as he shows by giving him some of his most immaculate and moving blank verse. Lucretius's predicament is appalling because he is becoming monstrous and 'filthy' (l. 220) in front of his own eyes and against his will. As Tennyson sees it, the implications of Darwinism are that we are all monsters.

Returning from 'Lucretius' to the 'Ode', Meredith is able to escape Tennyson's despair in part because he is not appalled at the loss of his human identity, either in death or in being one natural creature among many. Furthermore, although he celebrates 'the joy of motion, the rapture of being' (l. 180), the prospect of not being does not distress him. As he remarks:

> Behold, in yon stripped Autumn, shivering grey,
>   Earth knows no desolation.
>   She smells regeneration
> In the moist breath of decay.
>
> (ll. 186–9)

Earth is oblivious to death because she is undying. Meredith aspires to the same state of mind, in which the 'desolation' of mortality can be effaced by the knowledge of 'regeneration', and even 'decay' can be seen to participate in the 'breath' of life.

Like Swinburne in 'Hertha', Meredith identifies Mother Nature both with the world-tree of German mythology and with the Darwinian tree of life. Unlike Swinburne, however, he does not make the mistake of claiming that she has any special interest in humanity. Meredith prays to 'Great Mother Nature' (l. 141), 'Teach me to feel myself the tree / And not the withered leaf' (ll. 154–5). In 'In the Woods', Meredith asks us to accept our own deaths as 'we drop like the fruits of the tree, / Even we, / Even so'. Here he invites us to think beyond our own mortality, to set our individual selves aside entirely. By identifying with nature as a whole, and not merely with the transitory fragments of it that happen to be ourselves, we can transcend both our individual limits and our fear of death.

Like 'Lucretius', Meredith's 'Ode' ends with a death:

> Prophetic of the coming joy and strife,
>   Like the wild western war-chief sinking
>   Calm to the end he eyes unblinking,
> Her voice is jubilant in ebbing life.
>
>   He for his happy hunting-fields
>   Forgets the droning chant, and yields
>   His numbered breaths to exultation
>   In the proud anticipation:
>   Shouting the glories of his nation,
>   Shouting the grandeur of his race,

Shouting his own great deeds of daring:
And when at last death grasps his face,
And stiffened on the ground in peace
He lies with all his painted terrors glaring;
Hushed are the tribe to hear a threading cry:
   Not from the dead man;
   Not from the standers-by:
   The spirit of the red man
Is welcomed by his fathers up on high.

(ll. 190–208)

Throughout his 'Ode', Meredith sets before us a pagan vision drawing on Greek and Roman mythology and inflected by the Teutonic symbol of the world-tree. Here he invokes a third, native American, form of paganism. His verse takes on the quality of the ritual it describes. The triple rhymes that Meredith uses at key moments throughout his poem ('dyes'–'rise'–'skies', 'pain'–'brain'–'again') recur in the polysyllabic rhyme 'exultation'–'anticipation'–'of his nation'. The incantation in these rhymes passes into the repetition of 'Shouting' and, after a brief pause, into the faster, more intense repetition of 'Not from', as the ritual reaches its culmination and 'the dead man' is transformed from a lifeless corpse into the ascending 'spirit of the red man'.

The 'wild western war-chief' stands as an analogy for the Earth herself. But he also stands as a model human hero, facing death with equanimity. Meredith is typically unsentimental about nature. As his rhyme reminds us, 'life' is at least as tightly bound to 'strife' as it is to 'joy'. His portrait of the native American chief is idealised, but then he is another symbolic figure. Like the men whose 'love of Earth is deep' in 'The Lark Ascending', he embodies a willingness to subsume himself within a wider life, the 'grandeur of his race' struggling for its own 'savage freedom' in the face of the westward expansion of the United States. Of all men, he feels himself the tree and not the withered leaf, even as he does not lose his pride in his own 'great deeds'.

Both the Earth itself and the war-chief are 'jubilant in ebbing life'. But where her life ebbs like a tide, to flow back again in spring, his life is ebbing away for good. Because he looks forward as much to the 'coming joy and strife' as to his own death, and because he identifies as much with his race and nation as with himself, he is able to transcend this difference between them. His reward within the poem is a form of immortality. The war-chief's immortality is again symbolic, not literal, although Meredith does not stop us from reading it literally if we choose to. In rejoining his fathers, he is

— 258 —

subsumed wholly into the history and the lineage of his race, and by extension of humanity and nature as a whole. In death, his own 'spirit' becomes 'The spirit of the red man' at large. For Meredith, this is itself a fate worthy of 'exultation'.

Conclusion

At the end of *The Origin of Species*, Charles Darwin famously declares 'There is grandeur in this view of life' ([1859] 2003: 398). Tennyson and Meredith surely bear this out in their poems. But the poetry of Darwinism yields us more than grandeur alone. It brings into focus the spiritual, moral and psychological questions that the Darwinian condition forces us to ask. Through poetry, we can confront what it might mean to live in a purely material universe, if that is indeed the fate to which Darwinism consigns us. We can probe our own need for spiritual comfort and consolation and explore how that need might be answered within the Darwinian universe, whether by God or without him. We can enlarge too our sense of how, in Philip Appleman's words, 'to be, / knee-deep in these rivers of innocent blood, / a decent animal' ('The Voyage Home', v, ll. 42–4). We can reach across the divide that separates us from other animals. We can even hold science itself to account.

I want to close this book with one last poem that encapsulates the function of poetry in the Darwinian age. This is 'Kew Gardens', by the South-African born Scottish poet D. M. Black, written in memory of Ian A. Black, who died in 1971:

Distinguished scientist, to whom I greatly defer
(old man, moreover, whom I dearly love)
I walk today in Kew Gardens, in sunlight the colour of honey
which flows from the cold autumnal blue of the heavens to light these
    tans and golds,
these ripe corn and leather and sunset colours of the East Asian
    liriodendrons,
of the beeches and maples and plum-trees and the stubborn green banks
    of the holly hedges –
and you walk always beside me, you with your knowledge of names
and your clairvoyant gaze, in what for me is sheer panorama
seeing the net or web of connectedness. But today it is I who speak
(and you are long dead, but it is to you I say it):

'The leaves are green in summer because of chlorophyll
and the flowers are bright to lure the pollinators,
and without remainder (so you have often told me)
these marvellous things that shock the heart the head can account for;
but I want to sing an excess which is not so simply explainable,
to say that the beauty of the autumn is a redundant beauty,
that the sky had no need to be this particular shade of blue,
nor the maple to die in flames of this particular yellow,
nor the heart to respond with an ecstasy that does not beget children.
I want to say that I do not believe your science
although I believe every word of it, and intend to understand it;
that although I rate that unwavering gaze higher than almost
    everything
there is another sense, a hearing, to which I more deeply attend.
Thus I withstand and contradict you, I, your child,
who have inherited from you the passion which causes me to oppose you.'

D. M. Black's relationship with Ian Black and his science in this poem can
stand for the wider relationship between poets and poetry on the one side
and Darwin and Darwinism on the other. Like Darwin, the old scientist
sees the 'inextricable web of affinities' that comprise the 'entangled bank'
of life on Earth ([1859] 2003: 364, 397). For Black himself, this 'unwavering gaze' of science is 'clairvoyant', seeing beyond the 'sheer panorama' of
the visible world into the real relations between living things.

This clairvoyance marks science out as a form of transcendence. But
Black wants to transcend science itself. In the 'redundant beauty' of nature
he catches a trace of something science seemingly cannot explain, because
it serves no function. The switch from the bald, textbook vocabulary of
'chlorophyll' and 'pollinators' to poetic imagery and the details of 'particular' colours seems to mirror and confirm this new transcendence. But unlike
Tennyson, Black does not simply vouchsafe his transcendental beliefs and
values in the face of scientific materialism. Instead, the two are intimately
bound together.

Black dwells on the beauty of nature as beyond the reach of science,
yet the richest expression of this beauty in his poem – 'these ripe corn and
leather and sunset colours of the East Asian liriodendrons' – depends on
the literal and figurative resonances of botanical vocabulary. The word 'liri-
odendron' is beautiful in itself. Like the effect of a particular colour, such
beauty is hard to explain. I can observe that the first sound, 'li', is slightly
modified in the second, 'ri'; that 'den' is balanced by 'dron'; and that 'dron'
is also a reshaping of the elements that make up 'rioden'. I can point out

too that these internal resonances are complemented by the echoes of the words 'lyric', suggesting poetry itself, and 'dendron', the Greek word for tree, familiar to most of us through the word 'rhododendron'. Hearing the word, we can take pleasure in both the sounds and their associations. Yet this explanation does nothing to capture the effect itself. All it does is draw our attention to it, so that when we read the word or the poem again we are more sensitive to the experience it offers us.

In 'The Field Pansy', Amy Clampitt asks 'What difference do the minutiae / of that seeming inconsequence that's called beauty // add up to?' (ll. 29-31) Like life itself, beauty – in nature or poetry – remains a non-material fact in a material world, whether or not material explanations can account for it. Science cannot dispel beauty, but nor does beauty necessarily confound science. In 'Kew Gardens', Black half wishes it does. He wants to disbelieve, and yet he cannot, not least because he honours the old scientist's memory even as he battles against him. Even that very battle itself he understands through biology, as the product of an inherited temperament.

Ultimately, Black leaves it unresolved whether his sense of beauty goes beyond Darwinism, as he suggests at first, or whether it is itself a product of it. Perhaps, in the end, it does not matter. If we can find the beauty Black sees within the Darwinian world, do we need to look beyond it? If, like Black in 'Kew Gardens' and Meredith in his 'Ode', we can overhear meaning in nature, do we need something beyond nature to guarantee that meaning?

It is apt that Black and Meredith should put their trust in hearing over sight, as poetry is above all an aural medium. It is through its sounds, not merely its words, that poetry makes us feel. For all that it at times assumes the mantle of prophecy, poetry cannot tell us the final truth. Poetry is not revelation. But like revelation – which, to many Darwinians, is itself only poetry – it is a source of insight and wonder. Read receptively and with care, the poetry of the Darwinian condition opens our minds to forms of understanding and experience that can enrich that condition beyond measure.

Bibliography

POETRY

Ammons, A. R. (1974), *Sphere: The Form of a Motion*, New York: Norton.

Ammons, A. R. (1987), *Sumerian Vistas: Poems*, New York: Norton.

Ammons, A. R. (1993), *Garbage*, New York: Norton.

Ammons, A. R. (2006), *Selected Poems*, ed. David Lehman, New York: Library of America.

Appleman, Philip (1996), *New and Selected Poems 1956–1996*, Fayetteville, AR: University of Arkansas Press.

Barnie, John (2001), *Ice*, Llandysul: Gomer Press.

Black, D. M. (1991), *Collected Poems, 1964–1987*, Edinburgh: Polygon.

Blind, Mathilde (1889), *The Ascent of Man*, London: Chatto & Windus.

Bridges, Robert (1953), *The Poetical Works of Robert Bridges with The Testament of Beauty but Excluding the Eight Dramas*, London: Oxford University Press.

Browning, Robert (1981), *The Poems*, ed. John Pettigrew and Thomas J. Collins, Harmondsworth: Penguin.

Canton, William (1927), *The Poems of William Canton*, London: Harrap.

Clampitt, Amy (1997), *The Collected Poems of Amy Clampitt*, New York: Knopf.

Crane, Stephen (1899), *War is Kind*, London: Heinemann.

Davidson, John (1973), *The Poems of John Davidson*, ed. Andrew Turnbull, 2 vols, Edinburgh: Scottish Academic Press.

Eberhart, Richard (1988), *Collected Poems 1930–1986*, New York: Oxford University Press.

Frost, Robert (2001), *The Poetry of Robert Frost*, ed. Edward Connery Lathem, London: Vintage.

Gunn, Thom (1993), *Collected Poems*, London: Faber.

Hake, Thomas Gordon (1890), *The New Day*, ed. W. Earl Hodgson, London: Remington.

Hardy, Thomas (1930), *Collected Poems of Thomas Hardy*, 4th edn, London: Macmillan.

Hardy, Thomas (1981), *The Complete Poems of Thomas Hardy*, ed. James Gibson, London: Macmillan.

Hayes, Alfred (1891), *The March of Man and Other Poems*, London: Macmillan.

Heath-Stubbs, John and Phillips Salman, eds (1984), *Poems of Science*, Harmondsworth: Penguin.

Hopkins, Gerard Manley (1986), *Gerard Manley Hopkins (The Oxford Authors)*, ed. Catherine Phillips, Oxford: Oxford University Press.

Hughes, Ted (2003), *Collected Poems*, ed. Paul Keegan, London: Faber.

Jeffers, Robinson (1977), *The Double Axe and Other Poems Including Eleven Suppressed Poems*, ed. William Everson, New York: Liveright.

Jeffers, Robinson (1987), *Rock and Hawk: A Selection of Shorter Poems*, ed. Robert Haas, New York: Random House.

Jeffers, Robinson (2001), *The Selected Poetry of Robinson Jeffers*, ed. Tim Hunt, Stanford: Stanford University Press.

Jeffers, Robinson (2003), *The Wild God of the World: An Anthology of Robinson Jeffers*, ed. Albert Gelpi, Stanford: Stanford University Press.

Keats, John (1974), *Poems*, ed. Gerald Bullett and Robert Gittings, London: Dent.

Kleinzahler, August (2007), 'Anniversary', *London Review of Books*, 21 June, 2007, p. 17.

Leighton, Angela and Margaret Reynolds, eds (1995), *Victorian Women Poets: An Anthology*, Oxford: Blackwell.

Lucretius (1999), *On the Nature of the Universe*, trans. Ronald Melville, ed. Don and Peta Fowler, Oxford: Oxford University Press.

MacBeth, George, ed. (1965), *The Penguin Book of Animal Verse*, Harmondsworth: Penguin.

MacDiarmid, Hugh (1972), *The Hugh MacDiarmid Anthology: Poems in Scots and English*, ed. Michael Grieve and Alexander Scott, London: Routledge.

Meredith, George (1870), 'In the Woods', *Fortnightly Review*, O.S. 14/N.S. 8: 179–83.

Meredith, George (1909–11), *The Works of George Meredith: Memorial Edition*, 27 vols, London: Constable.

Meredith, George (1912), *The Poetical Works of George Meredith*, ed. G. M. Treveyan, London: Constable.

Meredith, George (1978), *The Poems of George Meredith*, ed. Phyllis B. Bartlett, 2 vols, New Haven, CT: Yale University Press.

Millay, Edna St Vincent (1941), *Collected Sonnets of Edna St Vincent Millay*, New York: Harper.

Millay, Edna St Vincent (1992), *Selected Poems*, ed. Colin Falck, Manchester: Carcanet.

Morgan, Edwin (1990), *Collected Poems*, Manchester: Carcanet.

Morgan, Edwin (2007), *A Book of Lives*, Manchester: Carcanet.

Morris, Lewis (1894), *The Works of Lewis Morris*, London: Kegan Paul.

Myers, Frederic W. H. (1882), *The Renewal of Youth and Other Poems*, London: Macmillan.

Naden, Constance C. W. (1887), *A Modern Apostle; The Elixir of Life; The Story of Clarice; and Other Poems*, London: Kegan Paul.

Naden, Constance C. W. (1894), *The Complete Poetical Works of Constance Naden*, ed. Robert Lewins, London: Bickers.

Oswald, Alice, ed. (2005), *The Thunder Mutters: 101 Poems for the Planet*, London: Faber.

Pack, Robert (1993a), *Fathering the Map: New and Selected Later Poems*, Chicago, IL: University of Chicago Press.

Pack, Robert (2004a), *Elk in Winter*, Chicago, IL: University of Chicago Press.

Pack, Robert and Jay Parini, eds (1997), *Introspections: American Poets on One of Their Own Poems*, Hanover, NH: University Press of New England.

Riordan, Maurice and Jon Turney, eds (2000), *A Quark of Mister Mark: 101 Poems about Science*, London: Faber.

Robinson, A. Mary F. (1888), *Songs, Ballads, and A Garden Play*, London: Unwin.

Robinson, A. Mary F. (1901), *The Collected Poems Lyrical and Narrative of A. Mary F. Robinson (Madame Duclaux)*, London: Unwin.

Rogers, Pattiann (2001a), *Song of the World Becoming: New and Collected Poems 1981–2001*, Minneapolis, MN: Milkweed.

Rollinson, Neil (1996), *A Spillage of Mercury*, London: Jonathan Cape.

Rossetti, Christina (2001), *The Complete Poems*, ed. R. W. Crump and Betty S. Flowers, London: Penguin.

Shelley, Percy Bysshe (2003), *The Major Works*, ed. Zachary Leader and Michael O'Neill, Oxford: Oxford University Press.

Stevens, Wallace (1954), *The Collected Poems of Wallace Stevens*, New York: Vintage.

Swinburne, Algernon Charles (1924), *Collected Poetical Works*, 2 vols, London: Heinemann.

Swinburne, Algernon Charles (2002), *Selected Poems*, ed. L. M. Findlay, Manchester: Carcanet.

Symonds, John Addington (1882), *Animi Figura*, London: Smith, Elder.

Tennyson, Alfred Lord (1892), *The Death of Œnone, Akbar's Dream, and Other Poems*, London: Macmillan.

Tennyson, Alfred Lord (1894), *The Works of Alfred Lord Tennyson Poet Laureate*, London: Macmillan.

Tennyson, Alfred Lord (1987), *The Poems of Tennyson*, ed. Christopher Ricks, 2nd edn, 3 vols, Harlow: Longman.

Thomas, Dylan (1988), *Collected Poems 1934–1953*, ed. Walford Davies and Ralph Maud, London: Dent.

Thomson, James [1874] (1993), *The City of Dreadful Night*, ed. Edwin Morgan, Edinburgh: Canongate.

Warren, Robert Penn (1998), *The Collected Poems of Robert Penn Warren*, ed. John Burt, Baton Rouge, LA: Louisiana State University Press.

Wilde, Oscar (1966), *The Complete Works of Oscar Wilde*, ed. J. B. Foreman, London: Collins.

References

Amigoni, David (2007), *Colonies, Cults and Evolution: Literature, Science and Culture in Nineteenth-Century Writing*, Cambridge: Cambridge University Press.

Anon. (1909), 'The Darwinian Celebrations at Cambridge', *Nature*, 81: 7–14.

Appleman, Philip (1965), *The Silent Explosion*, Boston: Beacon Press.

Appleman, Philip, ed. (2001), *Darwin*, 3rd edn, New York: Norton.

Appleman, Philip, ed. (2004), Thomas Robert Malthus, *An Essay on the Principle of Population*, 2nd edn, New York: Norton.

Armstrong, Isobel (1993), *Victorian Poetry: Poetry, Poetics and Politics*, London: Routledge.

Barnes, William (1878), *An Outline of English Speech-Craft*, London: Kegan Paul.

Barnes, William (1880), *An Outline of English Rede-Craft (Logic) with English Wording*, London: Kegan Paul.

Barnie, John (1996), *No Hiding Place: Essays on the New Nature and Poetry*, Cardiff: University of Wales Press.

Beach, Joseph Warren (1936), *The Concept of Nature in Nineteenth-Century English Poetry*, New York: Macmillan.

Beer, Gillian [1983] (2009), *Darwin's Plots: Evolutionary Narrative in Darwin, George Eliot and Nineteenth-Century Fiction*, 3rd edn, Cambridge: Cambridge University Press.

Behe, Michael J. (2007), *The Edge of Evolution: The Search for the Limits of Darwinism*, New York: Simon and Schuster.

Benton, Michael J. (2003), *When Life Nearly Died: The Greatest Mass Extinction of All Time*, London: Thames and Hudson.

Blind, Mathilde (1886), *Shelley's View of Nature Contrasted with Darwin's*, London: Shelley Society.

Bold, Alan (1976), *Thom Gunn and Ted Hughes*, Edinburgh: Oliver and Boyd.

Bowler, Peter J. (1983), *The Eclipse of Darwinism: Anti-Darwinian Evolution Theories in the Decades around 1900*, Baltimore: Johns Hopkins University Press.

Bowler, Peter J. (1992), *The Non-Darwinian Revolution: Reinterpreting a Historical Myth*, 2nd edn, Baltimore: Johns Hopkins University Press.

Bowler, Peter J. (2003), *Evolution: The History of an Idea*, 3rd edn, Berkeley: University of California Press.

Brooke, John Hedley (1991), *Science and Religion: Some Historical Perspectives*, Cambridge: Cambridge University Press.

Browning, Robert (1933), *Letters of Robert Browning collected by Thomas J. Wise*, ed. T. L. Hood, London: Murray.

Buell, Lawrence (2005), *The Future of Environmental Criticism: Environmental Crisis and Literary Imagination*, Oxford: Blackwell.

Butler, Samuel [1872] (1970), *Erewhon*, ed. Peter Mudford, Harmondsworth: Penguin.

Carroll, Joseph (1995), *Evolution and Literary Theory*, Columbia: University of Missouri Press.

Carroll, Joseph (2004), *Literary Darwinism: Evolution, Human Nature, and Literature*, London: Routledge.

Cartwright, John (2008), *Evolution and Human Behaviour: Darwinian Perspectives on Human Nature*, 2nd edn, Basingstoke: Palgrave Macmillan.

Cobbe, Frances Power (1872), *Darwinism in Morals, and Other Essays*, London: Williams and Norgate.

Conway Morris, Simon (2003), *Life's Solution: Inevitable Humans in a Lonely Universe*, New York: Cambridge University Press.

Crum, Ralph B. (1931), *Scientific Thought in Poetry*, New York: Columbia University Press.

Cunningham, John (2001), 'Human Presence in Frost's Universe', in Robert Faggen (ed.), *The Cambridge Companion to Robert Frost*, Cambridge: Cambridge University Press, pp. 261–72.

Daniell, Madeline M. (1890), 'Memoir', in Naden, pp. vii–xviii.

Darwin, Charles [1859] (2003), *On the Origin of Species by Means of Natural Selection*, ed. Joseph Carroll, Peterborough, Ontario: Broadview.

Darwin, Charles (1868), *The Variation of Animals and Plants under Domestication*, 2 vols, London: John Murray.

Darwin, Charles [1871] (2004), *The Descent of Man and Selection in Relation to Sex*, ed. James Moore and Adrian Desmond, London: Penguin.

Darwin, Charles [1872] (1998), *The Expression of the Emotions in Man and Animals*, ed. Paul Ekman, Oxford: Oxford University Press.

Darwin, Charles (2002), *Autobiographies*, ed. Michael Neve and Sharon Messenger, London: Penguin.

Daston, Lorraine and Gregg Mitman, eds (2005), *Thinking with Animals: New Perspectives on Anthropomorphism*, New York: Columbia University Press.

Davie, Donald (1973), *Thomas Hardy and British Poetry*, London: Routledge.

Dawkins, Richard (1991), *The Blind Watchmaker*, 2nd edn, Harmondsworth: Penguin.

Dawkins, Richard (1999), *Unweaving the Rainbow: Science, Delusion and the Appetite for Wonder*, London: Penguin.

Dawkins, Richard (2005), *The Ancestor's Tale: A Pilgrimage to the Dawn of Life*, London: Orion.

Dean, Dennis R. (1985), *Tennyson and Geology*, Lincoln: Tennyson Society.

Desmond, Adrian (1998), *Huxley: From Devil's Disciple to Evolution's High Priest*, Harmondsworth: Penguin.

de Waal, Frans (1996), *Good Natured: The Origins of Right and Wrong in Humans and Other Animals*, Cambridge, MA: Harvard University Press.

de Waal, Frans and Frans Lanting (1997), *Bonobo: The Forgotten Ape*, Berkeley: University of California Press.

Doreski, William (1995), *The Modern Voice in American Poetry*, Gainesville: University Press of Florida.

Dowden, Edward (1878), *Studies in Literature 1789–1877*, London: Kegan Paul.

Dupré, John (2001), *Human Nature and the Limits of Science*, Oxford: Oxford University Press.

Dupré, John (2003), *Darwin's Legacy: What Evolution Means Today*, Oxford: Oxford University Press.

Eliot, George (1992), *Selected Critical Writings*, ed. Rosemary Ashton, Oxford: Oxford University Press.

Epstein, Daniel Mark (2001), *What My Lips Have Kissed: The Loves and Love Poems of Edna St. Vincent Millay*, New York: Henry Holt.

Faas, Ekbert (1980), *Ted Hughes: The Unaccommodated Universe*, Santa Barbara, CA: Black Sparrow Press.

Faggen, Robert (1997), *Robert Frost and the Challenge of Darwinism*, Ann Arbor, MI: University of Michigan Press.

Fiske, John (1900), *Through Nature to God*, London: Macmillan.

Fletcher, Giles (1593), *Licia, or Poemes of Love*, London.

Foley, Robert (1995), *Humans before Humanity: An Evolutionary Perspective*, Oxford: Blackwell.

Frost, Robert (1965), *Selected Letters of Robert Frost*, ed. Lawrance Thompson, London: Jonathan Cape.

Frost, Robert (2006), *The Notebooks of Robert Frost*, ed. Robert Faggen, Cambridge, MA: Harvard University Press.

Garrard, Greg (2004), *Ecocriticism (New Critical Idiom)*, Abingdon: Routledge.

Gathorne-Hardy, Jonathan (2005), *Alfred C. Kinsey: A Biography*, 2nd edn, London: Pimlico.

Gelpi, Albert (1987), *A Coherent Splendor: The American Poetic Renaissance, 1910–1950*, Cambridge: Cambridge University Press.

Gottschall, Jonathan (2008), *Literature, Science, and a New Humanities*, New York: Palgrave Macmillan.

Gould, Stephen Jay (2002), *The Structure of Evolutionary Theory*, Cambridge, MA: Harvard University Press.

Gould, Stephen Jay (2004), *The Hedgehog, the Fox, and the Magister's Pox: Mending and Minding the Misconceived Gap between Science and the Humanities*, London: Vintage.

Graham, Peter W. (2008), *Jane Austen and Charles Dickens: Naturalists and Novelists*, Aldershot: Ashgate.

Gunn, Thom (1982), *The Occasions of Poetry: Essays in Criticism and Autobiography*, ed. Clive Wilmer, London: Faber.

Haas, Robert Bernard (2002), *Going by Contraries: Robert Frost's Conflict with Science*, Charlottesville: University Press of Virginia.

Hall, Donald and Robert Pack, eds (1962), *New Poets of England and America: Second Selection*, Cleveland, OH: World Publishing Company.

Hardy, Thomas [1873] (2005), *A Pair of Blue Eyes*, ed. Alan Manford, intro. Tim Dolin, Oxford: Oxford University Press.

Hardy, Thomas [1891] (1978), *Tess of the d'Urbervilles: A Pure Woman*, ed. A. Alvarez and David Skilton, Harmondsworth: Penguin.

Hardy, Thomas (as Florence Emily Hardy) (1962), *The Life of Thomas Hardy 1840–1928*, London: Macmillan.

Hardy, Thomas (1978–88), *The Collected Letters of Thomas Hardy*, ed. Richard Little Purdy and Michael Millgate, 7 vols, Oxford: Oxford University Press.

Haught, John F. (2006), *Is Nature Enough? Meaning and Truth in the Age of Science*, Cambridge: Cambridge University Press.

Hawkins, Mike (1997), *Social Darwinism in European and American Thought, 1860–1945: Nature as Model and Nature as Threat*, Cambridge: Cambridge University Press.

Hayes, J. W. (1909), *Tennyson and Scientific Theology*, London: Elliot Stock.

Hennessy, Christopher (2005), 'An Interview with Thom Gunn', *Memorious*, 5, www.memorious.org

Hobhouse, L. T. (1906), *Morals in Evolution: A Study in Comparative Ethics*, 2 vols, London: Chapman and Hall.

Hodge, Jonathan and Gregory Radick, eds (2003), *The Cambridge Companion to Darwin*, Cambridge: Cambridge University Press.

Hughes, William R. (1890), *Constance Naden: A Memoir*, London: Bickers.

Huxley, Julian (1942), *Evolution: The Modern Synthesis*, London: Allen & Unwin.

Huxley, Thomas Henry (1893–4), *Collected Essays of T. H. Huxley*, 9 vols, London: Macmillan.

Huxley, Thomas Henry (1910), *Lectures and Lay Sermons*, ed. Sir Oliver Lodge, London: Dent.

Inge, William Ralph (1925), 'Conclusion', in Joseph Needham (ed.), *Science Religion and Reality*, London: Sheldon Press, pp. 345–89.

Jablonka, Eva and Marion J. Lamb (2005), *Evolution in Four Dimensions: Genetic, Epigenetic, Behavioral, and Symbolic Variation in the History of Life*, Cambridge, MA: MIT.

Jeffers, Robinson (1968), *The Selected Letters of Robinson Jeffers 1897–1962*, ed. Ann N. Ridgeway, Baltimore, MD: Johns Hopkins Press.

Jones, Howard Mumford (1959), '1859 and the Idea of Crisis: General Introduction', in Philip Appleman, William A. Madden and Michael Wolff (eds), *1859: Entering an Age of Crisis*, Bloomington, IN: Indiana University Press, pp. 13–28.

Jones, Mervyn (1999), *The Amazing Victorian: A Life of George Meredith*, London: Constable.

Jones, Thomas Rymer (1865), *The Animal Creation: A Popular Introduction to Zoology*, London: Warne.

Kaati, Gunnar, Lars Olov Bygren, Marcus Pembrey and Michael Sjöström (2007), 'Transgenerational response to nutrition, early life circumstances and longevity', *European Journal of Human Genetics*, 15: 784–90.

Karr, Jeff (1985), 'Caliban and Paley: Two Natural Theologians', *Studies in Browning and His Circle*, 13: 37–46.

Kelvin, Norman (1961), *A Troubled Eden: Nature and Society in the Works of George Meredith*, Edinburgh: Oliver & Boyd.

Kingsley, Charles (1880), *Scientific Lectures and Essays*, London: Macmillan.

Kinsey, Alfred C., Wardell B. Pomeroy and Clyde E. Martin (1948), *Sexual Behavior in the Human Male*, Philadelphia, PA: Saunders.

Kinsey, Alfred C., Wardell B. Pomeroy, Clyde E. Martin and Paul H. Gebhard (1953), *Sexual Behavior in the Human Female*, Philadelphia, PA: Saunders.

Kitcher, Philip (2007), *Living with Darwin: Evolution, Design, and the Future of Faith*, New York: Oxford University Press.

Lack, David (1957), *Evolutionary Theory and Christian Belief: The Unresolved Conflict*, London: Methuen.

Lankester, Edwin Ray (1880), *Degeneration: A Chapter in Darwinism*, London: Macmillan.

Lankester, Edwin Ray [1910] (1932), *Science from an Easy Chair*, 18th edn, London: Methuen.

Leakey, Richard and Roger Lewin (1995), *The Sixth Extinction: Biodiversity and its Survival*, London: Phoenix.

Leavis, F. R. [1932] (1963), *New Bearings in English Poetry: A Study of the Contemporary Situation*, 2nd edn, Harmondsworth: Penguin.

Lester, Joseph (1995), *E. Ray Lankester and the Making of Modern British Biology*, ed. Peter Bowler, Oxford: British Society for the History of Science.

Levine, George (1988), *Darwin and the Novelists: Patterns of Science in Victorian Fiction*, Cambridge, MA: Harvard University Press.

Levine, George (2006), *Darwin Loves You: Natural Selection and the Re-Enchantment of the World*, Princeton, NJ: Princeton University Press.

Levine, George (2008), *Realism, Ethics and Secularism: Essays on Victorian Literature and Science*, Cambridge: Cambridge University Press.

Lewes, George Henry (1992), *Versatile Victorian: Selected Writings of George Henry Lewes*, ed. Rosemary Ashton, London: Duckworth.

Lewins, Robert, ed. (1894), 'Some Personal and Press Opinions on the Works of Constance Naden', appended to Naden, *Complete Poetical Works*.

Lockyer, Sir Norman and Winifred L. Lockyer (1910), *Tennyson as a Student and Poet of Nature*, London: Macmillan.

Lodge, Sir Oliver (1910), *Reason and Belief*, London: Methuen.

Lodge, Sir Oliver (1911), 'The Attitude of Tennyson towards Science', in Hallam Tennyson (ed.), *Tennyson and His Friends*, London: Macmillan, pp. 280–4.

Lomas, Herbert (1987), 'The Poetry of Ted Hughes', *Hudson Review*, 40: 409–26.

Lovelock, James (2000), *Gaia: A New Look at Life on Earth*, 3rd edn, Oxford: Oxford University Press.

Lubbock, Sir John [1892] (1900), *The Beauties of Nature and the Wonders of the World We Live In*, London: Macmillan.

Lyell, Sir Alfred (1902), *Tennyson*, London: Macmillan.

Lyell, Charles [1830–3] (1997), *Principles of Geology*, ed. James A. Secord, Harmondsworth: Penguin.

McGann, Jerome J. (1972), *Swinburne: An Experiment in Criticism*, Chicago, IL: University of Chicago Press.

McGrath, Alister (2005), *Dawkins' God: Genes, Memes, and the Meaning of Life*, Oxford: Blackwell.

McSweeney, Kerry (1981), *Tennyson and Swinburne as Romantic Naturalists*, Toronto: University of Toronto Press.

Mallett, Phillip (2000), *'Poems of the Past and the Present'*, in Norman Page (ed.), *Oxford Reader's Companion to Hardy*, Oxford: Oxford University Press, pp. 327–31.

Mayr, Ernest (1976), *Evolution and the Diversity of Life: Selected Essays*, Cambridge, MA: Harvard University Press.

Meldola, R. (1909), 'Evolution: Old and New', *Nature*, 80: 481–5.

Meredith, George (1970), *The Letters of George Meredith*, ed. C. L. Cline, 3 vols, Oxford: Oxford University Press.

Midgley, Mary (1983), *Animals and Why They Matter*, Harmondsworth: Penguin.

Midgley, Mary (2001) *Science and Poetry*, London: Routledge.

Milford, Nancy (2001), *Savage Beauty: The Life of Edna St. Vincent Millay*, New York: Random House.

Miller, Susan M. (2007), 'Thomas Hardy and the Impersonal Lyric', *Journal of Modern Literature*, 30.3: 95–115.

Millhauser, Milton (1971), *Fire and Ice: The Influence of Science on Tennyson's Poetry*, Lincoln: Tennyson Society.

Mitchell, Sandra D. (2005), 'Anthropomorphism and Cross-Species Modeling', in Daston and Mitman (eds), pp. 100–17.

Mivart, St George (1871), *On the Genesis of Species*, 2nd edn, London: Macmillan.

Murfin, Ross C. (1978), *Swinburne, Hardy, Lawrence and the Burden of Belief*, Chicago, IL: University of Chicago Press.

Myers, Frederic W. H. (1893), 'Modern Poets and the Meaning of Life', *Nineteenth Century*, 33:93–111.

Naden, Constance C. W. (1890), *Induction and Deduction: A Historical and Critical Sketch of Successive Philosophical Conceptions*, ed. R. Lewins, London: Bickers.

Naden, Constance C. W. (1891), *Further Reliques of Constance Naden: Being Essays and Tracts for Our Times*, ed. George M. McCrie, London: Bickers.

Nagel, Thomas (1979), *Mortal Questions*, Cambridge: Cambridge University Press.

Nordlund, Marcus (2007), *Shakespeare and the Nature of Love: Literature, Culture, Evolution*, Evanston, IL: Northwestern University Press.

Norwood, Kyle (1995), '"Enter and Possess": Jeffers, Frost, and the Borders of the Self', in William B. Thesing (ed.), *Robinson Jeffers and a Galaxy of Writers: Essays in Honour of William H. Nolte*, Columbia: University of South Carolina Press, pp. 69–82.

Pack, Robert (1991), *The Long View: Essays on the Discipline of Hope and Poetic Craft*, Amherst, MA: University of Massachusetts Press.

Pack, Robert (1993b), 'Afterword: Taking Dominion over the Wilderness', in Robert Pack and Jay Parini (eds), *Poems for a Small Planet: Contemporary American Nature Poetry*, Hanover, NH: University Press of New England, pp. 271–93.

Pack, Robert (1997), 'Naming the Animals', in Pack and Parini (eds), pp. 193–200.

Pack, Robert (2004b), *Belief and Uncertainty in the Poetry of Robert Frost*, Lebanon, NH: University Press of New England.

Pearson, Karl [1892] (1937), *The Grammar of Science*, London: Dent.

Peterson, Roger Tory, Guy Mountfort, P. A. D. Hollom and D. I. M. Wallace (1993), *Birds of Britain and Europe*, 5th edn, London: HarperCollins.

Pinkney, Tony (1999), 'Romantic Ecology', in Duncan Wu (ed.), *A Companion to Romanticism*, Oxford: Blackwell, pp. 411–19.

Ridemour, George M. (1971), 'Swinburne on "The Problem to Solve in Expression"', *Victorian Poetry*, 9: 129–44.

Reade, Winwood (1872), *The Martyrdom of Man*, London: Trübner.

Riede, David G. (1978), *Swinburne: A Study of Romantic Mythmaking*, Charlottesville, VA: University Press of Virginia.

Ridley, Mark (2004), *Evolution*, 3rd edn, Oxford: Blackwell.

Robbins, Chandler S., Bertel Bruun, Herbert S. Zim and Arthur Singer (1983), *Birds of North America*, 2nd edn, New York: Golden Press.

Rogers, Pattiann (1999), *The Dream of the Marsh Wren: Writing as Reciprocal Creation*, Minneapolis, MN: Milkweed.

Rogers, Pattiann (2001b), 'Twentieth-Century Cosmology and the Soul's Habitation', in Kurt Brown (ed.), *The Measured Word: On Poetry and Science*, Athens, GA: University of Georgia Press, pp. 1–13.

Roppen, Georg (1956), *Evolution and Poetic Belief: A Study in Some Victorian and Modern Writers*, Oslo: Oslo University Press.

Ruse, Michael (2003), 'Belief in God in a Darwinian age', in Hodge and Radick (eds), pp. 333–54.

Sagar, Keith (2006), *The Laughter of Foxes: A Study of Ted Hughes*, 2nd edn, Liverpool: Liverpool University Press.

Savage, R. J. G. and M. R. Long (1986), *Mammal Evolution: An Illustrated Guide*, London: British Museum (Natural History).

Shaw, George Bernard [1921] (1939), *Back to Methuselah: A Metabiological Pentateuch*, Harmondsworth: Penguin.

Simpson, Arthur L., Jr (1970), 'Meredith's Pessimistic Humanism: A New Reading of *Modern Love*', *Modern Philology*, 67: 341–56.

Sloan, John (1995), *John Davidson, First of the Moderns: A Literary Biography*, Oxford: Oxford University Press.

Smith, John Maynard and Eörs Szathmáry (1997), *The Major Transitions in Evolution*, Oxford: Oxford University Press.

Sober, Elliott (2005), 'Comparative Psychology Meets Evolutionary Biology: Morgan's Canon and Cladistic Parsimony', in Daston and Mitman (eds), pp. 85–99.

Stamp Dawkins, Marian (1998), *Through Our Eyes Only? The Search for Animal Consciousness*, Oxford: Oxford University Press.

Stevenson, Lionel (1932), *Darwin Among the Poets*, Chicago, IL: University of Chicago Press.

Strong, Archibald T. (1921), *Three Studies in Shelley and An Essay on Nature in Wordsworth and Meredith*, London: Oxford University Press.

Swinburne, Algernon Charles [1887] (1926), 'Dethroning Tennyson: A Contribution to the Tennyson-Darwin Controversy', reprinted as 'Tennyson or Darwin?' in *The Complete Works of Algernon Charles Swinburne*, ed. Edmund Gosse and Thomas James Wise, 18 vols, London: Heinemann, XIV, pp. 342–5.

Swinburne, Algernon Charles (1959–62), *The Swinburne Letters*, ed. Cecil Y. Lang, 6 vols, New Haven, CT: Yale University Press.

Symonds, John Addington [1890] (1907), *Essays Speculative and Suggestive*, 3rd edn, London: Smith, Elder.

Symonds, John Addington (1893), *In the Key of Blue and Other Prose Essays*, London: Matthews and Lane.

Symons, Arthur (1916), *Figures of Several Centuries*, London: Constable.

Tacitus, Cornelius (1935), *The Germania of Tacitus: A Critical Edition*, ed. Rodney Potter Robinson, Middletown, CT: American Philological Association.

Tacitus, Cornelius (1938), *De Origine et Situ Germanorum*, ed. J. G. C. Anderson, Oxford: Oxford University Press.

Tennyson, Hallam [1907–8] (1974), *Tennyson's Creed*, Lincoln: Tennyson Society.

Tillyard, E. M. W. (1948), *Five Poems 1470–1870: An Elementary Essay on the Background of English Literature*, London: Chatto.

Timko, Michael (1965), 'Browning upon Butler; or, Natural Theology in the English Isle', *Criticism* 7: 141–50.

Tomko, Michael (2004), 'Varieties of Geological Experience: Religion, Body, and Spirit in Tennyson's *In Memoriam* and Lyell's *Principles of Geology*', *Victorian Poetry*, 42:113–33.

Trevelyan, George Macaulay (1906), *The Poetry and Philosophy of George Meredith*, London: Archibald Constable.

Vendler, Helen (1995), *Soul Says: On Recent Poetry*, Cambridge, MA: Harvard University Press.

Walker, Cheryl (1996), 'Antimodern, Modern, and Postmodern Millay: Contexts of Revaluation', in Margaret Dickey and Thomas Travisano (eds), *Gendered Modernisms: American Women Poets and Their Readers*, Philadelphia, PA: University of Pennsylvania Press, pp. 170–88.

Wallace, Alfred R. (1899) 'Introductory Note', in Mathilde Blind, *The Ascent of Man*, London: Unwin, pp. v–xii.

Wallace, Alfred R. (2002), *Infinite Tropics: An Alfred Russel Wallace Anthology*, ed. Andrew Berry, London: Verso.

Watson, Donald and Bruce Campbell (1980), *The Oxford Book of Birds*, 2nd edn, London: Peerage.

Wells, Herbert George (1891), 'Zoological Regression', *The Gentleman's Magazine*, 271: 246–53.

Wells, Herbert George [1895] (1995), *The Time Machine: The Centennial Edition*, ed. John Lawton, London: Dent.

Wells, Herbert George [1898] (1993), *The War of the Worlds*, intro. Arthur C. Clarke, London: Dent.

Wilson, Edward O. (1999), *Consilience: The Unity of Knowledge*, London: Abacus.

Wilson, Edward O. (2000), *Sociobiology: The New Synthesis*, 2nd edn, Cambridge, MA: Harvard University Press.

Wilson, Edward O. (2004), *On Human Nature*, 2nd edn, Cambridge, MA: Harvard University Press.

Winters, Yvor [1937] (1960), 'Primitivism and Decadence: A Study of American Experimental Poetry', reprinted in *In Defense of Reason*, London: Routledge, pp. 15–150.

Woods, Gregory (1987), *Articulate Flesh: Male Homo-Eroticism and Modern Poetry*, New Haven, CT: Yale University Press.

Further Reading

Adams, Jon (2007), *Interference Patterns: Literary Study, Scientific Knowledge, and Disciplinary Autonomy*, Lewisburg, PA: Bucknell University Press.

Agyros, Alexander (1991), *A Blessed Rage for Order: Deconstruction, Evolution, and Chaos*, Ann Arbor: University of Michigan Press.

Amigoni, David (2006), 'A Consilient Canon? Bridges to and from Evolutionary Literary Analysis', *English Studies in Canada*, 32.2–3: 173–85.

Attfield, Robin (2006), *Creation, Evolution and Meaning*, Aldershot: Ashgate.

Banfield, Marie (2007), 'Darwinism, Doxology, and Energy Physics: The New Sciences, the Poetry and the Poetics of Gerard Manley Hopkins', *Victorian Poetry*, 45: 175–94.

Beer, Gillian (1996), *Open Fields: Science in Cultural Encounter*, Oxford: Oxford University Press.

Blackburn, Simon (2006), *Truth: A Guide for the Perplexed*, London: Penguin.

Bowler, Peter J. (1993), *Biology and Social Thought: 1850–1914*, Berkeley: University of California Office for History of Science and Technology.

Brown, Daniel (2004), *Gerard Manley Hopkins (Writers and Their Work)*, Tavistock: Northcote House.

Burrow, J. W. (2000), *The Crisis of Reason: European Thought, 1848–1914*, New Haven, CT: Yale University Press.

Bush, Douglas (1950), *Science and English Poetry: A Historical Sketch, 1590–1950*, Oxford: Oxford University Press.

Chapman, Steven (2004), 'On the Question of Science in "The Inhumanist"', *Jeffers Studies*, 8.2: 31–60.

Chapple, J. A. V. (1986), *Science and Literature in the Nineteenth Century*, Basingstoke: Macmillan.

Christie, John and Sally Shuttleworth, eds (1989), *Nature Transfigured: Science and Literature 1700–1900*, Manchester: Manchester University Press.

Cooke, Brett and Frederick Turner, eds (1999), *Biopoetics: Evolutionary Explorations in the Arts*, Lexington, KY: International Conference on the Unity of the Sciences.

Cordle, Daniel (1999), *Postmodern Postures: Literature, Science and the Two Cultures Debate*, Aldershot: Ashgate.

Cosslett, Tess (1982), *The 'Scientific Movement' and Victorian Literature*, Brighton: Harvester.

Crawford, Robert, ed. (2006), *Contemporary Poetry and Contemporary Science*, Oxford: Oxford University Press.

Dale, Peter Allan (1989), *In Pursuit of a Scientific Culture: Science, Art, and Society in the Victorian Age*, Madison, WI: University of Wisconsin Press.

Dawkins, Richard (1999), *The Extended Phenotype: The Long Reach of the Gene*, 2nd edn, Oxford: Oxford University Press.

Dawkins, Richard (2006), *The Selfish Gene*, 3rd edn, Oxford: Oxford University Press.

Dawson, Gowan (2007), *Darwin, Literature and Victorian Respectability*, Cambridge: Cambridge University Press.

Dembski, William A. and Michael Ruse, eds (2004), *Debating Design: From Darwin to DNA*, Cambridge: Cambridge University Press.

Dennett, Daniel (1995), *Darwin's Dangerous Idea: Evolution and the Meanings of Life*, London: Penguin.

de Waal, Frans, ed. (2001), *Tree of Origin: What Primate Behavior Can Tell Us about Human Social Evolution*, Cambridge, MA: Harvard University Press.

Diamond, Jared (1992), *The Rise and Fall of the Third Chimpanzee*, London: Vintage.

Distiller, Natasha (2008), *Desire and Gender in the Sonnet Tradition*, Basingstoke: Palgrave.

Domning, Daryl P. (2006), *Original Selfishness: Original Sin and Evil in the Light of Evolution*, with a commentary by Monika K. Hellwig, Aldershot: Ashgate.

Dupré, John (2002), *Humans and Other Animals*, Oxford: Oxford University Press.

Eaker, J. Gordon (1939), 'Robert Bridges' Concept of Nature', *PMLA*, 54: 1181–97.

Ebbatson, Roger (1982), *The Evolutionary Self: Hardy, Forster, Lawrence*, Brighton: Harvester.

Eibl, Karl (2007), 'On the Redskins of Scientism and the Aesthetes in the Circled Wagons', *Journal of Literary Theory*, 1: 421–41.

Fenchel, Tom (2002), *The Origin and Early Evolution of Life*, Oxford: Oxford University Press.

Fergusson, Christine (2006), *Language, Science and Popular Fiction in the Victorian Fin-de-Siècle: The Brutal Tongue*, Aldershot: Ashgate

Forster, Leonard (1969), *The Icy Fire: Five Studies in European Petrarchism*, Cambridge: Cambridge University Press.

Forsyth, R. A. (1962), 'Evolutionism and the Pessimism of James Thomson (B.V.)', *Essays in Criticism*, 12: 148–66.

Fromm, Harold (2003), 'The New Darwinism in the Humanities', *Hudson Review*, 56: 89–99, 315–27.

Glendening, John (2007), *The Evolutionary Imagination in Late Victorian Novels*, Aldershot: Ashgate.

Gossin, Pamela (2007), *Thomas Hardy's Novel Universe: Astronomy,*

Cosmology, and Gender in the Post-Darwinian World, Aldershot: Ashgate.

Gottschall, Jonathan and David Sloan Wilson, eds (2005), *The Literary Animal: Evolution and the Nature of Narrative*, Evanston: Northeastern University Press.

Gould, Stephen Jay (1977), *Ontogeny and Philogeny*, Cambridge, MA: Harvard University Press.

Gould, Stephen Jay (2002), *Rocks of Ages: Science and Religion in the Fullness of Life*, London: Vintage.

Green, Andrew J. (1944), 'Robert Bridges and the Spiritual Animal', *Philosophical Review*, 53: 286–95.

Groth, Helen (1999), 'Victorian Women Poets and Scientific Narratives', in Isobel Armstrong and Virginia Blain (eds), *Women's Poetry, Late Romantic to Late Victorian: Gender and Genre, 1830–1900*, Basingstoke: Macmillan, pp. 325–51.

Hall, Dorothy Judd (1984), *Robert Frost: Contours of Belief*, Athens, OH: Ohio University Press.

Henson, Louise, Geoffrey Cantor, Gowan Dawson, Richard Noakes, Sally Shuttleworth and Jonathan R. Topham, eds (2004), *Culture and Science in the Nineteenth-Century Media*, Aldershot: Ashgate.

Hollander, John (1997), *The Work of Poetry*, New York: Columbia University Press.

Holmes, John (1999), 'The Victorian Genetics of *Astrophel and Stella*', *Sidney Journal*, 17.2: 41–51.

Holmes, John (2004), '*The New Day*: Dr Hake and the Poetry of Science', *Journal of Victorian Culture*, 9.1: 68–89.

Holmes, John (2005), *Dante Gabriel Rossetti and the Late Victorian Sonnet Sequence: Sexuality, Belief and the Self*, Aldershot: Ashgate.

Holmes, John (2008), 'Lucretius at the *Fin de Siècle*: Science, Religion and Poetry', *English Literature in Transition*, 51: 266–80.

John Paul II (1997), 'The Pope's Message on Evolution', *Quarterly Review of Biology*, 72: 381–3.

Johnson, W. R. (2000), *Lucretius and the Modern World*, London: Duckworth.

Kaston Tange, Andrea (2006), 'Constance Naden and the Erotics of Evolution: Mating the Woman of Letters with the Man of Science', *Nineteenth-Century Literature*, 61: 200–40.

Kelleter, Frank (2007), 'A Tale of Two Natures: Worried Reflections on the Study of Literature and Culture in an Age of Neuroscience and Neo-Darwinism', *Journal of Literary Theory*, 1: 153–89.

Krasner, James (1992), *The Entangled Eye: Visual Perception and the*

Representation of Nature in Post-Darwinian Narrative, Oxford: Oxford University Press.

Kuhn, Thomas (1970), *The Structure of Scientific Revolutions*, 2nd edn, Chicago, IL: University of Chicago Press.

Langdon-Brown, Sir Walter (1938), 'Robert Bridges: The Poet of Evolution', reprinted in *Thus We Are Men*, London: Kegan Paul, pp. 152–71.

Leane, Elizabeth (2007), *Reading Popular Physics: Disciplinary Skirmishes and Textual Strategies*, Aldershot: Ashgate.

Levine, George with Alan Rauch, eds (1987), *One Culture: Essays in Science and Literature*, Madison, WI: University of Wisconsin Press.

Longenbach, James (2004), *The Resistance to Poetry*, Chicago, IL: University of Chicago Press.

Louis, Margot K. (1990), *Swinburne and His Gods: The Roots and Growth of an Agnostic Poetry*, Montreal: McGill-Queen's University Press.

Luckhurst, Roger and Josephine McDonagh, eds (2002), *Transactions and Encounters: Science and Culture in the Nineteenth Century*, Manchester: Manchester University Press.

MacDiarmid, Hugh (1961), 'John Davidson: Influences and Influence', in John Davidson, *A Selection of his Poems*, ed. Maurice Lindsay, London: Hutchinson, pp. 47–54.

Meadows, A. J. (1992), 'Astronomy and Geology, Terrible Muses! Tennyson and 19th-Century Science', *Notes and Records of the Royal Society of London*, 46.1: 111–18.

Midgley, Mary (1995), *Beast and Man: The Roots of Human Nature*, 2nd edn, London: Routledge.

Midgley, Mary (2002), *Evolution as a Religion: Strange Hopes and Stranger Fears*, 2nd edn, London: Routledge.

Moore, James R. (1987), 'The Erotics of Evolution: Constance Naden and Hylo-Idealism', in Levine with Rauch (eds), pp. 225–57.

Mordavsky Caleb, Amanda (2007), *(Re)Creating Science in Nineteenth-Century Britain*, Newcastle: Cambridge Scholars Publishing.

Morton, Peter (1984), *The Vital Science: Biology and the Literary Imagination, 1860–1900*, London: Allen & Unwin.

Morris, Richard (2001), *The Evolutionists: The Struggle for Darwin's Soul*, New York: Freeman.

Murphy, Patricia (2002), 'Fated Marginalization: Women and Science in the Poetry of Constance Naden', *Victorian Poetry*, 40: 107–30.

Myers, Frederic W. H. (1889), 'Tennyson as Prophet', *Nineteenth Century*, 25: 381–96.

O'Connor, Mary (1987), *John Davidson*, Edinburgh: Scottish Academic Press.

O'Connor, Ralph (2007), *The Earth on Show: Fossils and the Poetics of Popular Science, 1802–1856*, Chicago, IL: University of Chicago Press.

O'Neill, Patricia (1997), 'Victorian Lucretius: Tennyson and the Problem of Scientific Romanticism', in J. B. Bullen (ed.), *Writing and Victorianism*, Harlow: Longman.

Pack, Robert and Jay Parini, eds (1996), *Touchstones: American Poets on a Favorite Poem*, Hanover, NH: University Press of New England.

Paradis, James and Thomas Postlewait, eds (1985), *Victorian Science and Victorian Values: Literary Perspectives*, New Brunswick, NJ: Rutgers University Press.

Pigou, A. C. (1905), 'The Optimism of Browning and Meredith', *Independent Review*, 6: 92–104.

Peppe, Holly (1995), 'Rewriting the Myth of the Woman in Love: Millay's *Fatal Interview*', in *Millay at 100: A Critical Reappraisal*, ed. Diane P. Freedman, Carbondale and Edwardsville, IL: Southern Illinois University Press, pp. 52–65.

Rescher, Nicholas (2000), *Nature and Understanding: The Metaphysics and Method of Science*, Oxford: Oxford University Press.

Roberts, Philip Davies (1986), *How Poetry Works: The Elements of English Poetry*, Harmondsworth: Penguin.

Rose, Hilary and Steven Rose, eds (2000), *Alas, Poor Darwin: Arguments Against Evolutionary Psychology*, London: Jonathan Cape.

Rose, Steven (2005), *Lifelines: Life Beyond the Genes*, 2nd edn, London: Vintage.

Ruse, Michael (1999), *Mystery of Mysteries: Is Evolution a Social Construction?*, Cambridge, MA: Harvard University Press.

Ruse, Michael (2001), *Can a Darwinian Be a Christian? The Relationship between Science and Religion*, Cambridge: Cambridge University Press.

Segerstråle, Ullica (2000), *Defenders of the Truth: The Sociobiology Debate*, Oxford: Oxford University Press.

Segerstråle, Ullica (2006), 'An Eye on the Core: Dawkins and Sociobiology', in Alan Grafen and Mark Ridley (eds), *Richard Dawkins: How a Scientist Changed the Way We Think*, Oxford: Oxford University Press, pp. 75–97.

Shaffer, Elinor S., ed. (1991), *Literature and Science (Comparative Criticism*, 13).

Shaffer, Elinor S., ed. (1998), *The Third Culture: Literature and Science*, Berlin: Walter de Gruyter.

Shuttleworth, Sally (1984), *George Eliot and Nineteenth-Century Science: The Make-Believe of a Beginning*, Cambridge: Cambridge University Press.

Slade, Joseph W. and Judith Yaross Lee, eds (1990), *Beyond the Two Cultures: Essays on Science, Technology, and Literature*, Ames, IA: Iowa State University Press.

Small, Helen and Trudi Tate, eds (2003), *Literature, Science, Psychoanalysis, 1830–1970: Essays in Honour of Gillian Beer*, Oxford: Oxford University Press.

Smith, Jonathan (1994), *Fact and Feeling: Baconian Science and the Nineteenth-Century Literary Imagination*, Madison, WI: University of Wisconsin Press.

Smith, Jonathan (2006), *Charles Darwin and Victorian Visual Culture*, Cambridge: Cambridge University Press.

Stack, David (2003), *The First Darwinian Left: Socialism and Darwinism 1859–1914*, Cheltenham: New Clarion Press.

Sterelny, Kim (2001), *Dawkins vs. Gould: Survival of the Fittest*, Cambridge: Icon.

Sterelny, Kim and Paul E. Griffiths (1999), *Sex and Death: An Introduction to Philosophy of Biology*, Chicago, IL: University of Chicago Press.

Stocking, George W., Jr (1987), *Victorian Anthropology*, New York: Macmillan.

Storey, Robert (1996), *Mimesis and the Human Animal: On the Biogenetic Foundations of Literary Representation*, Evanston, IL: Northeastern University Press.

Swirski, Peter (2007), *Of Literature and Knowledge: Explorations in Narrative Thought Experiments, Evolution, and Game Theory*, London: Routledge.

Thain, Marion (2003), '"Scientific Wooing": Constance Naden's Marriage of Science and Poetry', *Victorian Poetry*, 41: 151–69.

Townsend, J. Benjamin (1961), *John Davidson: Poet of Armageddon*, New Haven, CT: Yale University Press.

Tudge, Colin (2000), *The Variety of Life: A Survey and a Celebration of all the Creatures that Have Ever Lived*, Oxford: Oxford University Press.

Turner, Frank Miller (1973), 'Lucretius among the Victorians', *Victorian Studies*, 16: 329–48.

Turner, Frederick (1991a), *Rebirth of Value: Meditations on Beauty, Ecology, Religion, and Education*, Albany, NY: State University of New York Press.

Turner, Frederick (1991b), *Beauty: The Value of Values*, Charlottesville, VA: University Press of Virginia.

Turner, Frederick (1992), *Natural Classicism: Essays on Literature and Science*, Charlottesville, VA: University Press of Virginia.

Turner, Frederick (1995), *The Culture of Hope: A New Birth of the Classical Spirit*, New York: Free Press.

Vance, Norman (1997), *The Victorians and Ancient Rome*, Oxford: Blackwell.

Vendler, Helen (1980), *Part of Nature, Part of Us: Modern American Poets*, Cambridge, MA: Harvard University Press.

Vendler, Helen (2004), *Poets Thinking: Pope, Whitman, Dickinson, Yeats*, Cambridge, MA: Harvard University Press.

Walzer, Kevin (2001), *The Resurgence of Traditional Poetic Form and the Current Status of Poetry's Place in American Culture*, Lewiston, NY: Edwin Mellen Press.

Widdowson, H. G. (1992), *Practical Stylistics: An Approach to Poetry*, Oxford: Oxford University Press.

Wilson, Edward O. (1992), *The Diversity of Life*, Cambridge, MA: Harvard University Press.

Zaniello, Tom (1988), *Hopkins in the Age of Darwin*, Iowa City, IA: University of Iowa Press.

Zwierlein, Anne-Julia, ed. (2005), *Unmapped Countries: Biological Visions in Nineteenth Century Literature and Culture*, London: Anthem.

Index

Bold refers to poems quoted in their entirety, including individual sonnets and lyrics taken from sequences.